Celtic Spirituality

The Ultimate Guide to Druidry, Irish Paganism, Shamanism, the Morrigan, and Brigid

Your Free Gift
(only available for a limited time)

Thanks for getting this book! If you want to learn more about various spirituality topics, then join Mari Silva's community and get a free guided meditation MP3 for awakening your third eye. This guided meditation mp3 is designed to open and strengthen ones third eye so you can experience a higher state of consciousness. Simply visit the link below the image to get started.

https://spiritualityspot.com/meditation

Table of Contents

Part 1: Celtic Magic

Unlocking Druidry, Earth Magick, Irish Shamanism, Tree Magic, and Scottish Paganism

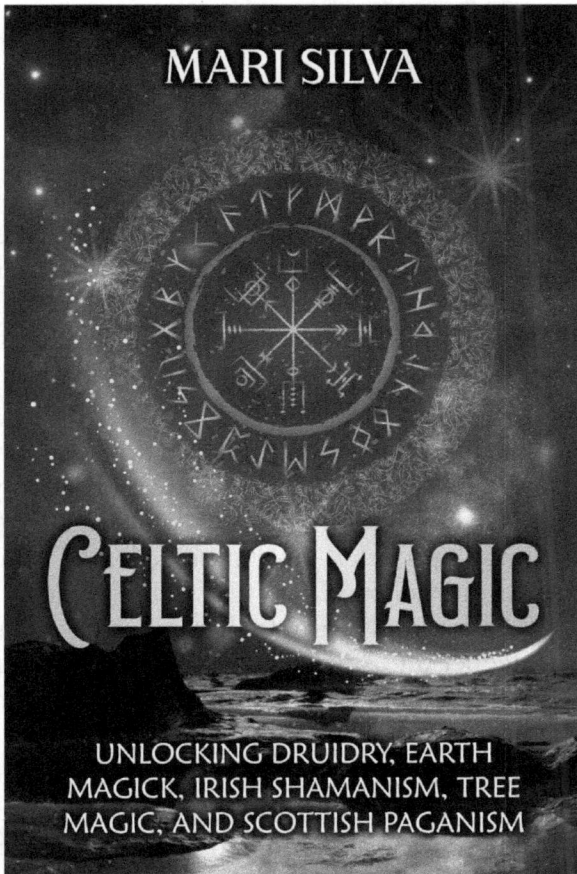

MARI SILVA

CELTIC MAGIC

UNLOCKING DRUIDRY, EARTH MAGICK, IRISH SHAMANISM, TREE MAGIC, AND SCOTTISH PAGANISM

Introduction

Modern-day Wicca has its roots in Celtic magic, and many practices taught these days are derived from these ancient traditions. Druids were known to dabble in divination and mysticism, from various forms still known today. Engaging in hymns and chants, creating incantations, and writing and reciting blessings and curses are the foundations of Celtic magic and, more specifically, Wicca.

This type of magic has been practiced for over two thousand years, and now, thanks to the handy guide you have in your hands, modern Wiccans can feel even more connected to their shared past. This book provides an unprecedented thorough yet comprehensible introduction to the transformative powers of practical magic. You will learn to harness your natural abilities while delving deeper into ancient traditions and honoring the work of so many who came before us. This book also covers the Celts' history and how their traditions influence us today.

The vibrant traditions, myths, and the magic of this uniquely beautiful part of Wales will be thoroughly covered in the following chapters. Turn the pages, and you'll discover the magical gods and goddesses whose presence is still felt today and the spirits whose magic forms the foundational vibrations that continue to carry the Wiccan religion. Various rituals are elucidated, and you will feel closer than ever to the divine energy of nature. You will learn to work with spells, invocations, and magical tools, made newly accessible in these pages but whose histories are derived from authentic Celtic resources.

Celtic magic retains its belief system and practices entirely unique to the Welsh region. Of course, the contemporary practice of Wicca draws plenty of inspiration from the Celtic systems of magic, and non-Celtic traditions, such as Teutonic, the Greco-Roman, and even Native American. However, these blends confuse contemporary practitioners and mislead people as to how these particular systems originated. In this guide, the Celtic sensibility and particular forms of magic will be studied within their specific cultural context, and no watered-down versions will be included.

Ultimately, reviving ancient folk traditions, practices, stories, and histories is about keeping an important legacy alive and its heart beating. Other narratives about the Celts and their magic observe them with the distant anthropologist's gaze, effectively "othering" the subject and flattening their characteristics with little regard for the specificity of its history. This book aims to do the complete opposite and provide a deeply immersive experience for the reader. If you're a new practitioner in the world of magic or someone who wants to learn more about this unique religion and practice, this book is for you. Other guides these days too much on parables and prettified stories. While there is always room for that, this book provides a more straightforward introduction to the fascinating Celts' magical practices and explores the ways they continue to influence contemporary magic.

Chapter 1: Celtic Magic Basics

It's essential to understand where the tradition of this magic comes from - the ancient Celts - to understand Celtic magic. If you've never heard of them, don't worry. This chapter discusses everything to know about the ancient Celts and Celtic magic basics and Celtic Neopaganism, Celtic Wicca, and Celtic magic today. By the time you've finished reading the chapter, you'll have answers to any questions you may have had on the topic.

The Ancient Celts

"Celt" is the collective name for several groups of ancient people who lived in Europe and Anatolia. Their related family Celtic languages link them, hence the use of the word "Celt." The Celts consisted of:

- Brits
- Gaels
- Gauls
- Galatians
- Celtiberians and many more

Additionally, these groups had several cultural similarities, which helped connect them.

They are believed to have a history tracing back to 1200 BC, if not longer. However, the word "Keltoi" was first used in Greek sources in the 5th century BC. In the 1st century BC, Julius Caesar reported that the Gauls referred to themselves as Celts, indicating that the tribes adopted the Greek name sometime between the four centuries. The modern word "Celt" was first used in the 1700s.

During their heyday, the Celts occupied territories stretching from Spain to the Black Sea, making them the largest ethnic group in ancient Europe. However, it's important to remember that the Celts were a collection of disparate tribes united by a common language, family, and cultural customs rather than a single kingdom. It makes tracing a single history of the Celts challenging.

The Celts thrived because of the vast territory they inhabited. For example, while the Roman Empire was expanding through Europe, the Celts on the islands of Ireland and Great Britain remained relatively isolated and grew as a culture. While Julius Caesar and his successors launched a targeted battle to destroy the Celts in Mainland Europe, their attempted invasion of Britain remained unsuccessful, making the islands a haven for the surviving Celts. Therefore, the Celtic cultural traditions are particularly prevalent in Ireland and the United Kingdom and the source of modern Celtic Neopaganism.

Though sources from the Greeks and Romans refer to the ancient Celts as barbarian warriors, it would be a mistake to think of them as such. The recorded barbaric nature of the Celts due to a combination of propaganda and war - the Roman Empire, in particular, benefitted from portraying their enemies negatively, as it made their armies more likely to fight and justified the war against the Celts. Additionally, when Caesar decided to abandon the invasion of Britain, the decision was justified in part by referencing the "barbarity" of the Celts and juxtaposing it against the "civilized" Mediterranean world.

However, there is significant evidence of the intricacy and richness of Celtic culture. For example, ancient Celtic burial mounds prove their skills as metalworkers and jewelers and the complexities of Celtic social culture. While Greek and Roman sources describe the Celts as "excessive drinkers," discoveries of burial mounds show that drinking was a way for tribes to strengthen allyship, and the presentation of alcohol (and other elements of a grand feast) was a sign of a good leader's generosity.

The Celts were also known for their intricate bronze and iron weaponry, which included highly personalized swords and shields with motifs tailored to each individual. These weapons helped them defeat the early Romans in the British Isles and established their reputation as fierce warriors. However, the detail of the weapons also shows they were often used for ritual purposes.

Celtic Languages

As mentioned above, one thing that tied disparate Celtic tribes together was a shared language family. Though the Celtic languages have evolved into many languages today, there were two main languages groups the ancient Celts likely spoke - Insular and Continental Celtic.

Continental Celtic has been extinct since about the 5th century AD, and the best-documented example can be found in Gaulish ancient documentation. Insular Celtic evolved into a range of languages, and some are still spoken today, including:

- Cumbrian (extinct)
- Breton (endangered but undergoing a revival)

- Cornish (recently revived)
- Welsh (still spoken today)
- Irish and Scottish Gaelic (still spoken today)
- Cornish (recently revived)
- Manx (recently revived)

The revival of ancient Celtic languages can be tied to opposition to British rule. The 19th and 20th centuries saw a revival of the Celtic identity in the British Isles (including Celtic religion, as we discuss later in this chapter) and was primarily driven by anger at British rule over other UK countries like Ireland, Wales, and Scotland. While the British government restricted the ancient Celtic languages, this embrace of Celtic identity also led to the revival of the languages and their use in everyday and formal situations.

Ancient Celtic Religion

While the Celts remain a fascinating subject of study to people around the world, the element of their culture serves as the biggest remains their religion and spiritual belief system. There is no "name" for the ancient Celtic religion, and some elements are shared with other contemporary belief systems, including:

- Polytheism
- Offerings to the gods
- A belief in the afterlife, characterized by leaving valuable and everyday items in the tombs of the deceased

With the Celtic people, there was no single unified religion shared by all the tribes. However, while primary gods, offerings, and places of worship may have differed from tribe to tribe, these disparate religions were extraordinarily similar in other ways, including:

- A reverence for the human head and a belief that it was the seat of the soul
- The belief that totems - especially animal totems like the stag and the boar - had a protective power

- Reverence for sacred sites, especially ones related to nature like groves, rivers, and springs
- Religious ceremonies that were, more often than not, led by Druids
- Religious and community rules were meant to be complied with and often ensured through the use of taboos for people who went against them.

There is a good chance that the ancient Celts practiced human sacrifice. However, human sacrifices were significantly rarer than animal sacrifices and offerings of other items, like food and weapons. Where human sacrifice was practiced, the sacrifice differed depending on the god the sacrifice was made. Some buried bodies discovered are thought to be local kings or people sacrificed by the Celts.

It should be noted that everything known of ancient Celtic religion today is based on surviving artifacts and the oral traditions passed on through centuries in closed communities. Druids and poets were frequently unwilling to commit sacred knowledge to write. Therefore, knowledge of Celtic magic and religious practices is from the Romans and Greeks, who extensively documented Celtic practices, and reconstructions based on existing Celtic artifacts. It's possible that many more Celtic artifacts were destroyed during the invasion of Celtic lands by the Roman and Germanic tribes. The existence of the Romanic counterparts of Celtic deities indicates Romans had a much broader knowledge of the nature and attributes of these deities than we can surmise from the artifacts existing today.

Most scholars agree that the Celts practiced a form of animism - a belief that all parts of the natural world had their own spirits. Some Celtic gods were local spirits. For example, the Irish Celtic goddesses Boann and Sioann were associated with Boyne and Shannon rivers, and The Morrígan was linked to the River Unius. Additionally, some gods and goddesses, like Artio (bear) and Epona (horse), are linked to animals.

Not only did the Celts associate their deities and spirits with elements of nature, but they also believed in the spiritual importance of these elements. According to the Celtic lore, these higher beings lived in mountain tops, trees, bodies of water - and when the time arose, they came out to assist people. The Celts often held their rituals at points where two major natural elements joined. These were the common areas where the inhabitants of the physical and supernatural worlds could communicate freely with each other.

In artwork that has survived the passage of time, Cernunnos, also known as "the horned god," is the best-known and most frequently depicted Celtic god. His role in the pantheon of gods remains veiled in mystery, although he is generally depicted in a seated position with stag antlers. Other major gods and goddesses include the healing goddess Brigid (known as Brigantia), the warrior god Lugh (known as Lugus and Lleu Llaw Gyffes), and the triple goddess Matrones. Triple deities were a relatively common phenomenon in Celtic religion. Some deities like Lugh and The Morrígan were often considered triple deities and individual figures, depending on the tribe and the religious tradition.

Ancient Celtic Religion and Magic

The Druids and the poets led the Ancient Celtic religion, and both groups were connected to magic.

The Druids were essentially the priests of the ancient Celtic religion and were tasked with linking humans and the gods. They were also the keepers of a community's history and respected for their knowledge of customs, traditions, and wisdom in all things.

They lead religious ceremonies, but this was only one part of their duties. They were also soothsayers who divined the future and interpreted natural events, made medicinal potions, and used sacred plants common people were not permitted to use (like mistletoe). Additionally, they were tasked with casting taboos (what we now call spells) on people who disobeyed religious and community rules.

As with ancient Celtic religion, knowledge of Druidic tradition comes from writings of Romans and Greeks. The Druids left little to no written sources for us to learn from. However, it's worth noting that the Celtic-based Roman written records contain the same elements as the ancient Celtic folk songs and oral legends passed down by the Druids, poets, and bards.

Becoming a druid was a complex procedure and could often take as many as 20 years of training. Some sources have Druids capable of:

- Producing snow storms
- Having power over the elements
- Creating illusions to fool enemies during wartime

Druids sometimes adopted specific postures while casting spells, but much of the magical power was in the actual words, which is why their extensive knowledge of these spells was so vital. It also explains the lack of written sources, as writing these spells down would allow others to understand and use their power.

Aside from Druids, knowledge of magic was also held by Celtic poets, especially in Ireland, known as the *fili*. Like the Druids, becoming a poet required extensive training, and poets were tasked with remembering numerous lengthy poems (sometimes hundreds). This extensive knowledge and memorization ability meant that poets were assigned as lore keepers for communities.

In Celtic Ireland, poets were seen and treated as people with a magical capacity; it was believed that poetry, or poetic expression, is intrinsically related to a form of magic or magical clairvoyance that gave poets unusual power in society. As mentioned above, spells and curses depended on the spoken word more than any gestures from the caster's side, and satirical poems spoken by a poet were often considered curses cast upon the person or persons being satirized in the poem.

It should be noted that poets were different from bards in Ireland. Bards were reciters of existing poems, while poets were artists with magical abilities who could create new poems. However, in Wales, poets and bards were interchangeable terms.

According to some Roman sources, a separate class of seers also existed, different from the Druids and poets. These seers were supposed to interpret natural events, like bird's flight, to tell the future. However, most sources combine the order of seers with the Druids.

Aside from codified magic from the Druids and the poets, there were instances of more "everyday" magic among the ancient Celts. The most significant of this "smaller" magic is using amulets.

Amulets were charms believed to have the ability to ward off danger. They were designed for living people (and the dead) and were often found in women's and children's graves. Furthermore, talismans were a different class of magical items believed to bring luck to the wearer or owner.

Celtic Magic Today

Over time, Celtic societies underwent gradual Christianization (as did much of Europe). The last Celtic country to convert to Christianity was Ireland, but by the 5th-7th century AD, the Church relegated traditional Celtic practices to irrelevancy, and the poets and Druids were rebranded as demonic and pagan practitioners. To further discourage pagan practices, fairies and other natural spiritual guides were also transformed into malevolent entities by Christian priests.

However, Celtic religion and tradition survived in pieces and folklore around the Celtic countries. If the Celts couldn't worship their gods and goddesses openly, they converted them into heroes and heroines in legends passed on to the next generations. In fact, the Celtic oral tradition was so strong that these stories are nearly the same today as they were recorded in older sources.

Some rituals, particularly those thought to have healing properties, such as a pilgrimage to clootie wells, the practice of well dressing, and using wish trees, remained in use even during the height of Christianity. In some isolated parts of these countries, like the Inishkea Islands located off the coast of Ireland, Celtic rituals were practiced well into the 19th century.

Additionally, the 1900s saw a resurgence of interest in Celtic traditions and Celtic religion. As mentioned above, it was a way of resisting British rule over other countries in the United Kingdom, especially Scotland and Ireland. Since using many Celtic languages was either outlawed or severely discouraged and penalized, this period also saw a resurrection of interest in these languages.

Celtic Reconstructionist Paganism

Celtic Reconstructionist Paganism is perhaps the best-known approach to Celtic neopaganism and takes a Reconstructionist approach to the religion. It prioritizes historical accuracy over combining Celtic religion with other pagan traditions, common in Neo-Druidism and Celtic Wicca.

Celtic Reconstructionist Paganism originated from various modern pagan religions of the 1970s and 1980s and grew as a religion in the 1980s and 90s. Core parts of this tradition include studying and reviving Celtic languages and focusing on Celtic cultural activities, including music, dance, and even traditional martial arts.

Practitioners also focus on preserving important archeological and sacred Celtic sites like sites around the Hill of Tara and have engaged in protests to ensure their survival.

Rituals include:

- Acknowledging the realms of the land, sea, and sky.
- Using the fire of inspiration as a force that unites and binds these realms together.
- Maintaining altars and shrines to personal deities.
- Some practitioners also practice divination with the help of the traditional Ogham alphabet or through interpreting natural happenings like the movements of clouds and birds.

Celtic Wicca

Apart from Celtic Reconstructionist Paganism, the other well-known version of Celtic neopaganism is Celtic Wicca. This subset of modern Wiccan practice combines Wiccan beliefs with Celtic mythology.

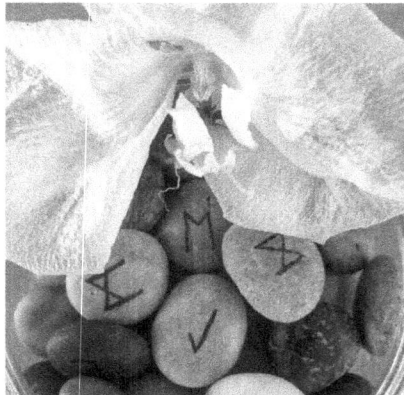

Celtic Wiccans believe the same basic customs as other Wiccans, including the Wiccan Rede and the Rule of Three. They also worship the divine Goddess and God. However, unlike traditional Wicca, Celtic Wicca is not duo-theistic. Celtic Wiccans also worship several other deities from Celtic mythology, with important deities including:

- Brigid

- Cerridwen

- Rosmerta

- Rhiannon

- Cernunnos (as mentioned above, Cernunnos is often known as the horned god. For Celtic Wiccans, he is frequently equated and combined with the divine male - the God)

- Lugh

It should be noted that how a person practices Celtic Wicca is often exceptionally personal. Many practitioners focus more on one aspect over the other, Wicca over Celtic religion, or vice versa. Celtic Wiccans who focus on the Celtic religion will often find the Wiccan Rede is incompatible with Celtic ethics of heroic mortality. Those who focus more on the Wicca aspect will incorporate the four elements into their spiritual traditions.

Celtic Wiccans generally celebrate the same eight Sabbats as other Wiccans do - the Wiccan Wheel of the Year and the Sabbats have origins in Celtic traditions, making it a core aspect of the Celtic Wiccan tradition. However, unlike Celtic Reconstructionist Paganism, Celtic Wicca remains a combination of two religious traditions rather than a movement focused on historical accuracy.

Neo-Druidism

As mentioned above, another Celtic Neopagan tradition is Neo-Druidism. It is, essentially, a revival of Celtic Druidism and its origins in the interest in Celtic religion during the 18th and 19th centuries.

During the 18th-century Romanticist movement in Britain, interest in the ancient Celts peaked. Early Neo-Druids aimed to imitate the original Druids and revive the Celtic culture.

As discussed above, there is little extant information about the original Druids, especially in primary sources. Due to this issue, Neo-Druidism was modeled on secret societies like Freemasonry and used Druids as a symbol of the indigenous spirituality of ancient Britain. There were several societies of Neo-Druids, and some were - and remain - purely cultural in nature. However, others have moved towards a more spiritual aspect, including nature worship, a belief in Awen (the idea of divinity and the Deity's spirit), goddess worship, and ancestor veneration.

It should be mentioned that, like Celtic Wicca, Neo-Druidism is not historically accurate. While modern Druids participate in ceremonies and rituals, celebrate during the Sabbats, and engage in several other magical practices, such as herbalism and divination, this does not mean they accurately represent ancient Druidic orders.

Even Celtic Reconstructionist Paganism is ultimately a Reconstructionist approach towards ancient Celtic religion. The lack of primary sources makes accurate replication of the religion challenging at the best of times, and practitioners have had to innovate their versions of the religion.

If you're interested in learning more about Celtic magic, including how to practice ogham divination, use tree magic, and conduct Celtic rituals, you're in the right place. The next chapter will detail the gods and goddesses you will encounter as part of the Celtic pantheon. You'll be introduced to Celtic magic in Ireland and Scotland, given a better understanding of druidism and the way of the druid, and learn much more. Keep reading to learn all you need to know about the Celtic religion.

Chapter 2: The Celtic Pantheon

Celtic mythology is always enchanting, and when we explore it, we are not talking about a particular group that happened to dominate a specific realm. Instead, we are focusing on exploring the dynamic culture of the Celtic era that strongly influenced many regions, including the Danube, Portugal, Ireland and more. Since it's multifarious, since the Celtic mythology as we know it today has numerous borrowed tales and traditions, an important note is to remember that their gods and goddesses have associated deities or cognates, depending on the region. For instance, Lugus, as it was known in the region of Gaul, was also known as Lugh in Ireland. Let's explore the most important gods and goddesses of the majestic Celtic Era.

1. Dana: Goddess of Nature

She is one of the oldest of all the ancient gods in Celtic mythology. Dana is known by many names such as Annan, Danu, Anu and is often recognized as the primordial mother goddess. This Celtic goddess is portrayed as a stunning and wise woman, deeply linked with nature and the spiritual essence of natural entities. Dana also stands for regeneration, prosperity, wisdom and death.

This goddess played a significant role in Celtic mythology and was regarded as the divine mother of Tuatha De Danann (the people of goddess Dana). Tuatha De Dannan was one of the greatest pantheons from Pre-Christian Ireland and considered a supernatural tribe or race of Celtic gods.

How to Honor Today?

Select a time when you can focus on the honoring ritual, about half an hour or, at the very least, chalk out 10 minutes. The best times are before sunrise or post-sunset, but you can select any time in the day if these don't suit you. Ideally, the ritual to worship Dana should be performed outdoors, but indoors will do just fine if you are uncomfortable with this. You will have to repeat the ritual basics, including grounding yourself, deep breathing to center and then going through the steps of a purification ritual. Now you are ready to connect with the deity Danu. You can call her with any name or title that feels closer to your heart. The invocation needs to be sincere instead of long-winded, and you must make an offering (wine, water, or ale). Afterward, sit quietly and visualize her. When she appears before you (perhaps you hear her or receive a sign), greet her, let her communicate with you, and listen with respect. Once you feel the communication has concluded, pour another offering to the goddess and drink some yourself. It is important not to rush the ritual and be polite and patient.

2. Dagda: Chief of All Gods

He happens to be an important fatherly deity and is called a cheerful god and chief of all the Celtic gods. Dagda is a deity linked with all the nourishing and earthly aspects, including fertility, masculine strength, weather, and agriculture. But this is not all; Dagda's divine powers were thought to encompass wisdom, knowledge, Druidry, and magic as well. It often intrigues the reader to learn about the physical appearance of deity Dagda as a simple and plump man who has aged. He is often represented wearing a rustic and old tunic. However, the one interesting element you will always see in the pictures or representations of the deity Dagda is the Lorg Mór (great staff or the club) with magical powers. His magical staff could resurrect the dead or bring death upon several simultaneously. You would notice the simple and nurturing deity, Dagda, never without his magical cauldron and a big ladle, known as "*coire ansic.*" The cauldron represented his connection with the magical, mysterious and surreal aspects of this world, while the ladle was a symbolic representation of Dagda's immense power over food, sustenance and abundance in general. He also had many lovers, including the goddess Morrigan.

How to Honor Today?

To celebrate the fatherly Dagda, simply make different offerings to him, like porridge or oat bannocks, ale, and butter to the fire while performing the ritual. Place different bounty and abundance symbols on the altar, including produce you have grown, and load a big cauldron with home-baked food and home-grown vegetables. Another way to honor him is to make food donations to the local food bank or be generous and hospitable to others around you.

3. Morrigan: Goddess of Fate

According to Celtic mythological folklore, the goddess of fate is also recognized as a mysterious deity known by the name of *Morrigu.* Moreover, she seems to be an ominous figure linked with terrifying wars and mysteries of fate. Morrigan was thought to have prophetic powers of premonitions of doom. There are several interpretations of her name in history that are quite intriguing, but one of the most interesting is the "phantom queen," as she was able to change her form or shape and would usually turn into a crow.

As mentioned earlier, Morrigan has been linked with foretold doom, and her reputation as an ominous deity stands true, as according to the stories, she lured soldiers to the frenzy of the battlefield. She is also popular among the believers as the deity of sovereignty and was considered a protector for the land and believers. When you peruse through the history of Morrigan, it is interesting to note the connection that has been established with other deities, including Nemain, Badb, and Macha. Not only this, but Morrigan also shared an interesting tryst with Dagda on Samhain.

How to Honor Today?

You must first get to know this deity in-depth, so spend ample time studying her and how she manifests in different cultures. Prepare a dedicated altar for her and place drawings or a statue of Morrigan. Use black or red candles, an altar cloth, and decorative deer and crows. Also, keep a bowl of water. You can perform shapeshifting shamanic rituals and practice meditation or shamanic drumming.

4. Lugh: Warrior God

He is the warrior god, known by Lugus, Lugos, Lugh Lámhfhada (Lugh of the Long Arm), and Lleu Llaw Gyffes (Lleu of the skillful hand), and represented as a powerful, courageous deity. He is among the most respected and celebrated deities that have been famous for their mesmerizing warrior persona and youthful appearance. However, one must not be deceived by the youthful appearance of deity Lugh, as his power was unmatchable. Lugh was the one deity who slayed the chief of Formorii, a formidable one-eyed Balor (an enemy of the tribe of gods, i.e., the Tuatha De Danann). An interesting irony or a twist of fate was that even though Lugh was heralded as the Balor slayer, he was one among Balor's descendants. Lugh was linked with lynxes, thunderstorms, raves and was known as Samildanach (skilled in all arts). Some various interesting mythical stories and folklores connect Lugh and Cu Chulainn (who was an Irish hero) as father and son. It is worth mentioning that Cu Chulainn is quite similar to Hercules/Heracles and Rostam. The folklores and mythology have a weird and spellbinding interconnection that does not cease to amuse the scholars to date.

How to Honor Today?

To honor the god of war, Lugh brings bread, grains, corn, or other harvest symbols as offerings. Before starting the honoring ritual for Lugh, spend time taking a personal inventory of your strengths, talents, goals, etc. Add items that speak about your talents onto the altar. You will need one candle to symbolize Lugh and place it in the center of the altar. When you light the candle, take another second to refresh all your life achievements. Make an incantation honoring Lugh and introducing yourself as a skilled devotee. Take pride in your skills (but don't be impolite or snobbish because you are speaking to a deity). Afterward, ask about the thing you want to improve. Make another offering, conclude the ritual with gratitude, and spend a few more minutes reflecting on your abilities.

5. Brigid: Triple Goddess of Healing

The triple goddess, Brigid, is quite popular for her reputation as a spring goddess and the deity of smithcraft as well as healing. She is also strongly associated with some peculiar brooding attributes of Morrigan. As far as, Celtic mythology and folklore go, Brigid is recognized as the daughter of the deity Dagda and has been an esteemed member of the divine tribe of deities, the Tuatha De Danann. One striking aspect of Goddess Brigid is her strong connection with the domestic animals, including oxen, boars, sheep. These animals would loyally warn the goddess of any upcoming calamity. This goddess was generally venerated as the poet, the healer, and the smith. In other words, she may even have been considered a triple deity.

How to Honor Today?

Start by learning more and reading mythical texts about her. The next step is to set up an altar for her, as Brigid loves having a dedicated small space in her followers' homes. She is a goddess of the hearth, so the kitchen seems the perfect spot. You can decorate the altar with a picture or statue of her, a glass of water, and a candle. It's as simple as that. While speaking to her, don't forget to light a candle purely to connect deeply with Brigid. You can also honor her by acknowledging other elements, like water. All you have to do is visit a nearby spring or well or any natural water body that would serve this purpose. Simply show your gratitude and humbly ask for healing your soul, body, and mind.

6. Epona: Guardian Goddess of Horses

Epona is considered the female deity and serves as the protector of horses, mules, and donkeys. This Celtic goddess is also linked with fertility. Roman Empire cavalrymen venerated goddess Epona, and they favored her strongly. Goddess Epona was quite popular among the Equites Singulares Augusti, who were the Imperial Horse Guards. These guards were the counterparts in

Praetorian Guards, and according to some stories, Epona was the one who actually instilled a spirit of inspiration in Rhiannon. The stories about mythical Welsh Rhiannon, who was also famously recognized for her tenacity and labeled as the otherworld's lady, are strongly linked with goddess Epona.

Epona's symbol is a horse since she is crowned as the goddess who protects animals. She is sometimes shown carrying corn in her lap or a goblet and is believed to inspire providence, love, and fertility. She can also help in situations when you need more authority.

How to Honor Today?

If you want to show her regard, eat corn and leave roses as an offering for her. You can also use rose incense or rose petals. If that is not an option for you, use sandalwood incense. The color most often associated with her is white, so don't forget to grab a candle of that color. She is a goddess linked to various aspects of our lives. You can ask her to fulfill your dreams, and she blesses the ones we see while asleep. But she is also the goddess of ambition and hope. So, if you want to manifest your dreams and seek protection, she is the goddess you should honor today. She is depicted as a caregiver, so pray to her for the protection of children, families, and pregnant women.

7. Belenus: The Sun God (Beli Mawr, Bel, and Belenos)

The Sun God was one of the most time-honored and idolized gods in Celtic history. He was often shown to be riding the sky in a majestic, divine horse chariot. He is also sometimes depicted as throwing thunderbolts, riding a single horse or using the mystical wheel as a shield. Romans linked him with Apollo (also known as the god of light). Therefore, Belenus is also cheered for his regenerative and healing powers.

How to Honor Today?

You can honor Belenus by offering ritualistic offerings similar to other gods and goddesses by first learning more about him before moving on to the purifying and grounding rituals. The general offerings typical of Belenus include terra-cotta horses and stone-carved swaddled infant statues.

8. Aonghus: God of Love

The name of this deity is often translated as "true vigor," and he is popularly linked with love. Like the deity, Lugh, Aonghus, or Aengus, is another deity who is celebrated for his youthful appearance. He is also popularly worshipped for the connection with spirits or themes of love and poetry. According to the mythological stories, Dagda and Bionn (the goddess of rivers) were supposedly his parents. As far as the folklore goes, Dagda and Bionn were involved in an illicit relationship, and as a consequence, Bionn got pregnant. However, Dagda tried to hide her pregnancy and the truth behind their illicit relationship by magically controlling the weather. The mythology narrates that Dagda froze or halted the sun for a whole nine months, and that's how the deity Aengus was born in a matter of a day! Despite the peculiar history of his parents, the god Aonghus grew up to be a lively deity full of love and affection for the creatures around him. You would see his representations with four birds always around him. Later on, Aengus tricks his father (Dagda) in an attempt to confiscate and rule over the divine tribe of Tuatha De Danann's Bru na Boinne. However, he was crowned as the deity of love, primarily because of his story. Aengus fell in love with Caer Ibormeith, who he saw in a dream. He eventually found and married her.

How to Honor Today?

Start with the same rituals of honoring and offering the gods and first learn more about him to connect with him on a deeper level. The prayer to Aengus should include his praise. Afterward, share what you are grateful for and ask him humbly for the things you need guidance for.

9. Taranis: The God of Thunder

Taranis was one of the gods among the triad of Celtic gods (along with Esus and Toutatis) and was called the god of thunder. This trait is particularly interesting because he was often compared to the god Jupiter and Zeus. The portraits or illustrations of Taranis often represent hum with a lightning bolt, and he looks physically similar to god Zeus. Another worth noticing thing is that Taranis was associated with fire (sky or air). He was shown in pictures, holding the solar wheel.

How to Honor Today?

There are several ways you can honor Taranis and express your devotion and dedication to this god. One way is to find lightning blasted oak and carry a piece of it with you. Another is to keep dried acorns and oak leaves with you in a mini sachet. When you are about to perform a ritual outdoors for Taranis, always make an offering to seek good weather. Making a fire-offering is recommended. Also, light a candle and offer a prayer to Taranis during lightning or thunder, showing your subservience to him. Another important detail to remember is to conclude the ritual by making the second offering showing your thanks.

10. Ogma: God of Eloquence

Deities that are linked with languages are not often seen in ancient folklore. This deity serves as an exception to the general rule because Ogma is the god of eloquence. Some stories represent the physical resemblance between Ogma and Hercules. If you observe the depictions of Ogma, there are amber or gold-colored chains that are linked to his believers through his tongue. He was also an important character in the Garlic mythological tales. He invented the Ogham, which was an ancient writing system in Ireland. He was famously labeled as a deity of Knowledge.

How to Honor Today?

To honor Ogma, start on the path to knowledge, and the best beginning is to gather as much information about him as possible. If you perform a ritual to show your dedication and praise to Ogma, the altar should be set in a specific way. As the god of eloquence, offer a knowledgeable asset piece or make an equivalent offering. Spreading knowledge or wisdom is also an indication of dedication toward Ogma.

11. Cernunnos: Lord of All Things Wild

He happens to be one of the most imposing and impressive of all the Celtic gods because he was the deity of everything wild. Cernunnos was given the "Horned One" title and frequently linked with forests, animals, and fertility in Celtic polytheistic mythology. In Celtic mythology, he is reported as the son of deity Lugh and struggled to ensure the survival of wild animals and woods. His depictions often mirror all the associated characteristics. He has quite conspicuous antlers on his head and poetic epithets and represents the fatherly masculine energy of mother earth. He goes through the cycles of death and life; after death, he was reborn and impregnated by the goddess of Beltane. Therefore, he was not only born through the earth but also played an important role in fertilizing it. However, this interpretation is quite a new one associated with Cernunnos. His weapons were made of natural materials, including the tree's roots.

How to Honor Today?

Offer brown ale, cider, roasted rabbit, fruit punch, bone carvings, acorns, toadstools, green candles, boar hide, and flower fragrances. Like other deities, an essential aspect of honoring him is to learn more about him to get closer to him. However, nature is a key component for honoring Cernunnos. You can honor Cernunnos by offering dedicated ritualistic offerings by purifying, grounding, and visualizing while waiting for the god of all wild things to respond.

The Celtic mythology does not conclude with merely the above few deities. Many other gods and goddesses can also be included as relevant. Each deity has its unique attributes, and to show your devotion, you must honor each deity bearing this in mind.

Chapter 3: Celtic Magic in Ireland and Scotland

People without a deeper understanding of Celtic mythology often assume that Celtic magic is similar to Wicca and many other forms of Neopaganism practices. In reality, this couldn't be further from the truth, and nothing illustrates this better than Ireland and Scotland's unique Celtic magic practices.

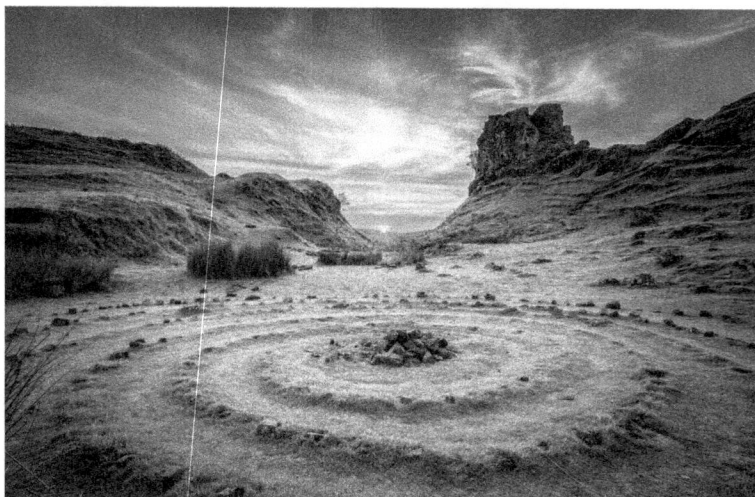

Apart from having a history that dates back to 400 AD, the Celtic representation of the universe is based on nature, while, for example, Wicca relies on the four elements. The belief system of most modern Pagans encourages using magic solely for healing and protection and never for harm. The Ancient Celts were mighty warriors who saw nothing wrong with harming someone if it meant their survival. This made it possible to occupy Ireland and Scotland, creating new territory to spread their beliefs. The most important characteristic differentiating Irish and Scottish Paganism from other forms is polytheism. This is another element leftover from the Ancient Celtic beliefs system, of which every god and goddess has its unique origin and function in the universe. While Wicca and similar modern Pagan practitioners often recognize the existence of multiple deities, these are said to be descendants of one god. This ideology is probably due to the mixed origins of these belief systems.

Celtic Magic in Ireland

Ireland is an island, isolating itself from the rest of the world. Due to this, there wasn't anything that could influence the spread of ancient pagan beliefs. Moreover, the practices of Ireland quickly evolved. First, it had to blend in with folk magic, also based on finding power in nature, and later Christianity, which was a much lengthier process. Nevertheless, this taught the Irish Celts a great lesson. They learned that sacred places could not be created. They could only be found, and once found, they did everything to keep it.

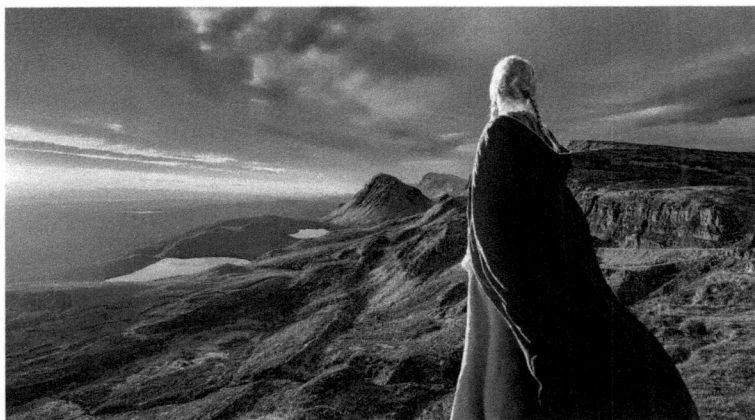

In Irish pagan mythology, birth, death, and rebirth are always intertwined, representing the elements of the same cycle. All creatures found themselves in three different realms, this world, the underworld, and the otherworld. The latter is often tied to the Tuatha Dé Danann, Ireland's well-known ancient Celtic tribe. According to legend, the "otherworld" was created as a world running in parallel to ours, so those banished from this world could continue living there. Deities and other elemental beings populate it. Using meditation and journeying, traveling between the realms is possible and often advised if one is seeking guidance. Practitioners typically do this with the necessary skills for gathering and sharing sacred wisdom in either realm.

The arrival of Christianity brought on the most substantial shift in the Irish Paganic practices. The priests took over the role of the Druids, causing their followers to change beliefs too. However, many Druids retained their pure Pagan beliefs, despite converting to Christianity or becoming priests.

Tuatha Dé Danann

The Tuatha Dé Danann (the People of the Goddess Danu) was one of the first Celtic tribes to take root in Ireland. Their gods were called Eriu and are still used as the name for Ireland in Celtic Pagan circles. Upon arrival at the Irish coastline, the Tuatha Dé Danann burned their boats, showing their absolute determination to take over this new land. After winning the battle with the ruler, the Fir Bolg, they succeeded and successfully ruled Ireland for over 200 years. Despite the sheer dominance they overtook Ireland with, the Tuatha were quite civilized. Their culture was admired by the conquered, and soon their skills and treasures became the source of tales still told today. According to these tales, the Tuatha Dé Danann possessed four talismans, and each was a testament to great power.

The four talismans were:
1. The Stone of Fal signaled when a true King of Ireland was standing on it.
2. The Sun God Lugh, with the ever-accurate slingshot.
3. The Magic Sword of Nuadha, which only inflicted mortal injuries.
4. The Cauldron of Dagda provided an endless supply of sustenance for the warriors.

Despite their arsenal and divine powers, the two-century rule of the Tuatha Dé Danann came to an end when the mortal Melesians defeated them. They were consigned to live underground and later to the magical otherworld but eventually took over a new role as the bearer of the fairies. They became known as the *people of the mound*, Aes sidhe or Aos Sí.

Aos Sí

Living in the otherworld, the Aos Sí are depicted in different forms. These mystical beings are sometimes described as elf-like creatures hidden from human eyes. In other depictions, they resemble tiny fairies. The latter is the modern characterization of Irish fairy folk, which in the case of Aos Sí, is the least accurate. Even though this interpretation seems to be the most popular, it's not reflected in descriptions provided by the oral sources available from ancient times. Most Irish tales describe them as tall as humans, fair, and beautiful.

They can cross between the two realms and often visit the mounds of Ireland, where they can be seen doing either mischief or good deeds. They must be treated with great respect to appease them, and regular offerings must be made to them. Since they have always been more advanced than mortals, they rarely show interest in humans who have learned to share their land with them.

In addition, modern pop culture often describes fairies as magical creatures with a penchant for good-natured trickery. However, according to Celtic lore, these creatures aren't always so benevolent. Some examples of malicious Aos Sí are the fairy vampire maiden, Leanan Sídhe, the headless horseman, Dullahan, an evil Leprechaun, Far Darrig, and the Bean Sídhe, or banshee (as it's known by its modern name.) The Aos Sí are often used in Irish mythology to answer something that cannot otherwise be explained. Natural catastrophes, diseases, birth deformities or even a simple case of bad luck could be attributed to them.

Legends about Aos Sí often have a recurring motif that emphasizes the importance of warding them off. Protective charms, wearing clothes inside out, and certain foods can keep these creatures away from people and animals. Since they are known to emerge from the otherworld through specific locations, one can avoid being led astray by avoiding these areas.

Tír na nÓg

The home of Aos Sí (and many other creatures) is said to be a magical place where time stands still, and no death, illness, or other mishaps happen. This part of the otherworld is located just outside the human realm. The only way to reach it is by using magic, which is how many have managed to find the pathway to cross. Some are taking this path searching for the eternal youth Tir na nOg offers, while others merely want answers to questions concerning their life in the human realm. According to Celtic lore, Tir na nOg (known as the land of youth) is home to many heroes whose fates were tied to this place.

A popular tale depicts the story of Oisin, a young Irish warrior who fell in love with Niamh, the daughter of the king of Tir na nOg. Niamh helped Oisin reach the magical land, where they lived happily together for three hundred years. However, Oisin missed Ireland, and Niamh eventually sent him back to his homeland. When he arrived, he realized that while time stood still in the otherworld, many years had passed in his own realm. His loved ones were long gone, and their home was abandoned. Deciding to go back to Tir na nOg, he started his journey when he noticed a stone he wanted to take with him. When he tried to pick it up, he fell, and time instantly caught up with him being over 300 years old meant he had crossed his lifetime. However, he was now at peace.

Irish Celtic Shamanism

Shamanism, in general, refers to a practice of reconnecting with nature as a form of experiencing divine consciousness. During their mystical journey, shamans extend a spiritual connection toward the outside world and their consciousness at the same time. Irish Celtic Shamanism is rooted in the spiritual energy of this land. It's an ancient tradition honoring the archetypes of the Celtic pantheon and sacred sites known from the oral shamanic lineages and tales of Celtic Ireland.

Through the practices of Irish Celtic Shamanism, you can learn to travel to the world of Spirit and retrieve the knowledge needed for guidance, healing, or divination. At the same time, the contemporary version often focuses on bringing you closer to nature and yourself. Taking this path will allow you to emerge from the experience as an empowered version of yourself who seeks the universal truth and isn't afraid to experience life to the fullest.

The terms "healing" and "retrieval" are interchangeable in the Irish (Gaelic) language, indicating that by revealing the hidden parts of yourself – or *retrieving* them, you can heal and become whole again. When all the damaged parts are recovered, you become a fighter instead of a bystander, or worse, a victim. In Irish Celtic Shamanism, there is no difference between the sacred vision of the soul and the love and compassion that come from the hearth. This is why it's so liberating to adopt the Celtic way of life, even in these modern times. By connecting to nature, we can recharge our spiritual energy to fill our entire day with positive intention. A strong intent, in turn, opens our hearts so we can perceive the meaning of life.

As you become more attuned to yourself, you will experience more powerful spiritual energies flowing towards you from nature. Your perception of the world starts to shift to a new insightful realm. Like it did in ancient times, Irish Celtic Shamanism is still a path that takes you on new adventures and allows you to forge connections to all the life forms that exist on this earth.

Celtic Magic in Scotland

While all historical evidence shows that Scottish Paganism has the same roots as its Irish counterpart, there are some notable differences between the two belief systems. Even though the Celts invaded Scotland shortly after taking over Ireland, the different geographical locations caused a significant divergence. Being connected to the mainland meant many other religions and practices influenced Scotland. For example, the nature-based folk had a substantial bearing on the Scottish Paganism development. Therefore, Pagans in Scotland came to respect nature as a sacred source of life. Human beings represent only a part of the whole and must learn how to co-exist peacefully with animals, plants, and every other living and non-living thing that exists around them. According to paganism, birth, growth, and death are interconnected and often carry spiritual meanings. Death is only a transitional phase in a person's life cycle, and it always leads to a new existence when the person is fully reincarnated.

In Scottish Paganism, even the deities are viewed as a manifestation of nature. The various divinities can take many different forms. Their gods and goddesses can send messages in many different ways, but the delivery is almost always connected to nature. They show up in animals, plants, and even human forms, particularly in dreams. Goddesses are thought to have a particular affinity to show up in the various elements of nature, so they are often held in much higher esteem. If one is looking for spiritual truth, they are much more likely to receive it from a goddess. The use of magical symbolism is one of the primary characteristics of Scottish Paganism, as is the case with its Irish counterpart.

The Sìth

Scottish Pagans have a very deep relationship with their land, evident in the traditional (ancient Gaelic) names they use for landmarks and events related to them. This is the result of honoring their ancestors buried in those lands. They believe they can maintain a relationship with the dead through the land. Similar to the Irish pagan belief system, the Scottish also recognize the existence of the otherworld. But the ancestor's spirits live on and provide guidance when needed.

However, according to most myths, the otherworld is also populated by many other creatures, including the Sìth. These creatures are similar to Aos Sí from Irish Pagan mythology and are described as luminescent, fairy-like beings. The most notable difference is that while their Irish counterparts are believed to have mostly neutral dispositions, the Sìth is almost described as malevolent creatures. They are said to lure humans in with their music, only to harm them. They can appear as cats, dogs, snakes, and ugly humans, representing danger for children and those unfamiliar with their lore.

According to another myth, the Sìth are descendants of humans who lived dishonorable lives. As the other dead spirits living in the otherworld can communicate with the living, so can the Sìth, except they always have an ulterior motive. If someone wants to communicate with them, they must understand the risk and must be prepared to bargain. Otherwise, the Sìth will seek to harm whoever they encounter.

Scottish Pagans have learned how to communicate with all spirits of nature, allowing them to understand and explore the realms behind theirs. This ideology is very different from modern magic practices, based on Celtic beliefs that have lost the true essence that lies in the heart of the Scottish Pagan way of life.

Cat Sìth

One of the creatures in Scotland pagans have learned to be wary of is the Cat Sìth. Although its size is closer to a larger dog, it has very distinctive catlike features, including the smooth black fur all over its body (hence the name Cat Sìth, or cat-fairy). It is believed to haunt the Scottish Highlands and is often mistaken for other larger animals living in the mountains. According to tales, many hunters and warriors have lost their lives hunting down this mysterious creature. Other myths suggest that the Cat Sìth are witches with human features and shapeshift into cats. However, they can only do this nine times before remaining a cat forever - a reference to the concept of cats having nine lives.

Whether they are fairies or witches, the general opinion is that they are not to be trusted. They lure people in, harm or steal from them. If the Cat Sìth crosses over a corpse of the dead before the burial, they can steal the deceased's soul. Gods cannot claim the dead without their soul, meaning they cannot remain in the otherworld. To prevent the theft of their ancestral souls, the Scottish set up guards to watch over the body until it's buried.

These guards were known as Feill Fadalach, and they were to draw the creature's attention away from the body with the usual methods of distracting a cat. They could play games with them, use catnip, riddles, and even music. It's also common knowledge that cats are drawn to warmth. Lighting fires near a body could attract the Cat Sìth to the area, so it is to be avoided as much as possible.

Cù-Sìth

Another malicious creature living in the otherworld was the *Cù-Sìth*, or fairy dog. With its intimidating size, dark green disheveled fur, and braided or coiled tail, the Cù-Sìth represents a truly terrifying picture. Like its cat counterpart, the fairy dog haunts the Highlands and is often mistaken for other, bull-sized animals. Most of the time, they hide in their homes, located in the crevices of the rocky mountainsides. They can only be noticed by their glowing eyes or when they suddenly appear in front of those crossing the mountain. Even when they roam around, they are stealthy hunters and only warn their prey from afar with their howls. Their appearance is believed to be a bad sign, as Cù-Sìth is also considered a forbearer of death and alarming news. A Cù-Sìth can take the soul of the dead to the afterlife after terrifying the poor victim to death. Those traveling the mountains are warned that if they hear one or two howls, they need to reach shelter before hearing the third one, as this is the last warning before the creature attacks.

There are also myths about the Cù-Sìth being the servant of the Daoine Sìth, the divine creatures fated to live in the underground fairy mound. They would ask the creatures to bring human souls for specific purposes. For example, women nursing children could provide milk for them, and their children were often used as bait to lure them out. To prevent them from being taken by the Cù-Sìth, these women and their children were locked up as soon as the howling was heard.

The Baobhan Sìth

Also known as the banshees of the pagan lore, the Baobhan Sìth are fairy-like creatures living outside human society. Keeping track of their every move, the Baobhan Sìth easily draws in their victims by inviting them to dance. Unlike banshees, succubi, and similar creatures from other cultures' myths, the Baobhan Sìth don't care much about staying young or powerful. However, their victims are almost always young people and are believed to have specific meanings. For one, this represents a bigger challenge when exhausting the victim with dance. When they see the victim is tired from the dance, they attack, cut their necks open with their long fingernails, and drink their blood. Young people have healthier and richer blood, and this is probably another reason for their choice of victims.

Highland warriors and hunters were particularly at risk of being lured in when roaming the mountains and forests. Due to the smell of blood from their kills, the Baobhan Sìth was drawn to the humans. They even used tricks like shapeshifting into wolves and other wild animals to stalk and lure in their prey. In another tale, the Baobhan Sìth shapeshift into women designed to entice the men, get close to them, and feed on them. These women could be recognized due to hooves instead of feet, which they tried to conceal under long dresses and skirts. Originally, they were also women, but once killed by the Baobhan Sìth, they turned into creatures.

Fortunately, these creatures also have weaknesses humans can use against them. As per a popular Scottish tale, horses and iron are the two main weapons used against the Baobhan Sith. According to this tale, a group of young hunters stopped to spend a night in an abandoned hunting lodge. To celebrate a successful day of hunting, they built a fire and made dinner.

As soon as they began to eat and drink, they heard a knock on the door. When they opened the door, they saw four beautiful women who claimed to be lost in the forest and asked if they could join the men and gain food and shelter from them. The hunters were more than happy to have female company and invited them in. When the women wanted to dance, the men willingly obliged. Before they realized what was happening, the women attacked them, revealing their long nails and hoofs.

One of the men had stepped away from the women at this very moment and stood by the door. Witnessing the death of his fellow hunters, he hurled an iron object toward the woman about to attack him and ran outside to the horses. He managed to kill the Baobhan Sith when the iron hit, but the others were on his trail.

However, as soon as he reached his horse, he noticed the creatures weren't coming closer to him. He stood among the horses until dawn when the women went back to their homes in the forest. After a quick look at the bloodless bodies of the clansmen, he went home to tell his clan what had happened and warned them of the dangerous creatures that lurk in the form of women.

Chapter 4: The Way of the Druid

While the Celts were known as great warriors, their elite formed a class of highly educated people responsible for maintaining their customs and order. Their wisdom played a fundamental part in shaping Celtic Paganism into the unique practice we know it to be. From this chapter, you will learn more about the beliefs of these distinguished Celtic groups called the Druids.

Who Are the Druids?

In ancient times, Druids were a group of Celts that enjoyed distinguished status in their society. They belonged to a highly educated class, with many responsible roles. Among them were teachers, judges, healers, and magicians possibly described as the equivalent of modern priests (men and women.) Despite this, the only evidence about their lives and roles in Celtic society comes from oral sources. What made them suitable for their roles was that their knowledge resulted from decades-long education. They were forbidden to write anything down, which meant all their knowledge had to be memorized. The early evidence of Druidry comes from over 2000 years ago, while the most prominent work of this class was documented during the Iron Age. During this period, Druids were held in such esteem they were often granted more responsibility and liberty than the tribe leaders.

Druids were able to consult otherworldly spirits and predict the future, so they were often asked for advice on matters ranging from personal to the entire tribe. A particularly known method for providing guidance before making an important decision was pouring liquid between two spoons (one spoon had a hole, and the liquid was poured from above into the second spoon below). If their answer was unfavorable, they advised the tribe against making the decision in question.

Druids also issued judgments in legal matters and handed out penalties, such as banning the offender from sacrificial rituals. This was considered one of the gravest forms of punishment because it meant that the person could not receive the blessings, protection, or any other protection the rest of the tribe received by their sacrifice. Sometimes a matter would be decided by an assembly of Druids, all having equal merit in the decision-making. The Druids typically gathered in a sacred place to vote on important matters once a year.

Most of their offerings consisted of animal sacrifices, but some sources describe human sacrifices. According to these tales, when someone was wounded in battle and came close to dying, the Druids offered a human sacrifice to save them. This was done by building huge wickerwork, filling it with criminals, and burning them alive. Their lives were exchanged for the life of the wounded innocents.

They rarely engaged in physical combat and mainly left matters of warfare to the chief of their tribe. Many young people joined the class because it meant being spared from fighting in battle. Some did this after encouragement from their families, while others came to this resolution on their own. As opposed to fighting and managing battlefields, Druids spent most of their time and energy learning the most they could about philosophy, astronomy, deciphering ancient verse, and the lore of the Gods.

While there is little known about how they conducted their rites in their early days, it's possible they were done in a large clearing under the open air. A location often associated with Druidry is Stonehenge. According to myths, Stonehenge was built by the Druids and used as a temple for their rituals. The structure was built approximately 5000 years ago - long before the first evidence of Druidry. However, since all this is based on oral recollections passed down through many generations, it's unclear whether the Druids were around the time the stones were put in place. The only solid evidence of this theory is that the stones align perfectly with the winter and the summer solstice. This place has a central role in festivities held for the summer solstice - a Sabbat celebrated by many Pagans. The Druids and Celts travel on the longest day of the year every year, even today, to Stonehenge for a small ritual at sunrise. Whether this is a result of the Druids elevating the structure or not, Stonehenge was and still remains a place of spiritual significance for them.

In modern Druidry, it's safe to say that it is somewhat different from its ancient roots - after all, it has been through many changes. Some of the changes were essential for the survival of the practice. With the arrival of Christianity, Druids were replaced by priests, and their functions were reduced to poets and historians. Yet, they managed to pass down the knowledge throughout centuries of oppression. During the 19th century, the interest in Druidry began to rise again, and new communities were formed in Europe and the United States. Modern Druidry represents a mixture of traditional practices and modern ideas and solutions. For example, animal or human sacrifices are no longer held in their communities. Instead, they offer food, alcohol, and symbolic structures built for this specific purpose, such as a structure stuffed with herbs, candy, etc.

While modern Druids are still required to undergo rigorous training before they are given any responsibilities, they are allowed to learn from books, write down anything they want, and use technology for educational purposes. Retaining the ancient ideology of Druidry, modern Druids are still focused on establishing a reciprocal relationship with their ancestors and between the members of their community. Although their roles are much tamer compared to ancient times, finishing their education grants Druids highly respectable functions in their community.

The Main Druid Philosophy

The central philosophy of Druidry has three equal parts: ancestral veneration, respect for nature, and the belief that everything is infused with nature. The different Druidry associations often have different views on the afterlife. However, almost all believe that the souls move on into another realm or body, continuing a predetermined cycle. They also agree that ancestral spirits hold much wisdom and provide guidance and protection, whether they come back in another form or only convey messages from the otherworld. Nature plays an essential role in each process as it either allows the spirits to visit this world as a living creature or carries the messages through spiritual passageways. Druids often hold rituals for honoring nature's role in their life. Each ritual is built around a particular myth selected by the presiding Druid. One of their grandest festivities is the welcoming of the spring solstice. They celebrate the awakening of nature's spirit during this festival, bringing them sustenance throughout the year.

Awen

One of the central concepts used in Druidry is Awen - the spirit that provides inspiration. Druids are often required to go on the quest for Awen, pursuing and fulfilling their purpose in life. Whether they become poets, historians, linguists, magicians, priests, or philosophers, is determined by Awen. Finding Awen means understanding where the Druid's strengths lie so that they will follow the path of their destination. Awen is unique to every soul, making it even more challenging to find. When a Druid finds Awen, they gain access to the wisdom of their ancestors in many vital matters. However, each Awen can only be recognized by the person to whom it is linked.

Finding and following their Awen is a sacred rule for the Druids, and it requires paying close attention to their inner spirituality. They must learn to ignore their ego, and everyone and everything else they come into conflict with, and only focus on their intuitive thoughts. This allows them to gain a deeper understanding of themselves, a step that's crucial for finding Awen. Druids are also required to set aside all convictions and prejudice about certain beliefs and their ability to make someone a better person. Since each person has a particular Awen unique to them, the different beliefs also provide a distinctive quality.

Druidry and Celtic Magic

Nothing illustrates better the long-standing relationship between Druidry and Celtic magic than the quest for Awen. The rites, spells, poems, and sacrifices designed to find one's spirituality are all inspired by nature. Celtic magic relies on forging spiritual connections through nature and natural forces. Druids use nature as their muse when enriching their practice and extending their creativity toward finding their life purpose. By spending time in nature and observing its colors, sounds, movements, and overall flow, they become profoundly inspired to create a piece of art, write a poem or a spell, design a ritual or dance, or do whatever they need to uncover the path of Awen. Or they can even create in open air, letting nature permeate their work as the inspiration flows through them.

Nature helps Druids gain a deeper understanding of Awen and how to harvest its benefits. According to Druid teachings, Arwen flows, similar to natural energy. It can travel from one person to another like the wind and touch them like the river touches its bank until it finds its corresponding soul. When this happens, Awen pours into a soul, inspiring its owner to make necessary changes in their life. However, for this to happen, Awen must be allowed to flow freely. The more it flows, the faster it finds the soul it's designed to inspire.

A great way to cultivate the flow of Awen is by reciting the following incantation:

"Awen, I sing of you

As I call you from the abyss

I am ready to receive the Awen that is granted to me

I welcome its call

Even if its power is limited

I know after it will well up

And the inspiration will flow again

You can also use this spell to call upon Awen:

I wish to behold Awen, the source of spiritual inspiration

I wish to find the muse that will guide my voice

So, I can call upon nature and earth

My ancestors and my guides

I ask them to inspire my craft

And let their creativity flow through me

May I receive the blessings of my souls Awen

So, it can stay within me from this day on."

Ritual for Invoking Awen

Another method for invoking Awen is performing a small ritual before any activity requiring higher creativity.

Collect water from a sacred place, like a natural spring or rainwater, and place it on your altar or the place you will perform the ritual. A small amount will be enough, as you can always make more, by adding water from any source. It will remain effective as long as it contains a drop of water from a sacred place. Pour some of the water into a small bowl and start your ritual. Take a few deep breaths, and allow your body and mind to settle. When you feel that your mind has calmed down, close your eyes, and recite the following sentence:

"Let the Awen come to me and inspire me through nature."

Visualize the Awen flowing toward you from the land, sky, and sea, permeating your soul and remaining within you. You seek inspiration when you sense it, open your eyes, and proceed with the endeavor.

Modern Druids

Nowadays, Druids live in smaller groups or are solitary practitioners but often meet with fellow Druids to share their life experiences. They also perform rituals on momentous occasions or celebrate Pagan festivals. Unless the weather makes this impossible, the meetings are held outside, either in someone's garden, a park, or a forest clearing. The people who celebrate together usually belong to one Grove, a group with at least two members who meet from time to time. Grove meetings can be held at times other than during the holidays, depending on the geographical distance that divides the members and people's schedules. For example, initiation of new members or sharing and exploring new teaching can also be an occasion for Druid gatherings. These are typically viewed as social gatherings to strengthen the spiritual connections within the community.

Many Groves are located across the continent, each having a unique way of conducting the teachings and organizing their membership structure. One of the most popular Groves is the UAOD or *United Ancient Order of Druids.* Founded in England, UAOD first spread its teaching through the European continent, later conquering Australia and the United States. This grove is open to all social classes - and in many countries, its purpose is to unite people facing unique challenges. Apart from providing an excellent opportunity for members to improve their knowledge in a specific subject, they often organize charity events to help their community.

Another example of famous Groves is the *Order of Bards, Ovates, and Druids,* known as OBOD. This Grove has a unique hierarchical structure based on the members' years of training and experience. The lowest grade they can occupy is the bardic grade. Once, the Celts' poets made it possible for this belief system to survive by creating various tales about the Celtic culture and the Druids. The second grade is reserved for the Ovates. They taught their community about the benefits of relying on nature in magic and life in general. The highest grade with the highest level of experience is the Druids, versed in journeying and magical practices through which they service the Druid traditions.

The Roles within a Grove

While their lower education level may suggest the Bards occupy a lower rank among the three, it couldn't be further from the truth. Being the custodian of the sacred magic is the greatest honor and influences all three functions of Druidry. These functions are spirituality, education, and politics - all part of a triangle that unites them. It means that while the Bards play an enormous role in education, they are closely connected with the other grades.

Being the masters of divination, the Ovate is responsible for informing their community about all the relevant prophecies and spiritual connections. Additionally, the myths bestow on them the ability to travel in time, allowing them to heal those in need or at least obtain the means to do so. When the Christian Church oppressed Druidry, the Ovate was the only way for the Celts to seek assistance from traditional sources. It taught them how to heal their wounds and persevere in difficult times while carrying on their ancient customs. Although they face different challenges nowadays, Ovate still uses spirituality to heal and guide others. Through spirituality, they even uncover a deeper meaning of life, while ethics guide them towards a path of light.

Druids are often described with the highest ranking, but this is only because of their role; namely, they are responsible for establishing laws or, in modern times, challenging them. Once, they were counseling kings and sovereign on how to achieve peace. Now, their role is reduced to resolving differences within their community and providing legal or financial assistance to those in need, so they need a deeper understanding of the social balance within a community. It's not uncommon for Grove members to train up to 20 years before they gather enough wisdom to occupy this function.

Typically, the purpose of a Grove is to set up a system where all individuals receive the highest education resulting in a class of beings with superior knowledge, allowing them to persevere in life. No matter which grade they specialize in, all members learn Celtic history, genealogy, and the current laws. This allows each grade to rely on the other two with confidence, as together, they can deal with any hurdles much more effectively.

Chapter 5: Ogham, a Magical Alphabet

The Celtic culture is not commonly remembered these days. However, it is a rich and dynamic culture with a long history. Today, the Northern European culture, including the Vikings and other clans that existed in the region, are diluted with the culture of new immigrants and settlers. Moreover, the culture has been exported to several different places across the Western world. It is hard to differentiate from modern Western culture. However, some jewels of the past beautifully preserved have managed to live on. One of the unique elements from the ancient Northern European cultures is the language. Even though it still exists today, it is very different from what it used to be.

The Origins

Ogham, known as the Scared Druidic Alphabet and the Celtic Tree Alphabet, is a language used to write primitive Irish. However, this same alphabet was also used to write several other languages common in the North European region, such as primitive Welsh and Latin. Today, there are few remains of this ancient script other than a few historical artifacts with inscriptions indicating that this language was widely used in much of the Western UK and some regions in Germany.

This language was typically carved onto stones to mark territories and, in some cases, as signs. There is evidence that this language was used in communication, though there aren't many artifacts to back this up. Most experts agree that Ogham is a very old language, probably around in the first century – or even earlier. However, most of the stone artifacts found with Ogham inscriptions are from the 4th century onward. The most recent of these artifacts were dated to the 6th century.

How to Read It

This language is unique from modern languages because the individual alphabet's characters are named after certain objects, a phenomenon known as the Briatharogam tradition. In Ogham, the alphabets are named after different trees, making the language unique and showing the importance of the trees in the culture. The alphabets themselves are known as Feda (trees).

Traditionally, Ogham had 20 alphabets, but five more were added later. The individual alphabets are grouped into 4 "Aicme" (tribes) of five alphabets each. The five alphabets added were Forfeda (special) alphabets but were not commonly used, increasing the number of Aicme to 5, making a total of 25 alphabets.

Similar, but not identical, to some language systems in East Asia, the Ogham alphabet is meant to be written and read vertically, from bottom to top. Nearly every letter other than the exceptional characters is a series of lines drawn through one main vertical line that serves as the "trunk" of the alphabet. All the letters have their unique sound, and some even sound similar to the modern English alphabets. However, pronunciation does vary with the dialect and the language they are being used for. Also, Ogham was commonly used to write names and label things so that people could tell who the object belonged to. Therefore, the structure of the language is not only a name, but rather it is in the third person where the statement sounds like "this belongs to so-and-so" instead of "this is so-and-so's item."

How to Remember It

Traditionally, Ogham was taught in schools alongside modern languages such as English and French. The process was very similar to learning any other language. Students were taught the alphabet through reading, writing, and phonetics and taught how to use these alphabets to construct words. However, since it was never used as a medium of communication, it was only taught to the extent where children could read it and get a good idea of its meaning and how it was constructed.

Suppose you want to memorize the Ogham alphabet and learn the language. In that case, a good starting point is to understand the structure of the letters and put this to your memory. While some sounds might be similar to English alphabets, the text is very different yet simple to remember. You can make things easier by following the alphabet according to the different *Aicme*. All the different Aicme have a specific structure. One Aicme will only have lines jutting out of the trunk to the right, while another will only have them jutting out to the left. In this way, you can simplify the process and remember the alphabets according to Aicme rather than memorizing 25 random characters.

Ogham and the Trees

Ogham has a deep relationship with trees. All the alphabets are named after trees, as previously mentioned. For instance, Beith is named after the Birch tree, and Sail is named after the willow tree. In many illustrations, the tree is part of the alphabet and is meant to make it easier for the readers to associate certain alphabets with the appropriate trees.

The Celtic culture of the past had a very close relationship with trees. Trees were a valuable resource physically and metaphysically for the people of those times. Most importantly, trees are a source of sustenance from the nuts and fruits they produce. They are also home to many birds and animals, which was another way for the Celts to find food quickly, especially during the harsh winter when hunting wasn't always as profitable. Similarly, the wood was used to build structures, make weapons, and, most importantly, make a strong fire to stay warm and cook on.

The significance of trees can also be seen in mythology and folklore, where they play a significant role. Countless Celtic stories are about how metaphysical forces and supernatural beings were related to trees, or the trees had a role in these stories.

Modern Uses of Ogham

The Irish language has gone through many stages of development, and what is considered modern Irish is very different from Ogham in how it is spoken and written. For instance, in modern Irish, the letter "gh," which traditionally had a "g" sound, is no more of a dip in tone than a complete sound. If you were to say Ogham, which technically sounds like Oh-G-Ham, now in modern Irish, it sounds like Om, or Ohm, where the "g" sound is omitted entirely.

There is little functional use for the Ogham language in the modern day. Even the languages it was designed to depict, like Irish and Latin, have very different alphabets. At most, Ogham stands as a memoir of what the Celtic culture used to be. Today, most Ogham is either used in tattoo art or wearable decorations and accessories. The popularity of using Ogham tattoos and other beatifications using the design cues of Ogham is vastly recognized.

Also, due to the relationship of Ogham and divinity, many uses for Ogham words and written depictions are in divinity and magic. Many people still believe in the supernatural power of the Ogham language and practice it according to their beliefs. For others, the Ogham language is the only path to connect with the Celtic gods, and various mantras and chants are used to call upon certain gods from this school of thought. As with many other cultures, there are different gods associated with different things, such as food, protection, and wisdom, and practitioners call upon the different gods depending on their needs and practice.

Ogham in Druid Culture

People in the Celtic culture, like many other cultures, had a caste system, with the Druids being the highest-ranking because they were concerned with metaphysical affairs. The Druids were responsible for all religious matters in the Celtic culture and were also the religious leaders and scholars of the Celtic people. In many cases, the Druids were ranked higher than other state leaders and even kings because they had direct contact with the gods. It was believed that the Druids possessed knowledge, power, and abilities that average humans, including kings and others of high status, lacked.

There were different roles within the Druids category, such as Priests, Shamans, Healers, and Fortune Tellers. In Celtic culture, trees have been the center of many matters similar to Druids. It is believed that the term Druids comes from the Celtic word "Doire," meaning "oak tree." The oak tree symbolizes knowledge and wisdom in Celtic culture and has a very high status among the trees. In the Celtic culture, the trees were usually placed in three categories; The Chieftain Trees, The Peasant Trees, and the Shrub Trees. It is important to note that the different categories of trees didn't make a difference to the tree's hierarchy or status. Instead, it was a way to organize the trees based on their unique characteristics. The oak tree belongs to the Chieftain trees. Examples of Peasant trees include birch, willow, hawthorn, spindle, and honeysuckle. Shrub trees include the apple tree, white poplar, elder, and reed.

Studying the Druids is challenging since so much information is based on information provided by neighboring cultures, such as the Romans. What makes it more complicated to keep track of is this was not a culture with very clearly defined principles. Unlike other religions, such as Islam's Quran or Christianity's Bible, there was no solid framework in place. There is no defined method of prayer, no weekly or daily prayer process, and no other concept that we can say has stood the test of time. Even though Druidism is still practiced today, it has undergone a series of changes and modifications depending on who and where it is practiced. Interestingly, many regional differences between people who practiced Druidism in the UK, where it was quite cold with long winters, and in Rome, where the temperature was much warmer and longer summers.

Ogham and Divination

Understanding how the Druids worked with divine matters, it is important to note that they used a lunar calendar and not the modern Egyptian solar calendar. This calendar is known as the Celtic Tree Calendar, and it is closely related to the Ogham alphabet. According to this calendar, the year is divided into 13 months, each 28 days long. Similarly, the major holidays are based on the transitions of the weather, and the natural environment is significant in the overall scenario. A new year begins every 31st of October, which is the same day as the last harvest in the United Kingdom. However, this is different for a Druid in the Roman region.

It's also important to note that the Ogham culture and Druidism are based on the concept of *Bnwyfre*, which is similar to the idea of Chi in Eastern philosophy. It relates to the life force we all have within us and how the different religious practices maximize this energy. Also, the culture is based on the Beth-Luis-Nuin concept, that there was first darkness and then light replacing this situation. This also refers to how religion is measured from new moon to new moon.

One of the most important traditions in the Druid culture pertaining to divination is the idea of the Finger Ogham. This is a technique where the hand is used to receive information from higher sources by the Druids. The hand represents the different alphabets of the Ogham alphabet. The consonants are at the tip of the fingers and also represent the lunar months, whereas the vowels are at the base of the fingers. In line with the five fingers, the number five also had a holy status and is usually associated with goddesses and the idea of the changing life cycles. It is also the number that shows the five critical elements of our lives: fire, water, air, earth, and the soul.

Finger Ogham is used as divination. The left hand is held over a person or an object meditated upon. The answer is based on the sensations the person feels in different parts of their hand. The hand is already measured out with letters, vowels, months, and other characteristics, which aids in understanding what the sensations in hand refer to.

Chapter 6: Unlocking Tree Magic

The Celtic culture places much importance on the environment: mountains, rivers, animals, and even plants have a unique place in the culture. However, the most important of all these are the trees. Trees are cherished for multiple reasons and numerous resources, with a spiritual and holy place in the culture. It is reflected in the literature where it praises the trees in many places and highlights how the most affluent people in Celtic cultures had a close affinity with trees.

Importance of Trees in Celtic Culture

For the Celtic people, trees provided several natural resources. Including shelter, building materials, food, protection, and, more importantly, served as the connection between the worlds. We can see that trees have greatly impacted literature, religion, mysticism, and the Celtics' way of life in different ways. Through the surviving Celtic lore, trees have become markers of the ancient cultural heritage of the Celts and allowed their spiritual identity to survive.

Many trees are found in the region where the Celtic people settled, and, for them, all the trees were precious and worthy of respect. The northern UK and bordering European regions are home to some of the thickest forests. Of the many trees within these forests, the Yew tree is given a higher rank than the others. It is seen as the tree that balances everything and brings together the male and female forces in the world.

Trees were so respected because they provided healing. Through the bark of the tree and the oils extracted from it, together with the leaves used as medicine, the Celtic people were able to cure a range of illnesses. Whether it was just a fever or a serious battle wound, there was a tree to provide assistance. Moreover, the Celtics believed that every living thing has a physical and metaphysical side, but they were unique because they extended this belief to plants. Trees were more important in the Celts' culture than in any other, even though general respect and fascination with trees are evident in different cultures of the same period.

Plant Spirit Allies

Many shamanistic approaches in cultures worldwide give plants an exalted status in their ideology. Whether it is things extracted or the physical form of the plant, they are unique creatures with energy and value. In the modern world, medicines derived from plants are chemicals and extracts, whereas, in traditional medicine, especially alternative healing, the plant from which the resource is derived has a value.

In Celtic culture, this concept is encompassed as the plant ally. It is the process where a person identifies with a plant at a much deeper level. They feel the plant's energy, understand what the plant is communicating, and, consequently, better their lives in the process. It is more than being one with nature. It is about internalizing nature and even receiving guidance from the plant ally.

In some cases, the relationship with the plant ally is a momentary interaction. For example, you walk down a path and see a plant reminding you of something or bringing a new thought into your mind. This was the purpose of the plant's interaction. In other cases, the plant ally has a much more permanent position in your life. The plant becomes an entity you can talk to, communicate with, and play a role in your life as with any other human relation. However, plants do not communicate with us as humans do. They are very different beings. The nature of the plant and human is a direct contrast, yet it is still very closely linked. Plants provide in countless physical ways and even more ways spiritually and metaphysically.

Getting a plant spirit ally is not about buying a plant, growing a plant, or even directly interacting with one. Rather, it is about waiting for that moment when a plant genuinely speaks to you. For some, this might be something they discovered in their youth, while many die in search of their plant ally. While there are certain plants you connect with more efficiently, all humans and plants can connect if you are willing to put in the time and effort required.

Tree Meditation

The idea of plant allies is put into motion more effectively when you combine it with a practice such as a tree meditation. Like any other form of meditation, tree meditation can have a range of benefits for both the physical and mental health of the practitioner. The core of tree meditation is aligning the human and plant energy so they are focused and expand as one.

Three main parts of the tree correlate with our existence that we can focus on during tree meditation. The first is the roots. They are buried deep within the soil, far from sight but hugely impact the overall growth and stability of the tree. Moreover, the tree begins its journey underground since the seed is underground and develops first. This relates to the world of dreams and the deep wisdom behind this phenomenon. Even though we don't see dreams with our eyes, we still "see" dreams, and they impact our lives. In the same way, we don't see the roots, but there is no denying they significantly impact the health of the tree.

The second part of the tree is the trunk, and it relates to the material world. As we use the tree trunk for wood to make a range of different things, the visible, physical part of our existence is what we usually do to remain alive – whether working a job you don't really like or tending to physical needs that cannot be avoided. This is the physical part of our existence, which, for some, is the core of their existence, and for others, it is the stepping stone leading them to higher consciousness.

The third part is the branches and the top of the trunk that extends towards the sky. It relates to our consciousness and how we work towards a more elevated level of awareness through meditation. This is where we have access to higher powers, divinity, and energy beyond human capacity.

Like a tree, if we get the right resources, we can continue to grow and develop into strong individuals who are successful in physical and metaphysical aspects, in our personal and professional lives, and ultimately, leading a balanced life.

Important Trees in Celtic culture

Oak

Oak is very close to the Druid people, and even the word Druid comes from the Celtic word for oak, "*Duir.*" Oak has been associated with the most powerful gods in a few different cultures.

The Greeks associated oak with Zeus, the god of gods, and the Celtics associated it with Taranis, the god of thunder. Interestingly, oak trees are associated with the god of thunder, or the god has some control over thunder, and thunderbolts and lightning most commonly hit the oak tree. The strength and longevity of the oak tree have been the subject of discussion for many poets, thinkers, and writers.

Ash

The ash tree also holds a very special place in Celtic culture. It is one of the three sacred trees, the other two being oak and hawthorn. Ash is part of the olive family, although it is much taller and stronger than an olive tree. This tree is not as common today as it was extensively cut down by the Christians in the 7th century when they invaded the Celtic region, and this practice symbolized their victory. According to tradition, St. Patrick used a wand made from ash to protect against snakes, and even today, the preferred material for a magic wand is ash. It is also believed that this wood has power over water, and when Irish immigrants were moving to America, they often carried a bit of ash wood to protect themselves from drowning.

Apple

The apple tree is commonly found in fairy tales in Celtic culture. There are countless accounts of a magical maiden with access to another realm using the apple as bait. In many stories, this apple also had superpowers. It either provided privileges like never-ending youth or regenerated as soon as it was consumed. In nearly all cases, this maiden used the apple to lure a handsome man to the other side of existence, possibly to a parallel universe. Apples were a fruit that not only gave good health, but which also gave life and were associated with rebirth, and why apples were often buried with people to give them fuel in the next life and to assist them with their rebirth. Interestingly, slices of apples were found in graves in Africa and other parts of Europe. These tombs and graves date as far back as 5000 BC, and, in some cases, there are graves from 7000 BC with traces of apples. We can assume those people used apples similarly or, at least, apples had some value for those passed on to the next life. However, Ireland is home to a unique species of apple known as the crab apple. The traditional apple was most likely brought to the region by the Romans as it does not naturally occur in the region.

Elder

The elder is also an important tree, and while it isn't part of the sacred trees, it does share similar status. Similar to rules concerning the hawthorn tree, it was forbidden to cut down an elder tree. The elder tree was used for many different purposes in the culinary, mystical, and medical departments since the flowers and the berries can be used to make wine. However, the wine made from the flowers was used as a celebratory drink, whereas the wine made from the fruit was used for divinations as it induced hallucinations. The elder tree was challenging to deal with. For instance, if the wine-making process isn't done properly, it could be fatal. Everything from the seeds, leaves, the bark, the flowers, and even the fruit can be poisonous if not harvested at the right time.

The culture of not cutting down the elder tree is common to other parts of Europe, and while the reasoning differs, not permitted to cut this tree remains the same. Later, the elder tree got a bad rep due to the Christians of that time, as they believed the cross on which Christ was crucified was made from elder wood. Similarly, Judas, who betrayed Jesus, is thought to have hung himself from the elder tree, so it was inherently an omen of bad luck. This is most likely where stories of the elder witches came from, as it was a tree associated with the devil.

Alder

Growing along streams, rivers, and swamps, the alder is linked to mysterious forces, secrecy, and bad fortune. Being a historically engrained cultural and spiritual orientation all these years, people in certain Irish communities still believe that running into an alder tree is a sign of bad luck or misfortune. The gloomy atmosphere of the alder woods makes them the ideal hiding place for fairies and other spirits – good or bad. The green flowers and leaves of the alder are perfect for concealing supernatural beings from human eyes. To walk amongst them would mean to disturb their lives. Therefore, these woods were seldom visited, particularly around the spring when fairies are said to be the most active.

However, since alder grows in wet conditions, the older trunks become very hard. The Celts made use of this quality by drying out mature trees and using them as charcoal to light fires with intense heat, like those needed to forge their weapons. As the alder tree burned under the heated-up metal, it also imbued the weapons with natural spiritual power.

A living and healthy alder tree is usually pale in color; you can find out that it has been cut or affected one way or another if a deeper, warmer color starts spreading across it; almost as if it's bleeding. This picture gave another reason for the Celts to develop a series of negative associations with this tree, linking it to death, injuries, and ailments. At the same time, they revered alder and even linked its roots to fertility. The same way alder roots found their way to thrive in wet soil; they can be used in rituals for enhancing the fertility of the land and one's own life.

Yew

While most sources tie the yew to Roman mythology, their records show that this tree has been revered long before its dominion over Europe. Native to the British Isles, the yew tree has been part of Druidic practices ever since the Celts arrived there. They observed that fallen branches of the tree could take roots and form new trees, revealing the yew's incredible regenerative abilities. Due to this, the yew becomes the symbol of death and resurrection. The dead were buried with yew tree branches to help their souls move on, a practice that continued well into the Christian era. A similar symbol of cultural resistance was planting yew trees besides churches and using branches during Christian ceremonies.

Another connection between the sacred yew tree and death was its toxicity. Druidic teachings indicate that even slips of yew needles were enough to cause an illness or even death. However, a tincture made from the flesh of yew berries can cure ailments, especially those caused by an inflammation of some sort. The yew's power is the strongest if harvested during the new moon.

Hazel

The Druids revered the hazel tree for its ability to grant higher wisdom; "*cno*," derived from "*cnocach*," meaning wisdom, is the Gaelic word for hazelnut. According to ancient Celtic lore, nine hazel trees grew around a sacred body of water in which salmon grew. When matured, the nuts fell into the water and were eaten by the fish. The salmon absorbed all the wisdom the nuts contained and were a suitable vessel for its distribution amongst humans, becoming the Salmon of Knowledge. If a Druid wanted to expand his knowledge, he needed to catch salmon with bright spots on its body. The brighter spots the fish had, the more hazelnuts it consumed - and the more wisdom they received.

According to Celtic mythology, hazel is also associated with other magical springs and wells, not only the one containing the Salmon of Knowledge. Mature hazelwood contained just as much wisdom as the nuts did. Wands made from this wood could settle arguments or, in some cases, even administer the law. Whichever part of hazel was used, it was fundamental to preserve the tree's ability to survive and regenerate.

Due to all this, cutting down an entire hazel tree often carried the death sentence as punishment.

Parts of a hazel tree were also used for Druidic rituals as an offering, fire, or containers for other tools. Forked twigs of hazel were used for divination – as it was known to help locate bodies of water and other natural sources of magic. The Celts also believed that young hazel leaves have healing abilities for humans and animals. They would make tea out of it to aid digestion and feed the leaves to cattle to improve milk yield.

Willow

Since most willow species thrive close to waters, there is little wonder Celtic folklore is full of tales based on this watery theme. The moon is also often associated with both the willow tree and the water. When covering the trunk, the water empowers the willow with spiritual magic, and the cycle of the moon affects how much of the tree will be covered. It's believed that willow contains less power during the waning phase of the moon. Therefore, if one wants to take advantage of the willow's benefits, they should wait until the waxing phase to harvest.

Willow has found many uses in Celtic healing rituals and practices. When made into a bitter infusion, willow bark alleviates fevers, pain, and inflammation. Deities associated with the power of the moon are often offered willow parts as an expression of gratitude, reverence, or need for assistance. Being a hunter-gatherer nation, the Celts have also used willow for building boats, coracles, houses, and much more.

Apart from the Celtic lore, the power of the willow is also illustrated in Greek mythology. Their priestesses and healers used this sacred tree for water magic, healing, and other witchcraft practices. The Greeks also linked willow to wisdom and inspiration, and the tree was revered by poets and philosophers alike.

Holly

Nowadays, holly berries and leaves are linked with Christmas, a Christian religious holiday. This symbolism stems from the similarities between the spiny leaves of the tree and Jesus' crown of thorns and between the red berries and savior's drops of blood he shed for humanity. Historical artifacts show that holly was part of similar pre-Christian Yule celebrations. The Celts would bring Holly berries and leaves into their homes to brighten up the cold and dark winter days. Young men would adorn themselves with holly leaves, while girls would wear ivy and walk around in their community. This ritual is said to cause winter to end soon and the New Year's fertility to re-emerge.

The use of holly around Yuletide emanates from the tales of Celtic mythology. According to these, the Oak King ruled over half the year from the winter to the summer solstice. Then, he battled with the Holly King, who, defeating him, took over to rule the other half of the year. His rule lasted until the winter solstice came again, and another battle between the kings ensued – and this time, it ended up with the Oak King`s victory.

The stories depict the Holly King as a giant wielding a holly bush and covered in holly. A similar illustration is found in the Arthurian legend - where the Green Knight arrived wearing a similar ensemble challenging Gawain during Christmas celebrations.

Apart from adding color and a piece of nature to their home, the Celts brought holly into their homes for several other reasons. They used the leaves as a source of winter fodder for livestock because they believed the magical properties of holly would protect the animals. Planting holly near houses was another common practice used to ward off malicious spirits and bad intentions. The fall of the entire tree was believed to be the work of these spirits and was considered bad luck. However, if only parts of the tree had fallen to the ground, they had already fulfilled their protective function outside the home and were safe to bring inside.

At other times, holly branches with leaves served as shelters for benevolent faeries inside the home. The leaves allowed these beings to hide from the harsh winter as well as from the people living in the home. Another Celtic tale depicts how holly was used to decide who had the most say in the household. Holly leaves come in two forms; prickly and smooth. Whichever type was brought into the home first around Yuletide determined whether the husband or the wife would rule their household through the following year.

Hawthorn

This tree is commonly associated with fairies and is often thought to be a gentle tree with magical powers. Out of respect, it is often referred to as the lone bush or simply the thorn as it is considered bad manners to mention fairies by their names. If one tree could be even worse to cut down than the elder tree, it would have to be the lone bush. It is considered a bad luck omen if one even hurts the hawthorn tree. It is so highly esteemed that many people won't even talk about it, let alone damage one due to respect and fear. However, Hawthorn trees have always been considered a source of protection from threats not visible to the human eye. Evil spirits, witches, and other threats are thought to be powerless in front of the majestic hawthorn tree.

Interestingly, in modern Britain, the hawthorn tree is considered a sign of love and prosperity. In the summertime, lovers would frequently meet under the loving shade of a hawthorn tree. Across the border, in Greece, brides often wore a decorative hawthorn crown. Even the wedding torch was made from hawthorn tree branches, and it was good luck for the couple exchanging vows.

On the contrary, Christians (not in the modern-day) believed the crown of thorns placed on Jesus Christ's head during the crucifixion was made from the hawthorn tree. Naturally, this school of thought would not favor this tree quite as much.

Many of the beliefs associated with the different trees of the regions have managed to live on. Even today, we see many people, even those not from Celtic culture, abide by these ideologies and respect the trees as the Celtic people did. While trees may not play such an essential role in our lives today, they are still crucial, especially for the Druids.

Chapter 7: Practicing Ogham Divination

The Ogham text is used for divination by Celtics and those wanting to participate in the Ogham culture for the divinity aspect. Similar to tarot cards used by fortune tellers and other systems used by palmists, the Ogham alphabet is used to decipher information about the past, present, and future. The Ogham culture gives insight into any situations you might face. Many people use the Ogham divination system daily to understand how they should pursue their day, what challenges they might face, and how they should deal with these matters. The other thing that makes this form of divination quite interesting and unique is that different people can interpret various things differently. The meaning can be adjusted to suit your personal preferences. This is an important aspect that requires time to perfect. This doesn't mean that you will read what you want to read or that would kill the purpose of divination. Instead, it means that the meanings you assign to different characters may be different.

For instance, if a certain character means something positive, this may indicate something good is coming your way. But, for someone else, this may mean a day when they won't have to make stressful decisions, or they can take things a little easier. So, the way you interpret the signs may be different, and that is fine. Many people who practice divination through the Ogham letter find that the meanings they associate with the letters change over time. Since all the alphabets are named after trees, or at least associated with a tree, they all have different characteristics reminiscent of the nature or structure of the tree they represent. For instance, the olive tree is generally seen as a feminine tree. It gives plenty of nutritious fruit, has healing properties, is small compared to an oak or mahogany tree, and is rather slow growing.

When one person looks at these factors, they may think they will have a fruitful day, a day where things will be warm and happy as the olive tree prospers in warmer weather, or find something that yields multiple benefits or expect a small positive surprise like the olive tree. On the other hand, a different person may interpret this as a challenging day since it takes a while to develop, or a day when they have to be careful about the environment as the olive tree requires consistent weather to fruit properly. They may be considering multiple risks since the olive tree gives multiple things, but even if one thing goes wrong, multiple things could be lost or wasted.

So, it depends on how you look at things, your situation, your walk of life, and other factors. Again, the more you learn about the alphabet, the more you will know and the better your understanding can be drawn from this divination. Let's look at the two ways Ogham divination is practiced.

Ogham Divination through Staves or Tiles

The process for divination through these tools is relatively straightforward and can be modified to meet your requirements. Generally, it is suggested that you use at least three staves or three tiles to uncover the message. However, in some cases, where the question is a simple yes or no, it is suitable only to draw a single stave or tile. In other situations, and depending on your needs where you seek a more in-depth answer to a more open-ended question, it may be appropriate to use more staves or tiles.

When performing the actual divination, there are a few ways to do it. Some people prefer to allocate a certain time of day to practice divination, which is somewhat of a ritual. Unlike tarot cards, where the expert merely reads the cards whenever you visit, when doing your divination, there are different ways you can choose to do it. Some people prefer to say a prayer, light candles, or even cleanse themselves before they do the reading. For others, it is something they do casually, whenever they feel the need. Also, some people prefer practicing in a particular part of the home, or outdoors or doing it during the day or at night. Once you start, you may feel better doing it before going to bed to help you through the next day or prefer to do it first thing in the morning.

These are variables you can work on according to what suits your needs, and they will get more refined as you practice.

When using the Ogham alphabets for divination, you only need to use the main 20 characters as the exceptional characters will not yield much value. Also, it is helpful to compile a list of traits and features of the various alphabets and learn the history of each. The more you know about each character the stave, or the title expresses, the more intricate and accurate your deductions.

For instance, the oak tree, known as Duir in Ogham, is represented by a vertical line with two perpendicular lines pointing outwards to the left. Duir is the name of the alphabet, and as a word, it means door. In this way, this tree is seen as the doorway to higher consciousness and the unseen world. Similarly, the oak tree is considered the king of the forest, or the king of the trees in the forest, a slow-growing tree that develops a strong and large structure with deep roots and a broad and tall network of branches. The oak tree is a very resilient plant and can withstand very long cold winters.

The wood is known for its quality. It is extremely smooth and hard, and the grain goes in the same direction. This wood doesn't deform very easily and can withstand various harsh conditions if processed correctly. Due to the toughness of this wood, it is not common for termites or other insects to cause harm, and it is very durable. Even though the original color is light, thanks to the natural patterns, just a bit of varnish or light tan can really make the wood stand out. Just looking at the tree, you can see its presence demands respect, and it oozes strength in every way. It is a majestic tree associated with wisdom, strength, patience, and resilience. It also represents justice, equality, prosperity, health, and protection.

Also, the Duir is a calendar star, and it governs people born between June 10th and July 17th. It is also associated with the number 7. The associated color is gold, the main feature is strength, the associated animal is a white horse, and associated plants include the mistletoe and the coltsfoot.

If you find Duir in your divination, know that you must handle the matter with courage and strength to walk through the door of change. You also need to maintain integrity and think things through as the wise oak tree takes time to grow and expands in every direction. Consider all the possibilities, and whatever you decide, be prepared to hold this stance for the long term. The oak tree yields acorns that are also very dense and solid protection for the seed within them. In the same way, when you see Duir in your divination, know that you have to act with wisdom, or the wisdom is already within you, and you must have the courage to act on it. Within these steps you are about to take, there is wisdom and a precious result, one that may yield a very strong outcome like the little oak seed that yields a mighty tree. It's essential to remember that the Duir is the doorway to experience, knowledge, information, and an overall up-gradation of consciousness. Even though the decisions are challenging, they are the way to go.

In this way, the Ogham alphabets can be interpreted in different styles, and the deeper your understanding of the alphabet, the more information you will draw from the stave or tile.

How to Create Ogham Staves

Some people prefer to make the wooden staves out of the wood they are associated with. So, the Duir stave would be made out of oak. However, others argue that they should all be made out of the same wood so that you can't tell the difference when picking them out. Similarly, some prefer to have staves of a smaller size, small enough to fit them all in your hand. Others like to have rather large staves, a foot long and a few inches thick. If you want something portable, stick to a smaller size, but you can make them larger if it's a home kit.

The process is quite simple. You have to inscribe into the stave the different alphabets. Some people prefer to burn the alphabet into the stave, some prefer to scratch it in, while others merely stain it into the wood. It all depends on what you have and what you are comfortable doing.

Also, you can finish and polish the wood as you prefer or leave it plain and raw.

How to Create Ogham Tiles

You can create the tile from clay, wood, ceramic, or any material you like. Some people even make small tiles the size of dominoes made out of marble or a different stone and made with a nice finish in a color of their choice. Usually, the tiles are made in a rectangular shape, although you can use squares, hexagons, or triangles. It's all a matter of preference and what is viable for you. The alphabet must only be written on one side of the tile as the orientation can change the alphabet entirely. Also, consider the material depending on how you want to use the tiles. Some people prefer to pick up a few tiles and throw them onto the floor, while others like to pick each one individually and place it gently in front of them. It is recommended that the staves and tiles be made from natural materials rather than man-made materials, so they are more connected with the earth, and this helps to keep their energy as pure as possible.

Also, when creating tiles or staves, it is important to mark the tiles from the first and third families of alphabets as they look the same, the only difference being the direction in which the lines are pointed. If you see the same tile inverted, it can cause confusion. Similarly, even the tile with diagonal lines has an orientation, so it's good to make a small mark on the stave or the tile to ensure you have placed it down in the correct orientation and you are reading correctly. Usually, these tiles will not require washing, but some people prefer to wash their tiles and staves to cleanse the energy and recharge for the next use.

If you prefer, say a prayer before your question or simply move directly into your question and pull out the alphabets to see the responses. Saying the question out loud or in your mind is fine either way. However, be thoughtful about the question. Make it as concise and accurate as possible so that you don't have to ask too many follow-up questions and get the most out of each question. At the end of the divination, it is considered good etiquette to say a word of thanks to the forces that helped you find your answer and treat your alphabets with respect. If you prefer, you can sit outside under a tree or on the ground to get your energy better connected to the Earth's energy.

Chapter 8: Conducting Celtic Rituals

Ceremonies and rituals are practices dating back to the first recorded human history. For example, Paleolithic cave paintings dating back more than 10,000 years suggest that our ancestors gathered around fires performing fertility dances. They also partook in other spiritual ceremonies that celebrated their hunts. Regardless of religion, ethnicity, geographic location, or culture, all societal groups in humanity have distinctive rituals, traditions, and ceremonies that give meaning and purpose.

Unfortunately, we no longer hold rituals and ceremonies of the same significance and importance as we once did. In this age, we use science and evidence to lead our lives. Rituals and ceremonies have become widely frowned upon due to their lack of functionality and scientific corroboration. They are now typically exclusive to native tribes or peoples and religious institutions.

While we don't need ceremonies, traditions, and rituals in today's digitally-driven world, many people don't realize they are an intrinsic part of humanity, a human instinct, even. Our ancestors needed the power of rituals because they gave them a sense of structure. They helped them make sense of a world they truly understood as they prayed for rewarding hunts, stable weather, and fertility. Today, we can check the weather predictions a week ahead and not worry about harvesting or hunting for food. Although we now have more access to life's riches and a deeper understanding of the world around us, the magic of life is no longer imminent.

The diminishing role of rituals has deprived us of a very important aspect of life. Not only are our rituals important for our happiness, but they also allow us to maintain and build communities, essential for a healthy society.

Food, water, clothing, shelter, air, sleep, love, hygiene, and communication are important for human survival, and we also need rituals and ceremonies. Rituals help instill an inner sense of belonging. They remind us that life and our human experience are a lot greater than we can ever comprehend. They reach beyond our physical existence. Ceremonies and rituals help us develop a deeper appreciation for the universe and enrich our perception of archetypes like continuity, faith, devotion, and unity. Rituals help us build a connection to the divine and serve as a pathway to recounting the capacity of existence, which is rather baffling to the human mind.

This is why rituals are vital to finding success and thriving in life. They donate a sense of direction in our physical experience. They allow us to forge deeper connections with ourselves and our souls and the higher power that grants life. Connecting with people interested in Celtic magic is awesome. However, conducting ceremonies and partaking in rituals establishes a sense of unity rather than separation. Even if they don't necessarily live in your area, sharing your experiences online, through Facebook groups, blogs, or forums shows that others strive and long for the same things as you.

While modern science undoubtedly allows us to comprehend the numerous mysteries of life, the need for belonging, especially regarding something we feel so deeply for, still persists. We need rituals and ceremonies in times of great uncertainty the most. They help us stay grounded through transformative experiences and big changes in life, such as marriage or death.

Even though some rituals, like funerals, birthdays, and weddings, are still present and celebrated, many others have been abandoned. Perhaps it is because many traditional rituals are too complicated to fit into our modern-day lives. The rituals don't cater to our deepest needs and yearning for meaning. Sadly, the lack of important rituals in our lives disconnects us from ourselves, our culture, or our beliefs. Therefore, it's important to incorporate them into the fast-paced life and ever-changing nature of the world we live in.

Choosing rituals or even making your own can be challenging, especially if you don't follow a certain belief or show an interest in a solid spiritual endeavor. If you're reading this book, you're likely to be interested in Celtic magic and traditions. Fortunately, this chapter includes various simple Celtic rituals you can try. It also explains the five Celtic rituals and how they were conducted in ancient times. You will learn how to conduct a modern Celtic ritual and its Druid, Scottish, and Irish variations.

Ancient Rituals

The Celts held rituals when the community was subject to great stress. They also conducted rituals for specific purposes and followed certain situations. Scholars also believed that the Celts followed a certain astronomy-based schedule, particularly a schedule based upon the phases of the moon. They offered incantations and prayed to their gods. They also made votive offerings to gain the favor of the gods. They believed that this would help them get outcomes in their favor and ward off disasters like famine, floods, drought, or wars. These offerings typically took the form of jewelry, bejeweled armors and weapons seized from the enemies, pottery vessels, and other precious goods. They also offered foodstuffs, and, in case someone had recovered from an illness, they'd offer the affected body part.

The Celts were very concerned with rituals as they helped bring structure and order to their lives and keep up with changing seasons and the passage of time. Rituals also allowed them to make sense of and find meaning in the world around them. They used rituals and celebrations to understand and explain happenings they couldn't control. For instance, they used the Wheel of the Year, which split the year into eight portions, and celebratory feasts, to mark the change of seasons and comprehend the changes in land fertility, hunts, etc. The way they attempted to understand natural phenomena and happenings shows how they tried to go beyond the material world and forge connections with the forces they believed affected the dynamics of life. There are five main Celtic rituals; magic rituals, curative rituals, divination rituals, transmigration rituals, and rituals performed at seasonal feasts.

1. Magic Rituals

As you can infer from their name, Magic rituals involved the use and concept of magic. The "Magic of the Head" was one of the most significant magic rituals. It revolved around the belief that the human mind, or head, is vital to magical practices. They also believed that it was of great potency and power, which is why the Celts often beheaded their enemies at war so they could preserve and put them on display.

• Human Sacrifices

Magic rituals involved curative plants (more on that later), and they are portrayed in various Druid tales. Evidence of calling onto a god to invoke blessings and curses is apparent on lead plates and other artifacts. Human sacrifice was also an aspect of magic rituals. There is evidence of a man from Lindow moss in England who was ritualistically hit on the head, strangled, and drowned. Other stories suggest that Celtic people often practiced the ritualistic killing of humans. Various Druid spells are linked to Druid priests and women, claiming they could control or influence natural elements. Many tales included claims of invisibility and the ability to turn rocks into armies of armed men and move mountains.

• Wands

Wands also played a great role in Druid magic rituals. Druids believed that wands were living objects, metaphysically speaking, because they believed trees have dryads or special spirits or souls. The significance of dryads (the human spirit in its essential nature) is that they're divisible. They're considered a quality of wood, like color, texture, luster, grain, and other properties. Therefore, the dryad is distributed throughout the entire tree or log. So, when the pieces are used to make wands, they still contain a whole dryad, like the entire tree. While using or making wands, Druids often employed rituals and recited blessings to activate and awaken the wand's dryad. Wands were considered more than just tools. They were also a practitioner's magical partner.

• Smudging

Smudging was also another aspect of the Druid magical practices. Smudging involved the burning of a stick or bundle of dried herbs. The purpose of this practice was to clear away negative energy and create positive vibes. A smudge stick differs from incense because it's made of plenty of leaves and has to be waved or moved around so that the smoke spreads effectively. On the other hand, incense is mixed with essential oils and is often transformed into granules, cones, or attached to sticks, and you don't need to wave it around.

Druids paid extra attention to the types of herbs that they gathered and used for smudging. They also typically made, and still make, their smudge sticks because each herb has its own characteristics and traditional uses. Your choice, along with your intentions, determines what your smudging practice attracts into your life. For instance, you can use the same herb to get rid of negative energy and attract good fortune and love into your life. Look up the characteristics of various herbs to know their purposes.

2. Curative Rituals

Curative rituals are associated with restoration and healing. The Celts believed there were ten elemental constructs for healing: water, stones, herbs, fire, nature, music, deities, symbols, rituals, and storytelling. Each element connected to or supported another element, acting as a dimension of Celtic daily life.

• Alternative Healing

In essence, Druid healing practices promote the support of spiritual and physical health through energy manipulation, exercise, and balanced or healthy diets. Although Druidry is a long-established spiritual tradition, Druids are always encouraged to experiment with their preferences and beliefs regarding magic, deities, and other spiritual endeavors. This is particularly important because there is no solid method for conductive rituals. Ancient and modern-day Druids typically incorporate alternative healing methods, such as healing rituals and spells, herbs, and Reiki, into their personal practices.

Druid healing practices involve the use of healing herbs the Celts traditionally used. Some herbs like vervain and St. John's Wort are used to make tinctures and teas, while others are used for their symbolic meanings. Plants were also popularly used by the Irish for their healing properties.

Many individuals accompanied the use of plants with spells and charms. It was believed that bladder stones could be cured with wild garlic infusions, epilepsy with juniper berries juice, and intestinal worms with tansy infusions. Sores and cuts were also widely healed using figwort. There is evidence of hemlock removing cancer growth with the right invocation.

- **Animals and Their Products**

It was believed that passing an individual under a horse's belly would cure their cough. The Celts believed that the horse had to be white, while many areas around the British Isles believed the horse needed to be piebald. Of course, where you lived as a Celt came with a few unique rituals. The Irish Celts, for example, believed that dandelion potion could cure asthma. The Scottish Celts, on the other hand, believed asthma could be cured if you smeared deer grease on the soles of your feet.

- **Spells and Charms**

In Celtic customs, fairies have always been known to be especially dangerous during childbirth. To save a mother and protect her child from being abducted, a piece of iron was usually placed in the mother's bed. The infant also had to be baptized as soon as possible to be kept safe from the evil spirits. Charms were also routinely used to protect people from injuries, especially those caused by the evil eye or obtained during battle.

Druid healing rituals and spells are often a combination of invocation and serve as a healing plea. They also visualize healing light or energy delivered to the suffering individuals. Many also use healing herbs to enhance the effect of the spell. They may also indulge in meditations that help rid undesirable energy and reduce stress levels.

- **Water**

It's known that the source of all life is water, and with that in mind, it comes as no surprise that it was used in many rituals. Add to that, if the water came from a specific well or river, it was thought to have incredible medicinal powers. The Irish believed that ailments such as mumps could be cured if the suffering individual drank water from specific rivers three times. Certain wells were also thought to reduce toothaches. They were also associated with local gods, and so, their healing characteristics were linked to the deities.

3. Divination Rituals

Apart from being associated with fortune-telling, divination also involves revealing hidden inner or external dynamics. It can also be defined as a very deep self-understanding and knowledge and the ability to know the unapparent reasons behind happenings.

Druids used numerous methods of divination, encompassing simple methods, such as weather-witching, to more complex ones like the observation of bird flight. They also examined animal behavior and elucidated planetary configurations. The Irish Druids used cloud divination or Neldoracht and a more sophisticated method, Tarbhfeis, which required the individual to wrap themselves up in a bull's hide. It was believed that the clairvoyant person could refine their abilities by doing so.

You can enhance your clairvoyant abilities by indulging in a wide array of divination rituals better suited for modern-day life. For example, you can work with sacred animals and traditional Druid and Celtic plants and herbs.

4. Transmigration Rituals

Transmigration is also known as reincarnation. In a spiritual, religious, philosophical sense, transmigration is the concept that a person's soul or spirit starts a new life in a different body or physical form following their physical death.

The Celts believed in life after death. Therefore, they buried individuals with their ornaments, weapons, and food. The Druids taught the principle of the transmigration of souls. They also explained the significance of nature and the power of the gods. The Celts practiced urnfield burial, which involved creating the body and placing its ashes in an urn. However, this only lasted until the 6th to the 8th century BCE, when they started practicing Inhumation burial rites (full-body burials). However, the process differed according to a person's class. Slaves and lower-class individuals were buried in normal graves, with a few prized possessions, while the nobles were buried with swords, jewelry, wine flagons, chariots, and more. They usually scattered large rocks and mounds around the burial site to ward off evil spirits.

The Irish believed in the existence of an otherworld. The otherworld was thought to be an island in the vast seas or located underground. They explained it as a country free of death, illness, and aging. They thought it was a happy place where a day was equivalent to a hundred Earth years.

5. Rituals at Seasonal Feasts

As we mentioned above, feasts were a significant aspect of the Celtic culture. They had season feasts to celebrate important changes and dates in their calendars. They used a Wheel of the Year to split the year into eight portions to mark the cyclical alternation of seasons. They mainly celebrated four fire festivals every year; Samhain, Imbolc, Bealtaine, and Lughnasadh. Equinoxes and solstices are also integrated into the wheel, with these four main festivals. The so-called quarter-festivals are Yule, Ostara, Litha, and Mabon. Each celebration accompanied a set of unique rituals, discussed in more depth in the following chapter.

Rituals are a vital aspect of humanity. They help keep us reminded of purpose and donate a sense of structure and were conducted in every culture throughout history, and played a vital role in Celtic, Druid, Irish, and Scottish traditions. The most significant traditions were magic, curative, divination, transmigration, and seasonal feast rituals. There are numerous modern-day-friendly ways you can incorporate these practices into your personal routine.

Chapter 9: Sacred Celtic Holidays

Celtic holidays hold a special place in ancient and modern pagan rituals and can significantly affect druidic magic and Celtic rituals. Each holiday is associated with a seasonal event and falls between solar events and turning points of the year. Although ancient, these holidays are still celebrated throughout the Celtic culture, with many traditional rituals carried out specifically on these holidays.

When learning about Celtic rituals and spells, it's important to understand the significance of these sacred holidays to best channel their energy through spells and rituals. While the ancient Celts had specific rituals for each holiday, their importance in modern paganism cannot be understated. Therefore, it's best that you understand the sacred Celtic holidays and their energies before carrying out special rituals on these holidays.

Listed below, in chronological order, are the eight most important sacred Celtic holidays throughout the year, starting with St Brigid's day in February through to the winter solstice in December.

1. St Brigid's Day - Imbolc

The year's first Celtic holiday, St Brigid's day, marks the first day of spring and is celebrated on February 1st. This day is associated with Ireland's first native saint, St Brigid, the Abbess of one of the first convents in Ireland. The symbolic representation of this day is associated with a straw or a red cross. Brigid day is associated with poetry, healing, and fertility and marks the beginning of a new season of hope.

Historic Celtic Rituals

According to ancient Celtic tradition, St. Brigid's day marked the beginning of the year. It was, therefore, celebrated with great fervor to secure St. Brigid's protection and promise of great abundance for life ahead. Ancient Celtic rituals during St. Brigid's day included the following:

- Ancient Celts celebrated Imbolc as one of the quarter days that marked a transition from one season to the next. The festivities took place on the eve of the day because this time was considered effective for spells and rituals.

- The traditional festive meal of St Brigid's day included a supper of potatoes with freshly churned butter, followed by apple cakes or barmbrack and tea.

- St Brigid's crosses held a special place in tradition. Many people believed that St Brigid would pass by and bless the homes with these crosses hung in her honor on the day of the festivities. There were many regional variations in the making and hanging of these crosses, but most served the same purpose to attract the saint's blessings.

- Leftover material from the crosses and old crosses from the previous year was sprinkled on the land to protect crops and livestock or incorporated into the animals' bedding.

- The tradition of a Brat Bríde or Ribín Bríde was common in ancient Celtic traditions. People would leave a piece of clothing or ribbon on the windowsill, which was endowed with healing or curative properties by St. Brigid on the eve of her feast.

- Many wells were dedicated to St. Brigid and visited by people on the eve of St Brigid's day every year.

Modern Celebrations

Modern paganism celebrates Brigid's day in various ways. While some modern pagans follow most ancient Celtic rituals, others have defined newer ways to celebrate this feastful day. Some modern pagan celebrations include:

- Special Imbolc feasts with traditional meals like dumplings, baked bread, eggs, milk, colcannon, etc., are dedicated to the saint Brigid.

- A cleansing bath ritual is customary to wash away the negative energy from the dark season (winters) in preparation for the new season.

- Brigid crosses are made through various methods, styles, and materials and hung outside homes to attract blessings and positive energy.

- A fire lighting ritual is followed to beckon the warmth of the coming sun. Whether you light a bonfire, fireplace, or even a candle depends on you.

Self-Purification Ritual

A self-purification ritual on Brigid's day is perfect for harnessing the purifying energies that St Brigid brings. As the mistress of fire, the saint has immense power over this element's cleansing and purifying capabilities. Use this simple ritual to cleanse away all the darkness and debris from the winter.

- For this rite, you will require a candle, incense, a bowl of water, and some salt.

- Find a quiet place to sit and center yourself by taking in a few deep breaths.
- Invite St Brigid into your ritual space and feel her presence.
- Light the candle to represent fire, and ask Brigid to purify your life.
- Next, sprinkle some salt on your skin, representing the earth, and ask Brigid to cleanse your body.
- Light the incense to represent air, and ask Brigid to clear your mind.
- Finally, take the bowl of water and sprinkle it on and around your body to purify your emotions.

2. St. Patrick's Day - Spring Equinox

One of Ireland's and the Celtic traditions' biggest holidays, St. Patrick's Day, or the spring equinox, is celebrated on March 17th as a tribute to the patron saint of Ireland. The time of spring equinox has certain significance in Celtic tradition because the Celts determined seasons using natural time. Hence, the solstice and equinox events hold tremendous importance, especially for certain rituals and spell work to be effective. As the name suggests, spring equinox is a time of perfect balance, where the day and night are almost entirely of equal length and considered a sacred time by Celtic ancestors.

Historic Celtic Rituals

While the spring equinox holds greater importance compared with St Patrick's Day in Celtic tradition, both are celebrated with equal fervor annually. Historically, the spring equinox has held great importance for Celtic rituals and spell-work as it represents the perfect balance between day and night, and many spells work best during this time. In Celtic tradition, the spring equinox was celebrated as Ostara, where rebirth and renewed life were celebrated. Historical rituals included:

- Initially, Easter originated from Ostara, where ancient Celtic people decorated eggs.
- New fires were lit as a symbol of new beginnings and rebirth.

- Ancient feast celebrations included meals that honored the coming of spring, including eggs, shoots and sprouts, and other early spring greens.

Modern Celebrations

Modern pagans all over the world celebrate the spring equinox or Ostara and practice specific magic and spell-work during this time. Here are some of the celebrations and rituals carried out during the spring equinox.

- The Ostara altar is set up using balancing symbols to represent the spring equinox.

- Many pagans practice earth meditation to ground themselves to reconnect with the earth and nature.

- Magic related to rebirth and growth is practiced during the spring equinox. This could include egg magic, serpent magic, flower magic, and magical gardening.

Rebirthing Ritual

As spring symbolizes the completion of the rebirth cycle, many pagans use the spring equinox to complete a rebirthing ritual to balance their energy and find harmony within themselves. The following steps should be followed.

- You will need to use your Ostara altar with a black sheet, a bowl of soil, water, candles, and incense.

- Wear the black sheet or ritual robe, and draw a circle around your Ostara altar.

- Enter this circle, kneel, and recite the Ostara ritual verses.

- One by one, move the items around your body to represent each element.

- Start with the salt, then the candles, the incense, and lastly, some water.

- Finally, take time to meditate and feel the balance of the rebirth within yourself.

3. May Day - Beltane

Mayday represents the beginning of the long days of the summer season. It is considered a holy day in Irish and Celtic culture. Beltane was considered a time to celebrate, especially through bonfires and extravagant feasts. This was a very special day for the Celts, one when the veils between the worlds was thinnest. Beltane symbolized a time to celebrate life and included huge feasts, festivals, and fairs.

Historic Celtic Rituals

Celtic tradition believed the time of Beltane welcomes the season of harvest and was considered the most important throughout the year. Although the season involved many rituals and customs, most were associated with fire, so this festival was sometimes called the Celtic fire festival. Ancient rituals included the following:

- One, two, or several huge bonfires were lit as a symbol of life and celebration.
- The flames, ash, and smoke were declared sacred, and people and cattle would walk around the flames for protection, wealth, and health.
- Animal blood was used as a sacrifice, and milk and honey were poured across thresholds to be found by fairies.
- An integral part of the festival was the Beltane feast. Although not as extravagant as the other festivals, it still held significance.

Modern Celebrations

Although the traditional festivities have largely died out in the modern pagan world, the fire festival has been enjoying a revival over the past few years. Neopagans and Wicca groups come together to celebrate the May Day festivities on weekends or hold fairs on weekdays. While the activities and rituals might have changed over time, the sentiment behind this festival remains the same, which is to welcome summer and hope for good fortune.

- Beltane is a fertility festival, so an altar setup symbolizes rebirth and celebration of life.
- The tradition of a maypole dance has been around for a long time and is still prevalent in many pagan cultures. The maypole celebration usually occurs after sunrise, the day after the fire festival.

- Bonfire ritual to celebrate fire and fertility is done in groups to celebrate the love partners have for each other.

- The Beltane planting rite is perfect for a solitary celebration and is a simple rite that celebrates the fertility of the planting season.

Handfasting Ritual

Today many pagan cultures follow handfasting ceremonies instead of traditional weddings, usually done during May Day celebrations. It can be a simple ceremony without the benefit of a state license. Many people also prefer jumping the broom, which is another non-conventional pagan wedding rite.

4. Midsummer - Summer Solstice

The summer solstice occurs when the sun hits the axial tilt of the earth, or in simple words, it's the longest day of the year, i.e., June 21st. This day celebrates light and sun and is closely associated with herbs, flowers, and candles. The Celts dedicated this day to their Celtic goddess, who went by many names. The day is marked and celebrated as the first day of summer.

Historic Celtic Rituals

The Celts had many beliefs regarding the summer solstice and considered the day of utmost importance for many rituals and spells. The Celts believed the sun's power would help banish darkness and evil and, in turn, open gates for an abundance of wealth. The sun was associated with vibrancy, warmth, and light, and the following rituals took place during the historic Celtic periods.

- Numerous bonfires were lit around which lovers danced and jumped over for luck.

- Wheels of fire were cascaded downhills as a symbol of light spreading.

- Delicious feasts were prepared, and people danced around the bonfires for the Druids.

Modern Celebrations

Although much of the old culture surrounding the summer solstice has faded, many people still come together to celebrate the summer solstice with great fervor. These prominently include the pagans, neopagans, Wiccans, and other cultures. Midsummer festivals all over the world include maypole dancing, mountaintop bonfires, and other rituals.

Midsummer Herb Ritual

You can use herbs in numerous ways in pagan summer rituals. Herbs represent nature and have significant power in healing and soothing. Beyond cooking with herbs, you can also turn them into incense or make relaxing candles. Here are some of the best herbs for summer solstice or midsummer rituals and spells.

- Fennel
- Lily
- Chickweed
- Frankincense
- Lavender
- Heather
- Rose
- Vervain
- Mugwort

5. Lughnasa

Lughnasa (August 1st) marked the beginning of the harvest season for ancient Celtic people and celebrated joyously to represent growth and celebration. Due to the joy of an abundant harvest, Celtic people would light bonfires and celebrate the oncoming of a full season. It was considered a time of gratitude or thanksgiving.

Historic Celtic Rituals

For the Celts, Lughnasa celebrates the fruition of the year's harvests and represents the harvest festival of the Celtic culture. In ancient tradition, the Celtic harvest festival used to last a month, with the festivities starting from mid-July and lasting two weeks into august. An old custom was to pick the ripe apples first to make a celebratory drink for the festival. Other Lughnasa rituals included:

- Bilberries (Blueberries) were collected first to gauge the crops' yield. If the blueberries were bountiful, so would the crops be.

- Garlands of flowers and greenery were placed around holy wells dedicated to patron saints.

- A feast containing seasonal fruits and vegetables and baked bread was prepared and enjoyed.

Modern Celebrations

Although Lughnasa celebrations have faded, and it's the least recognized of all the Celtic holidays, Lughnasa festivals and fairs still take place annually in the open-air museum of Craggaunowen. Many pagans celebrate this festival today with bonfires, feasts, and dancing.

6. Autumnal/Fall Equinox

Similar to the spring equinox or St Patrick's Day, the autumn or fall equinox celebrates the balance brought with the day and night of equal length. This sacred day falls around September 21st, somewhere in the middle of the fall season. It is considered a time of harvest, where people come together to gather, store, and preserve their food for the upcoming winter season. According to Celtic traditions, this time holds significant value for rituals and spell-work because of the changing of seasons.

Historic Celtic Rituals

The autumn equinox, known as the second harvest, brings either joy or suffering, depending on the outcome of a farmers' crops. The autumnal equinox brings a pause between autumn and winter seasons, considered the dark season among the Celtic culture. The following rituals were practiced during the fall equinox.

- According to Chinese tradition, the autumn equinox was celebrated with a moonlit dinner after successfully harvesting rice and wheat crops.

- Many people meditated before sunrise to find the balance an equinox might bring into their lives.

- Sustenance through foraging was an important part of the Celtic culture and was usually done during the autumn equinox in preparation for the oncoming winter.

- The ancient Mabon ritual included a bonfire festival to honor the changing season and celebrate the successful harvest.

Modern Celebrations

Modern celebrations during the autumn equinox are based on the same principles and beliefs in ancient teachings. Gratitude campfires, fall foraging hikes, and sunrise yoga meditation are all examples of modern pagan celebrations of the fall equinox.

7. Samhain

Samhain was when where spirits could cross the veil between the living and the dead and communicate with them as possible. Falling on November 1st, Samhain is a fascinating Celtic holiday. Paired with the spooky Halloween, it is considered the beginning of the darker half of the year.

Historic Celtic Rituals

During Samhain, many Celtic rituals that took place were to ward off evil spirits, while the ancestors of a family were invited and honored. Feasts were prepared for the living and the dead. People wore masks and disguised themselves as evil spirits to ward off danger. Essentially, this is where Halloween originated from.

Modern Celebrations

Modern Samhain pagan celebrations include setting up a Samhain altar, making an ancestors' altar, visiting a cemetery, holding a séance to communicate with the dead, finding divinatory guidance through tarot cards, or using Samhain herbs and spices for spells and rituals.

8. Winter Solstice

This is the shortest day of the year (pretty much the opposite of the summer solstice) and is around December 21st. It's considered a time of rebirth where people celebrate by attending festivals, gatherings, or performing rituals. While historic rituals include bonfires and spell-work, modern pagan rituals usually take place at a popular winter solstice site, i.e., the Newgrange burial chamber.

Chapter 10: Spells and Charms

While black magic is believed to cause suffering to other people, "white witchcraft" keeps danger at bay, cures diseases, and grants luck. This chapter discusses different Celtic, Irish, Scottish, and Druid spells. Other spells are used for healing, charms to attract fortune, beauty spells, love, and romance.

Spells to Attract Good Fortune

At some point, we all aspire to attract good fortune in life, and since we usually attribute bad luck to evil spells, we need good spells to counter that. Performing this spell involves a candle, some string, and a trinket.

First, you want to loop the string through the trinket and then tie it. Swing the trinket above the flame of your candle and chant, asking for good energy.

Repeat this three times and wear the necklace around your neck. The spell will give you a lot more power when you continuously do this.

Irish Beauty Spell

This spell is believed to make you prettier than you ever imagined. You will need a mirror, a pink candle, or incense for this spell. When there is a full moon, take a mirror and go outside or open the window and ensure the moon reflects in the mirror. Take an image of anything you want to improve and place it in the mirror.

Now, say, "Moonshine, Starlight, let the wind carry your light, let your glow cover my body, and let your shine cover every eye." Like most spells, you need to focus on what you want for it to work, which in this case would be the part of you that you'd like to change. Do that, and repeat the incantation three times.

Next, say the following three times, "Moonshine, Starlight, shape and mold my body, as a rose is granted beauty, let me blossom in your light, the light that brings me beauty, and grant me beauty three times three."

When you're done, light a pink candle or incense.

Spell to Recover Stolen Goods

Losing any valuable possession can be devastating, especially when it's stolen. No one wants to lose their hard-earned belongings since they may be difficult to replace. That's where this spell comes in.

1. Take two keys and place them in a sieve, crossways.
2. Have two people have to hold the sieve.
3. Make a cross sign on the suspected thief's forehead, calling their name aloud three times.
4. If the person you suspect is guilty, the keys will be around the sieve. If they're innocent, they won't move at all.

You can take appropriate measures to recover your stolen items when this happens. However, be careful to avoid false accusations since this may impact your relationship with others.

Four Leaf Clover Charm for Luck

Who hasn't heard of the lucky four-leaf clover? These four leaves are rare and are rumored to possess mystical powers representing positive attributes. The Celts believed in their powers and attributed them to hope, faith, love, and luck. Other people believe the four clover leaves will bring wealth, fame, faithful love, and health.

The four leaves are a genetic mutation and very rare, and only about one plant in 10 000 leaves carry the lucky leaves. While getting the leaves for the lucky charms can be challenging, there are different crafts you can use in their place. For instance, buy jewelry designed to symbolize the four clover leaves. It will give you the same results if used properly.

Charm against Danger

When men went into battle, they needed protection against dangers, such as injury, being captured by the enemy, or drowning. Different colored strings were used alongside a mixture of rhymes to evoke cures. The chords were believed to have powers to protect the fighters against harm. If you are going on a mission that could meet some challenges, you need this charm for protection.

Charms to Cure Sicknesses

These were usually administered by what were known as the "wise women" or "wise men." The "knowledge" from these wise people was a charm that could be used to cure ailments in man or animal – things like bruises, toothache, and the sort. The wise person would recite a chant over the sufferer, as well as over the water that would be sprinkled on them or drunk. If you sought the help of the "wise woman," you were not allowed to talk to anyone afterward until they reached home. There were a few other rules attached to this. Going to bed before sunset, no reading, no meat on the day the charm was administered.

Bond of Trust

An interesting custom in Ireland was for men to use their hair and braid it as a bracelet. This would then be presented to the woman they loved as a gift representing trust. For the binding powers of the spell to actually work, the woman needed to accept the gift. Basically, you can't force this spell on someone without their knowing of it or accepting it. This particular spell meant that the parties involved agreed to form a lasting union. When you use this spell, its main purpose is to give you focus and strength to achieve your aims and to make your intentions known.

Irish Charm for Money

Many people aspire to have a fortune of money in their lives. In Irish tradition, it is believed that a black rooster's feather coupled with a gold-colored coin can bring great fortune. You need to hold the coin and feather and go to the crossing points consisting of three fairy paths and call the name of the Goddess Aine three times. This charm will bring you everlasting prosperity, and you will always have money for various purposes. Also, use the charm to solve financial problems you may encounter.

Lucky Horseshoe Charms

Since the 10th century, this tradition continues to be used as a symbol of luck to this very day. You can usually see them over a door where they're meant to bring good fortune into homes and keep bad luck out. The horseshoe is commonly used in different cultures, although there are some disagreements about how it should be hung on the door.

There's a little discrepancy in terms of how to hang the horseshoe. A vast majority believe it should be facing upwards, in a sense collecting and capturing good luck. There is also the notion that it should hang downwards so luck can pour over anyone passing beneath it. Either way, it's believed that the horseshoe possesses luck because blacksmiths were able to bend any material provided by God. The talisman also makes a perfect wedding gift since it symbolizes the tradition of long-standing and is often presented to the bride. A horseshoe was also believed to represent a crescent moon, making it a very potent fertility charm.

Lucky Number Seven Charm

In many cultures, the number 7 is considered lucky and represents perfection and knowledge. This is mainly because of its special mathematical properties. The square and triangle are considered "perfect forms," and the number 7 is a combination of the four sides of the square and the three of the triangle. Hence, perfection. Seven is also significant in many other cases:

- How many days are there in a week?
- How many visible planets are there?
- How many colors does a rainbow have?

That's right, seven. Now all you have to do is involve seven in whatever you want to achieve. For example, seven can act as your winning number the next time you're out betting. Maybe create a charm with seven lucky symbols, like crystals.

Healing Charms

While many charms and spells are specifically meant for practices related to luck, protection against evil spells, love, and romance, others are used for healing different conditions. The following are examples of charms believed to possess healing properties.

A Cure for Mental Health Issues

This treatment should be performed on Thursdays only. The patient sits atop a gray horse and is taken for a ride where the animal gallops at its fastest speed three times around a boundary mark. They will move to an immovable stone where the patient will be asked to speak to the stone. This is the healing procedure, and afterward, it is believed the victim will recover. The process is based on the belief in the powers of the gods that will remove evil spirits causing the mental health challenge.

Irish Charm to Heal Depression

When someone becomes low and experiencing depression, they are said to have a "fairy blast." It is treated by pouring blast water over the victim. A fairy doctor will pour the water, while chanting in praise of the gods with the power to heal the condition. If water is left after performing the procedure, it must be poured into the fire. The entire healing system is based on religious beliefs and invoking the powers of the deities.

Evil Eye Charms

This charm is not as evil as the name suggests but offers protection to the wearer from persons with distrustful eyes. It can guard against negative forces coming from people believed to possess negative eyes. The evil eye charm functions by diverting any harmful intent caused by the harmful eyes when they look into your face. It acts as a protective amulet – the belief being that evil can only be harmful if it looks directly into your eyes.

The eye charm tricks the evil forces so they do not harm you. Most protective eye charms are worn, placed in homes, or carried in a pocket. The charms are also used to guard corporations and individuals against financial losses caused by poor business dealings. Consider this charm if you want to enjoy general protection against evil forces.

While black magic is believed to be harmful, white witchcraft is used to benefit different people. For instance, spells and charms are utilized for various purposes such as luck, healing, love, and romance. However, you need to consult a knowledgeable practitioner for insight into various spells to resolve your challenges. Like in any other religion, these charms and spells are based on belief systems.

Appendix: Glossary of Magical Symbols

Now that we have covered everything about Celtic magic and the Druids, we end this book with some of the most important Celtic symbols, their meanings, and uses. The Celtic symbols hugely influenced how the ancient Celts lived their lives. To this day, these symbols are associated with their culture and Ireland. Even if you don't know much about these symbols or their meanings, you are probably familiar with them. You have seen them somewhere, like in a movie, TV show, or you own a piece of jewelry with a symbol on it, but you don't know what it means. Understanding these magical symbols will make performing spells and rituals a lot easier.

Unfortunately, the exact meaning behind some Celtic symbols will never be known to us because they were not documented. However, many have been interpreted due to their popularity and our curiosity. When it comes to symbols, notice that there are several recurring themes, including but not limited to love, strength, unity, and, of course, loyalty. Also, the number three is incorporated in many symbols because of the Celts' beliefs that all essential things come in threes.

The Meaning behind Celtic Symbols

The Ailm

The Ailm symbol, like the Dora Knot discussed later, represents strength. Although the design behind each symbol is different, the meaning is the same. This symbol is taken from the first letter of the Celtic Ogham alphabet, where the Ailm is supposed to be a tree called the silver fir tree. According to ancient Celts, it was associated with healing one's soul.

The Celts believed that the trees represented strength, and for a good reason. For instance, the oak tree can grow and survive in extremely harsh conditions for hundreds of years. The Ailm symbolizes purification, fertility, strength, health, and healing. It is considered one of the most important Celtic symbols. Nowadays, many brands use it since it promotes many positive notions.

The Awen

Awen is a Celtic word meaning essence or inspiration. There is more than one interpretation of this symbol's representation. Some believe the three lines on the Awen represent the mind, body, and spirit, or earth, sea, and air, or love, wisdom, and truth. It is also believed to have represented the three pillars of awakening:

- Understanding the truth.

- Loving the truth.

- Maintaining the truth.

According to the NeoDruids, a person won't proclaim the truth if they aren't awakened. Nowadays, this symbol is popular since it is used in tattoos, artwork, and jewelry.

The Bowen Knot

The Bowen knot was created in the 17th century and is often called the knot of true love. The knot consists of tangled loops without a beginning or an end. Although this symbol has different variations, the pattern is always the same, with endless loops. The Bowen Knot represents devotion.

The Celtic Bull

The Celtic bull is known for its strength, and it played a significant role in ancient Celtic mythology. The relationship between strong animals and powerful warriors was depicted in Celtic myths. Additionally, animals were included in everything like clothing, carving, and jewelry. The ancient Celts believed that every animal had its virtues, like the bull that was fearless and strong. Bulls also symbolize fertility in women. In addition to strength and fertility, the bull represented wealth. To this day, many people attribute the bull to strength, and why many people choose it for a tattoo.

The Celtic Cross

The Celtic cross is one of the most common and popular Celtic symbols. Since it is a cross, many people have associated it with Christianity. However, this symbol has been around for centuries before Christianity. There are different theories as to what the four arms of the cross represent. Some believe they represent the four elements of earth, fire, air, and water. Another theory says the four arms represent the four sides of the earth, being the north, east, west, and south, while there is another theory that says the arms represent mind, body, heart, and soul. It is also believed that the cross represents the four seasons of the year; winter, spring, summer, and fall, or the stages of the day; morning, midday, evening, and midnight.

There are different theories and legends about the origin of the Celtic cross. Although the cross predates Christianity, one of the legends regarding its origin suggests that either St Declan or St Patrick introduced the cross to Ireland. It is believed that it was created for converting Druids. According to another theory, the Celtic cross is inspired by the ancient Celts Sun Cross. This symbol is still widely popular and used by many people as it is believed it will protect whoever wears it from dark forces and bring them wisdom.

The Celtic Five-Fold

You may not have heard about the Celtic Five-Fold symbol since it isn't as popular online as the other symbols. However, it is everywhere. For instance, the Olympics rings are a variant of this symbol. There are various interpretations as to its representation. Some believe it represents the four directions: north, south, east, and west. Others believe it represents the four seasons: summer, winter, spring, and autumn, while there is another belief that it represents the four elements: earth, air, water, and fire, or god, faith, spirituality, and heaven. The fifth ring is what connects us to the universe.

The Celtic Knotwork

The Celtic Knotwork is another old symbol that originated during the ancient Celts. However, we don't know much about how it came to be. It is believed this symbol can bring health, wealth, and good fortune. Nowadays, people use it in decor and tattoos.

The Circular Knots

The circular knot is considered one of the most important symbols for the Celtics. The circle symbolizes inner life, infinity, and the sun.

The Claddagh Ring

A strong symbol of unity, the Claddagh Ring consists of two hands (friendship) holding a heart (everlasting love) wearing a crown (loyalty). You will find this symbol on many items, but the most common place is on rings.

The name of the ring is derived from "An Cladach," an Irish word meaning flat stony shore. It is the Irish village where the ring was first designed.

The Dara Knot

The Dara Knot is considered one of the most beautiful Celtic symbols. Dara is derived from the Irish word Doire, an oak tree that the Celts and Druids considered sacred and whose roots are represented by the symbol's knots.

The Dara Knot symbolizes strength, wisdom, power, destiny, community, connection, and leadership. During troubled times, the Celts would seek its help for wisdom and strength. This symbol was considered a spiritual charm and also used for decorations. The Dara Knot has become very popular in the last few years and is now used in tattoos, jewelry, and clothes.

The Double Spiral

The double spiral represents the duality of life, death, nature, and balance. For this reason, it often represents things like the equinox (the one day of the year when the day and night have the same duration) as well as how opposites complement each other like life and death, the sun and moon, femininity, and masculinity, yin and yang and light and darkness.

The Dragon

The Celtic dragon is considered invincible, and it represents eternity and wholeness. The Celtic dragon has a sharp arrow on its tail, symbolizing mortality and energy.

The Druid Sigil

The Druid Sigil represents Mother Earth and fertility. The sigils were used during magical rituals, but only a few people used them, and the rituals were kept a secret.

The Eternity Knot

The Celtic eternity knot has three loops since three is considered an important number for the Celtics, and they build everything around it. It is one of the popular Celtic symbols representing immortality, beauty, and eternal youth.

The Green Man

This symbol consists of the head of a man surrounded by leaves. This man has different names, like the man in the tree and Jack O' the Green. He represents rebirth and life and the relationship between man and nature. It is considered one of the oldest Celtic symbols since it dates back to 400 BC and is part of ancient Celtic culture. This symbol is still popular today, as you will find it on many religious buildings. Additionally, it is now regarded as a symbol of the environment.

The Griffin

The griffin is a symbol of nobility, balance, and loyalty. It is a combination of an animal's power and intelligence, represented as a mythical creature with a lion's body and eagle's head.

The Motherhood Knot

You have probably noticed by now how the Celts incorporated various knots into their style and decoration. The Motherhood Knot, obvious by the name, represents the relationship between a mother and child. This symbol transcends any belief or faith since it shows the unbreakable bond and everlasting love between a mother and child, which exists regardless of faith.

The Quaternary Knot

The Quaternary Knot is four-sided and has many interpretations of what it symbolizes. It can either represent the four seasons: summer, winter, spring, and fall, the four directions: north, south, east, and west, the four elements; earth, water, air, and fire, or the four Celtic festivals; Samhain, Imbolc, Beltane, and Lughnasadh. Nowadays, many people opt for this symbol as a tattoo.

The Sailor's Knot

Since sailors would spend weeks or months at sea, the sailor's knot is a symbol of endless love, separation, and parting. This symbol was probably originated by sailors who left these knots for their loved ones at home, so they would remember them when separated for extended periods.

The Serch Bythol

The Serch Bythol represents everlasting love. The word itself means everlasting love in Welsh and is considered a Celtic symbol for the family. It consists of two triskeles joined together to form a circle representing eternity. The three arcs of the triskele symbolize the mind, body, and spirit. This symbol proves the ancient Celts had a profound understanding of their feelings, emotions, and relationships. Since it has a deep beautiful meaning, many people choose to incorporate this symbol in jewelry and as a gift.

The Shamrock

"I'll seek a four-leaved shamrock in all thy fairy dells, and if I find the charmed leaves, oh, how I'll weave my spells." Samuel Lover.

One of the first things that come to mind when we think of Ireland is the shamrock. Nowadays, the symbol is associated with St Patrick's Day celebration and good luck. It is believed that St Patrick used the shamrock to explain the Holy Trinity's unity and convert pagans to Christianity. However, the shamrock's origins go way back to the Celtic culture and are symbolic of the Druids. They believed the leaves of this plant symbolized the triad. Since, as we have mentioned, they believed all important things in life come in three.

They believed that it served as protection from evil, bad eyes, and bad words, and the shamrock would warn them of a storm by standing in an upright position. The shamrock is supposed to represent good luck and fortune, something many people in and outside of Ireland still believe. It is also the national flower of the country.

The Shillelagh

The Shillelagh is a short wooden club that was used to settle disputes, made from blackthorn wood or oak.

Solomon's Knot

This symbol was named after King Solomon and represented strength, wisdom, and masculinity. Usually, people who hope to represent themselves as authoritative or powerful wear this symbol.

The St. Brigid Cross

St Brigid was born in 400 AD in Dundalk. She was the daughter of a Christian woman called Brocca, who St Patrick baptized. Brigid became a nun, and the cross is attributed to her. It is believed that she created this cross after a dying pagan that wanted to be baptized, but some believed to be her father. However, it is also associated with the life-giving goddess, who also goes by the name Brigid and belongs to the Tuatha de Danann, a supernatural race in Irish mythology. The cross is usually used during the beginning of the spring celebrations and the festival of the goddess Brigid occurring simultaneously. The Irish hang this cross in their houses to protect them from fires and evil spirits.

The Tree of Life

The tree of life has always been associated with the Druids. They believe the earth and heaven are connected, and the tree of life represents this connection. According to the ancient Celts, it is a symbol of wisdom, strength, and long life. The tree also represents harmony and balance. The Celts considered trees a symbol of rebirth since they associated rebirth with how the trees change every season. Additionally, they considered trees the spirits of their ancestors. Trees were so sacred to the Celts, especially the oak tree, they would hold important meetings under them. They believed the tree of life was a doorway to the land of the fairies, and it protected their lands against enemies. Nowadays, this symbol is used in many jewelry pieces, as it is very popular.

The Triquetra

The Triquetra is also known as the Trinity Knot. The word Triquetra is Latin and means three-cornered. This symbol has been around ever since the Iron Age, and you can find it in Irish architecture, art, and design today. This symbol represents the three stages of the neopagan goddess's life; as a virgin, mother, and wise woman. Some Celts considered this symbol to represent earth, fire, and water, while others considered it a representation of the earth, sea, and the sky. The Triquetra is also called the Irish Love Knot and symbolizes eternal love. This knot also represents eternal spiritual life without a beginning or an end.

Not much is known regarding the origins of this symbol, but some believe it was inspired by the lunar and solar cycles. If you think this symbol looks familiar, then you aren't wrong. This symbol is everywhere today in jewelry and illustrations, and if you saw the original TV show, Charmed, it was drawn on the "Book of Shadows," they used for spells.

The Triskelion

The Triskelion, or the Triskele, reflects the Celts' belief that all-important things come in threes. The name of this symbol is derived from the Greek word Triskeles, meaning three legs, or the third time's the charm, something we still say today. It is believed the Triskelion has been around since the Neolithic era. The symbol consists of 3 clockwise spirals and is one of the oldest symbols known to man. The three spirals signify the earth or harmony. However, if the spirals are anti-clockwise, they are believed to be pagan symbols that control and manipulate nature. Since the spirals look as if they are moving, they signify moving forward and defeating hardships. They can also symbolize progress and strength.

The Wheel of Taranis

Taranis is the Celtic god of thunder, and he is the brother of the Roman god of thunder, Jupiter. They are portrayed as bearded heroes holding lighting and a wheel in their hands. According to Celtic mythology, Taranis united the lighting, sky, and the sun.

The Celtics have a rich and fascinating history, and their symbols represent it exceptionally well. These symbols are thousands of years old, and that they still intrigue people is proof of how great their culture was. Not only do these symbols look beautiful, which is why they are incorporated in buildings, designs, jewelry, and clothes, but they also have beautiful meanings making them even more fascinating. Beautiful meanings like everlasting love and loyalty make it seem like these symbols are out of a fairy tale. Irish culture is extremely famous for its mythology, and they introduced many mythical creatures we are very familiar with, like fairies and mermaids.

There is something very beautiful, mysterious, and enchanting about the Celts and their culture, especially since there are so many things we still don't know, making them all the more intriguing.

Conclusion

When you first become interested, Celtic magic, plant shamanism, paganism, Druidry, and other ideas within European folklore seem quite intimidating and even aimless. However, armed with the principles outlined in this book, together with the numerous techniques and strategies we have covered, you have everything you need to dive deep into this sea of knowledge and discover a new world.

The most challenging part of the entire process is going through the exercises and determining how you perform in the real world. If you come from a spiritual background and have some training in meditation or yoga, that knowledge will certainly help you during this process. For those completely new, it might be challenging to get in touch with your feelings and thoughts and understand how you channel different parts of the process. Most newcomers to this field will constantly argue among themselves about whether or not it is working or whether or not they are feeling the right sensations. You must understand there is no clear right or wrong. It is not about getting to the finish line first. It is about being true to yourself and developing as a person.

The various things we covered about the Irish people and their unique heritage are not limited to that region, religion, or race. These are universal concepts that can be applied by anyone, anywhere in the world. It will definitely help if you have the resources mentioned in this book at your disposal, but there are many things specific to this region. However, there are different ways to work around this, and with the interconnected world today, it should be no problem to get your hands on the things you need.

The most important thing to note is the time you invest in this practice. This is not a degree that will take several years. The elder Druids in the Celtic culture spent an entire lifetime perfecting their specialization. Students weren't considered masters even after twenty years of being a master's disciple. The various colored robes were not achieved by spending a certain amount of time but awarded when students showed mastery of their work and thought of the greater good.

The purpose of Druidry and the various shamanistic practices was to bring about good, starting with the individual who practiced it and slowly spreading it to the world around them, including everything tangible and intangible. In reality, we can only be happy when we are cOntent with everything inside and out. By going through these practices and lessons and complimenting them with research, you will develop a higher level of consciousness to enlighten you and allow you to see things from a holistic view. With this guide by your side, you are well on your way to developing a happier, healthier life.

Part 2: Irish Paganism

Unlocking Pagan Practices and Druidry in Ireland along with Welsh Witchcraft and Celtic Spirituality

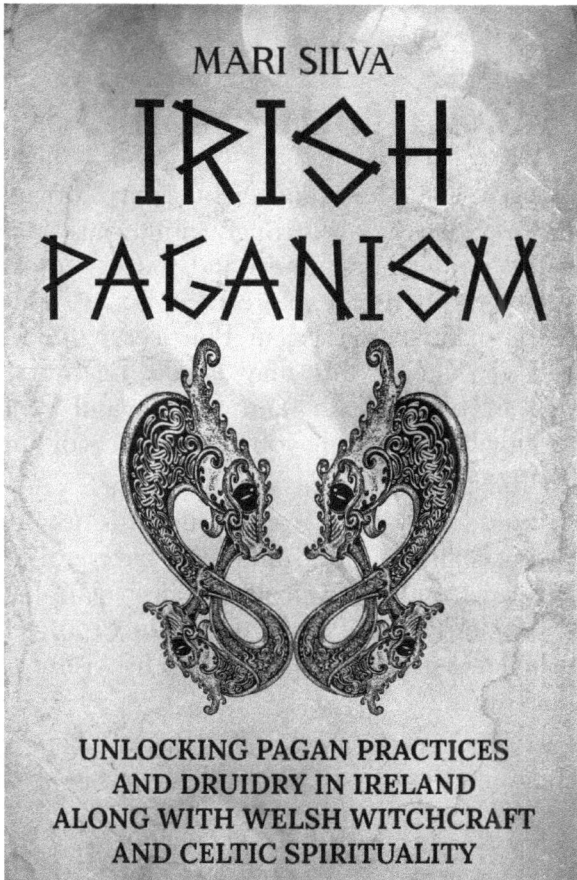

MARI SILVA

IRISH
PAGANISM

**UNLOCKING PAGAN PRACTICES
AND DRUIDRY IN IRELAND
ALONG WITH WELSH WITCHCRAFT
AND CELTIC SPIRITUALITY**

Introduction

Irish Paganism enjoys a long and rich history, originating from ancient Celtic religions and through numerous changes over centuries. In the modern era, more and more people with Irish Pagan roots have decided to explore their legacy, and with good reason. The spirituality-based Pagan Practices come in handy in times of need - whatever this may entail. Learning about the universal cycle of birth, death, and rebirth and venturing into different nature realms will guide you in all aspects of life.

Amid all the technological advancements and uncertain expectations of modern society, losing yourself is not unusual. The boundaries change all the time, and you have no control over them. The answer to all these problems lies in discovering your spiritual self. Modern Irish Pagan magick incorporates elements from various belief systems, so tapping into its wisdom allows you to find parts of yourself.

Apart from the historical aspects, this book explores the differences between the Irish and Welsh spiritual beliefs and magickal practices. Despite having the same roots, these two paths of Paganism have very notable differences. Many secrets will be unveiled, from how witchcraft was viewed in the two regions to the different branches both cultures have developed.

According to the Irish Pagan lore, we carry our ancestors in our blood, enabling us to communicate with them whenever we need their guidance. The innate appeal of this culture brings entire communities together during holidays on the Witches Wheel of the Year. The choice of becoming a solitary practitioner or performing spells and rituals with like-minded people should always be personal. However, many benefits are gained from belonging to an Irish Pagan community.

In Irish Paganism, the journey between worlds is also possible. However, acquiring this skill takes much time and effort. This fundamental knowledge will teach you many things about yourself and your magick. The Druids, Pagans, and even the Wiccans have done so for too many years to count. Now, you can do it too. All it takes is to unlock the secrets of their practices, and you can start your magical Pagan journey. You are provided with a practical guide of simple magickal tools and spells to take advantage of. Even people without much practice exploring their spirituality can take advantage of these tools.

This practice allows you to choose your spiritual guides, tells you how to approach them, and even the method to receive their messages. It all comes down to your tools and how you employ them during your spells and rituals. When you are versed in the fundamental parts of your craft, you are ready to grow your power even further, incorporating more and more of your background and beliefs and developing your unique magic practice.

Chapter 1: What Is Irish Paganism?

Celtic Paganism is typically an ancient religion with diversified practices and belief sets. The people who adhered to Paganism are widely known as Celts stemming from the Roman and La Tene periods. The British and Irish Iron Age carried much significance for Insular Celts. The oldest Celtic paganism records were written by Roman writers, whose personal hostile tendencies laid a particular biased hue on the historical records. Irish Paganism belongs to a larger category of polytheistic religions, and although there were many chronological and geographical variations between the finer details, there were also many structural similarities.

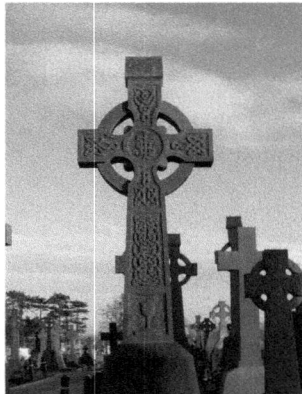

A Peek into History

Perusing historical manuscripts, you'll find that around 500 BCE, the Celts invaded Ireland. In essence, the Celts were practicing pagans and brought paganistic beliefs and rituals to Ireland.

Christian and other Abrahamic religious practices were at their peak during the Middle Ages, and ancient Celtic religious pagan practices were nearly extinct. However, Celtic religion was still alive in the Irish haven during this era, but the sources and written records existed in poems, usually written by Christian monasteries.

These historians were mainly ignorant of the gist of Paganism. Therefore, divine beings appeared as characters and heroes in the records instead of the pagan deities. One of the most significant examples of Irish records is Tuatha De Danann, depicted as merely an ancient human tribe. The Celtic belief was that Gods rest in the stars and worship the seasonal variations. However, as the core of the Pagan religion, they were free to choose a god and feel united with the universe and nature.

The Pagan Life of Ancient Irish People

During the Paganism era in Ireland, the Irish were predominantly taught Druidic religion. The Druids were the most powerful and highly educated members of ancient society, with immense power over others. They were the only available preachers and teachers and were tasked with imparting knowledge to the children of kings or chiefs.

The Druids were royal court advisors, and people would turn to them seeking advice on important matters. According to historical records and reports, they had immense magical powers, able to raise a magic fog with the ability to hide specific things.

They were also believed to possess other magical properties, like manipulating the seasonal and natural world attributes. Several Irish folklore tales talk about similar exemplary powers exhibited by these Irish pagans. Although pagans were widespread across Ireland, the city of Tara was an exception. The vast majority of Irish pagans inhabited Tara because it was the dwelling of over-kings, and evidence that pagan roots ran deep in the heart of Ireland during ancient times.

The Dominant Pagan Gods

Although, the information about Pagan Gods is minimal since the tales about those Gods were never documented by the ancient Celts. However, the paganism spirit and their rituals or beliefs survived through folklores and some historical records. To better understand Celtic mythology, it is essential to learn about the intriguing details and great connections with their gods and goddesses. Discussed below are a few of the dominant pagan divinities honored by the people of Ireland.

- ## Morrigan, The Goddess of War

   Morrigan is believed to be the phantom queen, translated to the queen of the demons. Merely thinking about Morrigan fills one with awe and curiosity. The ancient Celts thought she flew over battlefields in the shape of a crow and possessed the ability to foretell the battle's outcome. According to folklore, the deity Dagda was victorious in one of his most important battles because of her.

- ## Aonghus, The God of Youth and Love

   The god associated with the valley near the river Boyne is Aonghus. He was the son of god Dagda and goddess Boann. Boann was the goddess of the River Boyne, and why Aonghus, also known as Angus, is connected to this river and valley. He was exceptionally handsome and believed to be the god of love and youth, able to evoke love in others, and had four birds circling him at all times. His life revolved around seeking a beautiful maiden.

- ## The Pagan God Danu

   Danu had several names from Eastern Europe to Ireland, considered the earth mother goddess, and known as Dana and Anu. According to popular pagan belief, Danu is the one who nursed the gods. Perhaps because of these attributes, she was also known as the goddess of fertility and wisdom. In Irish lore, she is considered a highly skillful deity in magic. The Irish pagan lore also assumed that Dagda was her father; however, this story has various versions.

• The Good Pagan God Dagda

Dagda was a giant in stature and with a long and unruly beard. Popularly known as the good god, Dagda was a Celtic deity and considered the chief of Irish Tuatha de Danann. He always appeared as a fatherly figure, seemingly joyous and content. His superpowers were unique and not possessed by other gods and goddesses since he could give life and death. He was also associated with providing endless food and is also known as the god of agriculture. His children were Aengus Mac and Brigit from Boann and Morrigan, respectively. Dagda possessed vast skills and knowledge and was considered dominant over other gods. He could control seasons and provided endless food with the help of his cauldron.

• The Pagan God Cuchulainn

Cuchulainn was originally named Setanta, also known as the Hound of Ulster. He killed the dog appointed to guard Cullen and, after this act, was renamed Cuchulainn. People believed he could defeat death, as he was courageous in many battles, and why he declined Morrigan's gift of immortality. He did not consider it a favor because he had already defeated death several times. Morrigan, who hovered over battles as a crow, visited Cuchulainn when he died on the battlefield.

• Fearsome Pagan Goddess Brigit

As mentioned earlier, Brigit was Dagda's daughter and one of the most famous gods of pre-Christian Ireland. She was considered equivalent to the Roman goddess Minerva. Brigit had three central powers and attributes: the fire of the forge, fire of the hearth, and fire of inspiration. She was rightly known as the triple goddess, possessing diverse abilities and attributes.

• The Horned One, Cernunnos

As the name suggests, he was considered one of the most Celtic honored gods with very few other associations of his kind and connected to wild animals. Apart from wild animals, he was also linked to wealth and fertility. Not all the gods in the Celtic family are immensely represented through art, but Cernunnos was an exception and the reason he was easily identifiable and a popular god in Celtic ancient art.

- **Arawn, the God of Underworld**

God of the underworld or the dead is famous for darkness, fear, and his cloak. He was also known as the guardian of lost souls and a virtuous god. He represented war, fear, and terror. His biggest rival was Hafgan, who desired the position of god of the underworld or otherworld. It is believed that Arawn switched his place with Pwyll and defeated Hagan. Arawn rewarded Pwyll for this act of bravery with pigs.

- **Abandinus, The Defender of Water**

Out of all the Celts' ancient gods, very little information is available about Abandinus. Abandinus was the defender of the waters or seas. Most people associate this god with the inscription in Cambridgeshire, England.

These prominent pagan deities were quite popular in Ireland, and the gods and goddesses were thought to belong to the sacred tribe of deities. This tribe of gods and goddesses, known as the Tuatha de Danann, was considered the main Irish goddesses and gods tribe. The literal translation means "children of Goddess Danu." This particular tribe originated in the western islands and had the most magical powers, and the reason they settled in Ireland for so long.

Primary Beliefs of Irish Paganism

The beliefs of Irish Paganism are very humane and accessible, filled with kindness and an abundance of mysterious warm energy leading to great comfort. Irish Paganism's core belief revolves around love for nature and earth, overall harmony, and unity of the human community. It also greatly stresses being united with the universe.

Unlike the prevalent Abrahamic religions, Irish Paganism was a free-spirited religion advocated by beliefs in various gods. The pagan believers were encouraged to associate their subjective interpretations with the deities. Paganism proudly endorses three core principles keeping believers united across a common thread.

1. The first principle is about kinship and love for nature and others.
2. The second principle is about positive morality and advocates living your life your way as long as no one is harmed.
3. The third principle acknowledges and recognizes the divine (the feminine and masculine).

To better understand the Irish belief, it is best to discuss it from ancient and historical records and the modern perspective (which is more about neopagan spirituality).

Ancient Era Irish Pagan Beliefs

One of the most prominent resources often referred to in literature is Caesar's writings and records about the Gallic Druidism to the rich culture of Ireland. However, it may not be the most accurate depiction of what happened during the Irish pagan realm.

Interestingly, Ireland always opened its arms to soak in the traditions and culture of invaders and combine them with the existing culture. The result is an interesting and beautiful blend of cultures that created a curious cultural symphony. Some of the fundamental Irish pagan beliefs included the concept of "rebirth," revolving around the idea of the continuation of life in different cycles of birth and death.

The belief system in Irish Paganism signifies the importance of responsibility, honesty, loyalty, and justice – because without these attributes, an individual cannot be a good human being. This concept is among the most vital elements of pagan religion. They also believe in a "parallel world," which is nothing like an underworld but instead an entirely different world existing alongside this world. The Irish pagan folklore talks at length about the relevance and reality of this otherworld. The population of the otherworld consists of all beings, including goddesses, gods, royal or noble fairies (Sidhe), and elemental beings.

In addition to the belief sets shared above, Irish Paganism emphasized meditation and traveling between worlds. They firmly believed in occult power or hidden knowledge, and only certain people could develop these skills and could share them with others. Their belief included understanding and knowledge of prophecy, magic, and divination.

Even with rich religious beliefs and a firmly embedded pagan culture, Paganism shifted dramatically as Christianity gradually took hold. Over time priests replaced the Druids, resulting in various pagan beliefs' assimilation into Celtic Christian beliefs. The Celtic Christian Church was quite different from the Roman Catholic Church and advocated practices and beliefs not welcomed by orthodox mainstream Christian scholars.

As time passed, the pagan beliefs diluted even further as Christianity's influence became dominant. However, even with Christian dominance, Irish pagan beliefs survived. You can find numerous references to holy good observances (related to the pagan ritual of sacred spring and magic), crowds from the otherworld, Fairies or the Sidhe, etc.

Various folk practices and stories frequently refer to Irish Paganism resulting in several pure pagan beliefs and rituals surviving the sands of time despite the harsh and unwelcoming change. It brings us to the most recent era of Irish pagans. It is no wonder the modern pagan beliefs are nothing like the ancient ones, except for the essence still homogenizing and binding the pagan philosophy together.

Modern-Day Irish Pagan Beliefs and Practices

In today's surreal and chaotic world, Paganism appears to have acquired a prominent corner of solace for the Irish people. There is an innate appeal for pagan beliefs in Ireland, where a rich history of pagan religion still survives. Since 1970, steady growth in Irish Paganism, and although a few things have evolved, the change is subtle, and the primary ritual spirit and belief set is still in the original form.

These days the pagans organize a national Pagan Festival, the Feile Draiochta, for pagans to come together and recognize each other. However, because of the independent and tribal nature of

Irish pagans, it is challenging to bring the whole community together. Moreover, non-profit organizations in Ireland are working towards advocating and promoting Paganism. The primary purpose is to safeguard the rights of pagan followers and spread awareness about the religion. Several monthly moots are for pagans to network and meet periodically to establish lasting connections and experience a healthy exchange of knowledge and beliefs.

As far as the pagan festivals and rituals are concerned, several are still celebrated by modern pagans. However, some ritualistic practices have subtly changed to fit modern life. The most famous Irish pagan festival is Beltane (celebrated on May 1) and Samhain (celebrated on November 1). Modern-day Paganism is viewed as a reconstructed Irish pagan philosophy. However, reconstruction is not distorting the core beliefs and practices.

Since Paganism allows for individuality and subjective interpretation and construction of belief, many pagans nowadays define their rituals and practices. Some pagans practice a "stalking awareness," alert to their emotional and psychological state and the external world around them. Others find meaning in visiting pagan and Celtic spiritual sites and sites significant to other religions. In other words, Paganism welcomes a non-dogmatic and fluid ideology in religion and spirituality.

The principle of "polytheism" is at the heart of modern-day Paganism, honoring multiple goddesses and gods. The same belief was popular in the ancient era about females and males who embodied and related to different cultural aspects and natural forces. Worshiping nature is still popular and obvious because honoring nature is one of the foundational beliefs in Paganism and cannot be ignored.

Another core belief in modern-day Paganism is pantheism and animism, an integral part of this belief system. It's about the concept of entertaining a holistic worldview and interconnectedness. According to this belief, the spiritual or material universe and divinity are linked. Pagans believe nature is inseparable from divinity, with divine attributes spread around in nature (according to pantheism).

One of the central components of goddess-centered pagan witchcraft was understanding that everything in this universe is linked, like an organism. According to this belief, anything affecting one part has a ripple effect on the other parts. The other popular belief of animism was everything has particular spiritual energy or life force, or specific spirits are in the natural world, and it is possible to communicate with them.

It is evident that Ireland has a beautiful and strong pagan past, and, nowadays, a new wave of Paganism is growing stronger in Ireland.

Chapter 2: Who Were the Druids?

While most members of ancient Celtic societies were known as fierce warriors with a duty to protect their land and people, others had quite different roles. These were the Druids - a highly educated class of Celts occupying various leading positions in their society. Their primary role was as the repositories of their ancestors' accumulated knowledge, accrued since childhood. It was necessary to keep their traditions alive since the Celts would only pass on their wisdom through oral sources. It also secured Druidry survival, which is still practiced today, albeit in a modernized form.

The Origins of Druidry

Due to the lack of written records, the exact origins of Druidry cannot be determined with certainty. The few records we have on this practice come from the Roman Empire scripts and archeological findings throughout Europe. Regarding the Roman Empire scripts, these depictions of Druidry may be tainted by the centuries-long competition between the Romans and the Celts over European territories. However, since some archeological findings can be tied to the oral sources passed on by the Celts, it's possible to piece together some parts of the Druids' history.

The term Druid comes from the Irish word "Doire," meaning oak tree - one of the most telling natural wisdom symbols in Celtic Paganism. Druidry considers oak trees and the entire natural world a source of an immense power ready to be harnessed. Followers use this organic approach in their healing practices, along with the guidance they receive from the spirits. Some sources say that the same way Druids could heal, they could also inflict damage. However, this goes against the dogma of Celtic Paganism- which means it is unlikely to be true. Their knowledge of the earth and journeying between the realms was considered mystical. At the same time, their word was sacred among their followers.

The first reference to Druids comes from the 2nd century B.C. These accounts describe this Celtic class as a well-organized society. Not only did they have a hierarchy among their classes, but their life patterns also followed a natural order. Their life revolved around seasons, lunar, and solar cycles, and honoring the eight events on the Celtic Pagan calendar that coincided with these. Also known as the Witches Wheel of the Year, this calendar marked the most important celebrations in the Pagans' lives in Ireland and Wales. The Druids officiated ceremonies at Samhain (harvest festival), Yule (winter solstice), Imbolc (spring awakening), Ostara (spring equinox), Beltane (summer solstice), Lughnasa (first harvest), and Mabon (autumnal equinox). These holy days are repeated each year - as, according to the Druids (and Pagans in general), does nature itself.

Druid Hierarchy

Druids started their education in their early childhood and slowly gathered enough wisdom to perform all the prominent roles with which they were entrusted. They were taught by other, more experienced Druids, who had already accumulated a substantial source of knowledge during their life. This level of experience often took up to 20-30 years to achieve, so not all Druids could fulfill all the positions. Archeological findings show that many would wear clothes and headgear to emphasize their highly elevated status in their societies. Unlike the Celtic warriors, the educated class wore long robes and headpieces without a protective function. Due to the slight variations in these articles, it's also clear there was a separation between the different Druid classes.

For example, those with the highest ranks wore yellowish (once golden) robes and headpieces adorned with elaborate bronze carvings. They were typically teachers and other Druid masters with prominent roles. The novice was often discovered in dark robes and simpler headgear. Druids who acted as priests, healers, and advisors wore white, while those determining matters during battle wore red. The artistically inclined practitioners wore blue clothing. In some depictions, more experienced male practitioners also had long hair and an abundance of facial hair - another feature that separated them from the rest of the community. While the Roman sources deny the existence of female Druids, Celtic tales describe these women dressed similarly to their male counterparts.

Another proof of the hierarchy among the Druids is the traditional election of a chief Druid. Typically, this person was the most experienced and trusted member of their community, who - once chosen - held the position until the end of their life. They had the honor of deciding the most pressing matters concerning their clan and officiating the rituals during the main solstices. These leaders would also initiate Druid Masters and Teachers, responsible for carrying on their tradition. In many other societies, this separation existed because of the illiteracy commoners were afflicted with. In Druidry, it was due to the magnitude of the commitment required to master this craft.

The Roles of a Druid

Archeological findings and oral depictions agree that the Druids had sacred places for performing the most important rituals. Here, they would officiate deity worship, rule on all religious questions, and prepare for the major sabbats. These were secluded areas, like natural forest clearings and manmade stone circles. Stonehenge is a famous Druidic place of worship, a megalithic monument built around 2400 B.C. While it's unclear whether the Druids erected the structure, Stonehenge was a popular congregation site for Pagans during the major Sabbats. Today, this site is visited by Modern Pagans, Druids, and followers of other Neo Paganistic religions.

The Druids were seen as intermediaries between humans, deities, and spirits, so their help was sought whenever someone needed answers, guidance, or protection from malevolent entities. Druids were polytheistic and worshiped both male and female gods, meaning their practices were a true representation of the ancient Celtic belief systems in Ireland and Wales. Their offering could even appease the neutral spirits, so they weren't tempted to turn against humans. Due to this, many equated Druidry with the priesthood, calling practitioners Pagan priests. This knowledge was often reinforced because Druids were the most educated class among the Celts, and their opinion was considered sacred.

However, in reality, the roles of a Druid were wide-ranging. They would act as teachers, judges, scientists, poets, healers, and philosophers. They were respected because of their power to communicate with deities and spirits from all realms. Their rulings were also revered because of the infinite wisdom behind their abilities. Not only were they knowledgeable about natural phenomena, but they could also explain supernatural forces. They were often asked to distinguish between the two and take control of whichever they faced. While they could not always control these events, they provided insight on how to protect against them - often saving the lives of their clansmen, animals, or crops.

It is also believed that Druids could foresee the future to an extent. They did this by interpreting certain omens and pondering about upcoming events. Eventually, this leads to them predicting the consequences. The Druids' aptitude for divination granted them the astronomers' function. Using their keen sense of prediction, they could prepare for any event on the Paganic Calendar and signal the rest of the community when it was time for them to do the same.

Their role as famous poets is well documented by the Romans and is evidenced by how Druids carried on their traditions to our day. Poets were not merely busy crafting songs and mystical tales - they were historians retelling the lives of their ancestors. The stories they passed on to the next generations were part of their folklore and represented the meaning behind their laws. These were lessons learned from ancestral experience or prophecies left behind by an even older Druidic culture.

When they weren't busy performing spells, rituals, and divinations regarding important political matters or healing, Druids tended to more common affairs. When acting as a judge, their roles included dealing with minor crimes within their community and even resolving conflicts between family members. A person could have easily been banned from religious affairs and even banished from the entire clan if the Druids considered this a necessary punishment. What's even more interesting is that the Druids could grant divorces to men and women, something quite unusual for ancient societies. Yet, for this Celtic class, every human soul was considered equal and, therefore, deserved equal treatment.

The Druidic monopoly on religious events went far beyond the realm of merely officiating them. They had so much power in their communities that anyone who disregarded their ruling in any matters faced exclusion from sacred rituals and religious festivals. If anyone dared to disobey them, they would be considered unclean, and their energy threatened to taint the entire event. Therefore, they had to stay on the community's periphery and were prohibited from even glimpsing upon an upcoming ceremony. In Paganic Ireland, Druids imposed certain prohibitions known as geis. While much more mundane than a punishment for a crime, a geis was considered a sacred taboo. Those who disregarded this edict faced many misfortunes, including the death of close relatives. While this also sounds like an evil act, the application of geis probably served as protection against illnesses and other inflictions. For example, individuals could be forbidden to eat the meat of certain animals Druids believed to be tainted with a disease - hence the death warning.

Common Druid Rituals

Apart from their most sacred places, Druids often hosted rituals and other ceremonies at natural sites of importance. Spring, rivers, lakes, hilltops, bogs, and three groves could all serve as a place of congregation for Celtic Druids and their communities. Here, the line between our realm and the Otherworld becomes thinner, particularly around Samhain and Beltane. This allowed the Druids to offer sacrifices to the spirit inhabiting other realms in exchange for protection and guidance.

When their clans were at war, Druids often performed animal sacrifices. If they did this after a battle, it was to express gratitude to the deities for victory or the small number of losses. The offering made before a battle was typically for divination purposes. The sacrificed animal was watched very closely, as any part of their death (or dead body) could offer a clue about the future. If there was any message about the outcome of the upcoming battle, the Druids were able to interpret it. While benign in nature, the Druids showed no mercy for the captured enemy.

On the other hand, the fallen warriors from their clan were given peaceful funerals, representing the ancient Celtic culture in the Irish and Welsh Druids' practices. They believed that when a soul left a body after death, it simply moved on to inhabit another body. Therefore, courageous warriors and leaders needed to be buried with a lavish ceremony alongside their most cherished possessions, including weapons and jewelry. Besides the burial ceremonies, the Druids also officiated cremations and excarnations. This ritual involved exposing the body to the elements until only the bones were left. The practitioners buried or kept these bones for future divinations and other ceremonies.

Like in many other Celtic Paganic cultures, using objects to cast spells or perform ceremonies was common practice in Druidry. When performing a healing ritual, Druids often needed to prepare potions to enhance their spells and possibly cure the ailment they were asked to remedy. The Druids' mystical association with dark magic and the ability to cast curses is probably the result of other religions trying to suppress this practice. However, the Druids did use natural remedies with incredibly powerful effects. They would go on trips to sacred grows at night to harvest herbs; only they knew where to find and use them properly.

Mistletoe was particularly often used in Druidic rituals among the Celtic Pagans in Ireland and Wales. This perennial plant was a traditional symbol of eternal life and fertility because of its ability to keep its leaves, even in winter. Mistletoe often grows on oak trees - which made its importance in Druidry even more pronounced. Due to its wide availability, this plant was used to cure various common ailments. However, its dosage had to be carefully adjusted. If misused, the plant had a poisonous effect that could lead to dire consequences.

The practitioners gathered below the tree to prepare rituals, feasts, and animal sacrifices. They would climb the tree to cut the mistletoe and place it on a golden hook before preparing it for the actual ceremony. A prayer was said to express their gratitude to nature and ask for whatever service was needed. This mistletoe gathering was typically done before a specific day on the Witches Wheel of the Year - before a sabbat or the sixth day of the moon. At this time, the moon hasn't grown to half its size, but it already possesses enough influence to ensure a favorable outcome for the ceremony to be performed.

Link to Human Sacrifice

While animal sacrifices were common among the Druids, it's unclear whether they offered human sacrifices. There are some testimonies about the Druids performing rituals requiring a human sacrifice. Other sources say they only participated in offerings made by other Celtic classes. Again, most of these records come from the Romans, who may have used human sacrifice as an excuse to diminish the value of Druidry. There is no clear evidence about which Celtic cultures were doing these rituals. Much of their work was viewed as magic with a bad influence on those outside the Celtic Pagan culture. Witnessing Druids perform a powerful healing ritual on fallen warriors may have led to some common misconceptions about their practices. Druids who acted as intermediaries between the clans were always in favor of preserving the peace, but they sometimes used unconventional arguments to persuade the chieftains to maintain good relations. Some of their words were often viewed as threats, which, again, led to exaggerations about their practices.

How Celtic Druids Spent Their Days

On a typical day, a Druid would wake up before the sun was visible on the horizon. They considered the rising sun's energy the most potent source of natural energy, so they used this time for divinations and gaining answers to pressing matters. This was typically done through an offering accompanied by a prayer to the chosen spiritual leader. Most Druids had a preferred way to communicate with a deity's spirit of their choice, which was unique for every practitioner. Depending on the answer they were seeking, the offering could demand everything from a simple gift to an animal sacrifice.

If a Druid served as a teacher, they would continue throughout their day telling tales of Celtic ancestors to children and other would-be Druids. Large numbers of young people would gather in front of them, waiting to be empowered with new wisdom, which, upon receiving, they held in great honor. Afterward, a Druid would consult with their clan chief about what they learned during their morning ritual. If they uncovered something concerning the clan's safety, the chieftain would ask them for their advice on the matter.

If not, they moved on to discuss other important affairs, such as upcoming solstices, warrior oaths, criminal cases, conflicts with other clans, etc. Due to their infinite wisdom, the Druids were trusted to rule fairly on all matters and keep the community balanced.

Once all these matters were resolved, a Druid would take medicine to those who needed healing. They would also learn if anyone else required their guidance by interacting with their community. Arriving home, a Druid would prepare healing concoctions they needed to administer the next day. Late at night, they would ponder the issues they learned from others or prepare for upcoming rituals.

Decline and Rebirth of Druidry

Druidry played a fundamental part in Celtic Paganism, particularly in Wales. However, as the Roman Empire grew in strength, it eventually pushed the Celtic beliefs into the background. The Romans considered Druids a powerful binding force for the societies they were trying to take over, so they took it upon themselves to force it out as much as possible. Since Paganism emphasized spiritual values rather than worldly ones, Roman's early attempts to eradicate this culture weren't too successful. Unfortunately, this wasn't the case with Christianity - which during the medieval period, managed to render all the functions of the ancient Druids invalid.

They still managed to carry on their traditions. Some were forced to pass down their knowledge in total secrecy, while many Druids found a way to reach their followers by assimilating their teachings into the Christian practices. Due to their ability to adapt to other cultures, after the 17th century, Druids successfully revived their traditions. In modern times, Druidry is practiced somewhat differently than the ancient Celts, but its essence still lives on.

Like other remnants of the Celtic culture, modern Druidry represents a blend of ancient Paganism, Christianity, and modern Neopaganism religions, such as Wicca. In turn, other belief systems have also been influenced by this practice. For example, the number three, which was present in many Pagan symbols, and often used by Druids, is found in Christianity and Neopaganism practices. The circle is another symbol with great importance for the Druid beliefs and Neopaganism, and it still represents the circle of life and the wheel of the year.

Chapter 3: Pagan Feasts and Festivals

'Pagan' is a broad term used for many different groups, including the Wiccans, Celtic neopagans, Heathens, and others. Each group has its own religious beliefs, customs, and even languages. However, all these groups come together during festivities and celebrations at specific times of the year. This chapter discusses what makes the occasions so important for the different pagans and how the festivals are celebrated in the pagan culture.

Wheel of the Year

The pagan seasonal cycle is split into clearly defined moments throughout the year identified by changes in the seasons and the position of the stars. These different times are graphically represented through what is known as the Wheel of the Year. This circular depiction of the year divides the various celebrations into eight portions. Collectively these festivals and celebrations are known as Sabbath days/holidays. Four of the eight celebrations are of Celtic origin and are known as the Greater Sabbaths or the Quarter Days. The Greater Sabbaths are based on astronomical events, and for this reason, they can vary by a few days every year. The Minor Sabbaths are known as the Cross-Quarter Days, and these holidays are based on the solstices and equinoxes.

The solstices and equinoxes are changes in the tilt of the Earth and relate to season changes, and are determined by the way the sun's light hits the equator. As the Earth rotates around the sun, it also shifts forwards and backward on its axis, causing the change in seasons. If you are in the northern hemisphere, when the Earth shifts forward, you experience summer. When the Earth stabilizes and stands straight on its axis, this is the onset of autumn. When the northern hemisphere tilts backward and the Antarctic Circle faces forward, ahead of the Arctic Circle, it is the onset of winter. Also, while the earth is tilting sideways on its axis to one direction, it is also rotating irregularly around the Sun. It is like an oval circle around the sun, so we are very close to the sun at one extreme, whereas on the other end of the circuit, we are much farther away. This also plays a significant role in how we experience seasons and the intensity with which we experience heat and cold on earth during the summer and winter months.

The Wheel of the Year was an essential part of the Celtic and Pagan cultures as it was used to make sense of time – before calendars and clocks. With the Wheel of the Year, the Pagans could understand time and influence many life activities, such as what they grew and harvested, how they traveled, where they lived, and even their lifestyle.

Yule (Winter Solstice)

The winter solace is between the 21st and 23rd of December in the northern hemisphere and between the 20th and 23rd of June in the southern hemisphere. The winter solace is the shortest day of the year, accompanied by the longest night. In pagan traditions, this is the phase where the Child of Promise is born, the god that will overcome the darkness of the winter and guide people to a brighter, warmer, and fruitful spring. The days start to get longer, and the winter gets milder from this point on.

Yule is also closely tied to Christmas that Christians celebrate. Even though the Yule celebration has been part of Northern European culture since before Christianity, the festivals have overlapped and shifted from one to the other over time. For instance, the concept of giving gifts is common in both cultures. It is also a time to celebrate with the family, usually around a big feast. In Sabbath traditions, it is part of the culture to light a fire to Yule logs, whereas in Christianity, the tradition is to decorate trees. Pagans will burn Yule logs in their homes indoors and outdoors to bring good luck for the spring season ahead. Even the primary colors used in the Sabbath celebrations of Yule are commonly used in Christmas celebrations, such as red and green.

Pagans celebrate this time with sweet ale, hot cider, soups, and plenty of nuts and meat.

Imbolc (Candlemas)

Imbolc is a festive occasion built on the celebrations of Yule. This is celebrated on the 1st of February in the northern hemisphere, while the southern hemisphere enjoys this on the 1st of August. It is a festival signifying that winter is nearly over and warmer, more fruitful days of spring are just around the corner. This is when the last traces of winter start to fade. There is a lot more rain, and the sun and the Earth provide all living things with what they need to get back into the growth process.

In Pagan traditions, this is also known as Brigid's day, respecting the goddess Brigid. It is believed that if you leave an offering for Brigid, she will bless the harvest that is to come and save farmers from bad harvests. Since she is a god associated with growth and fertility, this is the most important time of year for her.

At the same time, this is a time for people to cleanse, just like how the Earth is cleansing itself of winter and refreshing for the year ahead. It is a time to sow fresh seeds, let go of the past, and be hopeful for a brighter future. If you want to make significant changes to your life and start anew, this is the time to do so.

The festival is highlighted by spring cleaning and making handicrafts symbolic of Imbolc. Using fresh spring flowers and eating fresh fruit is the norm at this time of the year.

Ostara (Spring/Vernal Equinox)

This is a special time of the year as it is the first time in the New Year that the length of the days and night become equal. In the northern hemisphere, this is celebrated on the 21st of March and on the 21st of September in the southern hemisphere. It is the pivotal point where the daylight hours start to increase, and we get a more positive vibe from Earth. There is plenty of growth during and after this phase transitioning into summer. For the pagans, it is the season of fertility. There is new life in abundance, and it is a joyous time. Like Christmas, this celebration is also reflected in the Christian culture during the Easter festival. The idea of decorating eggs with the symbolism of chicks and baby rabbits (among other animals) is all meant to demonstrate the coming of new life and a new beginning. It is the opposite of the autumn equinox.

Some people like to act out the role of the god and goddess, depicting the romance they experience that leads them to conceive the Child of Promise. Also, the way the night and day become equal is reflected by the god of nature as his personality is split between his higher consciousness and primitive sexual desires.

Beltane (May Eve)

The famous fire festival, Beltane, takes place at the end of spring and the start of the summer season. The northern hemisphere celebrates this on the 1st of May, whereas it is the 1st of November in the southern hemisphere. Beltane is also known as May Day. It celebrates fertility as much growth and development in all life forms occur on Earth. This festival is highlighted by fire, so many events and celebrations have bonfires at the center of the party, or there is a dance or performance using fire. Another essential component of the Beltane celebration is the Maypole, used to depict the reproductive part of the celebration. A pole has ribbons or multi-colored threads attached to it at the top, and people hold onto the threads as they dance and run around the pole, braiding it into a beautiful pattern. Women make crowns from flowers decorated with ribbons and wear them as they dance around the Maypole.

Families celebrate this festival with their children by planting seeds of small plants in pots at home, making wishes, and sending them out into the universe by casting them into the fire. It is a time when people look forward to the harvest they will get after a nice and bright summer. In pagan tradition, this is the time of the year when the sun god visits earth to fertilize it and play his part in the growth process. It is also depicted through the goddess and the Green Man, who symbolizes growth and rebirth. It also illustrates how the god transitions from being driven by lust and the urge to reproduce to committing to a relationship and raising the next generation.

It is also believed that this is when the veil between the living and the dead is at its thinnest. Therefore, people think they can communicate with the dead. Also, farmers will seek protection for their animals by taking them to open pastures and walking them through two large fires. This is believed to rid the animals of impurities and protect them for the coming season.

Litha (Summer Solstice)

Litha is the peak of the Earth's growth season as summer gets into full swing. Even though it is one of the lesser Sabbaths, it is still a much-celebrated time of year. In the northern hemisphere, it is between the 20th and 24th of June and the 20th to 24th of December in the southern hemisphere. It is also the longest day of the year, after which the length of the day shortens once again. In religion, this is the day signifying that the Sun god has reached the peak of his strength and maturity. It is the end of his youthful era where he roamed free and carelessly. Now it is a transition into a more serious part of life where the Earth is growing from the seeds to plants, and some plants may even have started to flower and give fruit. The Sun god is moving to a more protective phase in his life.

The monument of Stonehenge is also an important part of this celebration. Two large stones are located outside the main circle of stones known as the Heel Stone and Slaughter Stone. These two stones channel the sun's rays directly to the center of the circle on this day. All the activities and festivities on this day represent the sun's power and that the Earth is also entering a more mature phase of its life cycle.

Lughnasadh (Lammas)

Lammas is one of the greater Sabbaths and the first of the three harvest festivals. The word *Lammas* means loaf-mass, whereas the other name, Lughnasadh, means the gathering of Lugh, representing that Lugh has transferred his power. In the northern hemisphere, it is on the 1st of August, and in the southern hemisphere, the 1st of February. It is the first stage of preparation for the winter months ahead. The sun starts losing its strength from this point onwards, and the days get considerably shorter.

Pagans believe that during Lammas, the god sacrifices himself to the goddess, and she slays him with a sickle. The god's blood spills onto the earth and gives the earth the energy to last till the next Wheel of the Year. In this way, the god also transitions from the god of light and life to the Dark Lord of death, which is his role in the latter part of the year.

It is celebrated by baking bread in the shape of the god and making other artifacts representing the god. Celtics believe that the Sun god Lugh transfers his strength to the grains they are harvesting, and when they bake this grain into bread, the transfer of power is complete, and his role comes to an end.

Mabon (Autumn Equinox)

Mabon is the second of the harvest seasons and is another signal that the summertime is fading away and that people need to prepare for the winter. The northern hemisphere celebrates this during the 21st and 24th of September, and in the southern hemisphere, it is celebrated between the 21st and 24th of March. Once again, the day and night come into balance and are nearly in equal proportion to one another. The concept behind this phase of the Wheel of the Year is similar to what Christians practice during Thanksgiving. It is a time to reflect on the journey of summertime, how the earth gave us what we needed to stay alive and has even given us the fuel we will use in the winter.

While the spring equinox represented sexual energy, the Mabon period is a mystical phase of the year. It is surrounded by reincarnation, the cycle of life, the wisdom of planning for the harsh winter months, and the journey from the womb to the tomb. The god also contemplates these different ideas and concepts and reaches a higher level of consciousness. At this point, the god reconnects with the goddess as his higher level of consciousness grants him access to the underworld. By now, the goddess is the queen of the underworld, and it is another stage in their union taking place in a very different setting.

Samhain (Halloween)

Samhain is a well-known festival in Pagan culture and the modern world. However, the rest of the world recognizes this as Halloween rather than Samhain. This usually occurs around the 31st of October to the 2nd of November in the northern hemisphere and around the 31st of April and the 2nd of May in the southern hemisphere. Again, this is when the veil between the living world and the spirit world is extremely thin, so it is usually associated with ghosts, spirits, and extraterrestrial activity. It is believed that the spirits from the other world roam the Earth freely on this night. Since the spirits are so close to us, many people believe it is the best time to practice magic.

Samhain is the last of the three harvest festivals. The word Samhain is believed to come from an Irish word that translates to "summer's end." This part of the Wheel of the Year is also the opposite of the Beltane festival. Where cattle were initially sent out to graze on pastures in Beltane, this is the time of the year when they return and are again received with great blazing flames.

Some pagans and Celtics also view this festival as the witches' New Year as it is the end of the cycle for that year. It is a time when people think about the year, reflect on everything that happened, and pay their respects to those who passed away. It is a time when people practice gratitude and look at life differently as they prepare for the hard winter climate. They thank the gods for how they helped the people to achieve the resources needed for the winter and focus on how they can get through the winter successfully. In the modern-day, this is not that difficult, but back then, it was an extremely challenging part of the year that required as much, if not more, preparation than what was needed to get the plants growing and the crops ready for the summer.

During the festivities for this occasion, people sacrificed animals to the gods to thank them. They dressed up in animal skins and wore various animals' heads.

The god united with the goddess in the underworld dies at this point. The Sun child that is yet to be born is becoming more mature. The Sun god will be born in Yule, the next festival, completing the Cycle of Life.

All the various festivals in the Wheel of the Year are roughly 6 to 8 weeks apart, so there is always something to expect. How these events are celebrated has also changed with time, and people in different parts of the world also celebrate them differently. Due to the differences in weather, availability of resources, and other restrictions, people have found new ways to celebrate these events. However, the spirit of the festivals still lives on. Moreover, different covens have their specific way of celebrating the same events, and people from different backgrounds within the Pagan umbrella also have their festivals. But the essence of these events remains the same.

Chapter 4: Celtic Witchcraft and Branches of Belief

Witchcraft was a popular practice among almost every culture in history. Traditionally, the practice could be defined as invoking special powers to take charge of individuals or events. Magic and sorcery are two elements typically involved in the process. While it is elucidated differently in cultural and historical texts, most people, especially in the west, have always held inaccurate stereotypes of witchcraft. It is often perceived as witches meeting at night to partake in rituals with the devil and conduct black magic. These beliefs were particularly reinforced during the 14th-18th century witch hunts. However, these false perceptions are not merely similar to reality.

There are three main implications of the word "witchcraft" in the modern English language. The first is the regular exercise of sorcery and magic worldwide. The second refers to witch hunts that took place in the West during the 14th and 18th centuries. The last connotation is the variations of the modern Wiccan movement.

The words witch and witchcraft come from the Old English term *wiccecraft*. *Wicce* referred to female witches, and Wicca was the masculine term. Although there are terms that mean the equivalent of witchcraft in other languages, such as *sorcellerie* in French, *brujería* in Spanish, and *Hexerei* in German, none has the same connotation. It means they can't be used to translate each other accurately. It becomes even harder as we move away from Europe and into Asian and African languages.

The main issue with attaching a definite meaning to the term witchcraft is challenging because various concepts and underlying themes come with the practice. These concepts and themes are not fixed, and they change according to the time and place in history. It is not easy to find cultures other than the Irish and Welsh, who share reasonable, and somewhat similar patterns of beliefs attached to witchcraft. Besides sorcery, diabolism, magic, religion, the advances of time, and folklore, always influence and merge with these beliefs. For instance, some regions strongly believe that a witch's superpowers are intrinsic, while others are convinced mystical practices are learned and developed by any individual.

This chapter paints a picture of Welsh witchcraft and Paganism. You'll learn all about what mystical beliefs and perceptions of witches were like in Welsh society. As mentioned above, there are numerous overlaps between Welsh and Irish witchcraft. Yet, there are still some prominent characteristics and beliefs linked to Welsh Paganism, which we will be discussing in more depth. In this chapter, you'll discover what a typical Celtic witch looked like, whether witchcraft was accepted and revered among community members, and if Paganism has always been associated with it.

The Four Main Branches of Welsh Pagan Belief

There are four main branches of Welsh pagan belief: The Gods of Annwn (the Welsh underworld), the Protectors, the Skilled ones, and the Skies and Seasons. These characteristics of Pagan beliefs were very prominent elements among their pantheon of deities. Although many peoples or tribes within the Celtic Empire worshipped their own deities, some of the gods and goddesses were common among many Celts because they brought with their beliefs as individuals moved and conquered other groups. For instance, the Irish, Scottish, and English versions of the Welsh deities we discuss in more depth in Chapter 6.

The Four Branches of Mabinogi

The Mabinogi, referenced on several occasions, includes four branches. In the 11th century, the Welsh mythology tales were combined after being passed on through oral tradition. The Mabinogi were kept in medieval manuscripts and stored in private family libraries. Early modern scholars made strong efforts to restore and salvage the Welsh mystical tales. However, we only have two main versions, along with a few scrapes of the rest to this day. In the 1970s, the works were finally recognized as secular literature, which is only fair considering they contained elaborate characters and touched upon a wide array of gender-related, moral, ethical, and political themes. The mythology, unsurprisingly, also contained incredible, fantastical imagery.

Each branch of the mythology encompasses numerous sequential episodes of a tail. Each branch is named after its deity protagonist, who we'll be covering in more depth throughout the following chapters. The names of the branches are Pwyll, Branwen, Manawydan, and Math. However, it's important to note that this is a relatively modern alteration, and the branches were not named in the original medieval manuscripts. Pryderi is the only common character in all four branches of the Mabingoni, even though he is neither a central nor leading character in any of the tales.

• The First Branch

Pwyll, the Prince of Dyfed, is the tale of Pwyll's mystical and heroic visit to the otherworld. It delves deep into his shapeshifting abilities. Duels, and virtue, are all elements that led him to the creation of a powerful alliance. Pwyll is courted by Rhiannon, the goddess he married to grant freedom in this mythology, followed by his newborn son, Pryderi, being kidnapped and rescued; Tyrenon, the lord of the Kingdom of Gwent, then fostered Pryderi.

• The Second Branch

The tale of Branwen, Daughter of Llŷr, follows the goddess Branwen's betrothment to Ireland's King. The king starts abusing her after he is insulted by Efnysien, Branwen's half-brother. A war instigated by the brother erupts and results in genocide. The dead bodies are resurrected, and the head of Bran, the giant King, somehow remains alive after his death. Pryderi appears as a war survivor, and Branwen dies of guilt and heartbreak.

• The Third Branch

Manawydan, son of Llŷr, is the heir to the British throne and Branwen's brother. The war brings him and Pryderi closer, leading Pryderi to arrange Manawydan and Rhiannon's marriage. However, devastation looms in the land of Dyfed, and Rhiannon and Pryderi are suddenly removed from Manawydan's life due to a trap. Manawydan becomes a farmer and pleads for their release from the enchanted trap and the land of Dyfed's restoration.

• The Fourth Branch

Math, son of Mathonwy, the fourth branch of the Mabinogi, unfolds into a succession of treachery and deception. It revolves around the war with Dyfed and Pryderi's death, followed by a virgin girl's double rape and Arianrhod's rejection of an undesired son. Her magician brother, Gwydion, was the mastermind and creator of these happenings. He stirs in a synthetically incubated pregnancy with an artificial woman (Blodeuwedd). She gets involved in a deceitful love triangle that ends with a traitorous murder.

Gwydion then embarks on a Shamanic journey for redemption.

Was Witchcraft Accepted?

We started the chapter by explaining how witchcraft is perceived as an activity involving magic and supernatural powers to harm others. While many people still carry these misconceptions about witches, this stereotype was more popular in history. In the modern-day world, many think witchcraft is a mystical healing art.

Despite the popularity of witchcraft at the time, many people went on witch hunts to catch the practitioners of "black magic." Witchcraft was highly associated with black magic in ancient times. However, this belief grew more and more prominent during the later Middle Ages, after Christianity became the primary religion and the Roman ideology more widespread. The church officially prohibited divination, and they declared ritualistic magic as heresy. This triggered the onset of witch hunts in Italy and Spain during the 1420s. The Friars instigated a state of panic by spiraling satanic conspiracies and blaming all misfortunes on witchcraft and its practitioners.

The growing power of the Catholic Church and Protestantism spiraled the second huge witch hunt in Europe. Protestants targeted all forms of witchcraft during the 16th century, suggesting that witches were misled by the devil, which automatically garnered the Catholic Church's response. The allegations heightened, leading to the most vicious witch hunts in recorded history.

The History of Witch Hunts

When we think of Europe's early modern period, we immediately think of the great scientific and cultural advancements made at the time. Despite the academic and technological strides, the people grew more and more religiously intolerant as mass hysteria had struck the continent. This all contributed to the tragic witch hunts that overtook Europe between 1550 and 1700. Individuals were not only accused of witchcraft but were also executed for it.

The history behind witch hunts, alternatively known as the "witch craze," is very profuse and intricate. However, it's suggested that social issues, religious conflicts, and matters of gender and class were perhaps the driving forces behind this horrid historical occurrence. It is believed that the execution and torment the alleged witches endured were closely tied to particular problems in society. They were mostly victims of political and religious schemes.

When the witch craze came about, Europe was heavily divided and undergoing a socio-economic crisis. At the time, the European population was growing exponentially, pressuring the little agricultural resources they had to survive. Religious groups had been at war from the mid-16th century, during a time when Europe was already ravaged after the Huguenot and the 30-year wars.

No one had taken up a real interest in witchcraft, or even cared about it (other than those who were practicing it, of course), before the late 15th century. This changed when Henricus Institoris published Malleus Malefic arum, which was a treatise on witchcraft, in 1485, garnering the people's attention. This book served as a comprehensive guide for hunting witches and persecuting them. It undoubtedly left a great impact on the following two centuries of the European witch craze. The book aimed to provide a deeper understanding and a solution to the issues surrounding witchcraft at the time. It investigates the nature of the accusations of witchcraft, the trials, and Society's attitude toward women. The book remains one of the most prominent hallmarks of the history of witchcraft.

The church's main aim was to replace public beliefs with Christian ones. However, when it failed to eradicate the folk beliefs of the people who typically remained half-pagan, horror stories about the alarming practice of witchcraft and the potency of black magic were spread all over the continent. At the time, many people were practicing alternative medicine, which encompassed using charms and cures. This is the "magic" the authorities, and the church considered "sage and un-alarming." However, non-medicinal magical practices were deemed sorcerous and, therefore, heretical in the 15th century.

Christians began to grasp a sense or idea of witchcraft as a concept at this point, encompassing demonic and satanic worships, curses, harmful black magic, and Black Sabbaths. It led everyone to believe that folk activities and religious practices, particularly widespread in European rural areas, were associated with sorcery and the Devil. Ultimately, practitioners of folk religion, regarded as a satanic practice, were punished and criminalized. What further fueled these beliefs is that there were some malicious and widespread magical practices in these areas. Many individuals cursed others, which was evident behavior that cruel witches existed.

The tolerant and accepting individuals of the 15th century decided to take action. Anyone who wouldn't comply with the standard beliefs, systems of faith, and religious practices was marginalized. They were also terrorized and punished by other (typically the elite) members of society. During the 1500s, there was a popular notion that witches were part of a conspiracy and aimed to hurt Christians. People believed that the sorcerers had allied with the devil to eliminate Christianity. Many of the greatest Renaissance philosophers were convinced of the powers of occultism and magic, urging the elite to take matters seriously.

The Hussites and Cathars, along with other heretical groups of the time, were also put to rest by the Church before shifting its attention to the witches. In the 16th century, panic regarding sorcery struck Europe. The church's actions were sequential - they always followed a clear-cut pattern of some sort. For instance, an incident that gave rise to (typically unfounded) suspicions surrounding a person or a group occurred. Lower-class individuals, already marginalized and shunned, were most vulnerable to the accusations, and were the target group of the allegations surrounding witchcraft. Unsurprisingly, these allegations were made on false pieces of evidence. The accused were tortured in the hopes of getting a confession out of them before they were even trialed.

The trials were seldom fair, anyway. Even if it were a false allegation, those who were accused of sorcery expected to receive a death sentence right away. We don't know precisely how many people died during the European witch hunt. However, it is suggested that at least 40000 individuals were executed due to the witch craze. Anyone deemed guilty would be burnt alive, drowned, or hanged. The authorities claimed that barbarically killing them was "a must" since it set an example for others who were inclined to follow in their heretic footsteps.

Researchers believe that the witch hunts came in two waves, as we mentioned above. The first was to suppress heresy and, eventually, turned into a way to shut down political rivals. By the 1650s, the aim was not as explicitly about sorcery and witchcraft as it was previously, leading to a decrease in the number of witch trials.

The second wave of the witch craze was perhaps triggered by the intense rivalry that existed between the Protestant and Catholic churches. There was a growing need from both sides to ensure people conformed to their religion. Social tensions resulting from economic and social changes, inflation, and warfare also played a role in fueling these hunts because the need to keep control over the people was stronger than ever before. The authority used the witch hunts to threaten the lower classes, warning them against rebellion. Women, unfortunately, were the main victims. While some men were accused of witchcraft, women accounted for the greater number of allegations and executions because more women were becoming single, increasing societal tensions.

What Witches Looked Like

We don't believe there is a solid description of Celtic witches because they tried their best to blend in, considering they were being hunted. However, it is said that Dianonysic worship practices included drinking, feasting, animal sacrifices, and underground meetings in the Greco-Roman civilization. Horace, Aeschylus, and Virgil, among the most popular classical authors, also depicted sorceresses and witches as they illustrated harpies, furies, and pale-faced ghosts, dressed in decaying clothing with crazy hair. They also suggested that witches gathered at night and conducted human and animal sacrifices. During the late 20th century, Christians also accused witches of sacrificing children.

During the witch hunts periods, brutal practices were conducted on alleged witches. They used to prick them to find out if the Devil had made them indifferent to pain. They also searched them for the "devil's mark," which was thought to be anything that resembled an odd-looking wart or mole. They also threw the alleged witch into the pond. If the body sank, it was considered innocent because the water accepted it.

Paganism vs. Witchcraft

Wiccan beliefs started regaining popularity during the 1950s. The newly perceived religion started gaining more traction. However, unable to grasp what the practice of Wicca involved, many people confused Paganism with the new movement.

Witchcraft is highly associated with Wicca, a nature-oriented belief system. It includes rituals eminent during pre-Christianity times. In contrast, pagans, according to definition, are members of spiritual, religious, or cultural communities. Their practice revolves around the worship of the earth or nature in general.

Wicca, as a religion, can be traced back to Gerald Brosseau Gardner and England in the 1950s. Gardner spent a few years working across Asia before releasing the book *Witchcraft Today* in 1954. He started a movement built on pre-Christian traditions. It was based on three main aspects: respecting nature, magic, and worshipping a goddess along with other deities.

Pre-Christian traditions and rituals shape today's neopagan movement. Having a deep respect for nature is also a significant element of Paganism. This movement goes as far back as the 1800s before it was reshaped in the 1960s. It became a revival of fertility worship and nature. Pagans come from various belief backgrounds that particularly focus on equality and nature. They typically worship numerous deities. However, it all comes down to the practitioner's preferences.

It means that Wicca is different from Paganism but a subtype. As you know, there are many misconceptions about what it means to be a pagan or a Wiccan, and people typically mix both with each other. While technically all Wiccans are pagans, not all pagans are Wiccans.

In short, modern-day Wiccans are regarded as present-day witches. The aspect of magic is what sets Paganism and Wicca apart. While Wicca is a subcategory of Paganism, they share the core elements of fertility, nature, and spirituality.

The answer to the age-old question, "Is witchcraft real?" depends on many factors, including personal beliefs and the connotations attached to their time and place. Even though there is no solid definition, one thing is for sure, the depiction of witchcraft in literature, movies, and art is not at all representative of reality.

Chapter 5: Irish Spirits and Deities

Irish mythology encompasses details of ancient Ireland and the origin stories of deities, heroes, and kings. Among all the branches of Celtic mythology, ancient Irish beliefs and mythology are the best preserved. These ancient beliefs were passed down from generation to generation until the Middle Ages when Christian monks started writing down the narrations and placing them into historical records. The tales of ancient Irish beliefs and traditions might have evolved, but the deities and characters remain the same. Most Irish folklore and tales are chronologically placed into four cycles: the Mythological Cycle, Ulster cycle, Fenian cycle, and the Historical Cycle.

The importance of deities, gods, and goddesses varies a lot. Dindshenchas is an early Irish literature class focused on the origins of Irish mythological characters, places, and related geographical events. In comparison, most historical records hold great regard for warriors, heroes, and revolutionary leaders. Early manuscripts and texts like Dindshenchas emphasize the divinity of ancestors and goddesses. These primal deities are regarded as the region's ancestors and are deeply rooted in the land's sovereignty. Similar in attributes to Greek and Roman gods, Ireland's primal deities are immortal beings fostering various attributes that define their character. Many Irish deities portray human-like qualities of greed, anger, weakness, jealousy, etc., whereas others are linked to natural phenomena on earth. There are even Irish deities possessing the ability to transform their physical appearance.

In this chapter, we explore the realm of Irish deities, read about their personalities, and understand how to work with these deities and honor them.

Almost all Irish gods and supernatural beings are related to the Fomorians, Tuatha Dé Danann, and the Fir Bolg. The Tuatha Dé Danann maintained a positive image among these early descendants, whereas the Fomorians exhibited mostly negative, revolting, and gruesome characteristics. The Fir Bolg was the third race to inhabit the region but were eventually overthrown by the Tuatha Dé Danann, accepted as divine beings or gods having powerful skills and supernatural abilities.

According to folklore, the Tuatha Dé Danann were perceived as supernatural beings proficient in practicing Druidism, history, prophecy, and magic. The Book of Invasions, written by 11th-century monks, explains Tuatha Dé Danann as godlike beings in the form of humans who disappeared after the Milesians arrived. Some accounts say the Tuatha Dé Danann chose the underworld after leaving Ireland, while others propose the Tuatha Dé Danann blended in with the early Irish ancestors.

Here are a few key deities, warriors, and spiritual beings from Irelands' mythological past without further ado.

Dagda

Dagda, or the good god, is a key deity in Celtic Mythology and is portrayed as a chief god of the Tuatha Dé Danann. He is considered a leading figure with influential Druidism, kingship, and super-human strength characteristics. Manliness, strength, wisdom, fertility, and magic are attributes associated with Dagda. He ruled as the king of Tuatha Dé Danann and controlled life and death, weather, and agriculture. Accounts of Dagda from Irish mythology describe him as a bearded giant carrying a long staff called long mór and the ability to restore life. He also carried a bottomless cauldron that never ran empty, and a harp called "Daur da Bláo," which gave him the power to influence emotions and the weather whenever he played it. Dagda is often associated with the famous Celtic Goddess Morrigan and is the father of Aengus, Bodb Derg, Midir, Brigit, and Ceramic. You can gather several things around your altar to honor Dagda, including offering butter, pig meat, and porridge ale. Resembling the cauldron of Dagda, place one cauldron at the altar and fill it with produce and related food items to express your gratitude. As Dagda showed compassion towards others, you can honor him by helping others or donating to demonstrate generosity.

Morrigan

The wife of Dagda, Morrigan, has many titles like the queen of demons, phantom queen, and the goddess of war. The queen possessed the ability to transform into a raven and hover over the battlefield – as well as the ability to predict the outcomes. Tales also tell of Morrigan having enough power to influence whether one would triumph or die during a battle. Despite being associated with war and battle, Morrigan is held in high regard as having the rightful kingship of the land. Her tales from the accounts during the Ulster cycle depict her shapeshifting into a cow or a wolf. Some neopagan traditions have painted a negative picture of Morrigan by associating her role as a destroyer. However, many scholars don't agree with the portrayal and connect her attributes to sovereignty and generosity.

The Morrigan is regarded as a triple goddess as different texts refer to her by different names. Some historians also suggest the three names of Morrigan could be three different personalities having similar attributes. Here are the three personalities associated with Morrigan.

Badb, the Crow Goddess

Badb is portrayed as a fierce goddess influencing the battlefield. She can shapeshift into a crow, appear as an old woman, influence destruction, and convey prophecies. Her presence is heard as the flapping of large wings over the head. Badb is linked to the Crone aspect of the triple goddess.

Sun Goddess, Macha

Macha is often associated with motherhood as she is associated with sovereignty, love, and prosperity. Legends say the union of Dagda with Morrigan helped the land as she granted prosperity to the area after the union.

Nemain

She is the sister of Badb and has somewhat similar attributes, which influence the battlefield. Nemain translates to a dose of poison as she can cause chaos, confusion, and frenzy on the battlefield.

Study the goddess of war's characteristics, the three personalities she is portrayed as, to honor her. The more you study, the easier it will be to work with the deity. When setting up the altar, focus on placing items linked deeply with the Celtic heritage. You can offer her red wine, crow feathers, mead, and red foods. Place her statue or a picture, including candles and decorative items representing animals like deer, crows, and cows, on your altar. People with a higher degree of knowledge and expertise also perform shapeshifting rituals, crow magic, and shadow work to build a better connection with the deity.

Brigid

She was the daughter of Dagda and revered in Christianity as St. Brigit. According to the written tales, she has two sisters called Brighid, and each is associated with a unique ability. The three sisters are seen as a single deity possessing aspects of healing, agriculture, fire, prophecy, and poetry. Folk stories tell of Brigid possessing a green mantle that carried the power to heal and comfort the sick or distressed. Imbolc is a festival celebrated to honor the goddess Brigid, and devotees honor her to get her blessings.

To work with Brigid, dedicate a space to the deity and honor her with simple items like her representation, water, and candles. When you burn the candle, dedicate the flame to her as she kept the fire burning in ancient times and use it to connect with her. When honoring the healing aspect of Brigid, find a natural water source and ask for her blessings.

Lugh

Lugh is one of the top three deities in Irish mythology and the son of Cian and Eithne. Later records perceived him as a warrior and historical figure. Lugh was the chief of the Tuatha Dé Danann and played a vital role in introducing the civil aspects of the mythological period. He carries the Sleá Luin Lugh, a sacred treasure, and has a hound that fights alongside him during battle. He is an all-seeing deity possessing several characteristics like a craftsman, warrior, seer, and poet.

By honoring gods and goddesses, we build a relationship to seek their blessings and guidance and connect with them. Read ancient texts to understand the personality of the deity Lugh, as it will help maintain ritual purity. Lugh possesses musical skills and is attracted to music and related expressions while praying. You can offer food items like bread, butter, milk, and fruits to the deity to seek blessings.

Aengus

The God of love and youth, Aengus or Aonghus, is the son of Dagda and the goddess Bion. Folk tales depict him in his search for a maiden. The story tells that he searched all over the region until he found the maiden accompanied by 150 other maidens who were to be turned into swans. The legend says that Aengus transformed himself into a swan to be with the maiden he adored. Aengus is compared to the Welsh god, Mabon ap Modron, who has a similar personality. The Celtic god had a horse with magical powers to carry an entire household on the back. He wore a multicolored cloak that reflected only one color to the person struggling between life and death.

Besides having attributes of love and youth, Aengus could resurrect the dead using his breath of life. His shapeshifting abilities allowed him to turn into a swan and be depicted as a youthful man. To honor Aengus traditionally, use dairy products as an offering. Baked food items, cheese, mead, cooked water bird, and honey are other food offerings you can choose.

Aine

Praised as the goddess of fertility, love, sovereignty, protection, and warm summer, Aine is a powerful deity with multiple roles as the Sun and Moon goddess. She is believed to teach her people the true meaning and expression of love. Besides the above-mentioned attributes, Aine is associated with fertility, livestock, prosperity, abundance, and wealth. Lady of the lake and the Feary queen are two popular names given to Aine over time. The hill of Knockainy in Limerick County is linked to the goddess. With her two sisters, Fenne and Grianne, she is categorized as a triple goddess and a complex entity with whom to work.

During the summer solstice, or *Litha*, the goddess is most present, and an opportunity to connect with her. Summertime is the most feasible as her presence is not felt much in winter because she is less active. As a goddess of love, and fertility, she has the power to attract or cause harm to an unwanted adorer.

Make a dedicated space for the deity on the altar and include decorative pieces representing a horse, swan, or rabbit. Placing horseshoes are also a good option to consider. Incorporating music into the rituals assists in better connecting with the deity since she played the harp. The food offerings include meadowsweet, grains, corn, lavender, honey, and, in some rituals, menstrual blood. Most deities, including Aine, are best invoked during the full moon because it is associated with the motherhood of the goddess.

Nuada

Nuada was the first king of the Tuatha people and one of the founding fathers of the Irish region. He was a skilled fighter, warrior, and hunter who arrived in Ireland and claimed the land from the Fir Bolg. Nuada lost his arm during the battle and became ineligible to be on a throne. He possessed a sword called the sword of light with a blade sharp enough to leave his enemies in half.

Set up the altar and connect with him by offering basic elements of air, water, and fire. As the deity specializes in war and weaponry, you can seek blessings to improve courage, determination, and guidance to do justice.

Goibniu

Referred to as the smithing god of the Tuatha Dé Danann, Goibniu also possesses hospitality qualities. He was the first to work with metals and made weapons for his people. Most texts suggest that he worked alongside his two brothers. He made a silver arm for Nuada. Besides his smithing abilities, he possessed a cow who produced great quantities of milk. Goibniu is a deity who prepared feasts for the gods, and his prepared meals, when offered to warriors or the sick, protected and healed them from decay and illness.

Danu

Danu is a mother goddess of the Tuatha people and an ancestor of the Irish region. The goddess is linked to fertility, wisdom, regeneration, and strength but early mythological texts have limited literature available about Danu. She was perceived as an important character by modern scholars who wrote texts after the introduction of Christianity into Ireland. The Celtic goddess is described as a beautiful woman and was the divine mother of the people.

Mannan Mac Lir

Known as the god of the sea, Mannan Mac Lir is a popular Celtic god who ruled the seas and was revered as the master of illusions.

Mannan Mac Lir fostered his blessings and belongings to Lugh. Here's a small list of his possessions:

- A steed named Finbar could travel over land and sea
- A boat called an *ocean sweeper* that traveled according to the thoughts of the one who sailed and did not require sails, an anchor, or the relevant equipment to navigate the boat
- The cloak of mists changed color depending on the mood of the wearer. Stories tell that the cloak made thunder-like sounds whenever Lir got angry.

Some other belongings included a sword sharp enough to cut through armor and a spear.

The Manx people regarded Mannanan with great honor and sought his blessings. They offer the god rushes as tributes during the summer solstice.

Balor

He is a member of the Fomorians and a striking figure. Most Fomorian gods portray a negative character and possess destructive powers. Balor is depicted as having a human body with the head of a goat. The forehead has a third eye that can wreak havoc on anything in the surroundings. A legend suggests that when Lugh killed him, Balor fell face down on the ground, and his evil eye was open, which created a deep hole in the earth. The lake of the eye in Co Sligo is referred to as the hole made by Balor's evil eye.

Eithniu

Eithniu was Lugh's mother and the daughter of Balor and was locked away as she foretold her son Lugh would kill Balor. The stories suggest she was rescued and gave birth to three children, one of which was Lugh. Balor tried to drown the three kids, but Lugh survived and was raised by the sea god Mannanan.

Cú Chulainn

Cú Chulainn is a powerful deity talked about in the Ulster cycle. He is a heroic fighter and recognized as the greatest warrior of the region during his era. Cú Chulainn is believed to be a demi-god with supernatural abilities. He had unparalleled athletic abilities and could even handle sedating potions that would take an average person a day to overcome. The rage he portrayed during the battle made him undefeatable. Cú Chulainn used a slingshot called Gae Bolga, similar to a spear covered with deadly thorns.

The strength Cú Chulainn possessed was bound by two rules he had to follow at all times. He was forbidden to eat dog meat and always had to accept food offered by a woman. Ancient texts depict him as a youthful and beardless man popular among the females for his beauty.

Ogma

Oghma is another member of the Tuatha Dé Danann associated with intelligence, learning, and expressiveness. Besides these amazing abilities, Ogma was a great warrior and fought side by side with Lugh. He is portrayed as having long chains of gold and amber attached to his tongue that pursue the followers. He invented and introduced writing into the Irish region. As a warrior, Ogma possessed a sword that kept an account of his heroic endeavors and could recall on command.

Cliodhna

She had many faces and was called the mermaid, fairy queen, and witch. Cliodhna was the queen of the banshees and linked to beauty and love. She possessed an enchanting power to heal the sick. Three birds traveled with the goddess and sang songs that could heal anyone. Written mythological accounts say that whoever listened to the songs would go into a deep sleep state and wake up fully recovered from the illness.

A famous myth regarding the goddess is that she fell in love with a mortal man named Siobhan and wanted to leave the underworld to be with her lover. However, the other gods lured her into sleep and sent her back to the otherworld. Being depicted as a queen of banshees, she lived in cork alongside other fairies and turned into a banshee when an Irish ancestor died. In some texts, it is believed that Cliodhna became a witch after the spread of the church.

Working and connecting with Cliodhna can be a magical and unique experience for people practicing Paganism. Start by reading and understanding the goddess's stories, legends, and folk tales. Her representation at the altar is necessary alongside items like seashells, driftwood, shark teeth, plants, stones, and related elements. You can offer her fruits, vegetables, cakes, mead, and water as an offering.

Chapter 6: Welsh Spirits and Deities

Mythology is an important aspect of life for several good reasons: it makes up a significant portion of our heritage. Mythology always reminds us of who we are, where we belong, and where we come from regardless of our geographical location or what we've achieved in life. Each culture and civilization has its unique set of mythology, legends, and folktales. It's incredibly amazing how these myths have a lot in common and act as a unifying force, even though they each tell different tales and comprise different deities and characters. Our ancestors all used folktales and mythology to make sense of the world around them, regenerate their sense of purpose, and establish a system.

What is mythology exactly, though? By definition, mythology is a half-truth or a complete fiction that makes up an aspect of an ideology. It is a historical story that explains traditions associated with a particular culture, civilization, or group. These myths are typically cosmological and cover events – and even battles – between the deities. Some cultures also have mundane mythology that revolves around normal people having a supernatural experience. Mythology has served as the stepping stone of storytelling for ages.

Mythology is a significant aspect of life for another very important reason, and it acts as a building block for many religions. They are also a foundation for many moral questions and issues. For instance, most myths and tales are about the struggle between good and evil. Every myth and ritual tells stories; the protagonist embarks on a journey that teaches him the necessary morals and personal values to overcome obstacles or defeat the antagonist. Like *The Odyssey*, some legends and tales are so great they have become literary classics for the entire world to enjoy and learn from.

If you think about it, mythology still plays a huge role in our lives. Besides the cultural norms and traditions we live by or sayings embedded in our culture, mythology is reshaped and takes on a new form every day. For instance, one of the most popular examples of modern mythology is comic books. Ever since the creation of *Spider-Man* in 1962, the tale surrounding Peter Parker's incident turning into the renowned Spider-Man has been passed down from one generation to the other. Some comic books and fantasy tales are even based on actual ancient mythology. For instance, Thor is inspired by Norse mythology, while *The Chronicles of Narnia* encompasses characters derived from Roman and Greek mythology. Other examples, like the *Harry Potter* series and *The Hobbit*, have become major examples of modern-day mythology.

This chapter covers many of the most prominent Welsh deities and spirits. You'll learn about them and their tales and discover the importance of Welsh mythology today and its influence in the modern-day world.

Welsh Deities

There are over 36 prominent deities in Welsh mythology, but we will cover the most significant ones. As you may recall from Chapter 4, many Welsh deities were widespread among all Celts. Also, there are equivalent gods and goddesses in Irish, Scottish, and English mythology. You may also remember Rhiannon, Pryderi, Branwen, Bran, Manawydan, and Gwydion from the tales of the four branches of the Mabinogi.

The Goddesses

• Aeronwen

Many people believe that Aeronwen is the Welsh version of the Proto-Celtic goddess Agrona, and the Irish goddess Morrigan. Aeronwen is a Welsh goddess and deeply connected to fate. Agrona was the goddess of war, and the connection to Aeronwen is easy to see. They both determine how a battle would play out, each in their own way. As with most deities that determine how your life will play out, many sacrifices were made to Aeronwen. A battlefield, the number three, and the color black are commonly associated with Aeronern.

• Blodeuwedd

Blodeuwedd was Lleu Llaw Gyffes' (Arianrhod's son) wife. Most sets of deities have trickster gods, and that might have been Blodeuwedd. She liked to trick people, cheat them when she could, and go against her word – she even plotted to kill her husband. In modern times, she is seen as a beacon of female independence, the god who stood up against women being forced into a marriage that was loveless. Those who are single or in loving relationships will turn to Blodeuwedd for help.

• Arianrhod

Although we don't know much about Arianrhod, she is among the more popular Welsh deities. Her name translates to "Silver Wheel," a symbol of the moon and why she is the Welsh goddess of the moon. Don is

Arianrhod's mother, and Lleu Llaw Gyffes and Dylan ail Don (the twins) are Arianrhod's brothers.

- **Branwen**

The deity Branwen is renowned for her beauty. She is the daughter of Llyr and Bran and the sister of Manawydan. She found herself in a loveless marriage to a partner who was abusive. Through the help and strength of her family, she was able to free herself from her matrimonial bond. In order to save her, sacrifices had to be made, and legend tells that a great war ensued, killing almost everyone. It was only the pregnant women who survived. Feeling guilty and heartbroken, Branwen also dies. The deity is regarded as a "protector of abused women." She is also the goddess of healthy, nourishing marriages and true love.

The Bedd Branwen Period was a period of time spanning 1650 BC to 1400 BC – part of the Bronze Age. When the riverbanks of Alaw were searched, a ruined grave was found, and it was believed that this grave belonged to Branwen. This gives more credibility to Branwen being a real person

- **Rhiannon**

Rhiannon is the Welsh Goddess of horses and strength. She is a topic of great interest in the Mabinogi and other Welsh mythology. The fae is a spiritual place where deities, spirits, and other beings are said to dwell. Before she came to our land, Rhiannon was a dweller of the fae – some suggesting that she was a princess of the fantastical world. There are many stories told about Rhiannon. She left the far to marry Pwyll, a great hero of the human world. She had her baby stolen and was blamed for many years until she returned to the fae later in life to prove her innocence.

Rhiannon did not shy away from her destiny or from facing her problems, and this gives inspiration to women (and everyone else) around the world. She would often ride a horse, and the horse has become a symbol that is closely associated with the deity. Because of the tragic story of her son, she has become a symbol of motherhood, strength, and love. She is often prayed to when people are entering marriages, seeking more in life, or wanting to know what is to come.

• Cerridwen

The Welsh goddess Cerridwen is popular among many modern-day witches and neopagans. She is an herbalist, witch, and the guardian of the cauldron of knowledge. Cerridwen is also a shapeshifting moon goddess. Afagddu and Crearwy were the son and daughter of Cerridwen, and her husband was a giant. Cerridwen brewed a potion for Afagddu, granting him knowledge far beyond anyone else. The magic did not only come from the potion – Cerridwen was extremely knowledgeable, and she passed that on to her son. She is prayed to for knowledge and wisdom or when performing magic.

• Modron

In the Celtic Wheel of the Year, Modron is associated with the Autumnal Equinox, known as Mabon (the Divine Child). She is the Great Mother of the Divine Child. Many claim that Modron and Rhiannon are the same deities, considering their stories' similarities. For instance, Mabon's child was kidnapped in the middle of the night, only to be returned after they endured so much punishment and suffering.

The Gods

• Arawn

Annwn is the underworld or otherworld, and Arawn is the king of this world, protecting it and shepherding the souls that cross over. There is a story of Arawn paying for a misdeed by swapping bodies with the mortal Pwyll, a great human hero. While it must have been degrading for a deity to switch forms with a mortal human, they ended up becoming close friends. As Christianity swept into the land of Wales, getting rid of the "old ways," the title "god" was revoked from Arawn. The hunt has always been important in Celtic mythology, and many gods took part in the great hunt. Arawn took to the skies with the others when the hunt commenced, and he has become closely associated with not only hunting but the feast that comes after the hunt.

• **Bran**

Bran is popularly known as the blessed Welsh god. He was a Celtic god whose name is translated into "raven." Many people claimed him to be a kind hero and a giant. It is also said that he was deified after his passing. Many legends illustrate him as Llyr's (the mighty god of the sea) son. The god Manawydan and the goddess Branwen were his siblings. Bran was killed following a brutal battle; he asked his brothers to behead him so they could carry his head back to the kingdom. The head communicated with his brothers until they put it on a hill where the current London Tower is located. The head was meant to face France to take care of any potential dangers. If ever the ravens leave, the head will no longer be protected, and the country might fall into peril.

• **Mabon**

Mabon is the Celtic holiday that celebrates the arrival of autumn, the autumnal equinox. Mabon is also a god and is named after this holiday around this time of the year. Not only is Mabon known in other mythologies and religions by different names, but he is known in Celtic mythology by many different names. He is the Son of Modron and is considered the god of youth and rebirth. As we mentioned above, Mabon was kidnapped from his mother when he was only three days old. King Arthur plays a large role in the mythology and history of Britain. When Mabon became a man, Arthur's knights saved him. He is a man who is old but young at the same time, toeing the line between both, and he is most present on the equinox when night and day are equal in length. Mabon rides his horse with his hound by his side, protecting the beats of nature.

• **Hafgan**

What would a set of deities be without a plot to kill another? Do you remember when we explained that Arawn switched bodies with Pwyll? Hafgan was always a rival of

Arawn, and Arawn took his chance to remove Hafgan when the switch happened – Arawn asked Pwyll to murder Hafgan. After Pwyll's success, Arawn seized the throne and united the kingdoms into a sole otherworld.

- **Manawydan**

Son of Llyr, husband of Rhiannon, and brother to Branwen and Bran. Manawaydan is often conflated with the god Manannan Mac Lyr, the god of the sea of the Isle of Man – they share some distinct similarities. Manawaydan helped secure Bran's head at the London Tower. This Welsh Celtic god is expanded upon into two of the Mabingoni branches. The third branch tells that he saved Rhiannon from an evil curse. There is no solid proof that Manawaydan was a sea god. He was also depicted as one of King Arthur's knights in some Arthurian legends.

Working with the Deities and Attracting Them into Your Life

The deities are as relevant today as they were in the past. They are prominent spiritual figures, and their tales have significantly impacted the modern-day world (more on that later). Working with them and attracting their energy into your life can help you enhance your spiritual practice. Here are some ways you can connect with each Welsh Celtic deity; you may wish to place important items on the altar:

- **Arawn**

Put aside some time on the Winter Solstice when the night is at its longest. Arawn's energy is likely to attract dog owners or those who like to hunt.

- **Mabon**

Mabon should be especially honored when the day and night are balanced on the Autumn Equinox.

- **Manawydan**

To honor Manawydan, remember that he helped to secure Bran's head and was closely related to King Arthur. Find items that can represent either or both of those.

- **Rhiannon**

You can hang illustrations of birds and horses near your altar and also incorporate her colors: green, purple, and white.

- **Aeronwen**

The Welsh goddess of war appreciates items of battle; you might place a small knife or another weapon on the altar. Black is a color to focus on. You can also incorporate the number 3 into your altar.

- **Arianrhod**

Worship the lunar goddess Arianrhod on the Full moon. You can hang pictures or paintings of the moon around your altar or in your home to honor her.

- **Branwen**

Branwen encourages marriage filled with love – and love in general. You can place photos of yourself and your loved ones, flowers (pertaining to love and not death or sadness), and a mirror (to reflect your happy emotions and beauty).

- **Cerridwen**

If you want a significant attraction of Cerridwen's energy, you must use a cauldron. Make sure to dedicate this cauldron to her, and never use it unless you're working with her energy.

- **Modron**

Honor this god on the Autumnal Equinox. The deity loves apples and can be asked for help with problems related to motherhood.

The Impact of the Mabinogi and Welsh Mythology

To this day, mythology plays a huge role in Welsh history and culture. The national flag of Wales even has an image of a red dragon, Y Ddraig Goch, considered the mythological creature of Wales.

As you probably know by now, *The Mabinogi* is considered the most prominent source of folktales and myths. It encompasses a total of 11 tales dating back to the Middle Ages. The Mabinogi's author is anonymous, but the tales have been passed on from one generation to the other. Since storytelling is an oral tradition, each teller or group added their own take on the tales until they were finally written in the Middle Welsh language and kept in the *White Book of Rhydderch* between 1300 and 1325. The myths were also written between 1375 and 1410 in *The Red Book of Hergest.*

These stories were about the troubles and adversities of Welsh royal families, plagues, a Roman emperor, voyages, white horses, and mystical creatures. However, these books weren't translated into English until the 19th century. A woman from Lincolnshire developed an interest in the Welsh language and translated the stories to English. Not long after, they made it across Europe and the rest of the world.

Lady Charlotte Guest, the wife of the Dowlais Ironworks' owner, gathered the tales and titled them *The Mabinogion.* However, many people mistakenly thought this title was the plural of the word *Mabinogi*. A Cardiff University emeritus professor, Sioned Davies, translated the Mabinogion into English. She incorporated it into the Oxford World Classics and continued to study and teach it for the majority of her life.

The Mabingoni and the *Mabingonion* were by different authors and were created in different periods, even though they were all collected by Lade Charlotte Guest on a known date. As we discussed, The Four Branches of the Mabingoni encompasses the structure and overtones of Celtic mythology, including imagery and concepts like white horses, shapeshifting, and other greater worlds.

The Four Branches include the stories of Pwyll, Prince of Dyfed, Branwen, daughter of Llŷr, Manawydan, son of Llŷr, and Math, Son of Mathonwy. These, along with the other seven tales, were all collected in *The Mabinogion* by Lady Charlotte Guest. The Mabinogion, especially *The Four Branches of the Mabingoni,* significantly influenced Welsh culture and literature. Think of them as the Chaucer and Shakespeare of English literature. Many elements of these tales are also seen in internationally significant pieces, like *Star Wars* and the works of *Doctor Who and JK*

Rowling.

The Four Branches of the Mabingoni are considered more inspirational than the Arthurian legend because they are more relatable to the modern-day world because they have prominent themes like friendship. Their characters are more relevant to the present day.

The works have also been translated into numerous languages, including Hungarian, German, and French. Lady Guest's initial translation allowed the world to see the grandeur of *The Mabinogion*. It has greatly impacted the cultural landscape and filmmakers, writers, musicians, and artists ever since. Some illustrators like Alan Lee and Margaret Jones took an interest in illustrating the tales, while artists like Iwan Bala completed paintings inspired by the tales. Along with other writers, Jenny Nimmo was also deeply inspired by *The Mabinogion*. The impact of the tales could be seen in works like *The Magician Trilogy and The Snow Spider*. A Welsh national opera named The Sacrifice was also based on *The Second Branch of the Mabinogi*. Renowned writers like Gwyneth Lewis, Owen Sheers, Russell Celyn Jones, and Fflur Dafydd also worked on a modern re-telling of the tales by Seren Books, which was among the latest adaptations.

There are numerous Welsh gods and goddesses with remarkable tales. Calling on them as a part of your spiritual practice can enrich your experience. Their tales have influenced the cultural landscape and impacted the works of numerous filmmakers, writers, musicians, and artists. Mythology is incredibly important because it has been a pure form of storytelling and a source of entertainment and education since the beginning of mankind. We all love to listen and tell good stories – mythology or not.

Chapter 7: Paganism and Druidry Today

Given the proliferation of monotheistic religions, followed by widespread secularism in most societies, one would be forgiven for believing that paganism and Druidism went the way of other ancient practices and beliefs, forever disappearing into the ether. However, it's hard to completely eliminate religions that have lasted for longer than two millennia. Therefore, paganism and Druidry are still with us today and have taken root in their modern incarnations in various countries, specifically the west. It hasn't disappeared. On the contrary, many of the central beliefs and traditions have permeated the culture that many may not fully realize where this lore originated.

Simultaneously, there has been a steady revival of paganism and the Druidry for a few decades, with new followers adopting these ancient practices in droves. While followers remain part of a fairly niche religious movement, the numbers are growing. The exact numbers and stats aren't readily available, but given the growing market for books on the subject and stores devoted to this genre' of magic, it is easy to conclude its popularity is on the rise. Furthermore, as previously mentioned, the ways of the Druids and pagans are diffused throughout the culture and have never entirely disappeared. This chapter will devote time to understanding how paganism and Druidism take shape today.

More than Just a Holiday

Many of our most popular holidays these days, or the specific ways they're celebrated, possess pagan roots. One famous example is Christmas. Of course, the intention of this holiday is to celebrate the birth of Christ, which is about as far as you can be from the pagan or Druid beliefs. However, there is a great deal of historical evidence that the Catholic Church remade the pagan winter solstice to entice people into Christianity, and the traditions of Judeo-Christians and pagans have been woven into the holiday. The exact date of Jesus' birth is unknown, and there is no evidence in the Christian Bible. December 25th is a random date until you realize it most likely coincided with many festivities the pagans performed to celebrate the winter solstice. It was a clever intervention on the church's part to gently wean pagans off their religious practices and render the newer religion more relatable and palatable.

Next, of course, is Halloween. Unlike Christmas or the winter solstice, Halloween has managed to retain much of its original character. So much so that many strident believers in the major monotheistic religions will say celebrating Halloween is evil and has no place in the daily life of Christians or others. Halloween, or All Hallows Eve, originates from the pagan holiday of Samhain that occurs on October 31st, and is a time to honor the dead. It's also traditionally considered a spiritually discombobulating day wherein the boundary between our world and the next is at its weakest and most porous. This holiday and much of its attendant traditions are so powerful that non-pagans continue to celebrate it for thousands of years. Its popularity has continued to grow with time on a global scale, keeping a vital element of pagan religion alive and well.

Of course, Easter is another excellent example of a holiday with distinct pagan roots taken over to better accommodate the sensibilities of a growing Christian populace and the powerful church. Easter is a more modern incarnation of the spring solstice, and everything from the image of the Easter bunny to the act of finding eggs in a forest possesses deep roots in a pagan culture.

Aside from the major holidays, there are tons of traditions and mundane superstitions we've held onto for thousands of years, even though they derive from the beliefs of pagans and Druids. For example, our singular obsession with cats and all they symbolize have roots in pagan beliefs, as does knocking on wood to ward off bad luck or wearing flower crowns at a spring music festival. These are all things with pagan roots and sacred beliefs with a long history that continues with us today.

Neopaganism

Many religious practices of the pagans, Druids, and other polytheistic religions have been revived in the past few years. This "revival" of sorts has been referred to as neopaganism, is on the rise, and presents one key way paganism and Druidry have remained with us. At the same time, simply referring to these various trends in spirituality as neopaganism fails to recognize different nuances.

Neopaganism sets itself apart from these different practices in that it strives to revive authentic rituals of ancient culture, sometimes in seemingly strange or deliberately restorative ways. These days, most individuals with romantic feelings towards nature or who possess deep ecological concerns will turn to neopaganism and all the attendant dramatic, vibrant rituals as the very personification of nature and life. The pagan holy days and general motifs are sources of inspiration for neopagans and ensure that elements central to the lives of pagans and Druids survive.

Much of neopaganism has its roots in the Romanticism 19th century movement. Even organizations like the British Order of Druids originate from that, even though they claim to have an older, ancient lineage. Furthermore, instead of focusing solely on the customs of the pagans of Western Europe, neopagans are known to adopt other traditions, like Ancient Egypt or polytheistic African religions. This underscores another way of saying neopaganism is an extension of ancient pagan traditions is a bit of an oversimplification. Nonetheless, it proves that some central practices remain alive and well today through this revival of the ancient spiritual practices.

Neopaganism, as practiced these days, also has a dark side. There are quite a few neopagan groups associated with extreme nationalism, influenced by individuals such as Hitler, who deeply believed in a few pagan rituals representing white supremacy. Even before World War II, certain neopagan groups expressed anti-Semitic and deeply racist sentiments, although, arguably, much of contemporary neopaganism is a by-product of the freewheeling 1960s. So, the vast majority of neopagans do not entirely espouse negative beliefs but are more likely influenced by psychiatrist Carl Jung and writer Robert Graves. They loved nature and were not at all interested in *nationalism* of any kind.

Many neopagans these days would like to clarify that they are not to be confused with Wiccans. It is easy to conflate both spiritual practices since these groups honor old traditions in equal measures, but their attitudes and beliefs vary considerably. Wicca is one form of contemporary witchcraft, and witchcraft is only one pillar of paganism. Therefore, Wicca is a tradition of the pagan culture and was originally founded by Gerald Gardner in the 1950s – but it is not by any means the same as paganism. This will be further explained in the next section.

Wicca and the Rule of Three

"An it harm none, do what thou wilt." Does this adage sound familiar? If so, then you're more up to speed on the understanding of contemporary Wicca than you think. This saying is part of the Wiccan Rede, which, in essence, is a statement that provides the key moral system in the Wiccan religion. While other neopagans may identify with the rede, it primarily forms the spine of modern Wicca and other related witchcraft-based faiths.

The word "rede" means "advice" or "counsel," which makes sense when you think of the implications behind this verse. It is meant to guide the modern witch to use their magic without hurting others.

At this point, you're probably wondering how Wiccans define themselves and view their relationship to ancient paganism and Druidry. While they are a distinct religion and have their own set of practices and principles, Wiccans take the ancient rituals and prayers of pagans seriously. They have incorporated many facets of that belief system into their own. However, its origins are very modern, and the way it has entered the mainstream is fairly specific to its history.

As we know it today, Wicca seems to be either a hyper-feminine, new age-y religion with legions of female followers or something more akin to the scary teens featured in the cult 1990s film The Craft. Of course, Wicca is nothing like these common stereotypes, even though they bear some familiarity. The religion was developed in England during the first half of the 20th century and introduced to the public in 1954 by Gerald Gardner, who, ironically, was a retired British civil servant. Despite his buttoned-up occupation during the day, Gardner cultivated a deep appreciation for paganism and various ancient rituals, drawing inspiration from their theological structures and practices to create his 20th-century spin on the religion.

Because Wicca does not possess a central figure of authority, nor does it believe in centralized places of worship like a church or synagogue, there has been considerable disagreement on what constitutes Wicca. Its roots have consistently been up for debate, for better or for worse, making it difficult for many people to fully appreciate just how unique this religion is.

In terms of theology, Wicca is a purely duo-theistic religion, worshiping a goddess and a god. These higher beings are typically viewed as the Triple goddess and the Horned god. They each have specific divine aspects, and these characteristics have their roots in diverse pagan deities throughout history. For this reason, they are sometimes referred to as the Great Goddess or the Great Horned god. The word "great" denotes that the deity contains other deities within their nature. It's a nesting egg of sorts, and this distinction is important for Wiccans. It also indicates that Wicca was created as a patchwork adaptation of older elements; many were taken from pre-existing religions or pagan movements previously disconnected from one another.

While Gardner worked to formulate this religion, and it started practicing in the first half of the 20th century, it is clear from his writings that he never intended it to be a strict revival of Druidry or paganism. Rather, Wicca is a contemporary religion that prioritizes witchcraft and provides a fairly contemporary spin on many pagan precepts. While Wiccans celebrate the changes in season, and the most important holidays are the Winter Solstice or Spring Solstice, they diverge from other neopagans through a specific form of worship and newly written prayers or rituals. In general, Wiccans don't pretend to revive exact replicas of ancient traditions and festivities. Instead, they present paganism through the prism of 20th Century concerns and mores.

However, one belief that is shared among Wiccans, neopagans, and other occultists is the Rule of Three. This dictates that any energy a person puts out into the world, whether positive or negative, will be returned threefold to that person. Think of it as a Western version of beliefs like karma. Some practitioners believe this law is too strict and uphold a slight variation where the comeback would be less than threefold, but the general idea is easily understood.

Most occultists have stated in their research that the Rule of Three presents a direct "reward or punishment tied to one's actions, particularly when working magic." Wiccans, neopagans, Druids, and other occultists widely disagree on how to interpret such a tenet. Some historians have neglected the extent to which different groups believe in this adage. While the Rule of Three can be accurately ascertained to represent one of the central beliefs carried on by pagans throughout the centuries, not all Wiccans believe it. By that same token, because not all neopagans practice witchcraft, they may not find much truth in this rule.

Whether more experienced or new to the faith, Wiccans sometimes debate the Rule of Three and view it as an over-interpretation of the Wiccan Rede. Others still debate the extent to its representative of ancient beliefs and whether it is a more modern idea inspired primarily by Christian morality. On the other hand, Wiccans who firmly believe in this law often turn to a key piece of Wiccan liturgy Gerald Gardner initially printed in the influential 1949 novel, *High Magic's Aid*. All in all, The Rule of Three is not such an outlier for ancient beliefs, and different iterations of this basic idea exist throughout the world, either as the concept of karma, widely believed among Dharmic religion followers, or the more modern "Golden Rule."

According to recorded history, The Rule of Three was mentioned extensively by the famed witch Raymond Buckland who practically wrote the modern text on the Wiccan religion after Gardner officiated the spiritual practice. Prior to Buckland's innovation, the very idea of reciprocal ethics in Wicca was nebulous, ill-defined, and difficult to nail down. Any consequences of magical practice, whether negative or positive, were assigned a general understanding of karma and nothing more. There is some skepticism within the Wiccan community about applying The Rule of Three to their practice since Buckland expounded on the idea in 1968 – hardly an "ancient" date. Later, The Rule of Three became the basis of *The Wiccan Rede*, published by Lady Gwen Thompson in 1975.

The debates on The Rule of Three's exact application – and the Wiccan Rede, for that matter – are endless. However, the heart of these ideas is shared among many neopagans and others identifying as members of an occult. The core of this spiritual practice is seen as a vivid, thorough line from ancient beliefs to the contemporary moment, rendered tangible through writing and drafting poetry.

Celtic Paganism

One group of people with a tremendous influence in maintaining and shaping the contemporary understanding of paganism and Druidry today is Celtic paganism. This last iteration is very different from those discussed above, primarily because it adheres more formally to a polytheistic reconstruction of Celtic neopaganism. It emphasizes historical accuracy instead of romanticizing myths or rituals. Followers also emphasize specific theological concerns of Druidry in a more authentic effort to revive the pre-Christian Celtic way of life. These efforts are fairly modern, having originated in the writings of amateur scholars and members of neopagan communities in the mid-1980s, who were tired of how diluted some of these ancient beliefs came to be. While this movement is far from being a monolith and has several subgroups and denominations, they are united in a belief that the specific cultural context of the Celts must be upheld.

Celtic pagans believe ancient rituals need to be divorced from Christian incarnations that came later. Folklore, myths, and legends are excellent ways to introduce people to ancient ways without misinterpreting or peppering them with too many contemporary interpretations. They strongly believe in the beauty of these ancient traditions and that their rich legacies must be preserved for future generations. A thorough line that runs throughout these conversations among Celtic pagans is the sense of urgency and fear that much of the Celts' ancient culture and unique traditions are at risk of disappearing forever. Therefore, this sense permeates all their work and their specific paganism practice.

The movement had its origins in the 1980s but became a genuine phenomenon in the last thirty years, given the proliferation of the internet and the attendant online forums allowing free and open discussion among pagans. They established that an important part of their spiritual practice is advocating for the protection of Celtic archeological and sacred sites. This is why construction projects like the potential destruction of the Hill of Tara in Ireland a few years ago made the news. Historians, archivists, and passionate Celtic pagans joined forces to organize and protest the construction and worked hard to establish the site as a historical landmark worthy of protection by the state.

Celtic pagans don't have many centralizing texts of their own, and they acknowledge that the structure of their belief system may be perceived as a bit spotty given the obvious absence. While they work hard to revive these religious practices and the beliefs of ancient Celtic people as accurately as possible, they will always forthrightly acknowledge some aspects are reconstructions. They cannot verify the historical accuracy of some of the rituals and traditions they work hard to revive. Still, they take cultural survival seriously, and rigorous study is an important part of their practice. They augment their beliefs with scholars' and archeologists' work and downplay the importance of stories or myths if they do not have evidence – regardless of whether or not they are verifiable by historians.

The groups mentioned throughout this chapter work hard to preserve and maintain the legacy of pagans and Druids in their distinct ways. While there are many differences, they are joined by the desire to pay homage to the ancient ways and keep an important part of cultural history alive and thriving.

Chapter 8: Magickal Tools and How to Use Them

The word "magick" is not just a trendy spelling for the word magic, nor is it a spelling associated with pagans or Druidry. Magick is specific magic used for good. Generally, magic is associated with negativity causing harm to others or altering things for personal gain. Magick is about helping others through using different tools, spells, and skills associated with or connected to the spiritual realm. This chapter will explore the various magickal tools and how they're used in Wiccan and Pagan traditions. We'll also discuss the relationship between magick and Paganism and delve deep into the process of magical practice. Upon reading this chapter, you'll learn about the significance of animals in Irish pagan magical practices. Finally, you'll find out about the role that crystals play in magic and how you can select one that suits your needs.

Magical Tools

When people first develop an interest in any form of Paganism, they are quick to purchase all sorts of magical tools that they can get their hands on. Many people fail to realize that each tool comes with a significant and specific purpose; this is why you need to know which tools and ritual items to buy and what to use them for. It's worth noting that many of these items are not common across all traditions, and those that are aren't always used in the same way.

- **Altar**

  This book dedicates an entire chapter to altars and setting them up to incorporate them into your spiritual practice, which signifies their importance in the pagan practice. Altars play an important role in ritual and celebration. In most religions and mythologies, altars are used to honor gods, perform rituals, and offer sacrifice. This does not need to be a crafted altar; an altar at home is as simple as a small table with your tools and offerings. You can change the theme, decorations, and items to match the season you're celebrating. You can also dedicate an altar to the deity you worship by including their images, their associated colors, symbols, etc. Some people also have more than one altar in their homes. Ancestral altars are very common. They include ashes, photos, or heirlooms from family members who have passed on. Having a nature altar is not an uncommon practice either. Many people use it to showcase interesting and rare items that they collect, such as unique rocks, alluring seashells, and even patterned pieces of wood. If you have children you wish to introduce to the concept of spirituality and religious practices, you can have them help you set up the altar or even have them create their own in their rooms.

- **Athame**

  An athame is a double-edged dagger that you can make your own or purchase ready-made. This tool can be as simple or as embellished and personified as you wish. Many pagan rituals include the use of this tool to direct energy. The athame is mostly used when casting a circle. It is also used as an alternative for wands. This tool is not meant to be used to cut actual items. Creating your own athame can be a very fun DIY project. The process is as simple or as complicated as your metalworking skill level. This is why you should make sure to find online instructions that suit your abilities.

- **Besom**

Witches' brooms are not used for flying – they are used to help cleanse a room. A traditional broom is known as a Besom. This tool is used to clean a place by sweeping it before a ritual. When we sweep a room with a Besom, we are removing the negative energies that reside in the room – a practice that is essential if you are to perform a ceremony or a ritual in the room. The Besom is associated with the element Water because it serves as a purifier. Many pagans have a wide array of brooms since they're very easy to make. Brooms can be crafted from almost any material, but if you are making a traditional Besom, birch is used for the brush and oak or ash for the staff.

- **Bell**

Bells are common in many ceremonies, both religious and non-religious. Spirits are driven away by certain noises, and the act of ringing a bell in a room or larger area can drive away any evil or negative spirits in a room. This is due to the loudness of a bell and the frequency at which the bell rings. The vibrations move through a room and help to clear it. You can find other instruments to ward off evil spirits as long as there is a vibrational quality. While you can ring bells before performing a ritual or ceremony, you should try to bookend the ceremony by ringing the bell at the beginning and the end.

- **Candles**

Candles are one of the most commonly used tools in Pagan practices and rituals. Not only is it used to represent the element of Fire and as a symbol of various deities, like Badb and Brigid, candles are usually also an element of spell workings. This is because it is suggested that candles can absorb an individual's personal energy. As the candle burns, it releases this unwanted energy. You may be surprised to learn that it is customary to leave the candle burning for a set number of days as part of the spell in some traditions. Many people believe that creating your own candle makes it a lot more powerful than ready-made ones. This is why they prefer making their own candles. Others, however, believe that it is the intention that purely matters. They focus on the inter that they put into the spell rather than pay much attention to where the candle came from or how it was made. Most traditions, however, focus on the colors of the candle, as it is an important aspect when it comes to candle magic.

• Pentacle

The pentacle is used in May pagan practices, but don't confuse the pentacle with the pentagram – they sound very alike, but they are very different. A pentagram is a five-pointed star, while a pentacle is a flat slab with symbols carved into it. People incorporate this tool into ceremonial magic and use it as a protective talisman. Most Wiccan and Pagan traditions also view the pentacle as a symbol of the element of Earth. Pagans and Wiccans often place this tool on their altars to hold the items they will consecrate as part of a ritual. Pentacles can be easily made (all you need is a slab of sanded wood and a wood-burning kit) or purchased from a specialized store.

• Book of Shadows – BOS

The Book of Shadows should include all the significant magical information that belongs to its owner's tradition and spiritual practice. Despite what movies and novels have led us to believe, there is not just one book of shadows. The BOS is supposed to be personal and unique to its owner, as it serves as a notebook of all the information they believe is crucial. This book can contain rituals, spells, the rules of magic and relevant information, correspondent charts, lore and myths, tales about the deities, invocations, and more. Many pagans decide to pass on this book from one generation to the other. However, if you don't have a BOS passed down from your great-great-grandmother, you can make one yourself. While this will take a lot of effort to put together, you should enjoy the process as much as you can because it's very personal. Take the time to think about what you feel belongs in this book. Creating your own BOS can strengthen your spirituality and make you feel even more connected to your tradition.

- **Cauldron**

Cauldrons, like chalices, are very common tools in goddess-oriented beliefs and traditions. Cauldrons are very feminine and are shaped like a womb. It is symbolic of the vessel of life. Because they are vessels, cauldrons are connected to the element Water, and they can be used in many rituals and celebrations. Use them also in any celebrations where knowledge is sought. They are vessels of water, but they are also vessels for other things, such as knowledge and inspiration. For instance, you can use it to present offerings or burn candles and incense. Many goddesses of several traditions can also be represented through the cauldron. You can also use the tool to blend herbs and use them for magical purposes. Many people use cauldrons for moonlight scrying after filling them up with water. If you commonly use cauldrons for cooking purposes, make sure to dedicate a separate one for your magical practices. Many magical practices will make your cauldron no longer suitable for cooking.

- **Chalices**

As we just mentioned, the chalice is often strongly associated with female deities and archetypes. It is also a feminine symbol that is symbolic of the womb and is representative of the Water element. The chalice is often used alongside the athame in some practices. When re-enacting the Great Rite, symbolically, this combination is representative of the Divine Feminine. You can use a chalice of any material, like pewter and silver, on your altar. You can also use it to provide offerings for your deity. However, if you're offering wine, you should be mindful of untreated metals. Ceramic chalices are now more popularly used and are easy to get ahold of. Many individuals use chalices of different materials depending on the ritual they're conducting.

- **Divination Tools**

There are numerous divination tools and methods that you can choose from to enrich your magical and spiritual practice. Many people like to experiment with different types of divination tools rather than stick to one method. However, it's normal to feel most comfortable using a particular divination tool or feel that you're a naturally gifted area. Some methods may simply not work out for you. For instance, you may be able to grasp a natural understanding of tarot and oracle cards but feel completely lost when it comes to the Ogham staves, and that's okay. Some examples of common divination tools are:

- Numerology
- Tarot cards
- I ching coins and books
- Pendulums
- Essential oils
- Crystals
- Signs and signals
- Stream-of-consciousness writing
- The practice of opening books on random pages to receive messages
- Animal messages

- **Crystals**

You can select from and incorporate countless stones into your healing and spiritual practices. The stones that you choose to work with should depend on your intentions. This is why you should make sure to select ones based on their associations and characteristics rather than their aesthetic appeal. We will delve deeper into that topic and cover the uses and attributes of multiple crystals later throughout the chapter. Birthstones also work well in magical practices. Make sure to cleanse your crystal or gemstone before your first use.

- **Ritual Robe**

If you want to give your rituals a more special feel, you can wear a robe during the process. Ritual robes are very easy to make and can be worn in any color and style, depending on what your tradition or practice calls for. Many people don't care much about what they're wearing to perform their rituals. After all, it's the intent that matters. However, wearing a robe is significant for others because they think of it as a way to separate their spiritual practices from the mundane activities of daily life. Putting the robe on signifies stepping into a spiritual mindset or making your way from the physical realm to the magical realm.

- **Wand**

You can purchase a wand from a specialized store or make one that's as simple or as lavish and decorative as you wish. When we think of magic, a picture of a want immediately comes to mind. As stereotypical as this sounds, the wand is among the most popular and commonly used magical tools in the world of Wicca and Paganism. Wands are created to fulfill a wide array of magical purposes, including directing energy throughout rituals. Wands represent power, valor, and of course, masculine energy (it is a phallic symbol, after all). Wands are used in the air, and so they are connected to that element. Staffs can be seen as a type of wand, but they are connected to fire, and that is an important distinction depending on what you are trying to achieve. You can use the wand to invoke a deity or consecrate a sacred area. We associate wands closely with wood (and you might also think about items or ingredients infused into the wood), but wood is not the only material that can be used. Almost any material can be used, and the user is more important than the object. Many practitioners have a wide collection of wands, especially those who don't use athames.

- **Magic Staff**

Like the athame and wands, the staff can be used for the purpose of energy direction, according to some traditions.

Many Wiccans and Pagans incorporate the use of magical staff into their ceremonies, rituals, and spiritual activities. Even though it's not a vital magical tool, it can be of great help, considering that it's linked to authority and power. Some of them even believe that these divine figures are the only ones allowed to carry this tool. On the other hand, other traditions permit all practitioners to use the staff. Staffs are more closely associated with male energy and fire, but they can be used in place of wands and can represent air at times too. Like many of the tools we mentioned above, you can make your own staff instead of purchasing one.

Paganism and Magick

The idea of spirituality and magick is very closely related to Pagan beliefs. Even though different pagan groups have varying religious perspectives, the underlying framework that serves as the metaphysical phenomena basis and the magical activities is relatively similar. There are a few core tenants of this philosophy. The first aspect is the involvement of animals in the idea of god and the idea of magic. Secondly, the incorporation of various natural elements as spirits: the spirits of fire, water, air, and earth. Thirdly, the concept of God is not limited to one god but rather there is a god and goddess, and in some cases, there are multiple goddesses. Lastly, the spiritual or magical practices performed can be done individually or in a group.

The magical practices performed by pagans are used for a range of purposes. The most common are:

- To induct someone into the coven or group
- As a celebration of the season
- To honor the deity
- To get attuned with nature
- To attain self-realization
- For magical healing

The process of magical practice is split into three parts which are sometimes not that easy to identify. First is the separation phase, the second is a testing phase, and lastly, reintegration.

Separation

The first phase is the separation phase. The aim is to differentiate between the physical world and the spiritual world. Unlike most other religions, pagans do not have a dedicated place of worship like a church or a temple. Instead, the sacred place of worship is created wherever they feel like worshiping, and it is done whenever they wish to worship. The most common way is through a process known as "casting the circle."

It is physically demarcating a space, usually in the form of a circle, using things like salt, rocks, or candles, and consecrating the space by invoking the spiritual entities and deities. In some cases, casting the circle is done with magical and holy tools like a wand or a ritual knife. The practitioners ask these deities to bless the space they have created and invite the deity to the space to bless it with their presence, and also ask the deity to assist in the practices they will exercise in that space. Creating a holy space is common among all pagan religions. Mainly, people create this space in their home, but for some festivals, they create this outside where they can also make a fire to assist with the process. This sacred space is an area at the border of the physical and the spiritual world while not being part of either.

Testing

The second part of the process is the activity that takes place within the circle. It is known as the testing phase as it "tests" the strength of the circle. The practices that take place within the circle can vary a lot depending on the aim of the exercise. However, all practices have three distinct parts. The first part is to raise the energy level or create the energy needed. The second step is to give that energy a purpose and charge it to the desired level. The final step is to focus and direct this energy toward the recipient.

The different practices that happen in the circle are all dependent on the desired outcome and what is appropriate for that particular event. For instance, the festival of Beltane is highlighted by fire, and fertility is celebrated. However, the spirit of the festival is also celebrated metaphorically – writing down your desires and casting them into the fire, so they are delivered to the universe and the gods. Or the process of planting seeds into pots of soil in the sacred space to represent planting seeds of joy and happiness within ourselves. Then there are customized spells used for particular things like attracting money into one's life, enhancing love in a relationship, or healing from a physical or emotional injury. For instance, the practitioner will use relevant stones and tools to enhance love and induce positive energy.

Reintegration

This is the final step of the process. When the energy is raised, the interactions with the entities and the entire process of creating desired outcomes are directed to the person it is meant for. At the same time, this is also the process where the practitioner and the subject ground themselves and "seal" the portal they opened to connect to the spiritual realm. This final process is essential to ensure the energy that has been transferred to the recipient of the energy given to the tools used during the divination process is safely stored in them.

Grounding can be done in two ways. The first and most common way is through visualization. The practitioner and the subject visualize themselves becoming part of the earth and reconnecting with the physical world. People who practice tree magic often visualize they are growing roots into the earth like a tree grows roots and gets a stronger grip on the earth. It also acts as a way to discard the excess energy as the earth soaks up the excess energy dissipated through the roots.

The second way is to consume "blessed" food and drink that is believed to return a person to their normal state. Generally, this includes wine and cake, but some people also prefer other drinks like a lager or non-alcoholic juice. Cakes can be of any kind, and some people prefer to have a savory baked item. This is followed by dismantling the circle and thanking the entities that were there to help in the process.

Animals and Magic

Animals also have a special place in Irish Paganism. In some cases, they are used metaphorically, and, in other cases, they have a physical presence in the practices. One of the most common animal concepts in Paganism is the idea of the power animal. Also known as the Totem animal or spirit animal, it is when a person identifies with a certain animal as their spirit guardian. Similar to how people find spirit guardians from the spiritual realm that are other entities, totem animals take the form of an animal and play the same role. Another concept that resonated with spirit animals is the concept of "Familiars." An animal familiar is identified as an animal a person has a special bond with or feels a strong connection with. Familiars are physical animals existing in the real world but have a spirit belonging to the spiritual world. The person connects with them at a much deeper level.

Animal parts are used in various rituals and in the casting spell process. Usually, things like snake skins, a goat's jaw, a stag's antlers, or even a big cat's fur can be used in spiritual practices. Tools are often made from these items, such as knife handles made from the bones of an animal, or a shawl made from an animal's hide. In other cases, parts of the animal are used directly in the magic process, a snake's skin. Also, most of these items are collected rather than the animal being hunted down just for a specific part. These can be collected from animals used as an offering to the gods, animals that have died naturally, or things that animals leave naturally, shed skin, or broken antlers.

Birds also have a very important place in magic. Some are seen as a sign of bad news, danger, or even the onset of a natural disaster. Others are considered messengers delivering a message from the spiritual world. The challenge is to properly decipher what they are saying and use that knowledge for its intended purpose. Among the birds, the owl is one of the most important. The owl has a special place in many cultures, but it is associated with the goddess Athena in Paganism. It symbolizes the goddesses' wisdom and knowledge.

Crystals and Magic

It is unnecessary to have accessories like herbs, wands, and crystals when practicing magic. However, these assets can improve your magic's effectiveness tremendously. If there was one thing you could invest in, or you are starting to dabble with magic accessories and want something to make a tangible impact on your practices, it has to be crystals. Here are some of the best crystals to consider and their benefits.

• **Clear Quartz**

Of all the thousands of different crystals available, the clear quartz should be your choice if you had to choose just a single one. It is a neutral stone and can be used for practically anything, especially if you get a clear quartz stone with a pointed tip. This quartz can be a very powerful tool. The great thing about clear quartz is that it works extremely well with other accessories. It can amplify the power of other tools you are using. So, whether you have other stones, herbs, or anything else to use, it will get amplified using clear quartz. You can use this stone for meditation, therapy, magic, and even protection.

• **Citrine**

Citrine is part of the quartz family, and just like clear quartz, it is a very powerful crystal. However, this stone has a misty orange and sometimes yellow shade to it and is particularly efficient for cleansing and other healing processes. It is a stone with the ability to soak up energy in its surroundings, so it is fantastic for cleansing a space, your other stones, and magick tools, and even clearing out negative influences from your home. Other than cleansing, this stone is used to enhance your psychic ability, making it a great stone to have when you are meditating or things like astral travel.

• Rose Quartz

The quartz stone is a potent crystal for magic, and different variations are good for specific things. For instance, the rose quartz is extremely good for love, emotions, and even spiritual work. This is the crystal to use if you are casting spells based on emotions and, specifically, love. It's a very grounded crystal, so it can also be used to manage situations with intense emotional energy. For instance, this is the stone to use if you are trying to diffuse a matter between two people or helping a person get more clarity and peace in their mind.

• Amber

Amber is a very powerful stone if you are seeking something to offer you protection. It is often associated with the sun due to its color. However, it also has a deep relationship with the Earth. In reality, amber is not a crystal but fossilized tree sap, meaning it has spent millions of years deep underground and is a product of plants and not stone. For this reason, it has a very powerful connection to the earth and does a tremendous job as a grounding stone.

• Malachite

This is a favorite stone of the green witches largely because of its color. However, others can still use it, and it is great for meditation and even protection from danger. It is commonly associated with consciousness and is often used for things like fortune-telling and understanding at a deeper level. It is one of those stones that can be worn daily and used for dedicated practices and grounding rituals.

• Obsidian

This is another stone that is a favorite of the witches as it was also the favorite stone of the goddess of witches, Hecate. Although this stone is associated with protection and can absorb all energy forms, it is also typically used for scrying mirrors. Obsidian is a great source of energy and is known as a very powerful stone largely because of its origins. Obsidian is born out of volcanic eruptions and is, therefore, associated with fire. If you are practicing banishing magic, this stone will be very handy.

- **Tigers Eye**

Like the animal it is known for, Tigers Eye is used as a source of strength, courage, and fierceness. It is great for people wanting to improve their self-confidence and needing a boost of positive energy. It is an all-purpose stone that works exceptionally well in conjunction with other stones; white quartz will amplify its energy. It can also be paired with black obsidian to give you an incredibly holistic defense.

- **Blood Stone**

The bloodstone is named not because it is red. Instead, it is a green stone with flecks of red in it. This stone is excellent if you are working on your health or a patient's health and can also be used for protection.

- **Moonstone**

Milky white in color and ruled by the moon, this stone is excellent for everything with intuition, consciousness, dreams, and general matters of the mind. This stone can also be used in place of other stones, such as quartz, amethyst, or bloodstone.

You can easily buy these stones at your local metaphysics store or even find them at your local jewelry store. However, keep in mind that stones you find or are given to you hold more power than those you buy at a store. Also, if you have these stones as a necklace or a bracelet, you can still use them for your witchcraft.

Practicing Magick

Other than the main components of practicing magick, such as crystals or animals, other components make this possible. Whether you are casting spells or performing a spiritual cleansing, you can use different tools for better effect.

One of the most important instruments for witches practicing magick is a wand. Usually, this is made from crystals, such as quartz or ammolite, and comes in a variety of sizes and shapes. The most common shape is stick-shaped and 6 to 8 inches long with a blunt end or pointed end. The pointed wands are usually used in practices where reflexology is involved or if the practitioner wants to focus energy at a particular point. Blunt wands are commonly used in cleansing practices and in situations where the stone transfers energy to larger areas, such as a room in a house or a group of people.

As we mentioned above, altars are also essential equipment to have; they will be discussed in great detail in the next chapter. You can either have a specially-made altar designed to practice magic and other sacred practices or use a make-shift altar with any elevated table in your home. Altars are usually decorated with sacred items, such as sacred texts or objects used as symbols. What you place on your altar depends entirely on the purpose of the spell or ritual.

You should also use salt to demarcate an area for magical practices. Some people prefer to demarcate an area by digging a shallow trench around the area or using candles. Salt works particularly well as its energy is excellent for keeping unwanted forces out – and it also helps to retain all the energy within that space. You should also have some candles for your magic practice. In some cases, this is used to define the area. In other cases, fire and light are ingredients used in the process.

How You Can Get Started

Most of the things you'll need, like salt, crystals, or herbs, are items you can easily get at your local hardware or grocery store. If you are looking for something very particular and not available in your locality, you always have the option of ordering online. As Paganism, in all forms, becomes more popular and people worldwide gain interest in this philosophy, there is an increasing demand for tools and equipment. Many sellers worldwide manufacture these items, and many are accomplished witches who love to handcraft many products. Handcrafted versions can be a bit pricey, so there is no harm in getting a more economical option if you are just starting. Determine if you genuinely like it, then get a higher quality version. As a starting point, look into what you want to do and the spells you want to practice and get equipment catering to those needs. Some things, like quartz crystals, can be used for many things, so it is always a good investment. If you want to do very specific things, find out what you need and invest accordingly. Also, be sure to cleanse all your equipment after use, and refresh it before every use.

Chapter 9: Setting Up a Pagan Altar

To practice your pagan rituals, you need a special space, and you can achieve this by creating an altar. If you want to create a shrine, there are different steps you can take. This chapter outlines the significance of an Irish or Welsh pagan altar and the tips for building one. It also discusses different tools you can place on the altar and their purpose.

Significance of a Pagan Altar

A pagan altar is a sacred space where you place spiritual objects used for ritual, spells, meditation, prayers, visualizations, divination, and connecting to the deity. Pagans use this workspace, also called a shrine, to do their ritual work. An altar is a personal place where a practitioner puts different ritual items. This place is mainly used for religious spell works. If you cannot perform your rituals outside, you can create a shrine inside your home.

It is usually a raised platform or structure used for prayer or worship. The Wiccan practitioners often find several symbolic and functional items used to worship the goddess and god, say chants and prayers, and cast spells. You can also use your altar to connect with the spiritual world in various forms. You may use this platform for performing rituals, such as celebrating seasonal cycles, devotion to a deity, or rites of passage. The items you use to decorate your altar depend on your taste and preferences. Therefore, it is an excellent idea that your altar reflects your spirituality.

Your altar can be of any size or shape, and you choose the material you want. Many people believe that wood is the best medium since it comes from the earth. However, stone and metal also work well for your shrine. While there is no universal structure of the altar, it is usually believed that the left side is the goddess area. Feminine symbols like chalices, bowls, and other symbols representing goddesses and statues are placed in this area. On the other hand, the right side is meant for gods, and symbols like the wand and the athame are put here. The god statuary and his candle are also found on the right side of the altar.

The center area of the altar is known as the working space or both areas. The cauldron associated with four elements is placed in the center. You should know that Irish Pagan Practice is specifically meant for building a relationship. You can achieve this by showing up consistently at your altar and performing your religious work there. However, it should not be hard work. Instead, it must be something that connects you with your god or goddess.

How to Make Your Pagan Altar

Before creating your altar, the first thing to do is decide whether you want something permanent or temporary. You can create a shrine to dismantle and store in a specific place. Another thing you want to consider is the location of your sacred place. You can put your altar anywhere, and other people have natural shrines outdoors. Also, take your portable altar into your garden or inside the house if you have enough space.

The good thing about creating a natural altar is it offers you a close connection with Mother Nature. If you don't have a garden, create an indoor shrine, but make sure you have a room where you can place it. Choose a corner in your bedroom where you can create a special place to perform your rituals. A bedroom is a private room, and it's easily relaxing in this room when you are alone.

When you have selected the appropriate location for your altar, make sure you determine the size and shape of the altar. You can get a chest of drawers, a table, or any movable platform. When you choose a chest, use the drawers as storage for the items you need for your rituals, like lighters, candles, and others. When practicing Irish Paganism, fire is a critical component. Whenever you perform your rites, be sure to have some form of flame, usually obtained from candles. Your space should also have a place to put your candles and ensure safety.

You must have something that represents that place to create a connection. Find something that represents a deity, don't get caught in the predicament of attempting to find a perfect statue or painting. It does not exist since the gods are shapeless and formless. Therefore, anything that helps you visualize your god can go a long way in helping you build a strong relationship.

When you design your altar, you must begin by sticking to the basics. If you want to build the shrine from scratch, make sure you get appropriate materials you can shape into desired structures. It is important to start with simple items and develop over time. Constantly develop your altar depending on your needs. Aim to create something that resonates with your intentions and get things that make sense and are special to you. Make additions to your shrine depending on your changing needs.

What Direction Should a Pagan Altar Face?

To some individuals, the direction of the altar does not matter since it can face any side. However, others consider east-facing altars since this is where the sun rises. In most traditions, the sun is associated with bringing new life or air and supporting it. As it rises, it provides the energy required to perform different things. When your altar is facing the east direction, you are appreciating its power and helping to create a strong connection with nature. The northeast is another popular direction among most Pagans since it is symbolic in their tradition.

Most rituals are believed to be associated with the North Direction since it stands for the earth. An option is to get a portable compass to set your shrine in the appropriate direction. The south direction is believed to symbolize fire, while water is for the west. The center stands for the spirit. However, you can put your altar facing any direction you believe works for you. The most important thing is that the shrine must be in a place where you can see and connect with it every day. We all have different intentions, so do not copy others. Something that works for another person might not work for you. Prioritize your needs and believe in yourself.

If your altar consists of heavy items, it will be best to build a permanent one. Other areas to consider include drawers, tree stumps, trays, and windowsills. Make sure the space is free when you decide to build an outside platform. Use your intuition to choose an ideal area for your shrine. Select corresponding items to use for your rites when the platform is immovable.

Choose the Style of Your Altar

There are many different styles of altars, so your style should be heavily influenced by Celtic Paganism and other elements like deities. For Irish and Welsh Paganism, there are specific symbols you should familiarize yourself with and know how they can help you achieve your goals. You also need to consider your practice and how the shrine will reflect your spirituality. A carefully designed altar improves the appearance of your place. If the design is an essential component to you, choose something well-crafted.

Items to Use for the Goddess

When setting up a pagan altar, it's essential to determine the items you'll use for the goddess side. The side represents the divine feminine, the moon, the right brain, unconsciousness, and nighttime. Therefore, the goddess's components differ from the ones used for the god's side. You need to get a candle with the best color you believe represents the goddess. When you practice Paganism, you should understand the significance of light. The colors for the goddess side include green, blue, purple, and silver. Do your research first to know your intentions and how you can achieve them.

Crystal balls or divination tools are other vital components you should add when you set your altar. Crystals come in various forms, and they play different roles. Therefore, when you choose crystals, make sure they align with your intentions and understand how to use them. A statue is another vital component you can add to your altar since it represents the goddess. Various forms of goddesses are available, such as Isis, the moon goddess, or totem animals. If you don't get a statue, find a drawing or image of your preferred goddess. You can also use other lunar animals as long as they suit your intentions. Other things representing famine elements are water, like seashells, a bowl of water, a cauldron, or sea glass. Some of the earth items include brown or green-colored objects, for instance, plants, stones, bones, soil, and flowers. Depending on your intention and spiritual practice, you can get as many items as you want.

Items to Use on the God Side

Just like the goddess side, you also need to find appropriate items for the god side of your altar. The god side symbolizes the divine masculine, sun, elements of air and fire, consciousness, daytime, and the right half of the body or left brain. Some of the things you may want to put on the god side include a large candle with any color of your choice. Some colors to consider are yellow, red, orange, or gold. They should reflect your interests and other things you want to achieve.

A statue is another important item you need to add to your altar. You can use a masculine animal totem or solar imagery. The two masculine elements you may include are red or orange colors, a wand or athame, incense, candles, teeth, or claws. However, make sure you do not hurt animals to obtain these items. Also, include an oil burner or ash and feathers. Divination tools to put on the god side are also essential for your altar.

Your daily spiritual practice will determine the tools you need for your rites. Other objects special and sacred can be included on the list of items to put on the god side. The items come in different shapes and sizes, so get something that suits your altar. If your shrine is small, make sure you get portable tools to put on different sides of the gods.

Items to Put in the Center of the Altar

The center of the altar is crucial since it represents the core of your spirituality. This is the patron or matron of your deity you work with most of the time. It is important to know the deities you want to work with to get the appropriate items. Use crystals, candles, or skulls, and make sure you get something very important and powerful to represent the spirit element. These items should be white, rainbow, violet, or purple since these colors consist of great energy. Your zodiac sign should determine the candle for the center of the shrine.

If you have a pentacle representing the earth, include it on the goddess's side. A book of the shadow is another crucial item you can put in the center of the altar. An athame and wand can be placed on the god side of your shrine. If the alter is not very big, choose critical components only to declutter your space. More importantly, get things you can use, and they should also add value to your life. Always consult your paganism book of life to get the right things.

Additional Items to Put on Your Altar

The items you put on your altar mainly depend on your intentions and personal preferences. When you set your sacred place to perform your rituals, you know what you want to achieve. Therefore, feel free to include anything you think will help you achieve your desired goals. Add potpourri or herbs to your altar. You can add many different types of leaves to your place of worship, and these depend on your intentions. Additionally, include crystals since they also come in various forms. Before you get the stones, make sure you know their purpose.

Tarot or oracle cards are some items to add to your pagan altar. Cards consist of different images and designs and are usually used for meditation. You can also use them for divination if you want to know what might happen in the future. If your altar is big, add a small box you can use to store your sacred things. Spell objects are crucial since they play roles in the different forms of magic you intend to perform. Talismans and magical jewels are other items you can include when creating your altar.

Since you can use your altar for various functions, feel free to add anything divine and meaningful. Include a witches' ladder or hang a charm for energy and protection if possible. However, you need to be careful to avoid cluttering your altar with things you'll not use. If you do not know the specific function of a component, rather don't add it to your sacred space. As your needs increase, you can add the items, but do research first to get the ideal ones.

This chapter has discussed different elements to consider when setting up a Pagan Altar. You should know that everyone has a different approach when creating your sacred space for rituals. Depending on your intentions and needs, you can use any method with which you are comfortable. Make sure you put appropriate items in this sacred space since you'll need them for rituals, spells, meditation, prayers, divination, and connecting to deities. All these components should be in the right place before you begin your rites.

Chapter 10: Simple Pagan Spells and Rituals

Pagans use different rituals and ceremonies to celebrate or commemorate many aspects of life. This chapter highlights the simple pagan spells and rituals you can try if you are a practitioner. It also provides step-by-step instructions and ingredients for each recipe. Some common rituals and spells are meant for love, protection, luck, abundance, and others.

Bealtaine Rituals

In Celtic tradition, every year consists of two halves, one representing darkness and the other light. The end of the dark season heralds the coming of the light half of the year and is accompanied by celebrations known as Bealtaine. It was the most important and biggest festival on May 1st and is celebrated in Ireland and Scotland. Celebrating Bealtaine involves many rituals, and most include fire. During this period, supernatural beings were believed to be active, and their powers could freely pass to the mortal world.

These celebrations were meant to remind the farmers of when to sow and when to reap during the ancient period. In other words, Bealtaine festivals marked significant calendar events to mark the return of light. These celebrations were accompanied by several rituals explained below.

Fire Rituals

Fire played a critical role in these Bealtaine rituals since it symbolized the return of the sun after winter. Fire is also believed to have sympathetic magic that could enhance the growth of crops and animals. Smoke protects, and a bonfire means lots of smoke. Fire is also the great protector and provider, and the ashes have protective powers imbued in them. This is why dancing around a fire has been so prevalent in many cultures throughout history. Humans sometimes jumped over the flames.

Household fires were lit using the flames obtained from the central bonfire. In some instances, animal blood was used as a sacrifice to the gods. Bonfires were also markers for important events of the year, like the driving out of animals to pasture, and they would be a part of the celebration at these events. There were special places where the major celebrations were held every year, and the rituals were performed to protect animals, people, and crops. They were also meant to encourage growth.

Fires on the hearths inside homes were not supposed to go outside since it was believed they would carry the luck away. The fires were put out during May celebrations and rekindled using the flames from the main bonfire. From then, the fires were not allowed to go out. During this period, when the ritual was performed, people were urged to refuse requests, avoid strangers, and offer to share anything. The fire ritual was specifically meant to guard personal fortunes and other belongings. The link between the mortals and immortals was very close, so issues like death or injury were not expected.

Water and Flower Rituals

Water obtained from local wells was believed to be highly potent, and the flowers around these holy fountains were also said to be restorative. The dew on the grass on May Day was also thought to provide a cure for the entire year. According to the practitioners walking in the dew or using it to wash your face offered curative powers. Flowers were collected during the celebrations and used to decorate altars and other sacred places. Yellow flowers can ward off evil spirits, who are said to dislike the bright color. It could also be that yellow flowers contain the powers and spirit of deities, and evil spirits are repelled by such power.

Good Luck Rituals and Charms

The celebrations in May are often connected to harvest and abundance, and that brings joy and happiness. The rituals were used for luck and protection against unforeseen forces. It is good that so much power comes from celebrations and rituals at this time of the year, as it is noted that between May Eve and May Day is when evil spirits are at their most powerful. Water and yellow flower were often combined to ward off these evil spirits and bring luck. Other practices were discouraged in May since they were considered unlucky. For instance, getting married in May was considered unlucky.

In Ireland, the May Tree or May Bush is decorated. Ribbons are added to bushes or trees near to your house, and whitethorn bushes are the most traditional to decorate if they can be found in close proximity. Branches, leaves, and flowers are also hung over the door to help good luck and fortune enter the house.

Love Spells

Love spells were practiced in Irish Paganism, and these were specifically meant to bring back a lost lover or make your relationship stronger. If you wanted to bring back a lost lover, you would go to a pagan practitioner, and they would ask you the name, date of birth, and the place of birth of the person you want to reconcile with. The practitioner would also ask you the same details so they could bind your details with theirs.

There were certain ingredients required for the spell. For example, love spells would not work without ingredients like sandalwood powder and Rose petals. If you want to fall in love with someone, you have first to provide all the necessary ingredients to allow the practitioner to cast the spell. The spells were targeted, emitting an energy wave in all directions. The following are some of the basic ingredients required by the spellcasters to bring back ex-lovers.

- **Pink candles** represent your return to the lover and should be burned as long as possible before the spell is broken off.

- **Element of fire**: fire is an essential component in a love spell since it represents passion and destruction. It would destroy the negative feelings you might have destroyed.

- **Flower herbs and petals**: You increase your chances of reuniting with your lover with more flowers. A combination of lavender and marigold is said to be effective when casting your love spell. With your intention, mix these flowers in the right proportions to create a powder and use it for your lover's spell rituals.

- **Powder of sympathy** is a common ingredient used to speed up the love magic spell. It aligns the energies within the caster and the target to make the process faster.

- **Photos**: the spell caster will need your lover's photo or the two of you together.

- **Lovers' return oil**: Love oil can also be used to bring back your lost lover. Pick the flowers when the moon is waxing to make your spell more powerful.

- **Hair strands**: Get a strand of your lover's hair since this is an essential ingredient for casting a spell to bring your lover back. You can look for your lover's hair on a comb or follow them to hair salons.

- **Ex-lover's clothes:** a piece of your lover's clothing is another essential ingredient you should get for a love spell to be successful.

- **Nail clippings** can produce a powerful spell and play a pivotal role in bringing back your lover. However, it might be difficult for you to get these components, so see how best you can get them.

- **Jewelry** is another magical ingredient for your love spell to return an ex-lover. It should not be a very expensive piece, so an old ring or bracelet will suffice.

However, there are certain things you should never do even if you manage to get all the ingredients. For instance, you should never cast a spell to make your ex-lover stay with you against their will. Your spells should brick someone to the place where they want to be and not be forced. The other person should be ready for the love that comes with the spell.

If possible, you need to consult your ex-lover and let them know your intentions, so you don't take them by surprise. When it comes to love matters, never force things as it may produce undesired results. You need to set your differences aside with your lover if you want to enjoy your relationship once you reconcile.

Magic

Irish pagans also practice magic like other religions. Witchcraft was prohibited in Ireland and Scotland, but this later changed around the 18th Century. When honoring their deities, witches believe humans have the power to cause a change in different forms that cannot be proved by science. Witches also perform rituals and spells to heal people and help them with general life issues. Magic should never be performed to harm someone, and the following are positive examples.

Candle Magic

This is a good general-purpose spell anyone can do as long as they believe in it. You need to pick a candle with the right color for the job you want to undertake. For example, yellow represents wealth, pink or green for love, blue for good fortune, red for strength, brown for stability, and mauve for wisdom. If you wish to attract something, write its name from the candle's top to the bottom. Conversely, you can also write what you want to dispel from the bottom to the top of the candle.

Like other types of magic, it is best to do your candle magic after dark. It is a good idea to begin your magic on a new moon if you want to draw something to yourself. On the other hand, begin the spell on a waning moon if you want to dispel something. Light the candle and visualize what you want to achieve, and maintain your concentration. Blow out the candle when you finish and repeat the procedure the following night until the moon passes the waning or waxing stage. When you are done, bury the candle somewhere and don't throw it away. Forget about the spell, and don't talk about it.

Witches' Poppets

Poppets are wax, clay, or plasticine figures resembling the person you want the magic to focus on. When consecrated on the witch's altar, the poppet can be attached by a cord to a man and woman. A combination of female and male energy is believed to be most effective and provides symbolic treatment. The poppet's leg can be bandaged as part of the healing spell. The mouth can also be sewn closed to prevent the living person represented by the poppet from spreading gossip.

When the ritual has worked or achieved its goals, the poppet is buried or burned to release the spell. Essentially, when you undertake a particular spell, you'll be communicating with invisible spirits, and they will hear you as long as you do the right thing. If you think you want to heal someone, get the appropriate tools for the spell or ritual. It is crucial to visualize your intention and what you want to achieve when performing the spell to make it effective.

Spells for Protection

You must learn about your environment wherever you live and understand the folklore of the area. Honor the spirits of the land and seek energy from sacred sites honored by the people who lived before you. Weave your energy and relationship with the spirits of the earth for protection against evil spells. For example, Rowan trees are used for protection. There are also other trees with equivalent properties in other parts of the world. You must know how they can protect you against evil spells.

Look for a rowan tree and honor it as an ally by asking for a gift of the tree's wood or berries. Thread the berries into a bracelet to wear when you feel you need protection. You can also put rowan twig crosses tied with a red cord at your windows and doors to protect you. Make sure you thank the tree for the charms. Create a landscape where you can plant a single tree and treat it as a sacred space to perform your rituals. The spirits will recognize all the efforts you make to connect with nature. You must perform your rituals regularly to enjoy unlimited protection.

Healing Rites

You should understand and honor the water sources around you if you want to perform healing rites. The traditional folk healing method requires you to visit a holy well or sacred body of water and dip a cloth in the water. Wash the sick person while at the same time asking the spirits of the water to cure and bless them. Leave the cloth on a hawthorn tree and leave it to biodegrade. As the cloth rots, the illness is taken away from the sick patient. The process should happen naturally for the best results.

This practice is known as hanging clooties, and some people often misunderstand it. You should use biodegradable cloth, so the tree's growth is not affected. When something is bad for the land or nature, it is not good for folk magic. Therefore, using plastic or other non-biodegradable material may not give you positive results from your spell. Plastic impacts the environment in many ways since it does not rot like other compostable matter, so you should not include it in your spells if you want to achieve your goals.

Irish Paganism emphasizes the significance of developing close links with nature and achieved through different rites. This chapter discussed different pagan spells and rituals to help people resolve different aspects of their lives. Before undertaking these spells, it is essential to know the ingredients required and how to use them. Make sure you follow the instructions or enlist the services of an experienced practitioner.

Conclusion

After an overview of the Pagan history in Ireland, it becomes clear that Irish Paganism represents the perfect blend of ancient traditions, modern adaptations, and beliefs adopted from other religions. Due to the endless devotions of the Druids, many traditional practices remained, even in modern Irish Paganism. Followers are still free to choose their spiritual guides – whether a deity or any other creature inhabiting the natural realms. In many religions, only loyalty and honesty are emphasized as character traits to aim for. On the other hand, Pagans also believe in personal responsibility. Pagans honor their deities and spiritual guides with festivals and rituals and highlight the importance of respecting nature and its energy. Each solstice on the Witches Wheel of the Year holds a unique significance to the Celts' life. They are all related to events at specific times of the year.

Learning about Celtic spirituality will allow you to unlock the secrets of Druidry in Ireland along with the Welsh witchcraft practices. Many overlaps between Irish and Welsh witchcraft occur, but the latter is known for its unique characteristic, such as the four branches of belief. Due to being nature-based, Celtic witchcraft was more popular and widespread in Ireland than in any other country, allowing the Welsh branches to differentiate from it. In times of need, the spirits and the deities that followers turn to are also different for Irish and Welsh Pagans. While Paganism wasn't always associated with witchcraft, the local folk beliefs and healing practices in Ireland made it much easier for the connection to form between these two customs.

Nowadays, many ancient Paganism practices are long gone, and those that survived were only able to with the help of Druidry. Despite the Celts' oppression following the spread of Christianity in Ireland and the subsequent loss of influence they endured, the Druids managed to pass parts of the Celtic tradition to the next generations. Due to their efforts, even in modern times, the ancient legacy of Paganism is still alive - albeit mostly in neopaganism, and other similar contemporary Pagan beliefs, such as Wicca.

Lastly, this book empowered you with knowledge about magickal tools and their uses in Irish Paganism. Whether you are just learning the way of the witch or are well versed in spiritual practices, using the proper tools will make you better in your craft. Setting up an altar isn't always required for becoming an active practitioner, but having a sacred space will enhance your ability to cast an intention and make your wishes become a reality. An altar can be dedicated to the preferred deity and serve as a surface to prepare everything you need to perform a spell or a ritual. With so many candles, crystals, wands, and incantations to choose from, your sacred space will inspire you to find the perfect combination leading you down the right path whenever you need an answer or guidance in your practice.

Part 3: The Morrigan

Secret Celtic Practices, Devotional Rituals, Divination, and Magick Spells

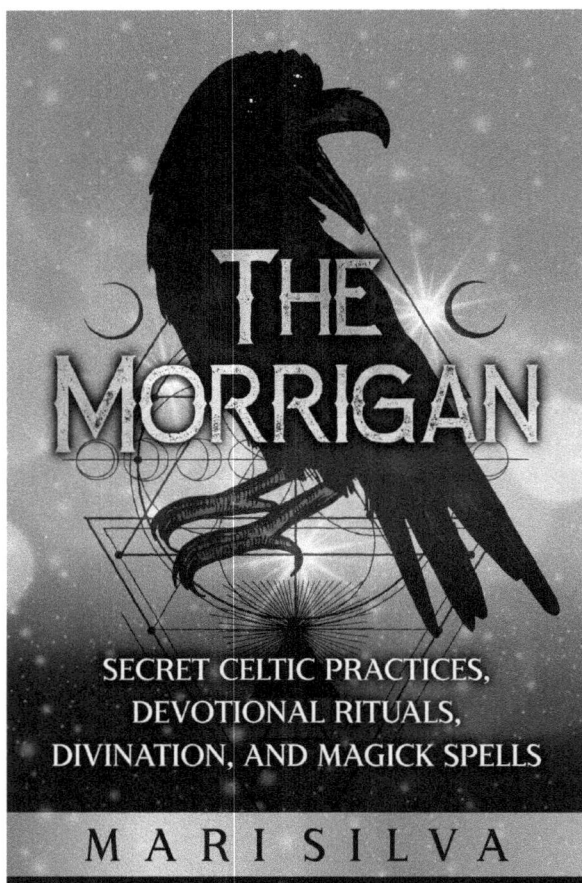

Introduction

The Celtic lore is full of legends about mighty gods and goddesses overseeing different parts of the lives of the Irish Celts. One of these deities was Morrigan (or "the Morrigan," as she is also known), who possesses an incredibly rich and complex history, not to mention her association with paradoxical roles. Those who only heard a few stories about her would typically refer to her as a war deity or a death goddess. Explaining this deity is a challenge as most of the information we have about her was recorded from folktales and changed with each retelling, depending on the person recounting the stories.

Only those who are more familiar with Morrigan's many guises can comprehend her contribution to the cycle of life, death, rebirth, and everything else in between. Like other supernatural Tuatha de Danann tribe members, Morrigan also has a deep connection to nature. There is archeological evidence that shows her symbols were found on objects indicating her role as an earth goddess, nourishing humans, and their lands. Similar evidence is found about her guise as the triple goddess of womanhood and fertility.

She wasn't only feared for her appearance before and after a battle but was also revered for it. This book will show how Morrigan brought solace in ancient times and how she can still do the same for you today. Suppose you regard Morrigan as a symbol of empowerment, intuition, justice, and wisdom instead of seeing her as a villainess. In that case, she will provide you with all these qualities. The roles of women depicted in the Celtic lore are all women of immense strength, and Morrigan is no different. She isn't seen and called by a collective name of the Morrigan - describing several powerful feminine figures - for no reason. She has the power of multiple women - and she can lend this to anyone who honors her. Her resources and qualities are all tied so closely together that when invoking one goddess to help you, your blessing will likely come from all of them.

Many think this goddess could only influence events taking place on the battlefield. However, Morrigan wasn't called the goddess of fertility based solely on her ability to ensure the reincarnation of souls who lost their bodies on the battlefield. As this beginner-friendly book reveals, the goddess also had some lesser-known roles as a healer, midwife, and protector of lands. The fascinating myths you'll read about her different guises are enough to have anyone on the edge of their seat.

The hands-on approach of the chapters will provide you with ample information about setting up a dedicated altar using symbols and various magical tools - all in the name of honoring Morrigan. Whether you want to use her abilities to predict the outcome of an important event, empower yourself to overcome a particularly formidable obstacle or require guidance or healing - you'll find everything you need for it in this book. All that's left for you to do is start practicing and get ready to receive your blessings. Remember, if you feel stuck with a particular task, putting your own spin on it will always make it easier to manifest your intentions.

Chapter 1: The Guises of the Morrigan

This first chapter will introduce you to the Morrigan (also known as Morrigu) as a single Celtic goddess with many faces and the trio of goddesses who live within her being that we will refer to as "aspects." Even her collective name - the Morrigan - is given to acknowledge the diversity of her forms and abilities. Because the Celts didn't keep written records, most of their legends have come to us through folklore passed down through the centuries.

These stories include tales of the one Morrigan - or at least the women who are often considered to be her. Each of Morrigan's faces or guises refers to her abilities as a shape-shifting Celtic goddess of war, sovereignty, fate, and death. At the same time, many of them describe her in different ways. For example, some tales attribute magical characteristics to her, while others deny this and only see her as a patroness of natural elements and battles. However, most descriptions of the Morrigan agree that while she is primarily associated with warfare, she also has a characteristic that gives her an earthly fertility goddess status. Despite her fame as the harbinger of death, there is a positive aspect to her. And this is true regardless of which of the following guises she was seen in.

Badb

Also known as the Battle Crow, Badb is probably the most well-known aspect of the war goddess in Celtic history. She is one of three sister goddesses collectively called the Morrigan. Sometimes she is also illustrated as one single being with multiple faces. This concept - of three in one - is most likely a consequence of the Celtic pagans' assimilation into Christianity and adoption of the doctrine of the Holy Trinity. However, there is no denying the link between all her abilities and other possible guises of the Morrigan.

What is even more confusing about the Morrigan is the use of her name for one member of the triple goddesses. Incidentally, out of the three sisters, it's Badb, who is often referred to by this name, who was herself known as a creator of confusion. Even though all three of them are associated with death during battle and wars, Badb appears more often than her sisters. And when she does, it is seen as confirmation of death or massacre in the future.

Badb would most likely appear on the evening before a battle was due to take place in the form of her favorite animal, the crow. This omen signals that bloodshed is most likely to follow. At other times, she would simply visit rulers disguised as hags and warn them of the outcome of the battle. However, if she really wanted to dissuade the parties from entering into combat, she would shape-shift into an even more terrifying form. Whether in the form of the hag, the crow, or another creature, she would sow panic and utter confusion amongst warriors in the hope of preventing them from fighting. Sometimes it was enough, if she flew over the battlefield as the crow, for the warriors to understand the outcome. If it wasn't, she would fly onto the battlefield and scream from there. She would also do the same after the battle to frighten the enemy so much that they would be too frightened to attack again.

Working alongside her sister, Badb was capable of much more than just making the enemy run. Together they could influence nature by summoning clouds, hiding the sun, and bringing out deadly storms and thunder. This magical weather could last up to three days to make certain the enemy were either killed or changed their minds from entering into warfare.

It said that her role was slightly modified after she lost her family and her tribe's territory fell into the hands of a rival tribe. From then on, she promised to bring them prosperity, peace, and victory in all her dealings rather than dealing with wars between the clans.

Badb is also one of the few interpretations of the Morrigan that appeared in most contemporary Paganic and Neopaganic cultures. She still appears as a crow which is her favorite form as a spirit guide when interacting with the Celts. However, now we are also familiar with how this bird came to be linked to the goddess of battle and warfare. Blackbirds such as crows and ravens often appeared on battlefields after the combat had ceased and after other disasters involving death and bloodshed. While this may seem like a particularly gruesome picture to paint of the animals associated with the goddess, there is more to this story. Crows are intelligent birds and are said to predict many outcomes in nature - which probably led to their association with war prophecy. They may have learned to recognize the signs of the impending bloodshed, causing them to fly over the troops before the fight even began. As unlikely as this may seem, it is backed up by research that has been conducted as recently as 2020.

Another form of Badb associated with prophecy is that of an older woman. Through Celtic lore, older women were often thought to have great wisdom and that they could see into the future and peek into people's fate. To once again draw a parallel with the triple goddesses, Badb could have been considered the *Crone*. After all, she symbolized both wisdom and the inevitability of death.

Yet another form Badb would take on was that of the Banshee, which she used when she wanted to terrify her enemies. These creatures were said to be malevolent sidhe, or spirits living in the other world. First, she would appear as a crow, then morph into a banshee while continuing to use the rasping voice of the crow. If this didn't have any effect, she would begin to shriek in a high-pitched voice. It's unclear whether this form of Badb would inhabit the spiritual world as the other banshees did, but there is also a reference to her acting as a harbinger of death outside battlefields. Since a Banshee's cry would have the same effect whenever someone encountered one, it's quite possible that there is a tangible connection between all these roles. However, this role of Badb is also common in modern interpretations. These may or may not have been tainted by the attempts of the Christian Church to reduce Celtic beliefs to occult and mystical tales. Due to this, most of their spirits have become mischievous creatures, and the legend of Tuatha De Danann is just a tale that was made up in the past. However, the Morrigan as Badb has retained quite a bit of power. This wasn't just due to her ability to instill fear but also referred to her courageous and protective nature.

Macha

Badb's sister, Macha, was also a powerful Irish war goddess, but her abilities were linked to the land more than any other dimension of life. Similar to the Maiden, Mother, and Crone trinity, the Morrigan was also known for a somewhat different trio of female deities. Macha, Badb, and Nemain were viewed as sisters, or sometimes sister aspects of the same deity. Macha was also known as the Raven, which also linked her to the Raven Queen. However, she was commonly associated with crows and horses, as well. Much like her crow sister, Macha would appear at a battlefield disguised as a bird, influencing the battle in several ways.

Another reference to the triple goddesses was Matchas' three aspects. She has had a maternal, reproductive element, rural elements often associated with nature, and an element of sensual fertility. These three parts united to form a mother goddess who protected her people during wartime and provided them with sustenance and protection for the rest of their lives. Because of her work in these areas, it is also possible that Macha was a member of the ancient Celtic Tuatha De Danann tribe, all of whom had supernatural abilities and relied on nature to sustain them in life.

Nemain

In Irish, the word "nemain" means frenzy, which is clearly illustrative of the type of role this goddess had in the Celtic pantheon. This female war deity was said to watch over a battle with an intense fury, which contradicts the calculating attributes with which the Morrigan is characterized. For this reason, she is probably one of the least known Irish goddesses. However, she did have some other qualities in common with Morrigan's other guises. For example, she would never fight a battle but would influence its outcome through other means. She is known to have chosen a side and then intimidated the other party with blood-curdling shrieks and an overall terrifying presence - as the Crow or a Banshee would. While using only her signature voice, Nemain could also become visible if she chose to. She has been the announcer of death, and seeing her would send panic through the enemy lines.

Nemain's death shriek could predict the demise of an entire army on the battlefield and even the rest of the clan's massacre by the enemy. Mighty warriors have dropped dead from fright upon hearing her shriek - so, in a way, this was an added tool to her deathly arsenal. Using this ability as a weapon, she was able to protect the soldiers and the civil members of the clan she chose - as long as they honored her in return. She may also have appeared to the souls of the deceased, directing them toward the other world.

The Washer at the Ford

Although it said that seeing the Washer at the Ford before a battle was a bad omen, the Morrigan in this guise had a much bigger role than simply being a harbinger of death. In this animation, she appeared as a young maiden washing the armor and weapons of those destined to lose their lives in the upcoming battle. She would also try to dissuade the warriors from fighting by claiming to be the daughter of a king who offers them many riches if they make peace. At other times, she would offer her love in exchange for her protection during combat. While she was seen as a young girl or woman on these occasions, she easily transformed into an old hag imparting wisdom and granting the gift of fertility in all areas of life. Those able to recognize her as the incarnation of the goddess were granted sovereignty and blessing from her. Their fields were always full of nourishing crops, their animals were protected from disease, and their own lives were secured during combat. On the other hand, those who failed to see her as the war deity were cursed in those same fundamental aspects. Warriors and rulers who disregarded her wishes were punished either by being made to lose a battle, death, or the fall of their tribe to the supremacy of their enemies.

The Great Phantom Queen

There aren't many records or even myths about Morrigan's appearance as the Great Phantom Queen. Some believe the reason behind this is that she was such a powerful shape-shifter that determining her guise or role was nearly impossible. Sometimes, she would appear as a black crow - announcing death to those who saw her. At other times, she would try to dissuade the feuding parties from entering the battlefield by appearing as a beautiful woman in front of them. Those who refused her and disregarded her pleading would suffer dire consequences during a battle. After a battle was concluded, she would appear again, but this time in the form of an old, haggard woman with wounds on her body, mourning all the lives that had been lost during the war. This also implied that she herself had participated in the battle, despite nobody actually having seen her fight.

The Fairy Queen

The folklore of Morrigan's incarnation as the Fairy Queen has survived through to modern times because of her importance to Pagans. For them, this powerful female figure represents much more than just a mythical figure. In their hearts, the Fairy Queen had transcended the boundaries between war and love, life and death, by natural and supernatural powers. She is honored during Beltane and Samhain for the blessings she grants for the harvest season. Fairies have been a common occurrence in Celtic lore since ancient times. They were seen as somewhat mischievous creatures - but nevertheless ready to help humans if they asked for protection, guidance, or healing. In Ireland, they are said to live in fairy mounds - also known as the land of the spirits. As the Fairy Queen, the Morrigan can cross over into their realm through bodies of water, burial chambers, mounds, and other natural landscape features.

Crossing the fairy mounds, she can communicate with spirits such as the Síth and ask for their assistance to help humans and other creatures of nature. It is believed she leads these fairies across the land around Samhain and Beltane when the veil between the worlds becomes thin. Together they come to the aid of humans, protecting them, their animals, and crops from malicious spirits who may also cross the realms around this time.

The Raven Queen

Much like many other aspects of the Morrigan, the Raven Queen was never seen participating in battles. In fact, it's said that she doesn't even care about mankind's struggles between law and chaos, nor does she align herself on the side of good or evil. As the goddess of death, she simply guards and guides the souls of those who have died. She helps everyone to transition from the mortal realm to the spiritual one. She even helps them start their journey toward the outer world if necessary. People also ask her to protect their deceased loved ones' souls from malevolent spirits who have been known to steal and feed on innocent mortal souls. The Raven Queen has very high regard for the natural processes of life and death and expects the same regard from her followers. Those who disregard her will often face dire consequences. And while she isn't concerned about how long a soul inhabits a body before it has found its way to her either, she does everything to make it easier for the soul to pass on. She is often said to assist those who have suffered a violent death at a young age.

Maiden, Mother, Crone (Triple Goddess)

After her fame as a war deity, Morrigan's second renowned aspect is that of the triple goddess. The number of interpretations of this iconic trinity in the ancient Irish role is too many to count. The modern Paganic and Neo-Paganism beliefs perhaps provide a clearer picture of the roles of these female deities. According to these, the Maiden is depicted as a young girl - most likely a virgin - who isn't yet awakened to her feminine nature. Full of youthful ideas, she finds stepping into womanhood enchanting. As such, she can bring a new beginning, particularly around the waxing phase of the lunar cycle.

Representing the next phase of a woman's life, the Mother becomes the goddess of fertility, who brings abundance, growth, wisdom, and fulfillment in all areas of life. Her power is greatest around the time of the full moon, especially in springtime and early summer, when she makes the ground fertile. Lastly, in her aspect as the Crone, she becomes an incredibly wise old woman, eager to share her knowledge with the next generation. She acts as a guide through dark times, including death and loss. In this incarnation, she is most powerful during the waning phase of the moon and watches over the frozen ground during the winter.

This triple aspect of the Morrigan is often used as an example of how ancient societies viewed women - and according to many, this can still be applied in modern times. After all, maidens are still revered, mothers are still honored, and crones have still been pushed aside. However, these days, more and more women are trying to claim the last role because of all the wisdom it promises. They ask the Morrigan to help them embrace and celebrate their later years in life instead of allowing the younger generations to push them aside.

Anand

Anand is the last of the trio of sisters named Macha, Badb, and Anand. However, unlike her sisters, she is also said to be the Mother of the Celtic gods. This characterization of her probably comes from the same source that claims the Tuatha dé Danann were a tribe of gods and not just humans with supernatural abilities. This also coincides with the depiction of Morrigan as the Mother in her famous triple aspect guise. Like Morrigan, Anand is also honored as the goddess of sovereignty and the fertility maiden, the second of the Morrigan's triple aspects. Anyone who wished to gain legitimate power over the land of her tribe had to marry Anand. She is also said to have shape-shifting abilities and was often symbolized by the horse - just like her sister Macha.

Ériu, Banba, and Fódla
(Irish Land Goddesses)

Ériu, and her sisters Banba and Fódla, formed a highly influential trio of feminine power in ancient Ireland. They were married to three chieftains of the Tuatha De Danann, and their husbands were all grandsons of Dagda, the first leader of this supernatural tribe. Their number and likely origins from this ancient tribe are their only connections with the Morrigan's other guises. While Ériu, Banba, and Fódla didn't have as much power as their husband did, these women showed incredible courage and an intense desire to defend their homeland.

They also had a very strong connection to nature and could tap into its power whenever any of their tribe needed its healing magic. When Tuatha De Dannan finally succumbed to enemy forces, these land goddesses had a special request to make from the ranks of their enemy. If the new rulers agreed to name the land after the Tuatha De Danann, the goddesses would grant them many blessings, ensuring a good harvest and many natural riches. Since it was Ériu who the enemy listened to first, they named the territory Ériu-land after her, and she has been granting the blessings ever since.

Danu (Earth Goddess)

Although much of her origin is still a mystery, Danu is most likely the namesake of the Tuatha dé Danann; the first Celtic tribe said to have inhabited Ireland. Also revered as the Mother goddess, Danu was an influential ancestral figure for the Celts. Due to her noble and possible supernatural origins, she wielded an immense power - something she provided for her offspring as well. Not only that, but she thought it necessary to maintain a good relationship with the nobility and the rulers of Ireland, often granting gifts to those of aristocratic birth. To help them maintain their sovereignty, Danu often presented kings and chiefs of Tuatha dé Danann with extraordinary talents. These rulers often had unusually high levels of creativity and were skilled in several daily life activities.

Danu is even said to have instilled wisdom for ruling in other gods in the Celtic pantheon. Since the Tuatha dé Danann often migrated from one territory to another, they asked Danu to provide them with plenty of successful harvests whenever they went. Some sources refer to her as the goddess of wind and earth, blessing all things in life. In this role, she is connected to the fairy mounds where she would communicate with the fairies, which many Irish dolmens can still authenticate.

The Mother goddess's relationship to nature extended to the rivers - allowing these bodies of water to nourish all creatures throughout many parts of the Celtic world. Thanks to these waters, the luscious greenery of Ireland still remains as breathtaking as it is said to have been centuries ago. It is also theorized that the Danube - one of Europe's longest rivers - is named after Danu.

While Danu was rarely present in the little written records obtained about the lives of the Celts, she is pretty much alive in several Neopaganic traditions. In those, she is revered as the triple goddess - a clear association with the Morrigan's other identities throughout the Irish lore. Due to her versatile powers, Danu can be used in various practices and is an excellent choice for beginner witches to turn to.

Chapter 2: The Morrigan in Celtic Myth

The Morrigan is certainly considered to be among the most influential and mysterious archetypes of Celtic lore and mythology. The Phantom, or great Queen, which is one of the implications of her name, has always been representative of concepts like death, fate, and war. As you are already aware, Morrigan was an ingenious shapeshifter who took the appropriate form for the messages she carried. When she appeared as a black crow right before battle, those who were unfortunate enough to see her knew that they were out of luck.

While the Morrigan is unique to Celtic and Irish mythology, similar figures have been found in other records of Celtic lore. For instance, Morgan le Fey, who appeared as a great foe or adversary in Arthurian legend, shared multiple characteristics with the Morrigan. Both figures appeared as prophets and shapeshifters who emerged in various forms. Many scholars also suggest that the names of both the Morrigan and Morgan le Fey have the same etymological root. However, both names have totally different definitions in Welsh and Irish, which means that there is not enough solid evidence to substantiate the connection (when it comes to the name, at least).

The figure of Irish mythology sovereignty goddess also shares several attributes with the Morrigan. For example, the figures of the goddess are portrayed as a conduit to Ireland's rule and land. In other words, the sovereignty goddess is associated with fertility, which is a symbol of the prosperity and fertility of Ireland and its land. Similarly, the Morrigan is highly associated with the vast lands of Ireland, especially ones that were named in her honor, according to the *Dindshenchas*. *The Dindshenchas* roughly translates to the "lore of places." It includes stories of how the different places of Ireland were named.

Many scholars suggest that the Morrigan is also associated with the banshee, or *bean sidhe*, which is a prominent figure in Irish folklore. The banshee is a figure that can foretell the death of family members. The announcement is recognized by her loud keening, wailing, and shrieking. The Morrigan is also characterized by her menacing shrieks when she is in the presence of death. It is believed that the Morrigan was either an inspiration for the *bean sidhe* or that the banshee came from the same oral tradition as she did.

The Morrigan does not only hold similarities with other figures in the Celtic world, but she also has ties to archetypes of other mythologies. For instance, the Valkyries (a group of women who determine those who live and those who die in battle) are figures in Old Norse mythology who hold a resemblance to the Morrigan. They appear in either ones or three's, three being the common denominator and very significant. They also have divination or prophetic abilities and are associated with birds. Some scholars suggest that the Morrigan, the Valkyries, and other mythological female figures embody an incredible power and strength of character and represent the full cycle of life. They can give life by giving birth and can take life away since they can determine who dies in battle. Throughout Celtic mythology and similar ancient mythologies, the female goddess or figure seems to be naturally aware of the destinies of men.

Morrigan remains relevant to this day due to her acclaim in the world of popular culture. She is a common figure in pop media and has made an appearance in numerous comic books, including Marvel Comics, TV series, and video games.

The previous chapter introduced Morrigan as both a single Celtic goddess – and as a triple goddess – without going into too much detail. In this chapter, however, you'll get to see how the goddess's traits and manifestations unfold in Celtic lore and myth.

Cath Maige Tuired

The Cath Maige Tuired is among the most significant mythological pieces when it comes to information available about the Irish deities and how they lived in the ancient lands, which comprise modern Ireland today. It tells of a war or battle that took place between the Fomorians and the Tuatha Dé Danann regarding the rights to rule Ireland. One of the most important deities happens to be the Morrigan, who plays a vital role, especially through her poetry and magical powers, in the rebellion that was conducted against the Fomorians.

While her role in the mythology is hard to pinpoint accurately, considering the English translations of the text cut out significant portions of her dialogue, her powerful role is still undeniable. Unfortunately, translations convey an inaccurate impression of her behavior and actions; however, when read in the original language, the role that the Morrigan takes on holds a much greater substance, and the nuances in the descriptions are easily felt, although the English language fails to convey some crucial overtones. With both of her appearances in mind, we intend to convey the significance of her efforts and actions in battle. Here, she employed her magical abilities to boost the fight of the Tuatha Dé Danann against the Fomorians, as well as using her successful intentions to drive them to victory before finally presenting a dual prophecy regarding the fates of the people comprising both sides.

The Battles

The Mythological Cycle of Irish mythology comprises two saga texts collectively known as the *Cath Maige Tuired*. This work is a reference piece telling of two different battles that took place in Connacht. The first one was in the Conmhaícne Cúile Tuireadh's territory, located near Cong, County Mayo, in Ireland. In Ireland, the second battle took place near Lough Arrow in County Sligo. The Tuatha Dé Danann fought the first battle against the Fir Bolg, and the second battle was fought by the Tuatha Dé Danann against the Fomorians.

In the first battle of Cath Magie Tuired, it is said that the Morrigan and her sisters, Macha and Badb, used their magic and spell-casting to affect the battle, and their sorcery left Tuatha Dé triumphant, allowing them to build a strong foundation in Ireland. However, it wasn't long before the Fomorian, who proved to be a lot more difficult to defeat, swept into the lands of Ireland, looking to set their own foothold. The Dagda sought help from one of his wives, the Morrigan, as the Tuatha Dé got ready to set out for battle against the Fomorians. In need of a prophet, the Dagda finally found her at a river drift, where they had intercourse. After they had finished, the Morrigan looked into the future and saw that the Tuatha Dé Danann would emerge victorious from the battle. However, she warned that this victory came at the price of a massacre.

The Irish gods gathered and readied themselves to fight against the assembly of Fomorians. Naturally, they asked Morrigan what helpful elements she could bring to the battle. She replied cryptically, saying anything she decided to follow became a target for hunting. It didn't take long for the battle to turn into a bloodbath. It only ended when the Morrigan instigated a thirst for murder and blood as she cried to the Tuatha Dé Dannan, causing the Fomorians to flee and vanish into the sea.

Cath Maige Tuired Cunga- The First Battle of Moytura

The Morrigan first makes an appearance in the lore of the First Battle of the Moytura, or the Cath Maige Tuired Cunga, in a rivalry between Tuatha Dé Danann and their supporters and the Fir Bolgs, who were indigenous to the lands.

Nuanda, the king of the Tuatha dé Danann, requested to be given half of the land, which Eochaid, the king of the Fir Bolg, refused. This quickly escalated into the battle of Moytura. Streng, a significant Fir Bolg figure, challenged Nuanda to a one-on-one fight, during which he cut Nuada's right hand. While this was considered a triumph of some sort, their happiness was cut short when the Morrigan killed the king of the Fir Bolg.

Cath Maige Tuired- The Battle of Moytura

The Morrigan made recurrent appearances in the tale to drive the Tuatha Dé Danann to battle, which was an effort she succeeded in. Her efforts to stir up a good fight were especially evident when her involvement was needed to guarantee victory. For instance, she emerged to push Lugh to fight after he armed himself up. It is said that she appeared in front of the army in a warlike manner, just as the warriors had sworn to take down Indech, the Fomorian King. She also emerged in the middle of the battle to work up the Tuatha Dé Danann, which was the turning point for them to rise and claim their triumph.

Every time she appeared, her exhortations were direct, strongly and carefully worded, and persistent. She made promises to hurt the king of the Fomorians, Indech, using her magical powers. She took his battle ardor and brought his blood back to the army. The magic she cast during the final battle contributed significantly to the death of Indech. At the end of the battle, the Morrigan foretold both negative and positive fates for the world, ensuring that her own side would emerge triumphantly.

If you take a look at the Irish text of the lore and its literal translations, you'll find that the Morrigan is an essential motivator in the battle. Her role was evident through both active participation and literal incitement and stimulation. The texts even end with her divinatory words, which is appropriate, considering the exceptional role she played in the victorious outcome of her people.

The Poems

There are three poems that are associated with the Morrigan, which are found at the end of the Vath Maige Turid saga. The first one is set right before the main battle, while the other two are set after it ends, marking the end of the entire saga.

The poems are created in a very dated form of poetry: roscaid. It has no rhyming factors and isn't metrical. Many scholars suggest that roscaid is so old that it may predate the Irish language's written records. The poems written in that form have connective alliteration, which is perhaps the only consistent element in these poems. When the words (or word) found at the end of one line alliterate with the words (or word) found at the beginning of the following line, this is called connective alliteration. This ongoing link makes it possible to use the imagery set by one line to create the one used in the next one. While it is a very clever form of art, it can be incredibly taxing to translate. Verbs, or their lack thereof, syntax, and long-lost words make it nearly impossible to convey the same meanings or maintain the poetic flow when translating them from the Irish into the English language.

The incredible thing about these poems is that even when they're extracted from the prose text that surrounds them, they still form an ongoing text of their own. Some academics believe that the entire saga was initially intended to be in this loose-verse format. The poem's structure and wording have been preserved in the old Irish language. Unfortunately, because it is so archaic and therefore unclear, modern-day storytellers of the poems are forced to keep adding prose to ensure better delivery and clearer meanings.

The first poem is told in the present tense and serves as a live narration of the battle. This poem concentrates on tales of preparations that were carried out before the battle and the following adverse effects of the struggle. The second poem is the second last portion of the saga. It is a wonderful classic tale that portrays a vision of timeless prosperity, abundance, and peace. This poem is perhaps a contrasting image of the first. The third poem, written in the future tense, highlights the prose as a vision and balances out the preceding poem.

Táin Bó

The Táin Bó, which can be translated into the cattle raid, is among the most prominent genres or pieces of early Irish literature. Irish literary works were especially divided by medieval academics into genres like Táin Bó, which is the Cattle Raid, Feis or Fled (the Feast), Echtra, which translates into Aventure, Imram or the

Voyage, Tochmarc, meaning the Wooing, Aided, which means Death, and finally Compert (Conception). Nowadays, these "genres" are more commonly known as literary cycles.

The Tains

Táin Bó Cúailnge, which means the Cattle Raid of Cooley, is among the most popular pieces of Irish lore. It was also particularly well-known among the literary audiences of the period between the 11th and 14th centuries. The Táin Bó Cúailnge is also the main story of the Ulster Cycle. It is largely believed that this tale was well known in oral literature before it was put into a written form by the recorders of medieval Christendom.

There are numerous other tána, or multiple táins, which were also translated into English. Others, however, are merely known by their names. These tána include Táin Bó Flidaise (The Cattle Raid of Flidais), Táin Bó Aingen or Echtra Nerae (The Cattle Raid of Aingen), Táin Bó Dartada (The Cattle Raid of Dartaid), Táin Bó Fraích (The Cattle Raid of Fráech), Táin Bó Regamna (The Cattle Raid of Regamain), Táin Bó Regamon (The Cattle Raid of Regamon), Táin Bó Ere, Táin Bó Munad, Táin Bó Ros, Táin Bó Ruanadh, and Táin Bó Sailin.

It was likely tradition in ancient Ireland to recite various short stories before telling The Great Táin and other similarly long tales. As a result, many people inaccurately regard these pieces, which are mere preludes, as a portion of the actual Táin Bó Cúailnge. This is especially true with written documents due to their static and bound nature.

Cú Chulainn and the Morrigan

The tales of Táin Bó Regamna and Táin Bó Cuailnge, which we will be covering, mainly revolve around Cú Chulainn and his interactions with the Morrigan. Cú Chulainn, who is also known as Cuchullin, Cuchulainn, and Cuchulain, is among the most prominent figures of medieval Irish literature. Cuchulain is the protagonist of the Ulaid or Ulster Cycle. He was also regarded as the greatest knight of the Red Branch, which is the name of the warriors loyal to Conchobar mac Nessa. Conchobar mac Nessa, or Conor, was believed to be the king of the Ulaids who inhabited the northeastern portion of Ireland during the start of the 1st century BCE.

Cú Chulainn, who was allegedly born with the name Sétante, was the son of the Long Arm and Dechtire's Lugh. Cuchulainn's skills and mastery were refined through his special gifts, which included having seven pupils in each of his eyes, seven toes on each of his feet, and seven fingers on each of his hands. Cú Chulainn was especially favored among the deities of the pantheon, which is why he escaped the curse of cyclical weakness that overtook all the men of Ulster. When compared to other great heroes and figures in history, like Achilles of Greece, Cuchullin was capable of completing extraordinary exploits, tasks, and labors. When enraged, the heroic Cú Chulainn adopted the characteristics of the berserkers of Scandinavia, turning into a deformed beast that was out of control. The Táin Bó Cuailnge, or the Cattle Raid of Cooley, at just 17 years old, kept a record of his singular and heroic protection of Ulster against Maeve (the queen of Connaught) and her forces. According to lore, Cú Chulainn was unfortunately deceived by his adversaries and lured into an unfair battle which got him killed at the age of 27.

Táin Bó Regamna- The Cattle Raid of Regamna

The Morrigan played a great role in the Ulster Cycle of tales as both a helpful figure and a foe of Cú Chulainn, the tale's protagonist. In the Cattle Raid of Regamain or Táin Bó Regamna, Cú Chulainn assaults an old woman riding a cow, driving her out of his territory, when the woman shapeshifts into a raven, which brings him to a very important realization; the shapeshifter, is, in fact, the Morrigan. To his great misfortune, the Morrigan punishes Cú Chulainn because he should have been wiser about his actions if he knew who she was. The Morrigan decides that predicting her presence at the death of Cú Chulainn in the Táin Bó Cúailnge would be a fitting punishment.

Táin Bó Cuailnge- The Cattle Raid of Cooley

Afterward, in the Táin Bó Cúailgne, the Morrigan shows up as a raven to warn the Brown Bull of Cooley. She advises him to leave Ulster before the Queen Maeve of Connacht lays siege on it. As Maeve made her way into the northern parts of the land, the men of Ulster were poisoned by an impending curse. Everyone but Cú Chulainn was affected, which is why he was left to defend the borders of Ulster on his own.

While he was on a break from the battle, a young maiden, the Morrigan, attempted to seduce him, but he managed to upset her by refusing to be swayed by her incredible beauty and rejecting her. This action had a predictable outcome, and Morrigan was furious. As soon as he was at battle again, she harnessed all her powers, transforming into an eel to trip Cú Chulainn as he fought a fjord. He was able to recover quickly. However, he attacked the eel and broke its ribs. The Morrigan shapeshifted into a wolf, which frightened the cattle and drove them right into the battle and toward Cú Chulainn. He used a sling-shot to protect himself, therefore blinding the wolf, or the Morrigan, in one eye. The Morrigan then shapeshifted into a heifer and charged at him once more. However, the Irish hero used another slingshot and broke the leg of the Morrigan. Beaten down, the Morrigan was forced to retreat.

Shortly after his great victory, Cú Chulainn ran into an old lady who was milking a cow. The woman had the same injuries as the ones he had previously inflicted on the army of animals that he had to fight off during the battle; broken ribs, a blind eye, and a broken leg. It was very clear that the Morrigan had transformed once more. However, the wounds hadn't caught the attention of Cú Chulainn. Offering him three drinks from her cow, the hero gladly accepted and blessed her with each sip he took. The woman's wounds healed with every blessing that Cú Chulainn uttered. After healing entirely, the Morrigan appeared in her true form as the goddess. She stood and reminded him of everything that he had done to insult her. Then, she warned him that his death would arrive soon before she left off.

Shortly before Cú Chulainn was killed, the Morrigan appeared once more right in front of him. On his way to the battle, he ran into a woman who was washing blood off armor. It was surely an omen of the doom that awaited him. In another battle with the army of Queen Maeve, the prophecy of the Morrigan was made true. Cú Chulainn was mortally wounded. He willingly tied himself to a boulder despite his intense and deep wounds. This foolish move was in an effort to scare his foes. It is also suggested that he knew he would die eventually, which is why he vowed to die as he stood up, tricking his enemies into believing that he was still alive. No one knew that he had died until a single black raven, which was the Morrigan, landed on Cú Chulainn's shoulder, signifying his death.

For centuries, Morrigan has remained among the most influential and prominent figures of Irish literature and lore. The archetype has played a significant role in helping her people emerge victorious from battles. Her powers also made her the enemy of one of the most powerful figures in Irish literary cycles, driving him to his doom.

Chapter 3: Sacred Animals and Symbols

In Celtic mythology, animals were generally believed to symbolize vitality and fertility because they are usually warm-blooded animate, and they breathe, move, grow, and reproduce. Many of the animals that had become domesticated were a source of nourishment and a useful source for materials used to make clothing and tools. Every part of the animal had some use; the skin was used for attire, and the bones were used by the tribes to fashion tools. They are a symbol of life continuation. Certain animals were also believed to be the conduit to the spiritual realm and the land of the gods. This incredible connection is illustrated during their use in the hunt, in which there was a quest for wisdom, knowledge, and secrets.

Just like any other deity in Irish mythology, The Morrigan is closely linked with several concepts, items, animals, and symbols. Each association explores and explains a different facet of this goddess. By becoming more familiar with each association, you become more familiar with the goddess herself. This will strengthen your connection to her and facilitate better communication with her during prayers or rituals.

Sacred Animals

The Morrigan and her three sisters were all conjoined or related to various animals. The Great Queens are associated with seven animals which were the most common apparitions used by the Morrigan.- the raven, crow, horse, wolf, eel, snake, and cow. She has shapeshifted into these animals on several occasions, and each circumstance brought her out in an appropriate guise. The chosen forms all conveyed different meanings and were used for specific situations to send messages or achieve a task.

To fully understand the meanings behind the forms that the goddess took, we must explore the significance that each of her sacred animals had in Irish culture. As you may recall from the previous chapter, the Morrigan transformed into a raven in the tale of Tain Bo Regamna. Badb took the form of a crow in the tale of Da Derga's Hostel. While they are both blackbirds, there is a difference between them both physically and symbolically - the raven's distinguishing features are its thicker beak and rounded tail. Crows are smaller and have a straight tail. The previous chapter also covered the appearance of the Morrigan in the Tain Bo Cuailgne, where she transformed into a heifer, eel, and wolf during her argument with Cu Chulain. Macha also has significant ties to crows, as well as to horses. Here is a more detailed breakdown of these animals and their associations with the goddess:

Raven and Crow

Ravens and crows are members of the Corvidae family. Since they feed on carrion, Celtic warriors (and people in general) began to associate them with death and foreboding. In addition to being messengers of death, crows and ravens are regarded as messengers from the divine as they straddled the worlds of the living and the dead. Ravens were also symbolic of war and prophecy, feeding on carrion and being attracted to the battlefields. Ravens were found imprinted on ancient Irish coins and armors. Scholars also found the bones of the bird at sacrificial deposit sites along with the ancient Celts.

Throughout history and mythological literature, the raven has always been known as a symbol or omen. Ancient people believed that whenever a raven was around, its calls, behavior, and flight direction could be observed and interpreted as a bad omen. For instance, if someone is about to start a new task and a raven appears, this is a very strong sign that the endeavor will not have a happy ending. Ravens appearing near homes were also symbols of death. However, if a raven flies to a person's right side and calls out, provided that it has white on its wings, this was interpreted as a sign of good luck.

According to academics, the majority of Irish lore surrounding the raven is also adopted by Norse mythology, representing the influence of the Vikings. The Morrigan is not the only Irish deity associated with the raven. Numerous other figures, including warrior king Lugh, are also prominently linked to the bird. The raven is regarded as a personification of death and was thought to be able to travel between the physical world, the otherworld, and the realm of the dead. Their significance as birds of omen perhaps comes from the fact that they're strongly linked to harbingers of doom.

In Irish mythology, the crow has slightly different associations and is thought to represent both good and bad omens. Badb was commonly known as Badb Catha, which translates into battle Crow or battle Badb. She, and the Morrigan, were believed to shapeshift from human form into the form of crows. The third sister, Macha, is also linked to crows. Her name holds several meanings, one of which is Royston crow, which is an old term for the hooded crow.

The Morrigan takes the form of crows often to signal those who will die on the battlefield. Upon the death of Cú Chulainn, The Morrigan transformed into a crow and perched on his shoulder. The hooded crow is different from the other types of crows in that it's not all black. Its chest, tail, head, and wings are black, but everywhere else is grey. This makes them easy to spot from their solid black counterparts. Hooded crows are a very common sight in the Shetland Islands, where mythology states that solid black ravens were believed to signal oncoming starvation. Like ravens, crows were thought to be omens of disaster or death. Spotting a hooded crow in the area was considered a symbol of bad luck in County Clare because it was believed that Badb, band side, fairies, and witches morphed into these birds.

Wolves

Long before they appeared in Ireland, wolves were already well known to the Celts. They were also significant to native Neolithic peoples as well. Archeological evidence suggests that wolves were hunted for their fur, and their teeth and bones were used to make jewelry. These animals were one of the symbols of war, and the carnyx or horn, which was an instrument that sounded during battle, was created in the shape of its head. Images of wolves were often used to decorate the armor of warriors. Appropriately, these animals are closely linked with war and all its accouterments because of their fierce characteristics. The ancient Irish used to call warriors "wolfs' heads." Additionally, Celtic tribes believed the wolf to be their ancestor. All these things made wolves representative of battle, wilderness, and even the dead, which naturally led to automatically associating them with the Morrigan.

Wolves are also known to have strong ties with shapeshifting and outlaws. According to mythology, there was a belief that outlaws shapeshifted into wolves. People used to keep dogs in the belief that it was the domesticated version of wolves. One of the forms that the Morrigan took when she came at Cu Chulain, whose name translates into the hound of Culan, was a wolf. At that point, Cu Chulain was defending Ulster, which is considered an honorable action, making the Morrigan's attack a form of outlawry.

Eels and Snakes

As you can recall, the Morrigan also took the form of an eel when she was fighting against Cu Chulainn. Many people also believed that her son Meche's heart had three snakes or serpents inside it, making it capable of destroying Ireland.

Snakes are seen as a symbol of fertility, regeneration, evil, death, healing, destruction, and water. Badb is highly associated with the themes of venom and serpents, and the name Neiman also means venomous.

Cow

Cows played a necessary and important role in Celtic lifestyle and culture, which led them to be cemented in Celtic mythology. Owning cows or a cow indicated a person's status and wealth, and the cows became a form of currency and monetary exchange. Numerous Irish goddesses were linked to cows in that they took their shape, owned cows that milked abundantly, or had magical cows. As a result, cows came to represent contentment and provision for daily needs. It was an animal central to a clan's survival and prosperity.

The cow represents the side of the Morrigan that provides stability and fertile growth. The Great Queen has appeared in several stories in the form of a cow or interacting with cows. Her first appearance in the form of a cow was in the tale of Tain Bo Cuialgne, where she was depicted as a hornless red heifer. Later on, she also took the form of an older woman milking a cow. This was when she tricked Cu Culain into drinking her milk and blessed her with his words so she could heal. Interestingly, the first time Cu Chulain and the Morrigan met involved the appearance of a cow. He tried to stop her from riding a cow that he thought she had stolen.

Horse

Horses were also another status symbol for Celts, and this led to them (the horses) being revered and well cared for. They have been pivotal in expanding Celtic culture as they were crucial to farming, war, meals (as meat), and transportation once they were domesticated.

The part the horse played in the war led to them becoming associated with victory, endurance, stamina, and faithfulness. The Morrigan is closely tied to war, and her presence on the battlefield determines who would be victorious in battle.

Symbols and Sigils

Any sigil or illustrative symbol that is associated with the Morrigan involves or is based on threes. These symbols are the Triskele, Triquetra, and the Triple Moon.

- **Triskele**

  Also known as the Triskelion, the Triskele has been used by Celtic people since 500BC. It is drawn or carved as three interlocked spirals and has several interpretations as to what it means and its significance to Celtic culture and mythology. The most notable interpretation is that it represents sacred triplicities and represents motion. It also symbolizes the unification or movement through cycles and worlds central to Celtic mythology.

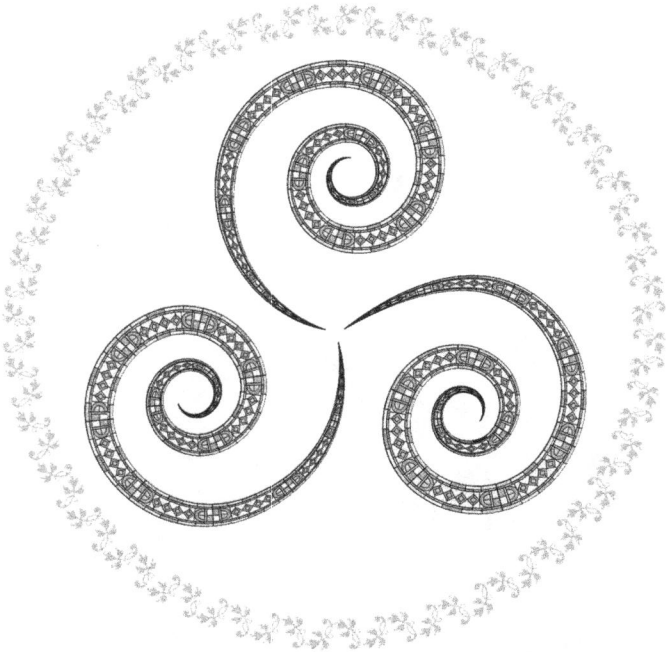

- **Triquetra**

Another symbol based on three's, the Triquetra, is also known as the Trinity Knot and has been adopted by various people and religions. It is illustrated as a single circle intersecting three *vesica pisces* or a triangular figure of three interlaced arcs. It represents the unity and significance of threes in Celtic mythology: earth, sea, and sky. Used since Europe's Bronze Age, it has been carved into many buildings and items as a symbol of protection.

- **Triple Moon**

The Triple Moon symbol is associated with the lunar cycle and the Triple Goddess. When referring to the lunar cycle, the Triple Moon represents the waxing, full, and waning moon. In relation to the Triple Goddess, it represents the Maiden, the Mother, and the Crone. Each phase of the moon is tied to an identity of the Triple Goddess: the waxing moon represents the Maiden, the full moon is the Mother, and the waning moon, symbolizes the Crone. The Triple Moon is a fitting archetype for The Morrigan since she, too, is a triple goddess.

What the Goddess Represents

The Morrigan was renowned for her prophetic abilities and how her presence could turn the tides of war, essentially shaping the rise and fall of clans and peoples. To her worshippers and those who had gained her favor, her presence gave them great courage and renewed resolve. At the sight of a flock of ravens or crows, their enemies would quake, and morale would fall.

As the goddess of war, she was able to predict the fall of warriors on the battlefield: washing the clothes or armor of those fated to die. Her association with battle and bloodshed also ties her closely to life and death. Her three identities each have their own representations and domains of power/control.

While both Badb and Nemain were deities of war and destruction, Badb was also connected to rebirth. Macha was connected to fertility. She governed sacred lands and horses that could grant people wealth and power. Due to the impact horses had on the advancement of Celtic culture. She also represented elite warriors such as the Celtic cavalry, which was widely honored at the time.

As The Great Queen, she was known for bestowing sovereignty or ripping it away from those who were no longer worthy. Her prominence in Celtic mythology is for a good reason, given her power and influence over Celts. Her ability to shapeshift enabled her to take on many different forms and also encouraged her worshippers to adapt to whatever challenges they faced. This flexibility became the dexterity that warriors leveraged on the battlefield to become stronger and fiercer.

The Great Queen's Sacred Numbers

There are three notable numbers connected to The Great Queen. She is associated with three, six, and nine9 for various reasons. Mostly because Celtic mythology is centered on triplicity or the rule of threes, and these numbers are multiples of three. This can also be seen in the sigils we discussed earlier based on threeness.

Like most other gods and goddesses in Celtic mythology, The Morrigan has three sides to her identity and divinity. This sacred number and philosophy inspired riddles and triadic phraseology rooted in the belief. It is quite widespread in Irish mythology since it represents unity and the creation of the different realms, and the process of action becoming a product of thought. Three is considered the first magical number in numerology, and from it, other philosophies have been based on or built upon.

Six represents the completion of two cycles, two times three. It represents equilibrium and ambivalence. In Irish mythology, the sixth moon signifies cleansing and achieving balance. As the triplication of the triple, nine is seen as the most magical number. This means that it is quite ubiquitous in Celtic mythology. It represents completion and newness in the churning of cycles. Since three is already a powerful number, repeating anything three times will increase its potency. This becomes evident in spells, rituals, and prayers.

Colors Associated with the Morrigan

The Morrigan has two main colors associated with her; red and black. Some sources include white and grey as well, but it's not widely accepted. Her colors feature in her stories in different ways - the clothes she wore, animals she transformed into, items she used, etc. Her association with red and black are inferred from the stories and texts she appears in. These colors reveal more about the goddess and her domain/power.

Red

Red is connected and associated with several different concepts, and the more we explore those connections, the more we see their relevance in the depiction of the Morrigan. Most notably, red symbolizes passion and desire. As the goddess of war, she herself was passionate about battles and the battlefield, often playing her part via magic. This inspired worshippers to also be passionate and zealous about battle and war, making them willing to die on the battlefield with little fear. It also inspired her worshippers to be passionate in other areas, including love, family, and kinship.

In line with passion on the battlefield is bloodshed, another symbolism attached to red. This association is quite apt based on The Morrigan's status as the goddess of war. Red represents the spilled blood during the war, whether necessary or needless. In texts, she appears as a red-eared heifer, a red dog, and wears red gowns/cloaks. In descriptions, Badb is also referred to as red-mouthed or The Red Badb.

Black

For a very long time, black has been associated with death and foreboding. Just looking at the color in certain scenarios can elicit feelings of morbidity. This is partly because crows and ravens are also black, closely tied to death. Without fail, people would see crows flock to corpses or piles of corpses. Watching these birds feed on dead flesh, especially of those they likely had strong bonds with, would certainly fill the witnesses with ill feelings.

Black is also associated with wonder, mystery, and the unknown. Covert and occult operations tend to integrate black into their practices. This could be through robes, masks, and candles, among other things. Black exudes power and dominance in a way that is subtle and final. The Morrigan, in her encounter with Cu Chulainn, appeared as a black eel during her first attempt to foil him in battle.

The Triple Goddess and the Phases of the Moon

We briefly mentioned the connection between the Morrigan and her connection to the moon phases. Here we'll go a little more in-depth about the phases that she is associated with. The moon is associated with feminine energy and cycles of death and rebirth, much like the goddess herself.

• The New Moon

The new moon represents the beginning of a new cycle. It is the first crescent of light that's seen after the moon and sun conjoin. This new light is quite potent and is the reason that it's recommended to set your intentions during the new moon. You can start projects or plan how you'll be tackling your goals. The new moon's energy will match and amplify your own energy as you set these intentions. Just as it is the best time for planning, it's also a good time for self-reflection as you determine how to enter this new phase of your life.

• The Dark Moon

In some circles, the dark moon phase is sometimes confused with the new moon. This mostly happens when only the astronomical aspect of the term is discussed. For witches or pagans, the difference is not only visible but also palpable. The dark moon phase comes just before the new moon phase; that's right before you can see any illumination on the moon's surface. At this stage, looking at it, the moon is completely devoid of light and dark. This phase represents rest and observance. You should do most of your shadow and internal work during this time. You can lean into the Morrigan's bountiful wisdom during the dark moon.

• The Waning Moon

As the moon transitions from full to waning, there's less visibility and light. All plans and goals have peaked or have been harvested during the full moon, and as we transition to the waning moon, it's time to pull back. Acknowledge your accomplishments and honor them. Whatever you had set out to do required effort and personal strength. At this point, you'll be exploring the personal growth you've undergone as you pursue your goals. These darker moon phases require gentle insight and to let go of pent-up energy or emotions.

Samhain

Samhain marked the division of the lighter half of the year (summer) and the darker half of the year (winter) and the physical world and the otherworld. It is usually celebrated between October 31 and November 1. When the Irish migrated to America, many of the customs would be integrated into the host country's culture and became the basis for Halloween traditions. Among these is mask or costume-wearing.

Since the barrier between worlds grew thinner during Samhain, malevolent entities could cross over and torment humans. There were several different monsters and creatures that would roam the village during this time. People would usually leave offerings to appease them so that they were not harmed or kidnapped. They would also dress up as animals and monsters for the same reason.

The disappearance of the sun played a part in the emergence of these monsters as well. It was believed that as the sun disappeared into the underworld, it was no longer able to inhibit the monsters' activities in the physical world. For this reason, fire (an element associated with The Morrigan) is a major part of the festival. Elementally fire has been responsible for the advancement of human civilization. It was not only used to keep us warm but was also essential to ward off predators and guide us through the darkness.

All of this makes fire symbolic of enlightenment, power, and energy. Fire is also associated with energy and is one of the four elemental energies in most beliefs/cultures. A wild element can consume what is in its path, and become a dutiful servant, once tamed. Even though it destroys and causes death, it also purifies and can enact births or rebirths, much like the Morrigan.

The earliest form of Samhain was the most important of the quarterly fire festivals. While the harvest was being gathered, family hearths were left to burn out. Once the harvest was done, the people would join the Druid priests to light a communal fire. During this fire lighting ceremony, the sun is honored as the source of all light and fire by being represented by a wheel that lights the communal bonfire. Each person would then take a flame from this fire and use it to relight their hearth.

In the Middle Ages, there was a shift from using communal fires to more individual ones. Families lit these fires on their farms to protect themselves from magical creatures and unwelcome visitors from the spirit realm.

The Cath Maige Tuired

The Morrigan plays a vital role in myths surrounding Samhain. It is about the Battle of the Plain Pillars (The Cath Maige Tuired), a fight that involves the Tuatha Dé Danann and the Fomorians. Coming up on Samhain, she meets Dadga, the chief Irish god, and they have sex before she instructs him to gather all the skilled people. Lying with The Morrigan at Samhain assured his victory as she rallied her people and motivated them to fight. On the night of Samhain, she rode on her chariot, pulled by a one-legged horse, out of the Sidhe of Cruachan.

Chapter 4: Fae or Phantom?

The Morrigan, as we know, was a shape-shifter, and according to mythology, she would rarely appear in the same form twice. Her shape-shifting abilities were as endearing as they were terrifying to the Celts, who were never sure what shape she would appear in next. Her mercurial nature is even echoed in her name, with some historians believing that "mor" may have been derived from an Indo-European word meaning "to connote terror" or "monstrosity." It may even be an amalgamation of the Scandinavian and Old Slavic "mara," which roughly translates to "nightmare," with the latter part of Morrigan, "rigan," translating to "queen." Therefore, the etymology indicates that her name could be translated appropriately as "Phantom Queen," which is an excellent way to summarize all her unique - and fearsome - qualities. The name Morrigan, with its unique spelling and pronunciation, would, of course, later be regurgitated in the Middle Irish period, and many of the attendant myths and stories we are familiar with today are deeply tied to this particular moment in time and the Celtic culture.

Unsurprisingly, as a result of Morrigan's guises, her legacy can be rather polarizing. She is sometimes referred to as the Fae, or Faery Queen, or as a Phantom or Ghost Queen. These archetypes are polar opposites, but this fact is illustrative of her dual nature more than anything. In this chapter, we will explore Morrigan's two main guises and deconstruct their meaning in a historical context. Morrigan's complex nature, in a way, reflects our own struggles with our dark sides. As we all know, both light and dark reside in one being, and most of humanity's spiritual work goes into ensuring that the light is not superseded by the darker forces. The figure of Morrigan bears many lessons for us today, and her spirit, coupled with the mythological stories, remains as relevant as ever.

The Faery Queen

Let's first begin by examining one side of the Morrigan's persona as the Fae, or the Faery Queen. Our contemporary understanding of a faery - or fairies, as we often refer to them these days - is different from their origins. The image of Tinkerbell, while lovely and perhaps mischievous, is not how the Celts' perceived a faery. To begin understanding Morrigan's disguise as the fae, it may help to better understand the context of the mythology of faeries first.

In the Scottish dialect, the word means "from." In the middle ages, it was used to refer to a being from another world or spiritual plane, which makes their applicability to mythical beings or legendary creatures more tangible. The fae is found in one form or the other in the folklore and legends of multiple European countries, although, of course, Morrigan has an elevated, highly regarded place in the literature and spirituality of the Celts. The fae, a supernatural spirit, can sometimes be associated with good, but they can also have a rather amoral approach toward their relationships with others, particularly humans. Within the intricacies of Celtic mythology, the term fae is generally only used when applied to magical creatures who possess a human appearance and are not shy about using their powers. They may also be prone to mischief, and the sneakiness of even the good faeries is not to be underestimated. In pagan religion, the fae is often worshiped much in the same way as the spirits of the dead or other spirits belonging to nature. It is a little wonder, though, that once Christianity became a dominant religious structure and appropriated key elements of paganism to avoid alienating new congregants at the church, fairies would become known as angels, with different terminology applied to those who have fallen out of grace and become demons.

This, in a way, weaves into the Arthurian legends and, in particular, the figure of Morgan le Fay, who many believe to have been one iteration of the Morrigan as the fae. The legend of King Arthur and the stories of figures in his world - Queen Guinevere, Lancelot of the Lake, and Morgan le Fay, among many others - actually have their origins in Celtic mythology. These stories are so much a part of the fabric of the pagan culture that historians have been able to easily identify their Christian counterparts later on.

Interestingly, modern interpretations of the Arthurian legends often go to great lengths to explore the stories against the background of a rapidly evolving Europe. Considering the wider scheme of events, Morgan's character can be depicted as the embattled pagan culture overwhelmed by the newly powerful Christianity. As such, it makes sense to focus for a moment on the most famous iteration of the Morrigan as the fae - or Morgan le Fay.

The Enchantress

In the earliest recorded mentions of Morgan, she is shown as a goddess who is generally a benevolent spirit and is related in some way to King Arthur. In some of the literature, she is listed as his half-sister, but in other stories, the blood relationship seems rather nebulous, even though it is always firmly established that she is Arthur's kin. Because she is often shown to be a goddess in these stories, historians have used this to help solidify the link between Morrigan and her literary equivalent of Morgan le Fay.

In any case, her early appearances in mythology are not exhaustive, and accounts of her and her activities don't provide a list of characteristics for us to follow, nor do they even provide the most basic of biographical sketches. However, we know that this blank slate situation is meant to let us know that she is some kind of magical savior to King Arthur, and her significance in the tales becomes more pronounced over time. With the increasing frequency of her appearances throughout the years, Morgan's ambiguous nature becomes more apparent, and we see her moral compass called into question more and more. Morgan's character transforms significantly over time. Whereas in the earliest stories, she takes on the role of a protector, she develops into an antagonist and is even portrayed rather cynically in the Lancelot-Grail and other mythological cycles. This is not entirely surprising, given that the rise of Christianity would eventually look to distinctly ethereal characters, be they goddesses or fae, with considerable distrust. In the Medieval interpretations of the Arthurian legends, which are arguably the most popular versions of the tale, Morgan is depicted as an unpredictable, dual nature entity that has both the potential for good and evil, although she is more inclined to produce the latter. Sound familiar? Morgan's evolution in these tales can be seen as the ultimate culmination of a wider understanding of Morrigan and the goddess' duality.

Before skipping ahead too much, however, we can uncover a bit more about the earlier iterations of the enchanting Morgan to allow us to better understand the connection with Morrigan.

In Arthurian legend, there is little debate about Morgan's childhood. It is well noted in several myths that she was drawn to the magic arts and wore a Druid stone as a special talisman. She worked hard to pursue knowledge from the nurse who raised her and then from the gods and faeries who populated the hallowed court of Avalon. Her pursuit of the dark arts is a fact that would be used to cast aspersions her way and for later authors or oral traditions to treat her with disdain. Like Morrigan, Morgan was depicted in earlier tales as a triple aspect goddess, each possessing a certain number of attributes. Another reason why Morgan is thought to be derived from the Morrigan is what we know of the former's origin story.

In Welsh mythology, Morgan was thought to share the same mother as Arthur, Modron. Interestingly, Modron and Morgan are both different localized forms of the Morrigan, who is depicted in Welsh tales as also taking the form of a raven or crow - a harbinger of death for our brave heroes. So, it can be assumed that Morgan le Fay is, in fact, the goddess the Morrigan in yet another guise. Many pagans believed that Morgan was in some way related to Morrigan, if not indeed the goddess herself. This further explains why Morgan was depicted in later stories as a harbinger of evil. Again, as Christianity became dominant, especially in Western Europe, the customs and culture of the pagans became subsumed by that religion and reframed within Judeo-Christian values.

The Phantom Queen

Morgan le Fay and the ever-evolving descriptions in Arthurian legends is a good segue to explore the darker version of the goddess Morrigan and what she means for pagans. Morrigan, as she appears in the Arthurian legends, is not always evil, but she is a deeply ambiguous figure who seems to vacillate between her duty to protect King Arthur and to curb her darker tendencies for mayhem and control. In Morrigan's guise as the phantom or ghost queen, most nuance is thrown out the window, and the goddess gives in to evil impulses more fully.

In Celtic mythology, Morrigan's symbol is the raven, the darkest and most mysterious of birds, often associated with death. Given that Morrigan is also referred to as the goddess of war, or even symbolically referred to as the "Warhammer," this makes sense. As a shape-shifting harbinger of battle and calamity, Morrigan had a massive influence on Celtic culture and, more to the point, Irish history. As you have read in previous chapters, Morrigan was actually a trio of powerful and dynamic sisters who struck fear in the hearts of many. Sometimes they went by the names of Badb, Macha, and Memain, but in other recorded mythological histories, Morrigan's sisters have been referred to as the Goddesses Eriu, Banba, and Fodla (or *Fotla*). In a series of important folklore works called the Ulster Cycle, Morrigan appears most frequently as this triad of goddesses. As we have read in previous chapters, the story is significant in Irish folklore and is worth repeating here with added nuances. The Morrigan is at the center of Cuchulainn's battles with the army of Connaught to protect Ulster against Queen Maeve. This infamous battle raged for months on end and is often considered to be one of the more traumatic stretches detailed in the history of the Middle Ages. One night, Cuchulain decided to invoke the right of single combat so that he could single-handedly defeat all the warriors. Morrigan appeared to seduce Cuchulainn in response to this invocation, offering herself to him before the battle. Cuchulainn, ever the focused and dedicated soldier, refused.

This outraged Morrigan, who then used her gift for disguises to transform into an eel, tripping up Cuchulainn as he traveled by fjord. As he tried to fight back against the vengeful goddess, the slippery eel transformed yet again into a wolf, driving away from the nearby cattle and causing them to gang up on Cuchulainn. The soldier, ever nimble, quickly responded with a slingshot, effectively blinding the fearful Morrigan in one eye.

This is perhaps the most famous story involving Morrigan, but it's far from being the only one. Her influence in mythology is so vast, particularly in the local history of Ireland, that it is often said that the country is named after her. The word "Ireland" can be broken down to the Celtic "aariu," meaning to watch over, and "eire," the latter of which means land. Combined together, both words are "Eriu-land," which is Celtic for Ireland. So, Morrigan has always been thought to watch over Ireland - whether this is a benevolent act or one meaning to denote something more fearful is up for grabs.

All in all, based on these myths, it is easy to see when and how the Morrigan's darker nature takes over - even when she seems to think she is helping or trying to care for others. Her anger, pride, or desire for control can consume her and cloud her vision of events in the world she is intricately interwoven in.

The Fae and the Phantom

Morrigan appears in different stories with slightly different characteristics each time. Written literature would suggest that the ways in which her characterization has evolved are deeply tied in with the shifting mores and religious structures of Western Europe. This is partly true. At the same time, it is also easy to surmise, based on the more popular stories outlined in this chapter, that the "good" Morrigan, or fae, is interchangeable with the phantom or ghost queen. At least, her struggles to find a spiritual balance between the two sides battling it out within her soul mirrors humanity's own fight to keep the dark phantoms in check. In this way, the Morrigan's legacy endures in the present for its reliability and the vulnerability inherent to her valiant fight. Even though she is a powerful goddess, what we know about Morrigan makes her feel tangible, which is funny given that she is famous for her mercurial nature.

So, is the Morrigan a fae or a phantom? Perhaps it is not a question of either-or, but rather a query on the ancient fight between good and evil and a rumination on the extent to which a person can contain a multitude of characteristics while fighting hard against their baser instincts.

Historically, Morrigan has been worshiped as the goddess of battle but was also thought of as the goddess of ecstasy, fertility, and magic. That fact alone seems to point to her dueling nature and confirms that her legacy is not a clear-cut one upon which easy moral points can be expressed. A second-wave or even third-wave feminist reading of Morrigan and what she has come to mean to pagans would support this, concluding that she was simply a talented witch or entity who desired in a way that feels more human. Likewise, given her gender, she has been taken to task for her actions more than other mythical figures with equally fearful legacies, with people holding Morrigan to a higher standard. As an independent, intelligent, yet essentially distrustful person, she did not always make the best decisions. She was hurtful, mercurial, and possessed an unknowable will that did not always earn her a great deal of popularity. However, calling her outright evil is unbalanced.

Even in the most flattering portraits, Morrigan is portrayed as a trickster, a sly shape-shifter who confused everyone, even while she intended to help them. This description falls more naturally in line with that of the faerie, or fae - a magical being with a good sense of humor but doesn't mean to hurt others. However, taking this tendency for trickery to its logical extreme could also spell trouble for Morrigan and those that fall foul of her.

A Quest for Balance

Ultimately, Morrigan is a very relatable supernatural being. While it isn't immediately obvious, Morrigan's ongoing journey - be it in her embodiment as Morgan le Fay or the fearsome being that terrorized warriors - represents an attempt to achieve harmony within the self. Some modern stories make Morrigan's spiritual battle rather explicit, but it's implicit in the ancient myths. For contemporary practitioners of Wicca and paganism, Morrigan is an effective vehicle for sharing our anxieties about not feeling grounded, without a sense of balance that would allow the phantom, or the dark side, to settle in and fester.

Ultimately, Morrigan is a captivating contradiction that has held millions in her thrall for centuries. She is simultaneously the spirit of fury and peace, joy and terror, a faery who is also a phantom. In her different iterations throughout time, she has been depicted as the caretaker of kings, a loving sister, mother, and devoted lover. She has also been depicted as an evil woman who does not enjoy being jilted by her lover, one who would mercilessly kill thousands of soldiers and destroy tons of homes simply to assuage some sense of grief. Morrigan is, in turn, healing and the stuff of nightmares - her dual nature consistently frightens and confuses. Of course, many of these labels can also be lobbed against mothers or women in general. The role in protecting society while also continuing the cycle of life through the physical demands of labor means that their power is at once feared and underestimated, same as for the Morrigan herself.

It is strongly advised for modern witches to tap into Morrigan's energy through a series of devotionals. They also need to make a thorough and rigorous study of her legacy and its multiple manifestations. Strengthening your relationship with (and understanding of) Morrigan will profoundly enhance your spiritual practice. While some of the work can be performed in groups, it is also advised to explore the various prayers and rituals on a solitary basis to deepen your understanding of such a complex being who possesses a great deal of wisdom for us all, regardless of gender.

We've mentioned how Morrigan remains a relatable figure, despite her outsized powers. While there are many pagan stories and rituals that deserve close attention, there is something about Morrigan and her ability - or sometimes inability - to harness her powers for good that is worth remembering and holding onto. Our modern world has become increasingly dark as of late, and it has been easy for many to fall prey to their baser instincts or to get wrapped up in feelings of vengeance and betrayal. However, these feelings have their limitations, and no matter how exciting or satisfying it may feel to give in and let the darker impulses take over your better judgment, they are of no use if you're not also acting as a protector toward those you love, or at least maintaining a fair assessment of balance within the universe.

Most religions and spiritual practitioners will say that the universe needs both good and evil in equal measures, and having one overtake the other completely will cause a serious imbalance in the world's fortunes. Therefore, it makes sense to uphold Morrigan - both the fae and the phantom queen- and learn as much as possible from her journey. Focusing on her legacy and becoming mindful of prayer rituals will only deepen the spiritual path and ensure continued enlightenment for all.

Chapter 5: The Morrigan as a Fertility Goddess

The Morrigan is one of the most powerful deities, usually discussed in scholarly literature concerning her association with war and bloodshed. However, she also possesses lesser-known and more intriguing personality traits. It is interesting to note that there are various aspects of her personality that are often discussed in the literature, but the more intriguing fact is that the mythological lore about her nature and attributes tends to change from one text to another. In this chapter, we will strive to better understand Morrigan as a goddess of Fertility and of the land.

Deriving Insights from Her Name

To better understand her role as the goddess of fertility and land, it is intuitive to review the origins of her personality as a goddess. Her name is a great starting point because it offers significant clues to her overall identity and nature as a deity.

There are, in general, three core theories that are commonly associated with her name, "Morrigan," which we have explained in previous chapters. Morrigan may be translated into "Sea Queen," "Great Queen," or "Phantom Queen." However, one of the most superficial translations of her name is "Great Queen" because the word "Mór" in Irish is translated as big or great. At the same time, "rigan" would mean "queen." However, in other texts, "Mór" appears as "Mor," indicating that it may have an absolutely different meaning and origin. "Mor" is very similar to "muir," an old Irish word that usually refers to the sea or any body of water.

The Many Forms of Morrigan

As we already mentioned, you'll find differences in tales about her personality dimensions and godly attributes. In some accounts, she appears as the solitary goddess, while in others, she is referred to as a triple goddess. She is often depicted as a beautiful girl and sometimes a woman of great power. You will also come across her image as a hag sometimes.

The most commonly associated role of Morrigan is the goddess of battle, and she is depicted as taking the shapes of a carrion crow or a raven. The folklore also reports her being the harbinger of death or victory for a soldier or an entire army, and she seems to be a foreteller. However, one of the least promoted and lesser understood attributes of this goddess is linked to the land and fertility, a position for which she is revered. She is also revered as a goddess of land and fertility and is specifically linked to the procreation and fertility of the cattle. Along similar lines, you'll find her impressive powers Center upon sexuality. According to folklore, the chief of the gods was victorious in the war and became acknowledged and turned into a hero because of the sexual energies of Morrigan. During a great battle, she slept with the hero and imbued him with added strength and motivation to ultimately succeed as she slept with him and contributed to his success in the battle. Because of her sexually attractive appearance, she is a renowned symbol of fertility.

Morrigan, Macha and Badb

There are two other goddesses that Morrigan is linked with, Badb and Macha. The three are collectively recognized as the Morrigu. However, according to some scholars, this trio merely defines different forms of the goddess Morrigan herself. This interpretation aligns with the Celtic philosophy because they tend to view gods and goddesses as bearers of potent divine energy. All three goddesses are believed to be the daughters of the mother deity, Ernmas.

Morrigan is seen as a goddess of abundance and fertility because of her place as a goddess of childbirth. She is often prayed to when a new life is starting or someone is opening a new chapter in life because her presence and blessings guarantee that life will eventually prevail and prosper despite destruction and death.

Morrigan and Other Deities

The great Celtic goddess Morrigan is one of the complex deities, and there are several layers to her divine persona. To better explore Morrigan's role as a goddess of fertility, abundance, and land, we must discuss her association with other deities, such as Anand, Danu, Eriu, Banba, and Fotla.

The Story of Anu, Macha, and Badb

According to folklore, the goddess Anand is another name for the goddess Morrigan, and she was one of the three sisters (Badb, Macha). Anand, Badb, and Macha were the divine daughters of goddess Ernmas (widely known as the Irish mother goddess). These three sister goddesses are often collectively called Morrigan or the Morrigans. Sometimes the names of Morrigan or Anand are interchanged with Fea or Nemain, but this varies from one myth to another myth.

To understand this triple goddess's appearance as Morrigan, it is worthwhile noting that this triplet nature is essentially inconsistent and ambiguous. The triplet nature of goddess Morrigan is quite representative of the lunar phases (i.e., waxing, full or waning moons), which is quite interesting to observe.

The goddess Anand, Anann, or Anu is one of the aspects or forms of the powerful Morrigan and is considered the Celtic Irish Maiden goddess. She is the goddess of fertility and earth and is deeply connected to the sea and rivers flowing around the world. On the other hand, goddess Macha (another form of goddess Morrigan) is depicted as the Celtic Irish mother goddess form of Morrigan. Macha is also strongly associated with the aspects of protection, fertility, sovereignty, and land, along with her warrior attributes.

She is generally represented with red hair and has been associated with the element of fire. Macha is commonly linked to horses and crows. Lastly, the Badb is considered to be a Celtic Irish Crone deity (yet another form of the goddess Morrigan). She is also recognized as the Badb Catha, which literally translates to "battle crow." Badb is also strongly connected to death, war, and prophecy. The animals linked with her include ravens and crows. All three goddesses are astoundingly powerful and bring along great divine energy with them.

Essentially the triple goddess appearance of Morrigan is primarily significant because of its relationship to the Celtic importance of the concept of trinity or the concept of threeness. At the same time, Morrigan can be viewed as a goddess who appears alone, which is why the concept of the Morrigan and her interchangeable names is challenging to describe and understand. It is also possible that you view Goddess Morrigan as appearing alone, and on rare occasions, her name is interestingly interchangeable with Badb.

Morrigan and Danu

No one has ever had the same ethereal status as the goddess Morrigan does among all the Celtic gods and goddesses. A core trait that runs through both Danu and Morrigan, linking them together, is their association with fertility and rivers.

Looking back at the mythological history closely, we have it established that the powerful deity Morrigan belonged to the divine tribe of Tuatha De Danann, who happened to be the people of great Goddess Danu. According to popular lore, Tuatha De Danann was the mythical tribe of divine beings who established a settlement in the Irish land, and this was before the ancestors of modern Gaels (i.e., the Milesians) arrived. Historically and mythologically, this tribe was of the descendants of the deity Danu, and the powerful Dagda (who was the son of Danu) happened to be the leader of the Tuatha De Dananns. This tribe consisted of gods, goddesses, and heroes who possessed great skills in science, magic, art, and poetry.

Danu has been respected and worshiped as the mother goddess, but there is a lot of mystery surrounding her origin. However, Danu happened to be the goddess of power, sovereignty, and being. Being a mother goddess, it was believed that several gods suckled through her to receive wisdom. Danu has been linked to various Celtic gods and goddesses outside and within Ireland. According to the neopagan traditions, it is interesting to observe that Danu was revered as one of the triple goddesses and is linked with the Morrigan. The name "Anu or Annan" and Danu are strikingly similar, and because of this, some pagan believers thought that great mother Danu was just one of many faces of the goddess Morrigan.

Goddesses Eriu, Banba, and Fodla

According to the mythological texts, the Morringa triplet is called the sisters of the triplet of land goddesses, Banba, Eriu, and Fodla. When you peruse the Irish mythological texts, Eriu (sometimes called Eire) is recognized as the daughter of Ernmas and Delbaeth of Tuatha De Danann.

Eriu is considered to be the goddess of entire Ireland and is also believed to be considered a personification. While Banba (also called Banbha) is revered as a patron deity of Ireland. She married the grandson of Dagda (Mac Cuill) and was one of the most important deities in Irish tradition. According to folklore (a variation of the Cessair legend), Banbha was the first deity who came to the Irish lands before the flood. When Milesians journeyed through Irish lands, they were hosted by met faery magic troops and the goddess Banba as hosts. It was written that this even took place. It was believed to have happened on the Mountain of Senna (Mes). Banba has been regarded as the earth goddess for this reason as well. However, she was also renowned as the goddess of war and fertility (just like the Morrigan). The third goddess,

Fodla, was also known by the names of Fotla, Fodla, Fodhla, or Fola and was amongst Ireland's giantesses.

These three sisters asked the Milesians to grant their names to the country, and their wish was honored. Although Eriu became the famous name, Fodla and Banba are also used to refer to Ireland in poetic texts. According to some historians, the divine goddesses linked with Banbha, Eire, and Fodla were the three Morrigan (Macha, Badb, and Morrigan).

Goddess of Fertility, Abundance, and Land

Looking through the texts of Celtic mythology, Morrighan is mostly described as the dark goddess of war or death. However, now that we have discussed so many other aspects of goddess Morrigan, it is quite evident that there is so much more to learn about her. As we now understand, Morrighan is also the goddess responsible for the sovereignty of the land. So, she also has the status of a protector added to her many-faceted authorities. Her association with animals and ability to shape-shift into any number of them further gives credence to her position as Goddess Morrighan is often represented by the animal forms of a raven or a crow. However, on some occasions, particularly in the Ulster cycle stories, Morrigan was represented by a wolf and a cow. These animal depictions of Morrighan suggest that she is also a goddess of land and fertility.

The goddess Morrigan is linked with animals (livestock or cattle in particular) and the fertility of the land. Even though the general and popular stories about Morrigan depict her as a dark, powerful, and sinister goddess and more folklore still attributes her authority over the domain of imposing female sexuality, we have already discussed the imposing sexuality of goddess Morrigan, and it was because of this that she had many earthly and fertile attributes as well. In fact, some historians even argue that the role of "omen bearer during battles" may not be the dominant or defining role of the goddess Morrigan because many of her activities and interests have had a tutelary aspect. She was the caretaker of the land, society, and livestock. These are the roles that require a nurturing spirit and a certain degree of earthliness. One of her dominant attributes or powers was the power of shape-shifting, and it can be interpreted as an overt expression showing her affinity with the entire living universe.

The Protector of the People's Interests

An interesting record entitled Cath Maige Tuired' (The Battle of Magh Tuireadh) is a dual saga text of the Mythological Cycle of Mythology in Ireland. This text refers to the two battles of Connacht, the details of which have been discussed in earlier chapters (the first battle happened in the Conmhaicne Cuile Tuireadh territory, and the second one took place near the Lough Arrow in the County Sligo). According to the Cath Maige Tuired, Morrigan is a protector goddess. To some, it may seem rather surprising to recognize the powerful goddess Morrigan as the protector goddess who safeguards the interests of her people. Not merely that, but in addition to the war, she was also strongly associated with fertility.

So, there is a lot of evidence that the goddess Morrigan has been mainly concerned with the prosperity of her land, its animal life, fertility, and keeping it and her chosen clan secure from all external forces and spiritual attacks. If you analyze this further, within the historical context, one prominent aspect of battles and wars has always been the security and protection of the people of that land against external forces or aggression. In the Celtic culture, it was quite common for women to partake in wars without losing their feminine attributes, and they were even allowed to fill leadership roles. They took their place alongside their men and were as fierce if not more so than them. So, it is quite easy to visualize how the folklore around Morrigan's involvement in the warfare is recorded goes because it has to be a protective act primarily as a defense for her people and land, as fiercely as any mother who is protecting her offspring.

Therefore, in this manner, the goddess Morrigan is illustrated as what seems to be a manifestation of sovereignty and earth goddess. This solidifies there a role of Morrigan as a guardian goddess that protects terrorism and people. She is seen to be this because she is actively involved in ensuring the political or military solidarity of the land by acting as a sovereign goddess (instead of merely a goddess of war).

Morrigan as a Mother Deity

This is another nurturing attribute that has been associated with Morrigan, but in order to visualize her in this role, it is important to challenge the stereotypical notions about a mother. An unhealthy and unrealistic preconception about "mothers" is that they must give themselves completely to the children, but this is not a reasonable, sane proposition. Motherhood is often associated with balance. A mother can be stern and authoritative at times, but a mother always loves her children, and the sternness that comes from being a mother is always from a protective and loving standpoint. Furthermore, she is represented as a powerful divine woman who directs her creative and nurturing energies toward her children or herself. Morrigan is depicted as the one who can give life or take it away as well.

Association with Water Bodies

In addition to the association between Morrigan and the land, she is also connected with water bodies, such as the rivers and sea. Many Celtic mother figures have ties to water, with many of the goddesses in Celtic culture connected to rivers. Danu is the same. The motherly goddess embodies the qualities of water, flowing with depth and purpose. This connection with water is further extrapolated to develop a strong connection to healing and fertility. Water gives birth to new growth, turning dry land into new life.

Dagda and Morrigan were mates. And where did they come together? On a river, of course. When Dagda was in battle, he had to cross a river. Morrigan took the form of an eel and offered her love to Dagda. It is only fitting that they came together on the flowing water, and this theme continued through Morrigan's life— she summoned blood-like magical rain to fight off her enemies, turned a foe into a pool of water, and interacted with water in numerous other ways to aid and rebuff.

Association with the Cattle

Another indication of Morrigan's status as the goddess of land is because of depictions of her as cattle in the mythology. As we mentioned earlier, Morrighan also appeared as a wolf and cow as well. In fact, a cow is a form that she took quite often. She is also associated with cattle and therefore has a strong link with fertility and land as well. Historically, the cattle were usually linked with different goddesses of rivers, as their milk was similar to the life-enriching waters which fertilized the lands. As has been said, the status and wealth of Celtic society was, without a doubt, measured by the quantity of sheep, cattle, and other livestock, as these were strong indicators of wealth and not merely thought of as a food source.

Morrighan was also linked with horses, and therefore, once again, it establishes her connection with the concepts of fertility and land. This is because horses were also an indicator of wealth and abundance, being as valuable as other livestock, as they were used for travel, agriculture, and even during wars. Moreover, since horses are solar animals, they are strongly associated with fertility.

Connecting to Morrigan as a Fertility Goddess

The goddess Morrigan is a powerful deity and can be called upon for support and blessings during difficult times. The primary purpose can be anything from overcoming a real-life battle or fertility or abundance in life. One of the best and simplest ways to connect with goddess Morrigan is through gaining mythological and symbolic knowledge about her. There are various rituals and invocations that you can perform to develop a deeper connection with the Morrigan (we will only be sharing the spells briefly because these will be discussed in greater detail in the next few chapters).

Below is just one of the invocations to the goddess Morrigan. With this invocation, you can perform a simple ritual that will require a black-colored cauldron (filled with water). Add a large-sized silver coin that will be a symbolic representation of the moon because Morrigan is also revered as the moon goddess. You can place a picture of the goddess Morrigan in front of you and begin invoking her.

> *"Mother Morrigan of life and death*
> *I call you for guidance and strength*
> *Help me to speak with you on my breath*

And fight my battles wisely at length

Help me to understand the situation at hand

And make the correct decisions to defend my land

Grant me wisdom in all that I do

I call on you now to see me through"

You should look intently into the cauldron once you have finished reciting the invocation with full dedication and focus. Focus on the silver coin and recall that Morrigan is the powerful moon goddess. You should try to focus on using your third eye and concentrate on listening to any possible message that the goddess Morrigan may have for you at that moment. Once you have finished the whole ritual, do not forget to ground yourself and close the circle. Another helpful thing is to put some bay leaves under your pillow before going to sleep that night because the goddess may visit you while you're asleep or send you messages in your dreams. These prophetic dreams of divination are intensified because of the bay leaves.

Chapter 6: Building an Altar for the Morrigan

For followers of the Morrigan, having an altar in your home is special and indicative of true homage to honoring the Celtic goddess. And that you have gone to the trouble of making it yourself and imbuing it with your unique energy and emotion makes it even more exceptional. While many people think that the purpose of the altar is to be solely a place of prayer and a place where they can celebrate Morrigan, the real purpose of the altar is to give you focus.

To make the most of your Morrigan practices, you need to be focused, and the altar is what will help you to develop that focus. For instance, if you want to make prayer, your mental acuity should be on studious concentration on the divine powers of Morrigan and contemplating how you can seek her help in your affairs. If you are trying to use magick for your own betterment or for the betterment of a friend or family, you are going to be focusing on your energy and the energy of Morrigan. If you are trying to seek guidance and enlightenment, then your focus will be on trying to connect with the spiritual guides, Morrigan, and your higher self to achieve this knowledge and wisdom.

In all these practices and others, the point of the entire process is to somehow develop a specific focus on the task at hand. You can use a range of instruments to do this, but the altar is easily the best choice.

When you are trying to achieve these goals, remember that we all operate in different ways and at different paces. For some people being indoors in a confined space is the best way to focus their mind, while for others, it is more efficient to be outdoors in an open space and closer to nature. Some prefer the early morning for their meditation, while others prefer to meditate late at night. We all have our own preferences, and different things work for different people. The altar is meant to give you a place where you can enhance your abilities in whatever you are doing, so it makes sense to customize and modify it to what works for you. Moreover, there is no hard and fast rule about what an altar can or cannot include, and it is really up to you to decide what you want to do with it.

There are a few issues to be considered when you build your altar. The Morrigan has distinct features and characteristics that make her who she is. Certain things are more conducive to Morrigan, and using them works better when connecting to her spirit, getting her attention, and attracting her energy. For instance, you could use any kind of cloth for your altar in any color, but traditional black and red work best because these are symbolic colors to her and will be more effective. Some people may find that blue works well for their intentions, as she is also connected to water along with her other influences. When you are just starting out, it is better to stick to tradition and try to find your place within that tradition. If you don't like black, you can choose red as both colors are excellent for a Morrigan altar.

This approach will make it much easier to put an altar together in terms of getting the right resources and help you create something that looks good and serves its purpose well.

In the most basic form, an altar can simply be a picture on a wall or a clean table in a space where there will be no distractions. Altars can be large, elaborate constructions of hard-to-find objects and art masterpieces in the most complex form. The average home altar will be something in between these two extremes. Also, it will be an altar that will serve a variety of purposes unless you want to build specialized altars for different activities.

Location

Where will you place your altar?

For most people, the best place is in their bedroom. It is a confined, intimate space where they can access the altar whenever they please without the worry of having distractions nearby or disturbing others while they use it. If you live in shared accommodation and you don't want to make others uncomfortable or if you just don't have the space in any other part of the house, your room is a great place to start. If you are making an altar for the entire family or something you would like to share with everyone else in your accommodation, consider placing it in the living room or in any common area where everyone has easy access to it.

It's important to note that an altar created specifically for you to use will be slightly different from an altar intended to be shared. So even if you have a family altar in the living room, it is still a good idea to have a personal one in your room or somewhere private where you can focus on yourself.

With the room decided, the next thing to consider is where to put your altar. Generally, people don't have a lot of free space in their rooms, so the altar just goes wherever it can be placed comfortably. If you are building the room from scratch or are willing to make major rearrangements to accommodate an altar, you should look into geomancy to get the best place in your room. Geomancy is a divination method based on the position of objects.

There are a few main principles of geomancy that you should consider if you are fortunate enough to be building your room and altar from scratch.

- North is the direction of wisdom.
- East is the direction of creativity and new beginnings.
- South is the direction of action.
- West is the direction of emotion and the subconscious mind.
- Everything to your right is considered to be "above" and is connected to god, matter, and manifestation in a physical sense.
- Everything to your left is considered to be "below" and is connected to the goddess, to the spirit, and to cleansing.

With these principles in mind, you can choose a location for the room depending on what you want to work on and what you want to manifest in your life. For beginners, it is advised that you start with the north since knowledge and wisdom are the foundation of everything else. Moreover, the north also incorporates aspects of all the other directions in healthy proportions. Going towards any other direction right from the get-go can end up with you getting results that lean too heavily in that particular area and create imbalances in other areas.

The other thing to know is that the altar itself can also be interpreted according to the rules of geomancy.

Some of the most important rules to keep in mind include:

- The right side of the altar is seen as the "warm" part. It is associated with God, the sun, physical energy, and the elements of air and fire.
- The left side is the "cool" side. It is associated with the goddess, the moon and stars, spiritual energy and magic, and the physical elements of water and earth.
- The center of the altar is associated with the spirit, who is a part of both the god and the goddess.

Preparing the Space

With your location decided, you need to prepare the area before installing your altar. Since the altar is all about your energy, helping you manage your energy, and helping you to focus your energy, you want the space to be clean of any kind of negative energy. Energy is constantly interacting with tangible and intangible things around it, so it is very sensitive to the things that are in that space. The best strategy to start building your altar is to do an energy cleanse of the space and then directly move into the build. Have your accessories, tools, and required materials ready beforehand. As soon as you have finished the cleansing, start making the altar and complete it in one go.

Altar Table

The altar table is any surface on which you make your altar. This doesn't have to be a table. It can be any kind of flat surface on which you can place all your altar accessories. Historically, altars were made outside the house in the garden or in a central place in the village neighborhood so the whole community could have access to it any time they needed to use it. In this case, the altar was made on the ground or on a log, or a large rock. The aim was to keep the altar as close to the ground as possible and hence connected to Mother Earth.

With indoor altars, this can be difficult to do, so it's best to use a table. As the aim is to connect to mother earth, is it preferable to use a table made of natural material such as wood or marble. At the very least, you should have a table with natural materials for the top, such as wood, and other materials such as steel or artificial materials used for the legs.

If you are tight on space, you can have a make-shift altar on an existing piece of furniture. You could make an altar on a small part of your work table, or you could use an empty bookshelf as the table or even have it on your dresser. Some people even add a jar of soil to the altar table in an effort to revive the connection with Mother Nature, though this is a less common practice.

Cloth

Having an altar cloth is the central item of your altar and needs to be carefully chosen or crafted. In ancient times all cloth was hand-made and was considered a luxury to own. Placing this on the altar was a form of respect for the space. Today, cloth has become a lot more affordable. It is still recommended that you use a natural kind of cloth rather than a modern synthetic material.

There are various ways you can customize the cloth and personalize it. For instance, you could get a simple piece of cloth and fashion some embroidery on it yourself. Another idea you could use if sewing is not your strong point is to paint it with signs and symbols that resonate with your philosophy. You could even specially cut and design the cloth to meet your specific taste and needs.

If you have an extraordinary kind of cloth, maybe an heirloom or something else that is very close to you, use that. The purpose of personalization is to create a connection between yourself and the items of the altar, in this case, the cloth. Working with the material during the customization phase or using something close to you helps create a unique bond with your altar.

Candles

Candles are always a crucial part of an altar, and, in this instance, they represent the element of fire. Some people prefer wax candles, while others choose oil lamps, but the idea is to have some form of fire and light on the altar. You can also combine this with the air element by having a scented candle. This way, you won't need to have separate incense.

Candles themselves have their own energy, and when you light candles on an altar, you increase the overall energy level. You also create energy in the form of the flame, which adds energy to the area and other items you use. There is no limit to how many candles you can have. Get them in the colors you most like, with the fragrances that you are comfortable with. Scented candles can be quite strongly aromatic, so just use a couple first and then take it from there.

Colors

The altar is decorated with many objects, but you'll often notice that they all have a similar color, or there is a dominant color theme throughout all the decorations. There is a range of colors that can be used for the Morrigan altar, and it depends on what colors the goddess likes and what works for you. The favorite color of Morrigan and the most prominent color on altars that are dedicated to her is red.

Whether that is the color of the cloth you use or the color of the candles you light, you'll find red on many Morrigan altars. Other colors that you can use include black, brown, dark blue, purple, green, and white.

If you are using stones to decorate your altar, then also look into stones of these colors, preferably natural stones, to keep the earth connection strong. Some stones can get extremely expensive, such as blue emeralds, so there is no harm in using much cheaper alternatives that have the same color but not the price tag.

Gems and Crystals

Speaking of stones, several stones are associated with Morrigan and can be used on her altar. The most common are jet, amethyst, obsidian, garnet, clear quartz, and emerald.

Some of these stones can be found in different colors as well. For instance, if you can't find clear quartz, get rose quartz, as that will work. All these stones have traits and properties attributed to them. For instance, clear quartz is a preferred stone because it encompasses the energy of all the other stones, it covers all the aspects of Morrigan, and it is a stone that can help to amplify your own energy as well. On its own, it is a stone with neutral energy, and it works well with other stones.

Then there are stones that serve a very specific purpose. For example, obsidian is a semi-precious stone used exclusively for protection and removing negative energy. It is a great stone to use to protect yourself in both the physical and the spiritual realms, and its deep connection with the earth helps in grounding your altar better than any other object could. This is the only stone to choose for people who need help with grounding. Other stones, such as clear quartz, can be substituted by a different type of stone, but none have the same power as obsidian.

Incense

Incense is equally important to have on your altar because it represents the element of air. Any kind of incense can be used, whether it be oil, stick, powder, or any other form. You may have to hold the incense for some rituals, so it is best to get an incense type that can easily be held in your hands.

Some incense can be unique, but it comes with its challenges. For example, powdered incense is meant to be burnt over coal. While this is a great addition to the altar, it will not be the best solution for an indoor altar, especially one in a closed room. Sticks and oils work best for indoor use.

You can also use smudge sticks. These are essentially just dried herbs that have been tied together to create a bunch that you can burn. These are great for cleansing spaces, but they can be hard to handle as they often have sparks and leave a trail of ash as you walk around with them, so be careful with these.

There are also several non-combustible kinds of incense that you can use if you are particularly sensitive to smoke or in an environment where it isn't possible to have an open flame. Electric incense machines are available, and they work with replaceable pods of aroma.

You can use an herb or plant for incense in extreme situations. If you get a fresh rose, some lavender, or some sage, these are appropriate because of their decorative value and fragrance. Simply heating these plants over a candle or placing them close to a fireplace will intensify their aroma and brighten up the entire space.

When placing your incense, keep it to the right of your altar.

Herbs, Plants, and Fruit

Different herbs, plants, and fruit are used as a decoration and an offering on the altar. Some of the best things to use in this regard include:

Traditional Oats – You can use these raw and place them in a bowl on the altar. Be sure to not use instant oats; the old-fashioned oats are the ones to get.

Apples – A favorite snack of the goddess and fruit that was extremely popular in a pagan culture. Apples are a sign of vitality and life and wonderful presents for the goddess.

Juniper Berries – Before these berries were made popular for the alcohol that is made from them, they were known as an integral part of pagan culture, especially when it came to the Morrigan. These berries were associated with protection and psychic abilities. They help the user to achieve higher states of consciousness during divination and are an important part of some protection rituals.

Mugwort – This common plant can be used in its plant form as a decoration, or you can make mugwort tea from the dried version of the plant and use this as an offering on the altar. It is associated with fertility and works extremely well on the altar of Morrigan.

Oak – This is one of the most significant trees in the pagan culture, and it is associated with knowledge, wisdom, magick, and wellbeing. The most common practice is to use the acorn from the oak tree. Traditionally, people wrote or drew an image of what they desired onto the acorn and placed it on the altar. It is a way of showing the goddess what you desire and giving her the responsibility of making it a reality in your life.

Chapter 7: Badb: Learn the Art of Divination and Prophecy

As you know, the Morrigan takes on numerous roles and manifests in different forms. People choose to connect with the goddess for many reasons. For instance, some people may be searching for guidance regarding their personal battles, while others may need to garner the strength to break cycles and let go of things that no longer serve them. However, in this chapter, the main focus will be connecting with the Morrigan in the form of Badb, or the goddess of prophecy.

Besides her shapeshifting abilities, the Morrigan is most popularly known for her activities of divination and prophecy. As you may recall, most of her mythology, if not all, incorporates omens and prophecies. Her most renowned prophecy was the one she made after The Second Battle of Moytura, predicting both positive and negative outcomes of the battle. In one of her several manifestations, particularly as Macha, she visualized the bloodshed and destruction that would take place as a result of the Cattle Raid of Cooley. The Badb even showed up in one of Queen Maeve's dreams as a phantom to warn her about the death of her son. She also appeared to Cú Chulainn as a woman washing blood off some armor before he went to battle, signaling that his end was near. There's a very strong link between prophetic abilities and speech and the Morrigan.

Connecting with the Badb as the goddess of prophecy is something that many people struggle to do. What they don't necessarily realize is that there are no clear-cut steps as to how this can be done. How a person connects with their deity, regardless of their role, depends on each individual, as well as the level of connection that they want. Building a relationship with the Morrigan is not a subject to be taken lightly or frivolously.

There are endless benefits to forging this type of connection with a deity. However, this endeavor comes with incredible responsibilities. To build this type of relationship, you must reshape some aspects of your life and make an effort and space to meet her demands. While this change can be very challenging, the Morrigan will also bring out qualities that you never knew you had. Working with the Morrigan gives you strength and heightens your intuitive abilities. When she's in your life, she will protect you and your children as if you were her own.

To build a relationship with the Morrigan, you need to make space for her both in your devotional practices and in your life. You need to indulge in activities that will facilitate your interactions with her and allow you to listen to her. Initially, you may feel uneasy with the changes you're making. However, when you find a spiritual practice that you feel comfortable working with, you'll profit from the experience on a more intimate level. Your practice should be personal and tailored to your needs. It should signify your desire to work with the goddess. The more consistent and persistent you are, the more committed you'll become.

When attempting to work with a deity, the most obvious place to start your journey is to research and study your deity as much as you can. Fortunately, after reading the previous chapters, you now know about the different guises and facets of the goddess. You also know about her roles in Celtic mythology and tales, which gives you insight into her character and behavior. After learning all about the deity you wish to work with, it's important that you build them an altar representing them and their heritage, which we covered in the last chapter. After this, you need to dabble in practices that bring you closer to the deity, ease your connection with them, partake in rituals, and provide offerings for your deity (more on that later).

This chapter is all about the various divination practices that call on the power of guidance, assistance, and foresight of the Morrigan. After all, there's no better way to work with Badb, the deity of prophecy and divination, than by learning as much as you can about her. This chapter will learn all about Celtic runes, black mirrors, and visualization techniques. You'll also learn how to use an oracle or tarot cards to work with the Morrigan.

Celtic Runes

Explanations and meanings of the Celtic Runes can differ depending on the source you're using. However, fundamentally speaking, the Germans of the medieval era used Rune, which is a type of font, to write scriptures on stones. The idea behind Rune is to convey mystical or hidden information. The word *Rune* is derived from a Norse term that means *secret* or *something hidden.* This is why only a few people knew the meaning of the signs used, and this was kept secret from the masses. While they were highly exclusive in honor of magic and mystical practices, Runes were eventually translated from German to modern English, making them more widespread and accessible.

People started using Runes less and less after the introduction and the accessibility of the Roman alphabet. Even though their use has significantly declined, they still remain very popular because of the mystery surrounding them and the divine, mystical energy they possess.

There is much controversy and inaccuracy regarding the origin of the Celtic Runes. However, one fact we are certain about is that the Runes were essentially linked to divinity and the higher powers. Scholars have found Celtic Runes on several objects, including spears, Viking ships, cups, and stones. They were most commonly found carved on pebbles.

Since the Celtic Runes are very powerful, they are still commonly used among pagans. Besides being used for predictive purposes, which is why we recommend incorporating them into your Badb devotional practices, they also have plenty of positive influence to offer. For instance, many people use Celtic Runes to revitalize their hope, reinforce their power, and attract abundance and good fortune into their lives.

Celtic Runes are also especially powerful when it comes to protection. You can engrave them into a ring or the pendant of a necklace and keep it with you at all times. This can help guard you against evil forces and bring different blessings into your life. Many people also like to use Runes to take control of their future. With the guidance they receive from the Runes, they are able to make anything they want out of their future. Runic readings can be conducted by focusing on their characters. The main aim is to allow the runes to guide your subconscious to its predictions. To complete the reading, the reader should spread out all the runes randomly in front of them. If they wish, they can ask specific questions to which they can receive guidance and answers through the Runes. You can seek out advice on whichever issue you desire. In turn, you'll get numerous readings and predictions. There's a mystery to the Celtic Runes, especially because their responses can take various forms. However, once you understand their powers, you can use them to enrich your life experience and work with the Badb.

Black Mirrors

Scrying or foretelling the future using a black mirror has some rules and stipulations that must be adhered to before you begin this art. To begin with, you need to have an oval or round-shaped mirror. You need to avoid using square-shaped ones. Many people believe that vintage or hand-crafted mirrors bring about the best results because of the very personal energy that they embody. Creating a black mirror is a very easy and inexpensive process. All you need is a photo frame you no longer want, and a black spray can. The paint should be matte rather than glossy. Make sure you clean both sides of the glass really well and ensure that they're entirely dry. Use the can to lightly spray one side of the glass, ensuring that you hold the spray around 20 inches (50 cm) away from the glass. Add a few more coats, allowing the paint to dry in between. After the paint has dried completely and nothing is visible through the glass, put it back into the frame. The unpainted side should be facing toward you. The glass should be clean and smudge-free to avoid distractions during the scrying process. The mirror should be dedicated strictly for scrying purposes. No one should look into the mirror unless they intend to participate in the scrying ritual.

The following is a step-by-step guide to demonstrate how you can use a black mirror for divination:

1. Position the mirror in a direction or at an angle to reflect almost nothing. This isn't always easy to do, but you should give it your best shot. If you want, you can position it on your altar.

2. **Optional:** you can skip this step if you want. However, you may cast a circle right in front of your mirror, which allows you to see the mirror clearly from its center. Perform a protection ritual and invocations if you want to incorporate them as part of your practice.

3. Light two candles, placing each of them on either side of your mirror. Your candles can be whichever color you desire, as long as they're not distracting. This is why it would be smart to opt for dull-colored candles or even tea lights. The most important thing is that you position them correctly, ensuring that the mirror is entirely illuminated without reflecting the candles.

4. **Optional:** many people find burning incense in front of the black mirror to be particularly beneficial. Use a slow-burning type on a piece of coal that allows the smoke to clarify the mirror. You can repeat this process as many times as you like throughout the ritual. Incense is also known to help to cleanse the space and raise one's

vibrations and intuition.

5. Meditate for as long as it takes you to get into, and maintain, a very relaxed state. If you can't stay deeply relaxed, we recommend that you work on your meditation skills before you attempt scrying.

Here's how you can use a black mirror for scrying:

1. Glare at the mirror with a *soft focus*. This means that you need to work on focusing your vision slightly behind the mirror. Your vision of the mirror should be out of focus and blurred. The entire mirror should be in view, but your pupils should be focused someplace about 1 or 2 inches away from the mirror.

2. Maintain this view for a few minutes. You don't need to stare - you can blink normally.

3. The longer you maintain this view, the foggier, hazier, grayish, or cloudier your mirror will become. At this point, your scrying experience has begun. This state isn't always easy to achieve. If you're having trouble, you may need to work on seeing things with a soft focus before returning to your scrying ritual.

4. Keep maintaining this soft-focus view even when the mirror fully fogs over. Maintain an open and clear mind. Thoughts and visions may float into your mind. Allow them to develop at their own pace and embrace the experience. These are the answers or the results that you're searching for.

It is possible that this ritual may not really work for you on your first try. However, the more you practice it, the more helpful your thoughts and visions will become. Your success in scrying using a black mirror depends on how in-tune you are with your subconscious, which is something that the following methods can also help achieve.

Visualization

Visualization is an invaluable tool when it comes to enhancing one's intuition. The process puts one's senses, mind, and imagination to full use, allowing the mind to formulate images of its own to help in divination. We already visualize things all the time. However, enhancing your visualization abilities to allow you to see things more vividly is important when it comes to prophesy and divination.

Here are some methods that you can experiment with:

1. Close your eyes and think of any color. Observe all the thoughts that flow in. What is the first thing that comes to your mind? Is it a thought about the word itself or something that you associate with the color? Write down notes and repeat the process with different colors. Then, visualize the words of the colors (in their colors). Think of as many objects as you can that are in that color. You should use this method before conducting rituals or spells.

2. Close your eyes and think about all the items you can find in your pantry. Notice the details about every food item that comes into your mind. After practicing this method a few times, notice if there's anything different about how you visualize these items. Perhaps, instead of just visualizing an apple, you now visualize biting into that apple and even hearing the sound that it makes.

3. Working on your imagination can also help boost your visualization. You can use an online random word generator to generate three words. Write the results on a piece of paper and try to come up with one sentence that incorporates all three words. You can also use a random word generator for animals. Visualize whichever animal comes up. Think about what it looks like, what it does, where it lives, etc. Try to imagine it in odd colors or in weird accessories. Continue making the image of the animal as silly as you can.

Oracle and Tarot Cards

Tarot cards are very insightful and helpful divination tools. The best thing about oracle and tarot cards is that they can be learned and used by anyone. You may want to start with oracle decks if you're a beginner since they're much easier to read.

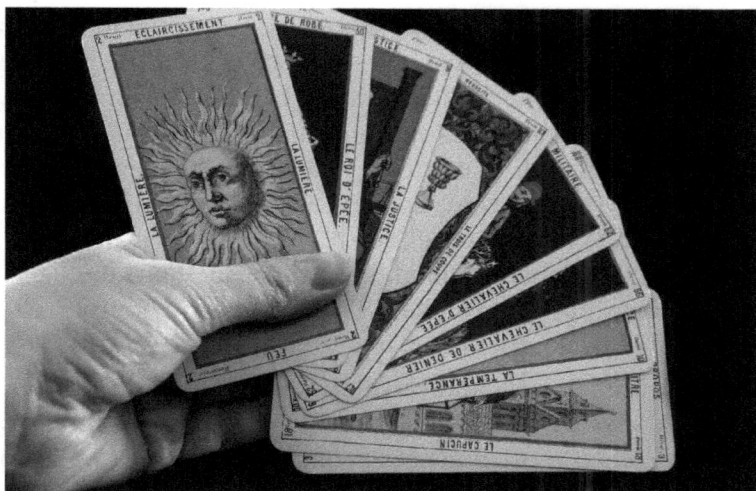

Besides being among the most popular divination tools, oracle and tarot cards can be used to help you work with the deities. The most important step toward incorporating them into your worshiping practice is selecting cards that represent the deity you want to work with.

The Morrigan is typically represented through the following cards:

- **Death** - Major Arcana
- **The Chariot** - Major Arcana
- **Nine of Pentacles** - Minor Arcana
- **Queen of Swords** - Court Card

To incorporate them into your practice, you can:

1. Use them as altar decor.

   You can frame them and place them on the altar.

2. Use them for Meditation and Journeying.

   Using cards can prove to be helpful when you are trying to get into a meditative state. To do that, you need to place your chosen card against the mirror at eye level. You can play music if you want (ideally, it should be associated with your deity. For instance, you can look up Samhain music for the Morrigan). Place two candles on your altar - one on each side of your card. Their colors should represent your deity (red, white, or black for the Morrigan). Turn the lights off and sit in front of your card. You should be comfortable and ready to meditate. Close your eyes and take three deep breaths. Open your eyes and focus on the card. You can even try to imagine yourself journeying into the card. Relax completely and interact with your deity. Ask about anything you want. You can receive your answers verbally or in the form of symbols. When you feel ready, bring yourself back to the present moment and thank the Morrigan. Turn the lights on and blow out the candles. Don't forget to journal all the details of your experience.

Note: Please keep in mind that you shouldn't light up candles during meditative or visualization practices if you're not going to be highly alert. Since most practices require the use of candles, you can ask someone you trust to stay around in case something happens.

Chapter 8: Macha: Spells for Protection and Sovereignty

The Morrigan is intricately associated with fate and war. She is renowned for foretelling death, doom, or victory in a battle. The goddess also encourages the warriors to be fearless and brave, and she can strike fear into the enemy. However, this can also be possible through performing spells for protection and sovereignty. This chapter discusses the rituals you can perform to call Macha for guidance and protection. While various spells are used, you can do your rituals and make sure you have an appropriate altar.

Macha: Sun Goddess

Macha is the sun goddess. When we think of the sun, we have thoughts of summer, new life, happiness, love, and power. While the sun is the light, it is also a destroyer and can engulf everything in its path. Macha is both a protector and a bringer of destruction.

Altar Space

First and foremost, you should set up an appropriate space for the Morrigan before performing any spells and rituals for protection and sovereignty. Make sure your sacred space reflects Irish Celtic heritage and decorate it with items like images of crows, their feathers, an image of the Morrigan, a bowl of water, candles, and other items. Then, having done a good deal of research, the first thing you should do is research the legends and myths surrounding the deity. You should be ready and able to do this, so you know more about how to perform your rituals.

While there are several rituals you can perform, you should understand the strengths and weaknesses of each. Macha, the goddess, believes and expects that you must show reverence by kneeling or bowing at the altar when you perform your ritual work. You have probably encountered conflicting and confusing stories and details about the Celtic gods. There are conflicting details about the Celtic gods and goddesses, but this should not sway you when you perform your rituals. This is one area where the instructions in mythology and research agree so that you can carry on without fear.

You should have already set up the altar for the Morrigan, and this can be decorated, as outlined in previous chapters. Place a simple feather on your dresser. The way you design your altar is a matter of personal preference. What is important is to set aside a sacred place where you can communicate with the goddess and nurture your relationship with her. The goddesses and gods are everywhere, so you can set your altar in any place. If your bedroom is convenient, you can have your sacred shrine there.

Essentially, your altar will be the place where you conduct all the activities that connect you to your deity. It's a sacred and undisturbed space that is dedicated to meditation, communication, ritual, and spirituality, regardless of what you are doing - asking for help, questioning, or making a thanksgiving offering. You can spend time performing rituals on your altar. You can use this space for meditation and communication with the goddess, while others provide offerings to their gods. When you want to perform a ritual meant to heal or protect you, it is vital to use the altar to communicate with the deity. Meditation is a key ingredient for all your rituals and is one effective way to communicate your intention to the goddess. When you meditate, you can ground your intentions and say whatever you want to the goddess. You should take deep breaths when you meditate and freely express your desires. It is important to end each session by expressing gratitude to the goddess.

Candle Ritual for Protection

To perform a protection ritual, you need a red candle since this is the color primarily associated with mainly used by the goddess, and it also reflects power. This ritual is an easy way to work with the Morrigan to ask for protection and the removal of obstacles. There is no need for formality when you perform this particular ritual, although you can be formal if you wish. The goddess knows what you want, so you must ask for help and always thank her for assisting you.

The candle ritual for protection is well known, given that it is easy to perform. The Irish goddess Morrigan is a threefold entity, and Macha is the elder, mother of death, and great goddess of ghosts. She can appear in different forms, but this should not surprise you. This spell is simple magic, but it is also effective. It is a spell that you can do at any time that suits you and is a universal spell. You can choose the best time to suit your needs to perform this ritual.

It is also a spell that can be taken advantage of. The moon's energy is potent and should not be abused. Use this spell to repel negative energy, but do not be tempted to use it negatively yourself.

You will need:

- A red candle
- Almond oil

- Fresh or dry chopped rue
- Unrefined coarse sea salt
- A flat plate
- A piece of aluminum foil

Once you have your ingredients, take the red candle and bathe it in almond oil, starting at the base and working upward toward the wick. Scatter the salt on the plate and roll the oiled candle in the salt. When it is soaked in the mixture, remove the candle, and wash the plate. After that, use your aluminum foil to line the plate and place your candle in the center of the plate. Light the candle with matches and make sure it is supported by dropping a little wet wax onto the foil and placing the candle into it to secure the candle in place.

Ensure that the flame is strong before you invoke Morrigan's spell.

> *"Goddess of strength and struggle,*
>
> *You are the wall to defend me from the evil and magic of my enemy.*
>
> *Above all, make it impossible for .... to reach me. (Say the name of the person who wants to attack you).*
>
> *And against this wall, the evil that is sent to attack breaks and moves away from me*
>
> *I remain under your protection, my goddess*
>
> *At the same time, this candle is consumed,*
>
> *The symbols of all evils are consumed."*

When you are incanting your spell, you can add your own invocations. This is a protection ritual, so add anything pertaining to protection in your life. Use whatever message or prayer you want to your goddess, and she will respond appropriately.

Make sure you remain in meditation and focus on your desire for protection. You can repeat the spell until the candle burns completely. When you finish the ritual, use the aluminum foil to wrap up the remains of the wax, and move it outdoors to take away all negative energy from you. Bury the foil containing the remains in the garden. And this is symbolic of removing negative energy away from you. You can repeat the spell whenever you want, and there is no limit to doing so.

Shape-Shifting Rituals

Morrigan is renowned for encouraging and motivating heroic warriors to win great victories in battle and heroes toward victory in a battle. She takes part in the conflict through the use of sorcery and shape-shifting. The goddess also terrorizes the enemy. She is capable of giving her people strength and providing strategic information to her people to help them win. The Morrigan is capable of shape-shifting, and she has a number of different animals and creatures she can change into. When you perform this ritual, you'll shift into different objects, and the enemy will cannot easily identify you. You can try shamanic drumming rituals or shape-shifting meditation to connect with her.

Some people can shift naturally, while others may require some form of training. With this ritual, the goddess can help you shift into different shapes or forms, including crows, cows, ravens, wolves, and eels. She can also fulfill crucial roles concerning prophecy and poetry. In the hour of need, the goddess will make prophetic pronouncements of doom or victory, especially on the eve of major battles. She can also do great things after the battle. It is believed that the goddess has power over life and death, and she can resuscitate all the fallen heroes in the battle.

When you perform the shape-shifting ritual before a battle, it means you'll not die. This kind of ritual can go a long way toward protecting warriors in different battles. It is essential to do some research into this spell so you know the items required. Like any other ritual, you should know that there is no single way of doing the shape-shifting charm. You need to communicate with the goddess to give you guidance in whatever you do.

Crow Spells

The Morrigan is linked to the Crow, which is viewed as one of the sacred animals. She is identified as the crow, and you can also use this to perform your rituals for protection and sovereignty. You can achieve this by gathering some crow feathers, which you can use as an offering to the goddess. Alternatively, you can perform a simple ritual where you invite the crows to your garden. Feed them to create a mutual relationship for everlasting protection. The presence of crows in your yard means you are protected against evil forces.

To be successful in this ritual, it is essential to study the behavior of the crows so you can imitate their mannerisms. You can call on the crow spirit to guide you when you perform a ritual or spell. Feel free to perform this kind of spell in any way you want. Remember, your intentions will determine what you'll ask of the goddess.

Shadow Spells

While shadow spells can be painful, they can help you in your journey toward creating a new life. Destruction can herald new things into your life, and you can also perform a ritual where you seek protection against negative forces. But shadow spells are not only about rebuffing the negative forces in your life; they are also about *facing them*. Look inside and find where you are hurt and what is hurting you. The Celtic Goddess of War will help to guide you in your search for what ails you emotionally. The spell is a healing process as much as it is about rebuffing negativity.

Before you undertake this particular spell, try to invoke the goddess's powers and communicate your intentions to her. The goddess knows all the things you need in life, and she will guide you accordingly. If she feels this spell is not ideal for you, you'll get a message from her voice. Additionally, if she is happy about the charm, she will also give you the green light to proceed. While communicating with the goddess about your intention, you should also ask about the items required for the spell work.

Use Prayers

The Celts believed that as they engaged in a battle or warfare, they should invoke the power of the Morrigan for protection. These powers can be summoned through a protection charm. The warriors chanted the following elemental protection charm against harm.

> *"Power and protection to those marching for a better world*
> *Power and protection from the earth to the feet that march upon it*

Power and protection from the winds to fill the lungs of the people

Power and protection from the water to cleanse the pain from the hearts of many

Power and protection from the fires that burn for justice."

Furthermore, a prayer to the Morrigan as Goddess of Sovereignty is another method you can consider while honoring her and asking for guidance. If you are going into a battle to defend your land and territorial integrity, it is critical to invoke the goddess's powers.

"A Morrigan

Singing spells of power, you shape the land.

From Odra's flesh and bone, you shaped a sleepy stream.

Anu,

The hills are your breasts,

Fertile, lush

Badb,

The barrows and claims are your womb,

The river ford's your mournful haunt

Macha,

The fairy mounds are your domain,

Emain Macha, marked out by your hand.

May I feel your power in the ground beneath my feet,

May I hear your words in the rushing sounds of rivers.

May I find rest in your barrows and shadowed realm."

One aspect you should know about these prayers is that you can alter them to include anything you wish to get from the goddess. You can recite your prayer before you undertake a major event that can pose a threat to your life. After saying the invocation, you should end up by giving thanks to the goddess to show appreciation.

Perform Sex Spells

The Morrigan goddess is associated with sex through her characteristics since she stands for rebirth and fertility. A sex spell will honor Morrigan for her sacrifices, connecting with her rebirth. With fertility and creation come territorial integrity or sovereignty. You can perform a sex ritual and ask the goddess to protect your offspring to defend your territory. Communicate with the goddess your intention to let her know what you intend to achieve. This spell should not be complicated, but make sure your partner is aware of your intentions. Avoid doing a spell against someone else's wishes since you may not achieve your goals.

Sacred Offerings

Sacred offerings bring honor to deities. When asking for Morrigan's protection, give generously. An offering to a deity shows your appreciation of whatever they do for you. When you work with the Goddess Macha, you'll be dealing with the brighter side of her energy. Therefore, presenting an offering is more like feeding the goddess with the energy and nourishment they may need to enhance your intentions.

The Goddess loves, comforts, and provides energy that makes you feel safe, secure, and warm. You can consider different things when making offerings, depending on your preferences and intentions. Red is a common color for offerings to Morrigan. Red food and wine are easy to come by. As with other gods of old, the symbols from the past are frequently used—add mead, milk, honey, crow feathers, and traditional food. The gods like poetry and artwork, and, of course, blood shows you are serious about the offering (you do not need a lot of blood, a drop is more than sufficient). You can choose anything your intuition resonates with (and you are satisfied with) to make an offering to the goddess.

The offerings are presented to her on the Morrigan's altar, and there is no strict formula for doing this. However, you need to say a prayer or communicate with the goddess about your intention while making the offering. If you are in a difficult situation and you need protection, she will remove the burden from you. All you need to do is surrender the burden to her, and this should be accompanied by your offering. She will provide a remedy for you that will ease your problems. If you are preparing to go into a battle, you should make an appropriate offering to the goddess, who tends to be a school teacher, nurse, and mother. If you want to learn new things which are herb-related, you can invoke Macha.

When you give your preferred offering, it shows that you are serious and willing to sacrifice something for Morrigan. Alternatively, you can ask the goddess what she wants before you present your offering. Again, there is no single way to communicate with her since you can do anything that feels intuitively right. If you want to make a unique offering, you should consider whether there is anything that has a significant meaning to you and offer it to her with a strongly reverential intention. You should feel that the deity has accepted your offering. When you do the ritual correctly, the goddess communicates with you. Remember to thank the goddess at the end of each ritual you perform to the goddess.

The Morrigan Goddess Macha is renowned for protecting different people who seek guidance in various things. While the goddess is associated with death and destruction, she is believed to promote rebirth and fertility. There are several Macha spells for protection and sovereignty you can consider, especially when you are going into a battle. It is essential to research the goddess, so you know how to perform protection spells.

Chapter 9: Nemain: Rituals to Find Your Fierce Self

While occupying somewhat similar roles to her sisters, Nemain is more often revered for her positive qualities. As the fiercest of the trio, this charming Irish goddess provides courage and strength for those who invoke her. Using the sound of her voice, she led Celtic warriors into battle and shepherded the souls of the fallen toward the other world. And she can guide you towards your goal - on whichever path you choose to take in life. Whether you need to find an inner strength to heal from the past so you can become more assertive in the future or simply want to get battle-ready for an upcoming hurdle, invoking Nemain's power will help you out.

Sometimes, she will already feel your need for her, so she will call on you and share her strength and experience with you. At other times, you will need to perform a ritual to invoke her and ask for her assistance. Keep in mind that your experience with her will always be personal and will differ from time to time depending on your current spiritual needs. This chapter will outline rituals addressed toward Nemain. All of them will need to be done at your altar and include an offering to the goddess. And remember, you should always offer thanks after you perform the rituals to ensure that positive energy keeps flowing through your connection with her. And the more personal you make the ceremony, the more likely it will bring you success.

Honoring Nemain's Strength

This ritual has the purpose of helping you to remember the changes the cycle of life brings. Through it, Nemain will bestow on you the power to find your inner strength and tap into that intuitive wisdom you require. The best time to perform this ritual is at night, during, or near the new moon.

You will need:

- 3 candles: white, black, and red
- A bowl of water, ideally from a natural freshwater source
- Representations of the Nemain
- An offering for the goddess
- A stone
- Writing tool you can use on the stone

Directions:

1. Place the bowl of water near the window in the room in which you have your altar. It must remain in a dark area.
2. Write your intention or words associated with it onto the stone, and wait until the writing is dry.
3. Place the representation of Nemain on your altar and the stone next to it.
4. Put the three candles in front of the symbol and the stone and turn the electric lights in the room off.

5. Step in front of your altar by assuming a position of power. Stand tall, with your feet shoulder-width apart so you can feel grounded to the Earth.

6. Take a couple of deep breaths and raise your arms over your head, palms facing each other. You should feel your spine lengthening and your shoulders extending towards the back.

7. Now that you are in a triangle that symbolizes the goddess, you should focus on her strength. Try to imagine her powerful blood flowing through your veins.

8. Hold this position until you feel strong enough to defend and heal yourself or lend your powers to others if needed. You must feel this strength coming from a place of self-love and with an acceptance of your life's changes.

9. Wait a few minutes to see if Nemain herself has any messages for you. Then, take the bowl of water and place it on the floor, and put the stone beside it as well.

10. After some stretching, sit down in a comfortable position and take a blanket to wrap around yourself.

11. By gazing into the bowl of water, allow your mind to relax so that positive thoughts can come through. Take the time to absorb anything you may feel, hear, or otherwise perceive with your senses.

12. When you feel your intuition rising and feel empowered enough to face whatever difficulty may come, take the stone, and place it into the bowl of water.

13. Wait a couple of minutes until the stone soaks up the energy. Whatever you wrote on the stone will now be assigned a great power, and you'll feel this when you take the stone in your hand.

14. Now it's time to express your gratitude for Nemain's wisdom and the blessing she has granted you with the following chant:

"Oh, Great Goddess Nemain,

I call upon your strength

For you are the one so many fear,

But I honor your power inside me.

You rule the cycle of birth, life, and death,

and create the rebirth of strength.

You are of heals and gives at times of need,

and you can protect and shepherd me on my path indeed.

And I know only you can stand so strong,

for only a true warrior shows strength when they are the most vulnerable.

May I receive your power now,

so, I can stand with you and be just as strong."

15. Take a deep breath and have a glass of water. Leave the offerings on the altar for a couple of hours before disposing of them.

16. Stand up and place the stone in a visible place to remind you of the goddess's power. You can also carry it with you and tap into Nemain's strength when you need it.

Asking for Nemain's Guidance

Sometimes to find inner strength, you don't only need to borrow the power of the warrior goddess. You'll also need her to show you how to use it. With this ritual, you can ask for empowerment and counseling on how to act after receiving her blessing. This simple yet effective act of magic can be done at any time you wish. However, if you take advantage of the growing moon's energy, it will be even more effective.

You will need:

- A red candle
- Dry or fresh chopped rue
- Coarse, unrefined sea salt
- Almond oil
- Aluminum foil
- A larger flat plate
- Matches
- The offering of your choice

- A representation of Nemain

Directions:

1. Spray or rub some almond oil on the candle to anoint it. Start from the bottom and slowly go upward, but be careful to avoid the wick.

2. Pour the salt and the rue onto a plate and mix them. Then roll the candle in the mixture and let the salt and the rue stick to the oil.

3. Wash the plate and line it with a piece of aluminum foil. Put the candle in the center of the plate and light it with a wooden match.

4. If you are using a thinner candle, wait until the wax melts, so you can make it stand up on its own on the foil.

5. Place the plate with the candle in front of the symbol of the goddess, along with whatever offering you have prepared for her.

6. Make yourself comfortable by assuming a position that will allow you to focus on your intent. Meditation techniques will be helpful to get you into the right frame of mind as well.

7. At this point, you should start focusing your mind on calling on the goddess of strength with the following spell:

   "Goddess of strength, I call upon you,

   for I know you have struggled before.

   I need your wall to defend me from those who wish me harm,

   and I need you to help me recognize the malicious spirit.

   Above all, I want to be impossible for evil to reach,

   so, I can ward its attack should it come.

   Show me how to protect myself from the harm

   they send to break me and set it far away.

   Help me find the strength to protect those I love too,

   Nemain, when my candle is consumed, let my power grow."

8. Stay focused on your intention and, if needed, recite the spell a few more times. You may do this until the candle is burned down, or make a few pauses and return to your mission as soon as you can.

9. Finally, when the candle is completely consumed, take the foil, and gather it slowly, ensuring the wax remains closed in the middle.

10. Take it away from your altar, and bury it. You can do this in a plant pot if you don't have a garden.

The candle soaks up any negativity that may be hindering you from acting intuitively. By burying the wax, you are getting rid of it and cleansing yourself of the negativity.

Strengthening Ritual

A negative state of mind can greatly impact your ability to invoke power when faced with stressful situations. If you want to overcome any hurdle in life, the first step is to strengthen yourself mentally. This ritual addressed to the goddess of strength will help you with that.

You'll need:

- A white, a black, and a pink or red candle
- Sage, cedar, or pine incense
- Rose or amber incense
- Sage, pine, or another banishing oil for the black candle
- Rose oil pink or red candle
- Moroccan oil for the white candle
- A black gemstone
- A piece of rose quartz
- Matches
- A charcoal block
- Offering for the goddess

Directions:

1. Place everything in front of you on the altar and anoint your candles with the oils.

2. Start the ritual by lighting the white candle at the center of the altar.

3. Let the charcoal block heat up, and sprinkle the loose herbs over it to make incense. Use only sage, pine, or rosemary at the beginning.

4. After letting the smoke purify your energy, visualize your intent - try to find any emotional trauma or mental blockage.

5. When you have identified all the hurtful emotional baggage and issues clogging up your mind, use smudging with the incense smoke to banish them.

6. Then, use the white candle to light the black one. Place the latter on the left side of the altar.

7. Call on both sides of the goddess - the fierce one to help banish your mental blockage and the peaceful one to wake up your intuition with this invocation:

    "Nemain, goddess of strength and wisdom,

    I invite you here to help me see.

    I refuse to let my bad thoughts cloud my judgment,

    and I choose to banish them forever.

    I ask for peace instead,

    to see what truly lies ahead.

    Help my work tonight, oh dear Nemain."

8. Now, you can start focusing on the black candle and recalling all the things you wish to change in your life. Think about everything your negative thoughts are preventing you from achieving.

9. When you have identified all your negative thoughts and emotions, acknowledge them. This will help you see past them and find your true strength.

10. When you find them all, blow out the candle in a quick motion and allow the dying light to take all the negativity from within you. Visualize this energy leaving your space with the smoke from your incense.

11. Breathe in the banishing incense aroma for a couple of minutes to ensure all the negative energy has dissolved.

12. Now that you are a blank slate, you can start to refill yourself with positivity. At this point, you should light the red or pink candle using the white one and place it on the right-hand side of the altar.

13. Sprinkle amber or rose incense on the charcoal block and let it fill your senses as you breathe in their energies.

14. Remember how the goddess herself found her inner strength in her most vulnerable times, and ask her to show you how she did it.

15. When you feel her presence, look at the candle flame and let it help you to focus on all the positive things in your life.

16. Continue repeating affirmative thoughts to yourself until you feel sated with them.

17. Take the rose quartz in your hands and keep breathing in the scent of the invoking incense and watching the candle flame. Draw this fragrance into your body and mind.

18. Thank the goddess for lending you her wisdom and strength so you can find your own power.

19. You can either allow the pink or red candle to burn itself out completely or, better yet, snuff it out and relight it later a few times and repeat the affirmations each time.

20. After the ritual has been completed, bury the wax from the black candle, along with the ashes from the incense.

21. Carry the rose pendant with you at all times wherever you go.

Visualizing your negative thoughts being buried with the candle and the ashes will help to keep them away from you in the future. You can then remain strong and able to overcome any hurdle in life. The first (banishing) part of the ritual should only be repeated if it's necessary. The blessing part should be done during every new and full moon, which falls on Saturdays.

The Memory Ritual

Sometimes the blockage in your intuitive power is caused by a trauma that lies so deep even you fail to recall it. However, doing so is necessary to become a more empowered version of yourself. Through this ritual, Nemain will help you hunt down those memories from the deepest corners of your mind.

You will need:

- 2-3 Yellow candles
- A representation of the goddess
- A box with a lid
- The incense of your choice
- Offerings for Nemain
- Paint or aluminum foil
- Decorations for the box
- Music - optional

Directions:

1. Paint the inside of the box black or simply line it with aluminum foil. Decorate the outside with symbols that will help you evoke memories, and add some that represent the goddess, as well.

2. Place everything else on the altar, close the box, and light the candles.

3. Get in a comfortable position and start focusing your mind on revealing its hidden memories.

4. Recite an opening statement greeting your past and acknowledging its effect on your present life. Then continue up with the following invocation:

   "I call Nemain to reveal my past,

   so, my future may be bright.

   I need you, goddess, to bring myself forth from the darkness,

   and help me find the light and make my mark.

   Don't let my past control my present and future; don't let my thoughts and actions remain dark as night.

   I now meet and greet you with open arms,

   as you shepherd me back into the light."

5. At this point, you should open the box and gaze intently at what you find inside it.

6. Visualize your memories staring back at you, ready to meet and greet you, so you can make peace with them during the following moments.

7. Accept your memories of negative experiences with a state of mind that won't let them hinder you from reaching your full potential. Take as much time as you need during this step.

8. After making peace with your past and diminishing all the negative thoughts and emotions related to the past, let your mind clear with a large exhalation of breath.

9. Express your gratitude toward the goddess and leave the offerings for her.

10. The box should be dealt with according to your preferences. You can choose to destroy it or leave it out in the sunlight, where all negativity from it is replaced by positivity.

Cleansing a box and keeping it for future uses is an excellent option, as it's a good idea to repeat this ritual a couple of times a year. You can do it any time you feel overwhelmed with negativity that is preventing you from finding the inner strength to deal with any issues lying in front of you.

Chapter 10: Honoring the Morrigan Daily

If you want to connect with the goddess Morrigan, there are a number of different things you should do to honor her. This final chapter explains some quick and easy daily micro-rituals you can practice to create and cement a lasting relationship with this powerful goddess. Some of these things include reciting a brief daily prayer, wearing a triskele, splashing water on your face three times, asking for protection, meditating, or pathworking with the Morrigan. You can choose one or more than one of any of these small activities to honor and worship your goddess.

Study the Morrigan

First and foremost, it is vital to study the deity if you want to know them better. You should read the legends and folklore about the goddess Morrigan and study the history of Irish mythology in your attempt to understand her convoluted make-up, sorcery, and powers. When you research Morrigan, keep a journal where you record critical aspects to remember. In your studies, you must focus on areas dedicated to the Celtic Goddess of War. Write notes about your experiences and thoughts. There are several sources of information about Morrigan you can find online, and if you check carefully, you can get free Irish studies online.

Altar Space for the Phantom Queen

The space is an important starting point for honoring Morrigan. Your altar should be in a dedicated space away from disruption and distraction. Have a representation of the goddess on your altar—either a picture or a statue. The altar should be covered in cloth—either red or black—with candles in the same color. She is connected with water, so add a bowl of water too. If you have a representation of a crow or crows, add that too (statues and not drawings).

A crow image is one of the most important things you should have to honor the Goddess Morrigan. When you cast your spells, you should try to win your battles and defeat all your inner demons. A statue on your altar is symbolic since it represents the presence of the goddess in your space.

The Number 3

The number three is a popular symbol for the Morrigan, and you can use it to honor the goddess in different ways. Three sisters exist within Morrigan, and three lines are often used to depict the trio of sisters or the three forms of energy that flow from the goddess. The magical number is associated with many deities and powerful figures, and in Ireland, there is a flower that has three leaves (four if you are lucky)—the shamrock. Use three lines or a shamrock to honor Morrigan.

The Goddess Morrigan is often associated only with destruction, but she also represents initiation. Morrigan is like a phoenix rising from the flames—from her own destruction comes rebirth. The triskele is a three-pronged symbol used to represent Morrigan. The triad comes from the three figures of Macha, Badb, and Nemain. The images of these three females represent birth, growth, and death. The word "Triskeles" is a Greek word that means "three legs." The Triskelion is a symbol that is found at the entrance of Newgrange, Ireland. It gained popularity in Celtic culture from as early as 500BC, and it continues to be used as a symbol to honor the goddess.

You can wear the triskele symbol since it is believed to represent motion. All three arms are created to make it appear as if it is moving from the center, and this kind of motion is believed to signify energies. The triskele encompasses numerous trilogies in our everyday life—the three components of a family (mother, father, and child), the life cycle (life, death, and rebirth), our timeline (past, present, and future), and many more.

The Celtic triskele is believed to indicate a forward motion, moving to eventually reach an understanding. The meaning is diverse, and it also has many possibilities. The triple moon also shows different sections of the lunar cycle. When the moon is full, we have the Mother. When it is waxing, we have the Maiden. And the waning moon brings the Crone. The Morrigan is understood to be a triple Goddess. Therefore, the symbol triskele can symbolize her essence.

While still on the number three, the other simple ritual you can do to honor the goddess is to splash water on your face three times each morning for each of the trio goddesses. You can do this while calling the goddess for protection and splash the water three times at night to thank them. This spell is easy, and it does not require any complicated tools. You can do it when you wake up and before going to bed.

Morrigan Meditation

In your daily rituals to honor the Goddess Morrigan, you could include meditation because of its many positive effects on the mind, body, and soul. You can erect a temporary shrine or altar, but it is recommended that you have a permanent one if you are going to be honoring Morrigan on a regular basis. Decorate the altar or shrine with red or black cloth, crow feathers (or raven), water, candles, blood, honey, and other traditional Irish foods. Your ritual should be simple since you need to meditate on anything that symbolizes the Morrigan.

When you visit your altar, find a quiet place to sit, or if you don't feel comfortable sitting, you can meditate while standing. Make sure you have appropriate items to use for this purpose. Say your intention out loud to the goddess while meditating. If you intend to ask for protection, make sure you communicate clearly. You may wish to offer the goddess something valuable when you feel her presence in your life. This can be any item that symbolizes her. For instance, you can meditate on a candle flame and a crow's feather. When you offer something to the goddess, you'll suddenly feel her presence in your body, indicating that your offer has been accepted.

Meditating or pathworking at a specific time every day is another way to honor the goddess. Shapeshifting can help you connect with and honor Morrigan. This can come naturally to some people, but it is not something that everyone can do. The ritual involves deep meditation to release yourself from your body to travel to another. Make sure you do something that satisfies your needs and something that will please the goddess.

Crow Magic

The Morrigan is closely connected to the crow. It is one common sacred bird that symbolizes the goddess. She can shape-shift into a crow. Therefore, one way of honoring her is to try to make many friends with the crows in your area. You can do this by feeding them or inviting them into your garden or yard. Crows in your yard symbolize the presence of the goddess Morrigan. If you see crows frequently, study them. You can invoke the spirit of the crow in your meditations and rituals, and Morrigan is always close when crows are.

The Morrigan chooses the crow or raven as the main symbol of war, conflict, and death. The crow is renowned for its wisdom and trickery. It is also viewed as a protector of sacred records. It also represents her on the battlefields. You can also choose a crow as a spirit guide or totem. It warns you if there is imminent danger and guides you on your path. Also, it allows you to overcome certain fears you may have, allowing you to take advantage of opportunities in your life. To make sure you get the most out of all these benefits, you should wear raven images or jewelry with bloodstone. Morrigan loves this stone, so wearing the jewelry shows your devotion to her.

Honor the Morrigan with Chants

As you develop your relationship with the goddess Morrigan, you should have a daily ritual devoted to her. You can honor her with chants that should be dedicated to her life and where she comes from. The main reason for honoring her is to allow her to contact you if she has any desire to fulfill. You'll strengthen your relationship with the goddess when you call upon her by name. Essentially, a strong bond with her means she will guide and protect you in the different things you do. The following is a common chant you can call upon the Morrigan.

"I Praise Morrigu, Great Queen!

Hail Morrigan, Queen of Phantoms!

I Call Morrigan, Goddess of Fate!

I Call You, Mistress of Battle – Come, Morrigan!"

Apart from using chants, you can also ask the goddess for guidance through the use of divination tools. You can ask for guidance using tools such as tarot cards, pendulums, runes, and other things. She is a goddess of prophecy, and she can help you get insight into the events likely to happen in the future, so you can make your plans with confidence.

Shadow Work

An important thing to know about the goddess Morrigan is that she is associated with destruction. However, it is not necessarily a bad thing because new life is able to grow from destruction. Shadow work takes you inside yourself to discover what is troubling you. When you do shadow work, Morrigan is guiding you, showing you where the negative energies reside and what is causing them. You might see your dark side within, but the goddess is there with you every step of the way.

This type of work can be hard to perform, especially when you are facing buried issues, but think of it as the tunnel you travel through to get to the light. Life cannot always be smooth since you are likely to encounter negative things that can impact you in different ways. However, Morrigan knows the things we desire all too well, and she can pull us through troubled times. Likewise, the goddess is concerned about teaching us that there is light at the end of the tunnel. Even if you are going through difficult times, you should call upon the goddess to guide you in whatever you do to achieve your desired goals.

Sex Magic

Sex is not something to shy away from. Morrigan engaged with Dagda in sexual intercourse. The goddess symbolizes new life and fertility, which can be achieved through sex. If you wish, you can try sex magic to honor The Morrigan. This is a noble way of honoring her since she stands for rebirth, fertility, and creation. It is essential to make your intention known to the goddess because if you practice sacred sex out of faith and respect for the goddess, she will bless you with many offspring. Bringing new life to earth is something that appeases the goddess.

Sacred Offerings to the Goddess Morrigan

You should have a routine to leave offerings to the goddess Morrigan on her altar when you conduct your ritual. Your altar is a sacred space where you conduct your rites and try to communicate with the supreme power. Offerings to the deities are critical since they show your appreciation for the good work she creates for and around you. When you present an offering, you'll be feeding the goddess with the energy she may require to help you in your intentions.

There are specific food items you can use as offerings to the Morrigan. You can use red foods or wine, traditional food and drink offerings like mead and honey, art like poetry or paintings, water, blood, blades, and feathers. These foods are regarded as acceptable offerings because of their connection with the goddess. The items also share some character similarities with the deity's energy. Place your offerings on the altar and focus your attention on her spirit. The Morrigan will provide her service in appreciation of your offering.

Use Prayers

One effective way of connecting with the goddess Morrigan is through prayer. There are many ways of praying to the goddess, so try to choose anything your intuition leads you to. You can recite the following prayer in honor of the goddess.

> *"Great Queen, the Morrígan*
>
> *Hear me; I am your Priest and your Warrior,*
>
> *Protect me from harm, be it by intent or by ignorance,*
>
> *In the face of life's trials and joys,*
>
> *May I be ever steady: calm in mind, body, and emotion,*
>
> *May I be centered, present, embodied,*
>
> *My mind like water; clinging to nothing and untroubled,*
>
> *May I act decisively, truth and wisdom as my guideposts,*
>
> *May my actions and words move from a place of honor, wisdom, compassion, and love,*
>
> *May I know when to cut and when to be cut*

Clothe me in guile and cunning;

That I may move with suppleness and resiliency between the worlds."

When you pray, you should feel free to include everything you want the goddess to do for you. She is a provider and committed to fulfilling the needs of her followers. It is vital to listen to the voice of the goddess and make sure you do as instructed. In your next prayer ritual, you should thank her for everything she has done for you. She will continue giving you more blessings.

Invocations for the Morrigan

When conducting a ritual, call on the Morrigan, and you'll feel her presence. When you develop a strong relationship with the goddess, she will come to your rescue every time as long as your relationship with her is strong and respectful. You must call her when you need her to accompany you to a battle. Morrigan protects everyone, but she often focuses on those who need it the most, those who cannot fend for themselves. When called, she will aid in healing and protection. The following is an invocation for Morrigan when you want help with different things.

"I call to you,

Daughter of Ernmas,

Sister of battle and sovereignty,

I call to you

Goddess of war-craft,

victory, and death

I call to you Great Queen

Morrigu, Lady of Phantoms

Be with me now."

Another method to invoke Morrigan Goddess is to light a red candle representing the color of power. As with most prayers to deities, you don't simply ask for what you need, but an easier path to get there. Ask Morrigan to be with you on your journey and remove obstacles so you can plot a path to your future. When you are invoking the goddess, be clear about what it is you truly need—vagueness will not get you what you want. The goddess knows what you want, so you should ask for help and thank her. This is something you can do in your way since there is no universal formula. All you need to do is ensure that the method you choose to honor the goddess is acceptable.

Spiritual rituals are unique, and your devotion to goddess Morrigan should help you connect with her. To honor Morrigan daily, it is recommended that you familiarize yourself with her history. You can achieve this by reading books related to this goddess. Furthermore, you can also honor her with prayer, chants, or meditation, but make sure your reason for contact or intention is known. You must be honest, truthful, and show respect to Morrigan for her to respond. Once you allow your inner self to receive her calling, you'll hear her voice. This will help you to create a respectful relationship with the goddess, and you can honor her daily using this line of communication.

Conclusion

This book tells the complicated, convoluted, and often confusing story of the goddess Morrigan, or the Morrigan, as seen by the eyes of the Celts. Wherever the Celts lived across the world, Morrigan would appear in one of her many forms, bringing a warning of death or a blessing of fertility. There are colorful tales of prowess and magical abilities. Most of these refer to her as a shape-shifter associated with war, death, and prophecy. However, her divination powers go far beyond just announcing death.

She could also reveal a higher destiny or fate in a different life. She is a protector and a guide to achieving fertility in work, art, or personal life. These controversial roles of the Morrigan are best described in her guises as the Phantom Queen and the Fairy Queen. The first one is known for appearing out of nowhere and announcing the death or forewarning about more bloodshed to follow after a battle. The second one is said to lead the fairy court across the realms to protect humans, animals, and crops from malicious spirits.

Irish mythology sometimes mentions her as one single being - working alongside her sisters Macha and Neiman. Together, they would influence the outcome of many wars. Morrigan predicted the impending massacre and warned the feuding parties. Neiman would cause panic amongst the warriors to deter them from combat, and Macha offered them protection and solace on the battlefield. Other sources claim that these three are all manifestations of one sole goddess. She would take on one role to warn warriors about their inevitable death and then another to shepherd the souls of the deceased toward the other world. More often than not, she would see to these duties appearing as a crow - a wise bird associated with prophecies and death. She could also appear as an old hag or even a terrifying banshee if she really wanted to deter the warriors from fighting.

However, the Morrigan would not only keep the parties from fighting. Sometimes she would inspire them to fight even harder - on the battlefield or for their goals in life. This aspect of hers is what many Paganic and Neopaganic practitioners use to empower themselves. Despite popular belief, Morrigan is not an evil goddess - even if she warns you about bad things to come. Seeing her as the representation of reincarnation and rebirth gives her followers hope that there will be better times to come after every hurdle in life.

Overcoming obstacles will make you wiser, and the knowledge you gain cannot be banished. She can help you heal, so you can assist others through the same process. Morrigan can guide you toward the path on which you'll find a balance between dark and light, which resides in all of us and which we try to keep on an even keel. If honored regularly, this mighty goddess will help you find your fierce self even when you feel the most vulnerable. All you need to do is to build an altar where you can honor the Morrigan, recite the spells, and perform the small rituals dedicated to this versatile goddess. You can also use meditation, write your own chants, or personalize the ones in this book according to your own beliefs.

Part 4: Brigid

Unlocking the Magick of the Celtic Goddess of Divination, Wisdom, and Healing

Introduction

The Celtic Irish goddess Brigid is among the most renowned and significant pagan figures in history. The deity managed to thrive and evolve, even with the rise of Christianity. Among very few other pagan deities, she somehow held out against the stringent and obstinate eradication of the "old ways." The reason behind Brigid's endurance comes from her popularity and the great love people have for her.

In addition to the endless roles that the goddess Brigid took on, she miraculously went from being a Celtic goddess to taking the title of a Catholic saint. She had since become a very prominent Catholic figure as well. This deity forged a wonderful bridge between two very different and opposing belief systems. This book covers everything there is to know about this incredible archetype. The book includes extensive yet easy-to-understand information, making it perfect for beginners and individuals with more knowledge on the subject alike.

Reading the book, you will find out exactly who Brigid is. We first explore her in the pagan Gaelic world and provide insightful descriptions of her, according to pieces of lore and tales. You will learn all about her names, her equivalents in the pantheon and other cultures, and how she was worshipped in ancient times. The book then walks you through her transformation into a Catholic saint. You will find out the differences between her role as a goddess and that of a saint in terms of appearance and duties. The first chapter explores Brigid from a different aspect, that of a Triple Goddess of the Flame. You will understand what a triple goddess is and why Brigid corresponds to that description. Then, you will find out how she was syncretized into the loa Maman Brigitte, which is Brigid's final form of transformation. Here, you will uncover her role as Maman Brigitte, her association with Baron Samedi, the offerings she prefers, and what her temperament is like.

A later chapter covers the connection Brigid has with animals and the symbols associated with her. It lists the creatures which are associated with the goddess, along with a few tales that clarify the connection. This chapter includes hands-on instructions on how to make the most important symbol, which is Brigid's Cross.

As you read through the book, you will find out what the Celtic wheel of the year is, where Imbolc falls on it, and why this festival is closely associated with Brigid. You will learn how to build an altar to dedicate to the goddess, as well as one that is suitable for celebrating Imbolc. Upon reading this book, you'll find out which colors, herbs, flowers, crystals, scents, and crafts to incorporate into your altar. You'll understand how to tend the altar and what you should use it for.

The last few chapters will walk you through the process of working with Brigid. Not only will you find out how you can honor her daily, but you will also come across prayers, chants, and affirmations dedicated to Brigid that you can recite in her honor. This book offers numerous healing rituals and spells and provides you with what divination methods work with Brigid.

Chapter 1: Who Is Brigid?

Brigid, who is also known as Brigantia, which is Celtic for High One, was the ancient Celtic goddess of poetry, prophecy, crafts, and divination, among a wide array of other things which will be explained later. In Ireland, this goddess was one of three other goddesses who shared the same name. They were the daughters of the Dagda, the great god of Ireland. The other two Brigids were mainly associated with healing and smith-working crafts. The Filid, a rather sacred poetic class, worshipped Brigid. The Filid were considered professional poets and were expected to know and maintain tales and lineages, as well as to write poems that recollected the past and current distinctions of the ruling classes. Many suggest that Brigid is the Irish equivalent of the Greek goddess Athena and Minerva, the Roman goddess. Brigid's among the most popular deities in modern paganism.

Brigid was later adopted by Christianity, reappearing as Saint Brigid. However, the goddess still preserved her prominent sacerdotal links. The Celts feasted in honor of Brigid on February 1st (more on the relevance of this date in chapter 2). St. Brigid's Day happens to fall on the same date as Imbolc, which is a pagan festival that signifies the start of spring. Being the goddess of spring, new beginnings, and growth, it goes without saying that she is honored on this day. It is said that St. Brigid's landmark, which was located in Kildare, Ireland, was built on a pagan sanctuary. Brigid's sacred fire at that location burned eternally. Her fire was tended by 19 nuns, and the saint herself also tended her own fire every 20th day. The goddess is still a significant figure in modern Scottish folk tradition. According to Celtic Scotts, Brigid served as the Virgin Mary's midwife. They dedicated several holy wells to her.

Brigid is considered the philanthropist of healing, smithcraft, and poetry, which are the three main Celtic skills. For this reason, she is considered a Triple goddess, which is a topic that we explore in-depth in chapter 3. On top of that, Brigid is the goddess of two very contradicting yet complementary elements, which are fire and water. She is also associated with midwifery, brewing, dyeing, and weaving. Being the daughter of Morrigan and the Dagda, who is the Great God, Brigid is connected to Tuatha Dé Danann. She was also the wife of Bres.

The Tuatha Dé Danann is Celtic for *People of the Goddess Danu*. In mythology, the Tuatha Dé Danann was a race that lived in Ireland before the arrival of the Milesians, who are the ancestors of the present-day Irish. These people were thought to be very proficient in magic. The first reference to the Tuatha Dé Danann explained that they descended on a cloud of mist down to Ireland from heaven, as they were banished due to their mystical knowledge.

Brigid had a large family. She had two brothers that were known – Midir and Aengus – along with many other siblings that are not named. Her father was Dagda, and her mother was likely to have been Danu, a powerful river goddess. Danu took on the roundabout moniker: the mother goddess of the Tuatha Dé Danann (the Children of Danu) – or the mother of her own children, to make it more concise.

Brigid married the High King of the Tuatha Dé Danann, Bres, and they had a son, Ruadan (relationships and names were more complicated back then). Bres and Brigid's marriage was intended to serve as an alliance between two families that were at war; she, from the Danu, and he, from the Fomorians. They had hoped that this marriage would be an alliance, averting any potential warfare. The Danu had revealed to Ruadan the smithing skills of Goibhniu (the warrior smith of the Tuatha Dé Danann) – explaining that nothing crafted by Goibhniu could kill him. Tragically, Ruadan challenged this knowledge against the Danu's wishes and decided to attack their smith, who was an incredibly sacred position to the tribe. The now wounded warrior smith, however, managed to kill Ruadan before he himself died. Brigid grieved not only for the death of her son but for the hatred and warfare that existed between both sides of her family. This incident marked the beginning of the end of the "Old Ways." Acting against the maternal family was then identified as a sin, marking motherhood as a sacred position.

Another tale, however, describes Brigid as the wife of Tuireann. In this story, she birthed three sons: Brian, Irchaba, and Iuchar. They were responsible for the death of Lugh, who could shape shift into a pig.

Brigid is seen by many as the guardian of children, particularly newborns. This is why it became customary to weave Brigid's cross over babies' cradles. She was also the deity of animal fertility. She had the strongest connections with geese, cows, swans, bees, ravens, owls, lambs, serpents, and snakes. The colors gold, white, green, yellow, blue, and red are typically associated with Brigid. It is also recommended that you honor her on Sundays. Brigid was both a fire and water goddess, which means that she had connections with both the sun and the moon.

In this chapter, we delve into who Brigid was and what she was like. You will find out what her other names and titles were, as well as the various roles she played as a goddess. Here, it also mentions the deity equivalents of Brigid from other cultures and explains how she was worshipped.

What Was She Like?

Brigid showcases the characteristics of many other goddesses, and some scholars postulate that she was created by amalgamating the archetypes of multiple deities. The name Brigid strongly associates her with the concept of dawn. Her name shares the same roots as the word Bright and initially meant high or rising.

Brigid's hair was bright red, and she is depicted as wearing a robe made from the sun. This, in turn, strengthened her link to the sun and the light it emits. Essentially, she became the goddess of the point of the year during which the sun shone its brightest. Brigid was also very popular for her green cloak. It was said that anyone who sought shelter beneath the mantle would be protected.

Brigid was typically regarded as the goddess of spring. This does not mean that she was not present at other times of the year. While she was more prominent in spring, she was always around. If we look to Scottish mythology and folklore, we see that she was still dominant through summer and was only driven back when the queen of winter appeared.

In Celtic history, the seasons were not set by date. Instead, they considered springtime over when the weather started to get very cold. This led to some Celts celebrating Brigid at different times of the year. When it started to get cold, spring and summer were over, and the last celebration of Brigid would be had. Others celebrated the end of Spring on a specific date, and Brigid would be commemorated on that date. It is believed that Brigid came to Earth to visit the Irish people and offer them blessings on Imbolc.

Brigid was associated with many cycles, the most prominent being the cycle of life and death. Even though she was mainly the goddess of fertility, her lore and tales also incorporated loss. One of the most popular Irish legends suggests that the light goddess left a great impact on the death rituals carried out.

The Cath Maige Tuired, which translates to the Battle of Magh Tuireadh and is the name of the Mythological Cycle texts of Irish mythology, tells that Tuatha Dé Danann came to rule over Ireland. They defeated the preceding ruling lineages, the Fir Bolg and the Fomorians, during two huge battles.

While Brigid didn't fight in the second battle, numerous people in her family did. Dagda, her father, along with her son both met their end in this battle. Her son, Ruadan, allied with his father during the war, and this pitted him against his mother and her people. This split Brigid's loyalties, with some of her family fighting on one side and some on the other.

Giobnui's, the smith god, death came shortly before Brigid's son's death. She went to Ruadan on the battlefield to be with him at the end, letting out wails that could be heard almost across the country. They say that her shrieking and weeping were the first time these sounds were heard in the lands of Ireland.

According to Cath Maige Tuired, Brigid's mourning wails were what led to the keening Irish tradition – a tradition where a woman would cry out in mourning at funerals and wakes to honor and mourn the dead. This tradition is no longer as eminent as it once was. However, Irish musicians still play that same style of music today. When someone passes, those around them (especially close family who are mourning) look to Brigid for consolation. The same is true for musicians at funerals, who want to convey mourning through their music, and they often try to mimic the keening.

The whistle is attributed to Brigid, an invention of her own design that was used to create music and sound as she traveled, especially at night. It started out as a helpful tool to be carried and soon transitioned into musical entertainment. The Irish believed that music was a great way to transfer knowledge. They recited their poems to music and passed on their legends, history, and tales by using performances.

Starting the tradition of keening did not make Brigid the goddess of death or mourning. These archetypes are rather linked to Morrigan, who is considered her polar opposite in various ways. She was, however, the goddess of agriculture.

Brigid's loss made her the protector of mothers and children of both humans and animals. The Celts have always reared farm animals, mainly cattle and sheep. They are both a source of milk, can be killed for meat when they are nearing the end of their life, and are strong enough to help pull a plow. When they have passed, they continue to give with skins and furs, not to mention tools and other instruments crafted from bone and sinew.

There was a lot of fighting over these animals, with attempted theft frequent in olden times. Brigid was often prayed to for the protection of flocks. And, when the mating season came around, she was prayed to for fertility.

The festivals that were associated with Brigid are indicators of her significance in the world of agriculture. Beltane, which is the Celtic May spring festival, and Imbolc didn't only rely on the sun's cycles. However, they were also strongly tied to the farming seasons.

Imbolc is the great festival celebrating Brigid, which occurs at the start of February. Lambs and calves are born around this time, and that would be accompanied by an increase in prayers to Brigid for the safety of the newborn when the weather was still cold.

Beltane celebrates the middle of spring when the cattle and sheep are let out to pasture. Again, this was accompanied by more prayers to Brigid for the safety of the livestock. The connection between Brigid and animals is discussed at length in Chapter 5.

Brigid's Various Roles

Brigid was thought to be a very personal goddess, and she was worshipped by people for countless reasons. As mentioned above, she was the goddess of fertility, the dawn, and spring. She was also the protector of mothers and their offspring, perhaps because she couldn't protect her own child. The hearth fire and the warmth and emotions associated with family homes are symbols of Brigid. Somehow, she is also famous for being a *Warrior Goddess.*

Many people may struggle to wrap their heads around the fact that this very deity is the goddess of warriors. This attribute may sound unreasonable when compared to all her other traits and associations. However, given a little thought, Brigid is merciless and ferocious when it comes to the safety of her children. Some people believe that Brigid was probably misnamed a warrior goddess because of her passionate and intense protectiveness. This fiery motherly instinct was likely misinterpreted in a period diseased with domination, ruthlessness, and violence. Despite her fighter archetype, Brigid was believed to possess healing properties.

The reason for Brigid's link to agriculture is because this goddess protected pastoral animals like sheep and cattle. She was also a source of inspiration to craftsmen and metal workers, especially smiths. This earned her the description of a fire goddess. On the other hand, she was also thought to have strong associations with rivers and wells. Evidently, Brigid's Well in Kildare, which is among Ireland's most renowned landmarks, is still named after her. She was also labeled the goddess of music and was incredibly popular among poets. Having inspired songs, wisdom, craftsmanship, and poetry, Brigid became known as the goddess of knowledge.

No wonder she was an incredibly popular and beloved figure. She was admired to the point where she didn't vanish with the passage of time like most of the other pagan figures – even after Christianity became the official religion of the country. Brigid was refurbished as a Catholic saint and managed to garner reverence far beyond the shores and borders of Ireland. She was among the most impactful and enduring Celtic mythology figures to have ever existed.

As explained earlier, Brigid is often referred to as the *triple goddess* due to her numerous roles. The concept of the triple goddess is prevalent in Irish and Celtic mythology. Morrigan, who is thought to appear as either one goddess or three entities, is the most well-known Irish example. However, the fact that Brigid had two sisters who also went by the same name leaves room for doubt. Since we already know that one sister was a healer and the other was a smith, there's a chance that all three may have been confused with one another.

Even though she is said to be a triple goddess with three facets, she was still depicted and referred to as only one goddess. She wasn't always the same age in stories either. She was sometimes referenced as a wise mother and sometimes as a young maiden.

A Paradoxical Goddess

Brigid, as you know, was the goddess of the waters and wells and the goddess of fire. She was an inspirational goddess but was also the goddess of action. Brigid was the goddess of the Sun and the Moon and the goddess of healing and warfare. She was a goddess with endless contradictions. She had dominion over motherhood, healing, and fertility but was still fiery and intensely passionate. She was deeply involved in a wide array of personal matters, which is a reflection of her significance and power as a deity.

A Wiccan Goddess

Being a pagan goddess, Wiccans find Brigid a subject of great importance. Like the Irish Celts, Wiccans look to Brigid for inspiration, deep wisdom, and help with creative expression. They seek her out in all matters related to divination, healing, and abundance. They believe that working with Brigid will allow them to attain peace and harmony with the planet to sustain life in itself. Brigid comes with the power of prophecy, magic, dreams, and music, which are all fundamental elements in Wicca. Being the epitome of compassion, protection, love, and, of course, feminine power, this goddess encompassed the values that matter the most to Wiccans.

Brigid is thought of as a personification of the Divine Feminine. She is the Great Mother Goddess, which is the Irish Celtic equivalent of the Wiccan Great Goddess – a core element in the Wiccan religion. The concept of the Triple Goddess is also prevalent in Wicca. Wiccans, however, use the title to describe the triad of Maiden, Mother, and Crone.

Her Counterparts

Her stories and lore included fragments of other goddesses that are derived from many different ancient worlds. She was thought to strongly resemble Minerva, the Roman goddess. Some of Brigid's symbols are also very similar to those of Isis, the ancient Egyptian goddess. Brigid's embroidery tools, which also resembled some of Minerva's symbols, are kept at the chapel in Glastonbury. Her bag and bell, which symbolize healing, are also preserved there. The colors red, white, and black are also Kali's colors, and Kali is the Hindu goddess of time, death, and doomsday. It is suggested that an ancient linkage lies between these figures.

People began suspecting that Brigid was the equivalent of Minerva after the Romans had conquered Britain and Gaul. Belisama and Sulis, who were other Celtic goddesses, were also potential counterparts and are referred to as *Celtic Minervas* by scholars. Since the Roman conquest never made it to Ireland, there was never a direct association between Minerva and Brigid. Either way, academics still sometimes include her in the family of the Celtic Minervas. The other goddesses in the said family usually reflect many qualities, like justice, the connection with poetry, fire, stars, water, moon, fertility, healing, wisdom, and the sun.

There are other goddesses that manifest some of Brigid's attributes but who aren't a part of the Celtic Minerva family. These include:

- The Welsh goddess Cerridwen
- The Greek goddess Athena
- The Egyptian goddesses Hathor and Isis
- The Phoenicians goddess Astarte
- The Babylonian and Assyrian goddess Ishtar
- The Hindu goddess Saraswati.

How Brigid Was Worshipped

Imbolc – another term for Saint Brigid Day – comes at the beginning of February and is a time when Brigid is celebrated – this is also the start of the Irish year. During this time, offerings are made to Brigid, with a focus on bodies of water. Money is a traditional offering, and coins are often dropped into wells or thrown into rivers and streams. When Brigid is honored, the person honoring her asks for good health, healing, inspiration, and more, but they do not do so only for themselves. If you are asking Brigid for something during this time of year, you should be asking for the same for your family and friends.

Brigid is a water goddess, and there is power in bodies of water. Many wells and rivers have been named after Brigid over the years:

- **Brigid's Well (Kildare)** – Ireland has many popular sites, and Brigid's Well is among them. Located in Kildare, the well is said to have healing properties, and people often go there specifically for healing, drinking the water from the well. Those not in need of healing will often travel there to honor the goddess and pray for other blessings.

- **Brigid's Well (County Clare)** – The well is located in County Clare, and was built as part of a cemetery at a church. The spectacular views add to visits, and a journey to the well is never wasted.

There is also a very prominent pre-historical symbol that is associated with Brigid, and that is the *Brigid Cross*. People usually make it from grass or rush, and it is still used to this day all across Ireland. It is typically hung over the doorways of businesses and homes. The symbol is particularly popular around Imbolc.

There were numerous goddesses in Irish tradition and mythology; however, Brigid remains among the most well-known to this day. The goddess of poetic arts, prophecy, knowledge, crafts, agriculture, midwifery, divination, and basically *everything* was one of the very few Celtic figures who remained significant even after the rise of Christianity. This just shows how incredible an archetype she was and how popular and admired she became. Pagans recognize Brigid as the Great Mother Goddess of Ireland; Christians, on the other hand, refer to her as Saint Brigid or Brigid of Kildare. Her existence in lore and mythology has created an incredible bridge, which may not have been present otherwise, between totally opposing practices and spiritual beliefs. At a time of increased brutality and violence, the two factions were able to find a compromise.

The energy she brings to the table reminds us of our unity and oneness. It also serves as a continuous reminder of the Divine Feminine's everlasting essence. The goddess acts as a symbol of life, compassion, and love for Neopagans and Wiccans. This is why, to this day, many people seek her blessings when they hope to find happiness, comfort, protection, and love in their lives.

Now you have a clear understanding of who Brigid was and how impactful she remains to her followers. There's no doubt that the abundant information above is quite a lot to take in – there is a lot more to this Irish goddess than meets the eye. However, this chapter only touched on a few of the aspects that make up this renowned deity. Continue reading to find out more about Brigid's second and very significant role as a saint. You will also be able to better understand the concept of the Triple Goddess in more depth, as well as her deep connection with animals.

Chapter 2: Brigid the Saint

Amongst pagans, Brigid is known as the most influential goddess of the Celtic Pantheon - in the Christian religion; she is St. Brigid, the patroness of Ireland. There are many who argue that the history of the two women isn't related, while others claim there is a clear connection between them. As with the rest of the Celtic culture, there are very few written records to examine should someone want to delve into this topic. We, therefore, rely on the oral traditions of both cultures, which - at least when it comes to Brigid - do have a few facts in common. Historical artifacts also show that the saint probably had the same origins as the pagan goddess and only took over her roles and worshiping sites out of necessity.

How Did a Pagan Goddess Become a Saint?

As Christianity overtook Pagan Ireland, the depiction of Brigid as a female icon began to change as well. While the new religion infused the lives of the Celtic pagans with fear, they were clearly not ready to lose their traditional role models. So, instead of banishing Brigid from their lives after around 453 C.E., they just syncretized her with a more acceptable Christian role as a saint.

Fortunately, Brigid was a supreme ruler and a kind spirit as well. So, making her a good role model in the new religion has proven to be rather effortless. Once Druids – and now monks and priests – those honoring Brigid were very well-versed in tactics used for similar purposes: they simply needed to spread rumors about a saint whose backstory contained similar elements to the life of the pagan goddess. Describing a woman who connected the two religions, they have managed to show Brigid in a new light while simultaneously staying true to her core essence.

Initially, the pagan traditions around her worship were continued in convents in a not-too-disguised form. Wanting to overtake as the ruling religion, the Christian Church built its monasteries and convents at sacred Celtic sites. This made it very easy for the Celtic pagans to pass on their culture and empower the new generation with their ancient knowledge through sacred pagan rituals.

Later on, during the middle ages, this practice was significantly reduced – but nevertheless, it was kept alive even in these dark times. Even though wars were decimating the ranks of the men, women found a way to embrace a new religion while keeping their own traditions alive as well. After all, both cultures had lost countless lives to political and religious ideologies, leaving behind many who needed help from Brigid – or as she has become known by then, Mary of Ireland.

After becoming the patroness of Ireland, Brigid was widely worshiped for her generosity throughout Ireland –and the Scottish Highlands as well. An almost cult-like devotion to her existed until the early 20th century, when the occult once again became an acceptable topic, and many new Neopagan traditions were born. Nowadays, her evolution acts as a bridge between these two very different worlds as the worshiping of the pagan goddess is very prevalent in modern pagan cultures – more so than it is the *Veneration of St. Brigid* amongst Christians.

The Story of St. Brigid

Born in 450 AD in Faughart, Ireland, Brigid lived on the property of her father, Dubhthach, who was a pagan chieftain. Legend has it that Brigid was named after the pagan goddess of fire by her Celtic Druid father. Her mother, Broicsech, was a Christian captured in Portugal, bringing her daughter up in her own faith. Brigid and her mother were both slaves tasked with the hard work of herding cattle and sheep and tending to other obligations such as cooking, cleaning, and feeding the animals. Despite her fate, Brigid became known for her generosity from a young age. She would share the butter she churned with the poor, then replenish the missing portion miraculously. She believed that God existed in anyone who believed in him, finding it hard to deny him his own food.

Apart from her extraordinary compassion for others, St. Brigid was also known for her profound spirituality. Brigid was inspired to do this by a contemporary charity worker, St. Patrick, who she heard preaching about the needs of the poor and ill in Ireland. Through this, she felt an even stronger call to God. Wishing to devote her life to charity work and spiritual enlightenment, she asked her father's permission to enter a convent, consecrating herself to God.

Initially, wanting her to marry another distinguished chieftain, her father denied her request. In a desperate attempt to dissuade her father from finding her a husband, Brigid prayed to God, asking him to take away her beauty, so no one would want to marry her. Fortunately, God granted her wishes, making her beauty fade. Seeing this –and that his daughter was willing to give away all her possessions – Brigid's father decided to allow her to remain unmarried and to live her life as she wished. Ultimately, when Brigid turned eighteen, she and her mother were freed, and she was able to continue with her charity work.

At this point, she entered the convent of St. Macaille and made her vows to serve God. After this, it is said that St. Brigid's beauty was suddenly restored, making her glow with purity and love toward others. As her story became known throughout Ireland, other young girls devoted themselves to religious life, wishing to follow her example. Soon the first convent became too small to accommodate everyone, which is why Brigid joined another monastery, where she was appointed abbess and led with the power of wisdom. St. Brigid died on February 1st, 525, in her monastery in Kildare. She is celebrated on the anniversary of her death.

St. Brigid's Actions, Veneration, and Depictions

Nowadays, the patronage of St. Brigid extends from Ireland to nuns and midwives to artists and sailors – and even to farmers. She is also said to protect all babies, particularly watching over children born out of wedlock. Upon becoming free to devote herself entirely to God, Brigid decided to set up a convent – a sacred place where women could be educated in recognizing the needs of the poor and empowered with ways to address these needs. She wanted everyone to remember that God instructs everyone to share what they have with others. A true example of how one can bring tenderness and love into the lives of others, she continues to inspire many to carry out similar work even in modern times.

The monastery she founded at Kildare has become the first of its kind – housing both monks and nuns who devoted their lives to prayer and God. Due to her charity work and contribution to their education, the Christian Church in Ireland became one of the most influential ones in the British Isles. Later in her life, Brigid also founded a school of art that produced exceptional Gospel manuscripts and contributed to the Celtic culture's survival. Albeit only with its pieces incorporated into the Christian religion, Paganism has managed to survive thanks to the influence of unselfish and devoted people like Brigid herself. Recognizing this, poets and bards from both cultures honor St. Brigid as their patron.

A practice that helped unite the two religions in hard times was *fostering*. Families taking in children orphaned at a young age was quite common among the Celts, especially after battles. According to legend, Brigid herself once acted as a foster mother of Jesus, taking him in to save him from imminent death when Herod ordered the slaughter of all the male infants. It is said that wearing a headdress made out of candles, she led the child to safety, bringing a new kind of charitable practice into the life of Christians. She is often depicted in art with Jesus in her arms – an illustration that has become popular amongst women who mastered the art of weaving mantels and similar household decorations.

Through all her actions, St. Brigid has become one of the most venerated patrons of Ireland, along with St. Patrick and St. Columcille. St. Brigid's death is commemorated by Christians on February 1st, which date is connected with the date on which Imbolc, the imminent demise of winter, and the growing power of the Sun, are celebrated in Paganism. Christians with strong Celtic roots will often honor both the saint and the goddess on this day.

Over the centuries, St. Brigid has inspired many artists – allowing us to witness her likeness before and after her transformation from a pagan goddess to a saint. As the latter, she is typically pictured as an abbess, with the traditional outfit of a 5th-century nun. Sometimes, she is shown standing beside a cow, representing her work as a humble slave on her father's farm. At other times, she is only pictured with her cross in her hand, illustrating her love for God.

More Legends and Stories Associated with St. Brigid

The Story Brigid's Cross

One of the symbols most commonly associated with Brigid is her cross. In fact, she is often pictured with it in artwork, along with a manuscript that represents her infinite wisdom. Legend has it that the first cross was made by St. Brigid herself after visiting a dying pagan chieftain. Upon receiving a fatal injury, the chieftain asked St. Brigid to visit him on his deathbed. Seeing the man in despair, Brigid began telling him about her faith while taking some rushes and weaving them together to form a cross. Then, he asked her what she was doing, and Brigid told him about the sacrifice of Christ on the cross.

Moved by the story, the chieftain asked to be baptized before his death, so he could die a Christian. As similar stories began to spread about St. Brigid across Ireland, people started to make crosses of their own. They would hang them over their front doors so she could help them ward off fire and evil.

The Legend of St. Brigid's Cloak

Another common legend associated with Brigid is the story of her green cloak and the role it played in her acquiring sufficient land to build a monastery in Kildare. The legend is also referred to as the first miracle performed by Brigid. Having lived most of her life devoted to God, around 470 C.E., she decided to form her own sacred institution. She has searched for an ideal place for a monastery and ultimately came across the land in Kildare. Surrounded by woods to build fires, a freshwater lake, and fertile soil on which healthy crops could grow, she knew she had found the right place.

However, as the land belonged to the king of Leinster, Brigid had to ask for permission to use it. Unfortunately, her first request was denied, even though it was done after a series of prayers to soften the king's heart. Then, Brigid decided to try a different tactic. When she asked for the land for the second time, she only asked for as much as her cloak would cover. Seeing her cloak was barely enough to cover her, the king granted her request – not knowing that Brigid had also asked for God's help in the matter. Her four sisters took the four corners of the cloak and started to pull in the four cardinal directions – it began to stretch, eventually covering many acres. Seeing how Brigid managed to acquire enough land to build her monastery, the king realized that she was blessed by God and offered to become a patron of her institution. He sent her money, food, and whatever she and her sisters needed and later converted to Christianity himself.

The 12 Year Prayers

These prayers were revealed by St. Brigid and honor the seven times Jesus spilled his blood for mankind.

• Opening Prayer

"O Jesus, now I wish to pray the Lord's Prayer seven times in unity with the love with which You sanctified this prayer

in Your Heart. Take it from my lips into Your Divine Heart. Improve and complete it so much that it brings as much honor and joy to the Trinity as You granted it on earth with this prayer. May these pour upon Your Holy Humanity in Glorification to Your Painful Wounds and the Precious Blood that You spilled from them."

- **First Prayer: The Circumcision**

Pray 1 Our Father, 1 Hail Mary, then:

"Eternal Father, through Mary's unblemished hands and the Divine Heart of Jesus, I offer You the first wounds, the first pains, and the first Bloodshed as atonement for my and all of humanity's sins of youth, as protection against the first mortal sin, especially among my relatives. Amen."

- **Second Prayer: The Suffering on the Mount of Olives**

Pray 1 Our Father, 1 Hail Mary, then:

"Eternal Father, through Mary's unblemished hands and the Divine Heart of Jesus, I offer You the terrifying suffering of Jesus' Heart on the Mount of Olives and every drop of His Bloody Sweat as atonement for my and all of humanity's sins of the heart, as protection against such sins and for the spreading of Divine and brotherly Love. Amen."

- **Third Prayer: The Flogging**

Pray 1 Our Father, 1 Hail Mary, then:

"Eternal Father, through Mary's unblemished hands and the Divine Heart of Jesus, I offer You the many thousands of Wounds, the gruesome Pains, and the Precious Blood of the Flogging as atonement for my and all of humanity's sins of the Flesh, as protection against such sins and the preservation of innocence, especially among my relatives. Amen."

- **Fourth Prayer: The Crowning of Thorns**

Pray 1 Our Father, 1 Hail Mary, then:

"Eternal Father, through Mary's unblemished hands and the Divine Heart of Jesus, I offer You the Wounds, the Pains, and the Precious Blood of Jesus' Holy Head from

the Crowning with Thorns as atonement for my and all of humanity's sins of the Spirit, as protection against such sins and the spreading of Christ's kingdom here on earth. Amen."

- **Fifth Prayer: The Carrying of the Cross**

Pray 1 Our Father, 1 Hail Mary, then:

"Eternal Father, through Mary's unblemished hands and the Divine Heart of Jesus, I offer You the Sufferings on the way of the Cross, especially His Holy Wound on His Shoulder and its Precious Blood as atonement for my and all of humanity's rebellion against the Cross, every grumbling against Your Holy Arrangements and all other sins of the tongue, as protection against such sins and for true love of the Cross. Amen."

- **Sixth Prayer: The Crucifixion**

Pray 1 Our Father, 1 Hail Mary, then:

"Eternal Father, through Mary's unblemished hands and the Divine Heart of Jesus, I offer You Your Son on the Cross, His Nailing and Raising, His Wounds to the Hands and Feet and the three streams of His Precious Blood that poured forth from these for us, His extreme torture of the Body and Soul, His precious Death and its non-bleeding Renewal in all Holy Masses on Earth as atonement for all wounds against vows and regulations within the Orders, as reparation for my and all of the world's sins, for the sick and the dying, for all holy priests and laymen, for the Holy Father's intentions toward the restoration of Christian families, for the strengthening of Faith, for our country and unity among all nations in Christ and His Church, as well as for the Diaspora. Amen."

- **Seventh Prayer: The Piercing of Jesus' Side**

Pray 1 Our Father, 1 Hail Mary, then:

"Eternal Father, accepted as worthy, for the needs of the Holy Church and as atonement for the sins of all Mankind, the Precious Blood, and Water which poured forth from the Wound of Jesus' Divine Heart. Be gracious and merciful toward us.

Blood of Christ, the last precious content of His Holy Heart, wash me of all my and others guilty of sin!

Water from the Side of Christ, wash me clean of all punishments for sin and extinguish the flames of Purgatory for me and for all the Poor Souls. Amen"

The prayers offer the following promises:

- Relief from purgatory
- Acceptance as Martyrs as though they have spilled their blood themselves
- The possibility of choosing three others who will stay graceful and become holy
- Saving the souls of their four successive generations
- Consciousness of one's own death one month in advance

Differences between St. Brigid and Brigid the Pagan Goddess

While the tale of the two Brigids clearly shows some similarities, there are definitely some differences between them. For a start, St. Brigid was said to be a daughter of a Druid, a spiritually educated Celtic class member, and a slave woman, both mortals. The legend of the goddess, on the other hand, portrays her as being a member of the first Celtic clan in Ireland, her father being a leader and a warrior. She was also worshiped as the goddess of smiths, poetry, and fertility, while St. Brigid was and still remains an icon of female spirituality and one of the most influential Irish saints alongside St. Patrick. This is a much more institutional view of her roles than the free-spirited view that pagans have portrayed her to be.

Due to her uncommon association with fire and smiths, the Celts also believe Brigid was born with supernatural powers. St. Brigid dedicated her life to God and never married, whereas the pagan Brigid was married and even had children. Even the appearance of the two female icons has some differences. While both women are described as having reddish-brown hair and pale skin, Ireland's patron saint is said to have worn a long, white robe, as was customary for those serving God, and a green cloak. The pagan goddess was described as wearing modest clothes, typical for the 5th century Ireland clans. Despite all these differences, both women have inspired and continue to bring inspiration to the lives of their followers. Some even celebrate both Brigids on February 1st with a traditional feast.

Chapter 3: Brigid as a Triple Goddess

This chapter looks at Brigid from a different angle, shedding some light on her roles as the triple goddess – as she was long revered amongst the Celts in pre-Christian Ireland. It will also show why Brigid is often seen as the keeper of the Sacred Flame and how she can enlighten your inner self. Honoring her at Ireland's sacred, healing wells isn't the only way of summoning her into your life. It's also possible to call upon her whenever and wherever you need her help – it's only a question of recognizing her signs around you.

Brigid and the Sacred Flame

Nowadays, Brigid's connection to the sacred fire of Kildare is mostly associated with her role as a saint. However, legends of the fire reach back into times well before Christianity overtook Ireland. In fact, to the Celts, Brigid was known as the goddess of the sun, the source of the most ancient flame of all. According to their ancient lore, Brigid was born when the sun had just begun to rise during the time of Faughart. Upon noticing its light, she ascended into the sky to come as close to the sun as possible. The rays have enveloped her head in bright light and created a tower of flame around her home, empowering everyone and everything inside of it.

She became associated with the sun, awareness, enlightenment, and inner warmth from that moment on. Even her celebration around the time when the warmth of spring starts to overcome winter speaks of her association with the flame. She encourages the sun to stay out longer, bringing the promise of spring and brightening our lives after the dark and cold winter months. She also brings hope and renewed enthusiasm toward life and a positive outlook toward a new beginning.

At Brigid's sacred well in Kildare, the sacred flame is still tended to this day by her followers. According to the tradition, there are 19 priestesses entrusted to tend the flame, each of them feeding it with a piece of firewood obtained from the sacred Hawthorn tree for 19 days. This practice was started in pre-Christian times to celebrate the new cycle of the Great Celtic Year – which occurs every 19 years. This is the time it takes for the new moon to fall again on the same day at the Winter Solstice. It's suggested that apart from invoking Brigid to provide a plentiful harvest, the fire was also meant to cleanse and protect herds from malicious spirits.

Legend tells us that on the 20th day, when no one tended the flame, Brigid herself would keep it alive to honor its light and those who fed it on the rest of the days. While only the priestesses were permitted to walk close to the flame originally, now anyone who wishes to honor Brigid at her sacred well can visit the site. Here is where Brigid brought a bright light into the dark lives of her followers many times during history and continues to provide illumination and healing for those in need.

The Triple Goddess of the Flame

There are several interpretations of the term "triple goddess." According to some, Brigid is depicted as three mothers with different individual characteristics. However, in most Celtic legends, Brigid's role as the triple goddess resembles her three aspects: the goddess of healing and herbs, smithing and building, and midwifery and fertility. Other sources may refer to these roles as aspects of Mother, Maiden, and Crone. Most sources will agree that all these aspects are actually three sister selves with three distinct roles, which are then multiplied by Brigid's countless responsibilities. The tales also agree that these roles were often self-imposed due to Brigid's charitable nature, which she possessed from a young age.

Her connection to the Sacred Flame also presented her with the ability to fulfill these duties. She could use the flame to light the following:

- **Fire of the Hearth** – Warming the hearth and the home.
- **Fire of the Forge** – Heating the forge.
- **Fire of Inspiration** – Inspiring through work of art.

The aspect of the triple goddess may seem very simple – but yet, complex at the same time. Ruling over battle and healing while also ensuring fertility may seem like an impossible task. Then again, she was able to do much more than that. However, the number of her aspects isn't a coincidence either. The number three was often present in Celtic culture, even more so in the traditions they used to honor their deities. While Brigid wasn't the only Celtic deity depicted with a triple aspect, she is one of the best examples of the significance of this number for the Celts. For them, this number represents the three parts of a life cycle being life, death, and rebirth.

The Goddess of Healing

As a healer, Brigid is often depicted in artwork carrying a bag of healing herbs and flowers. Her healing role is also associated with animals and water – often seen around natural springs and healing wells. Since we know that folk healers had sacred wisdom even before the Celts arrived in Ireland, it's easy to see why her ability to heal is revered in such a manner.

Not only that . . . but the knowledge she wielded as a healer is also connected to philosophy, inspiring scholars to delve into the history and poetry to reveal the secrets of their ancestors. It also said that Brigid could provide insight into prophecy and dreams through her wisdom, explaining these visions and using them for inspiration, guidance, and much more.

There are tales about Brigid teaching the Irish about the healing properties of herbs and their applications on humans and animals. She gave most of her lessons under an Oak tree near her well in Kildare. While the tree is long gone, her well is still associated with healing and divination and is often used to glean helpful guidance and insight. Other than the one in Kildare, there are several other wells in Ireland dedicated to the goddess, all with waters blessed with her healing grace. Here, she combines the warmth of the sun with the sparkling purity of the water, healing everything from body to soul.

There is also a legend about Brigid displaying her generosity and sense of justice at the same time. According to the story, two lepers came to visit Brigid in Kildare in a desperate attempt to find a cure for their illness. The goddess agreed to help them and directed them to the well, asking them to bathe one another in the water. Following her instructions, one man washed the other one until the man was healed. However, when it was the turn for the cured man to bathe the other man, he refused. Seeing the injustice in the man's unwillingness to assist a person who helped him to heal, Brigid caused the man's disease to return. She then took the other man under her cloak and allowed its power to heal the man instantly.

There is little evidence about how Brigid came to possess these powers. According to one source, she learned how to tend wounds when her own family members were injured in one of the many battles they had fought against other Celtic clans. Other sources claim she inherited her powers from her ancestors. Many other Tuatha Dé Danann clan members were said to possess supernatural powers, though not all of these gifts were as powerful as hers.

The Goddess of Smithing

Having participated in many battles, Brigid acquired exceptional metalsmithing skills. According to Celtic lore, her ability to forge was so great that she could create a whistle that could transport someone to another location. It is said that she gave this to the warriors for them to use at night to transport themselves one by one onto the enemy territory. She also went on to show them how to forge more effective iron and smith tools. Her ability to shape and transform wasn't only limited to weapons and other metal objects. It transcended to everything else in the world that could be reshaped and, with it, *reborn.*

But even after her lifetime, she remained the patroness of the warrior, providing them weapons, aiding them through questions, and helping them bring justice to the lands. For this aspect, Brigid is still revered as the overseer of law, order, and ultimately peace. The latter is probably the result of her deception in wars after her son was killed in a battle.

Legend tells that Brigid had three sons who were fierce warriors. One of them, Ruadan, suffered a mortal injury, and after his death, the feuding parties left the battlefield to honor their goddess's grief. From then on, Brigid would encourage feuding parties to forge peace instead of weapons, which is how she became the symbol of unity. And instead of being the patroness of war, she became a guide for metal workers and artists.

The Goddess of Fertility

As the goddess of fertility, Brigid was often associated with childbirth, livestock, and crops. She is often called upon at childbirths to provide midwives, children, and their mother's protection, but she can also shield the babies afterward by leaning over their cradle and enveloping them in her cloak. Providing a fire in the hearth also provided the children with a warm environment to keep them healthy and happy.

Although her connection to domesticity is said to go even further than that, it is believed that her power lay in every cleansing object, weaving, and embroidery decorating the home. Furthermore, her support also extended to the birthing process of people's creativity in work and art. By keeping the fire in the hearth burning steadily, she also provided transforming warmth, allowing people to channel positive energy into the tasks they had to do.

Brigid helped animals in childbirth and lent her healing grace to sick animals. She showed people how to keep cattle and livestock healthy and prevent illnesses. Brigid also shared her knowledge of making grounds fertile with a group of women, who then went on to tend the lands of the goddess. Despite this, she still brought prosperity through the abundance of the land herself. In fact, her green cloak was associated with protection and the fertility of the soil as well. The Celts believed that each spring, Brigid laid down her mantle, covering the land with luscious greenery. Through this act, she brought new life into the world, further ensuring our well-being and allowing us to remember our own ability to grow and prosper in life.

United Aspects

Apart from the three main ones, Brigid embodied many aspects, allowing her to participate in any part of the natural incarnation process. And even more importantly, these three aspects can rarely be separated from each other – a testimony to all of them being sister essences of one person. When the goddess of fertility brings change into any aspect of our lives, the process of rebirth is aided by the goddess of the forge, and she is responsible for this transformation. In turn, the goddess of healing will bless all of our creations birthed by the goddess of smithing. She could also heal the wounds of those the other sister couldn't protect, while the fertility goddess within her would provide them with fertile ideas to keep them safe.

All of her aspects show a creative side, which is why we can use them all together. Suppose you want to use the powers of the triple goddess to illuminate your path in a creative process or when facing a challenge. In that case, she will also envelop you in a protective embrace, shielding you during your journey. This ensures that anyone can enjoy the great benefits of the whole process, despite how different its polarities may seem. Because humans also have their own polarities, acknowledging them is the only way to achieve the balance that we seek.

Brigid in Modern Pagan Beliefs

In these modern times, sometimes there is nothing we need more than a source of inspiration. Bringing with her the Sacred Flame, Brigid can illuminate your way by showing you who you are in your own natural state. She can show up in your dreams and aspirations and become your muse if you lack something that would help your creative energies flow. Everything you do in life is empowered by some invisible force inspired to create something. This energy comes from you, and it helps you to realize your innate desires and establish a connection with an infinite source of spiritual wisdom. However, there are times when you may need help tapping into this knowledge, and this is exactly when Brigid can come to your aid. She will show you that piece of the sacred fame each of us carries inside of us. By doing so, she will reveal that divine source of inspiration you were looking for, even if you are not yet aware of it.

The goddess Brigid can empower you in any aspect of your life. Whether you want to find your purpose, release or transcend your fears, heal, or banish self-limiting behavior, she will show you how. Sometimes, you will just need her to show you the truth, so you can liberate yourself from your past or stop worrying about your future. In modern societies, it can be hard to communicate one's true desires, especially if they go against the wishes of our loved ones. Brigid will grant you her support while expressing your true desires to those around you.

Apart from encouraging creative expression, she can give you a voice to use when you feel you can't find the right words to communicate. Brigid certainly has a way of ensuring that the words you are saying are in complete alignment with your innermost thoughts. If you need help to ascend from your passive voice and find affirmative language to stand up for something you believe in, Brigid is the right guide to call upon. This is true for all aspects of communication – which is why she can help even in this day and age. Whether it's verbal communication, poetry, or a message you need to send via the phone, the goddess will help you channel the magic into your words. In this way, you express what you want to create or experience without fear of being judged getting in the way. Brigid will remind you that the true power lies within you and your desires and not in following others.

Brigid will encourage you to speak your truth, which can be a powerful gift in itself. Whether you're manifesting a goal you have in mind or expressing your honest opinions, when you feel the purity of your thoughts ringing in your voice, you will feel more balanced within yourself. The expression of one's self comes with such a blessed feeling that it will further empower your inner growth. It is believed that you are raising your spiritual energy by allowing Brigid to illuminate your truth with her sacred flame. Although having many faces (and not all of them peaceful), Brigid can bring harmony into your life simply by highlighting the essential truth. Through this, she will raise your confidence – which is something else we often struggle with in these modern times. But by being backed up by an influential goddess, like Brigid, it's so much easier to embrace yourself with confidence. You can finally experience the ultimate peace within yourself and in your relationships with others as well. Not only that, but she may guide you on a path so you can help others to experience the same bliss too. Everything she can do to help you, you can do for others with her help.

What Are the Signs of the Goddess Calling to Someone?

Like most spiritual guides, Brigid can come to you when being summoned or call to you if she needs you to do something for her or yourself. There is no predetermined way you can know she is calling you. However, you may suddenly come to a realization that you are doing something she would do, so you may as well seek her guidance to make sure you get the best results. You may also feel a presence in your life prompting you to listen to your inner self more. If this happens, it's a good idea to contemplate if Brigid is the one evoking these feelings. If you realize that your work could positively influence someone else's life, it may very well be the goddess's way of telling you that you are on the right track.

Brigid can also come to you in your dreams or visions if you practice journeying or similar spiritual exercises. She can come in the form of a human figure, an animal, or a symbol with a specific meaning. Either way, you will feel something different about them, even if they are a little evasive about who they are. It's recommended to do some research to see if the signs point toward Brigid. However, if she really wants to guide you in the right direction, she will be quite persistent. She will be sending you a series of messages, symbolic in nature.

Brigid typically calls people in such a way that they will be able to interpret what she says based on their religion, culture, gender, or experiences in life. She is all about spirituality, so she will try to contact you through the means you are the most comfortable with spiritually. She is also loving and nurturing, so she will be as gentle as possible if it's the first time she contacts you. In this case, the signs of her being there may not be obvious at first, so you may want to explore the connection by taking the first step.

If you want to ensure she is the one backing you up, you can set up an altar and make offerings, such as milk and butter. You can also deepen your connection with her through meditation, prayers, and by looking into her lore. More about working with Brigid is yet to be discussed in the following chapters.

Chapter 4: Brigid as Maman Brigitte

The Celtic Goddess and the Saint are only the faces of Brigid, most commonly known in Europe. However, her role as protector was known all across the globe – just a little bit differently. For practitioners of Haitian Vodou, she is known as Maman Brigitte, Grann Brigitte, Manman, or Manman Brijit. She is a loa who plays a paradoxical role in this diasporic religion, being the spirit of death and fertility at the same time. These two roles may seem worlds apart, but they have a lot more in common than one may think. Obviously, Brigid isn't a common goddess, and she isn't a common loa either. Her syncretization into this role was borne out of necessity brought on by slavery and the salvation she could provide to those who suffered this fate. While slavery has been abolished in a major part of our world in modern times, it still carries a significance we cannot ignore. Role models and guides like Maman Brigitte remind us that there is always something to look forward to, even in the darkest of times. And if a person needs to change to be able to do this, they must do this while they can enjoy the fruits of their labor.

What Is a Vodou Loa?

Like many other religions, Vodou is also based on natural spirituality, but spirits –rather than deities - guide its followers. They acknowledge a god (called Bondye) who may help the living – but usually does so through the loa. These are the most influential spirits in Vodou and are also known as the lwa. Legend has it that the religion was formed by African slaves brought to Haiti many years ago. The loa represent the souls of these slave ancestors. They oversee the spirits of those living in the visible world and guide them as needed. Furthermore, these spirits help this nation express a unique worldview, practice their traditional medicine, and establish justice in their own way.

As a loa, Maman Brigitte is typically summoned in a common Vodoun practice, in which the person who wants to communicate with a spirit allows them into their body. This is usually performed as an elaborate ceremony, which includes chanting, drumming, dancing, and using traditional Vodou symbols called *veves*. By letting her spirit take a temporary position in their body, the followers can communicate much more freely with Brigid.

How Brigid became a Loa

Unlike the other loa living in Vilokan, the abode of spirits, Maman Brigitte is fair-skinned, indicating her origins are not from Africa. Instead, she is believed to have been born in Ireland, around the time when many in the British Isles were forced to become indentured servants. It's believed that Brigid was transported to Haiti to act as a servant but received a similar treatment to many African slaves, which led to her ending up with the same fate they did and becoming a loa. While some argue about the truthfulness of this tale, the similarities between Maman, the Celtic goddess, and the Irish Saint are undeniable. Their appearance, name, and similar roles all indicate the connection between these female icons. Even the Maman's burial site – the grave of the first woman buried in a Haitian cemetery – is marked with a cross very similar to that of St. Brigid.

In her role as loa, Brigid was first seen as a patroness of slaves. Until the practice was abolished at the end of the 18th century, slaves, particularly women, relied on her protection, often carrying dolls with them, symbolizing the Maman's presence in their lives. Her becoming a carefree loa was a reminder that anyone can transform their lives – even if, for them, this change would only come after death. Upon being freed, the former slaves were ready to start their own quests but still relied on Maman Brigitte's guidance on their journeys. In fact, many Vodouists still ask for her help when wishing to speak their truth or find their purpose in life. After all, no one can tell you what you should believe in – and Loa Brigitte is the best example of this.

Brigid's Roles as a Loa

Much like her Celtic goddess counterpart, Maman Brigitte possessed incredibly powerful healing abilities. If someone suffers from a long-term illness, they may seek out Maman Brigitte to help them recover. She can also heal minor injuries like broken bones and is often called to assist with illnesses others refuse to tend to, such as sexually transmitted diseases. Her powers aren't limited to healing physical illnesses, either. She can help in situations where someone only needs a fresh start mentally to avoid a so-called "spiritual death" as well.

However, unlike the female deity, a loa also helps souls she can't save to reach the afterlife in a peaceful manner. Upon observing the state of the person's soul, she will decide whether she can step in and heal them or if she merely needs to ease their suffering and let them pass on to the afterlife. And if the person's death is already imminent, relatives may call upon Brigitte to watch over the poor soul during the final hours of their life. She will observe as the person takes their last breath and then start preparing their soul for the afterlife. Like her husband, she could also act as a protector of graves and cemeteries. In exchange for a small offering, she would stand over a tombstone, safeguarding the soul of the deceased. For her to be able to protect or bless a gravestone, it must be marked with a cross.

Apart from healing, she can also be called upon for several other matters. For example, she may help protect women in childbirth or in an unhealthy relationship where domestic violence is present. She can also provide guidance on relationship issues, such as dealing with unfaithfulness.

For all these roles mentioned above, she is primarily revered by women. However, she also deals with issues both genders can face. For example, suppose someone commits a crime or other wicked deed. In that case, they will feel Maman Brigitte's force upon them as they receive punishment. She will ensure everyone receives divine justice, regardless of the magnitude of their crime. She is one of the few loa who Vodouists prefer to call when they feel they have suffered unjust harm and wish to seek retribution for their damages.

In the same way, Voodooists believe God delegates their duties to the loa; these spirits will also share part of their responsibilities with mortals. Apart from promoting compassion towards others, this also teaches humans responsibilities they can't avoid. Maman Brigitte encourages people to accept death rather than fear it. Legend has it that she often held rather spirited lessons about the importance of respecting the dead and remembering their role in our lives. Besides caring for the dead herself, she also wants the living to help the deceased pass on toward the afterlife. If necessary, the relatives of the deceased may stand guard at the grave, helping Brigid and her husband safeguard the decease's soul. The purpose of this is also to make people face their mortality and realize that if they want to be treated with respect when they die, they must do the same for others. If anyone disobeys her and fails to tend to their deceased, they will face punishment from Maman.

One of the reasons Maman Brigitte is seen as such a powerful loa is because of her ability to inflict the verdict on whether someone will receive punishment or assistance. Summoning her must be done only after carefully considering all the factors that may affect her ruling. The fact that someone calls to her seeking help, claiming to be wronged by someone, doesn't mean they will automatically be seen as the innocent party. Maman will observe their actions, too, and only grant a judgment in their favor if they have made a claim with pure intentions. If they did it with malicious intent, they might very well be punished for their actions. So, if one does not want to be on the receiving end of one of her curses, or even a lecture using harsh language, they must appease her. She can be quite wild sometimes, and once she gets into high spirits, it may take some time for her to be sufficiently appeased. This is particularly true if she is confronted with foolish behavior, as she has no patience for this whatsoever.

Besides all her other roles, she is also associated with fertility in several aspects of life (much like other variations of Brigid). Rum and partying aren't the only things she enjoys. She is also said to be interested in the arts and poetry, encouraging all who want to pursue these careers. By enhancing their spirituality, she can help anyone express their creative side and give life to new ideas and projects. After all, life is too short to be stuck in the same position without the possibility to grow. Maman Brigitte understands this and therefore promotes fertility, allowing people to become a better version of themselves.

How Maman Brigitte Is Depicted

Maman Brigitte is often shown wearing simple yet feminine and sensual clothes, especially if she has been summoned to heal. At other times, when she is ready to party with her husband, she opts for more revealing and dangerous garb. She has light, reddish-brown hair and emerald-green eyes. Her favorite colors are black and purple, as is shown in several illustrations. When she isn't busy healing or following souls to the afterlife, Brigitte is seen drinking rum infused with hot peppers. The drink is said to be too hot for mortals to consume. She, on the other hand, would sometimes eat these peppers or chew on a cigar she had stolen from her husband. There are also several depictions of her and a black rooster.

She accepts most of these objects as an offering for her services – although her favorites are definitely black candles and pepper-infused rum – the hotter, the better. However, if someone only has a piece of black clothing and a prayer to offer, she will not deny her assistance as long as the person is honest about their intentions. For, there is nothing she loves more than speaking from the heart, even if this means using foul language. And she expects the same from the followers, not minding if they utter obscenities, as well.

Even though she is known for her rather mischievous tricks, she encourages others to speak the truth. She knows when it is time for a party and when it's time to return to her role as a loa. As a result, she can be protective, caring, respectful, or wild and rowdy if necessary. She can recognize whether someone requires tough love but also knows when softer, more compassionate words are needed. How she appears depends on what the soul in need requires.

Maman Brigitte and Baron Samedi

A former slave himself, Baron Samedi is a loa notorious for his debauchery, obscene behavior, and several mortal vices. Like Maman Brigitte, he too enjoys a good party, especially if plenty of dancing and rum are involved. With both of them being influential loas of death, the pair led the Ghede family. Essentially, he is her male counterpart, with the pair sharing many roles. And while both of them are known for consorting with mortals, they are often depicted as husband and wife. As outrageous as it seems, this behavior isn't without a purpose. Through it, the pair shows that the rules of the living no longer restrain them and that they are free from all the burdens they were destined to carry during their lives as slaves. The second purpose of their carefree demeanor is to show the living that they need to enjoy the benefits of being alive while they can. Death is imminent, and it will come for everyone, so they might as well do everything they can during their lifetime to die without regrets.

The Baron is typically depicted as a tall, slim black man wearing a stylish outfit, such as a tuxedo, a top hat, and even a walking cane. His appearance represents a contrast to Brigitte's fair complexion and simple style – but then again, she was quite unique amongst the loa. Both husband and wife are capable of seeing the spiritual realm and the world of the living at the same time. However, while Brigitte would often ascend amongst the living, the Baron prefers to spend his time in his spirit form. The pair rules over the dead and the cemeteries, but they have different, yet somewhat complementary, roles.

Baron Samedi would meet the souls waiting between the world of the dead and the living and welcome those destined to die to Vilokan. However, not everyone who meets him will end up dying – only those whose grave has been already dug by the Baron. In some cases, he can prevent a person from dying – in others, he would accept them into the realm of the dead. If he believes a person can be saved, he will refuse to dig a grave for them and let Maman Brigitte save their life. While her husband can decide whether someone can be saved or not, Maman Brigitte is the one to decide if a person deserves to be healed. If not, the person will die, and their soul is left in the care of the Baron. Or, if someone is particularly undeserving, she herself would personally escort them into the Vilokan to ensure they will stay dead.

By preventing a person from dying, together, they prove that the person is worth saving. Sometimes, all it takes for them to save someone is to lift a powerful curse that has been cast upon the person. Other times, it would take applying both of their extraordinary healing powers to cure someone of an ailment. Acting as the guardians of the cemetery, the pair will ensure each person is buried properly and remains in the ground undisturbed. According to the legend, they do this to prevent the souls of the deceased from coming back to the dead bodies, raising them from the grave. Naturally, they expect some sort of payment for their services, even if it's in the form of a simple offering of cigars, rum, and black coffee. They will also appreciate the followers honoring them by wearing purple, white, or black clothing.

It is said that Brigitte is more likely to be content with the latter, while the Baron will typically require a more elaborate ceremony, complete with dancing and even animal sacrifice. Without a good incentive, he won't be bothered to cross the realms. Due to this, Maman Brigitte has far more roles in the world of the living than her husband, but they will always work together to help a soul, one way or another.

Besides working together, the pair also have a playful relationship. Being the loa of money, Brigitte ensures people respect monetary transactions and assures they pay their debt when needed. At the same time, she doesn't care much about money and personal belongings – hers or anyone else's. She even enjoys stealing the Baron's top hat and cane and watching as he is looking for the objects.

The Veve of Maman Brigitte

A veve is a symbol used to draw out the loa – and is usually designed by keeping the characteristics of the specific spirit in mind. While some veves may share some common elements, their design and use are dependent on the loa. For example, just as Maman Brigitte prefers certain colors, chants, and drum beats, she is also characterized by a unique set of illustrations that unite in her veve. So, when her presence is desired, her veve is drawn on the ground with some kind of natural powder, and she will then notice that the ceremony is for her. The veve is typically erased at the conclusion of the ritual, which frees the spirit once again.

The veve of Maman Brigitte typically includes a triangle and a heart sitting opposite each other, depicting the cycle of life and fertility, respectively. Between and on these shapes are several crosses, symbolizing crossroads and the crucifixion of Jesus Christ. A black rooster is also added sometimes, representing rebirth and the dawn of a new life. During a ritual, a veve is used to make her spirit descend to the world of the living. Apart from specific ceremonies when Maman Brigitte is called upon for guidance, her veve is displayed on All Soul's Day, which falls on November 2nd. Vodouists may also honor her spirit with her symbol on February 1. Coincidentally, this is also the day on which St. Brigid and the triple goddess are venerated. On this sacred day, the veve is used to infuse objects with her healing power, empowering the followers' practice.

A Song Associated with Maman Brigitte

Songs and chants appeal to every loa differently, as every spirit has its own individual preferences.

Here is a song Maman Brigitte prefers in Vodou ceremonies:

Originally sung in Haitian Creole

"Mesye la kwa avanse pou l we yo!

Maman Brigitte malad, li kouche sou do,

Pawol anpil pa leve le mo (les morts, Fr.)

Mare tet ou, mare vant ou, mare ren ou,

Yo prale we ki jan yap met a jenou."

English translation

"Gentlemen of the cross, please advance for her to see you!

Maman Brigitte is ill, so she lies down on her back,

A lot of talking won't raise the dead,

Tie up your head, tie up your belly, tie up your kidneys,

They will see how they will get down on their knees."

This song is typically sung when someone is being prepared to receive punishment for a crime they have committed. It illustrates the Vodouists' relationship with Maman Brigitte, including an unusual choice of words used when addressing an ancestral spirit. As we know, this female icon isn't someone to mince their words, and she expects the same from her followers.

Chapter 5: Sacred Animals and Symbols

Each deity in every mythology has a certain set of symbols tied to them. Their followers or the people who sought their blessings incorporate these symbols in their worship practices. Symbols can be used to enrich the connection between individuals and their deities in many ways. For instance, they can place them on their altars, wear them as jewelry, and even decorate their houses with them. To honor the deity, these symbols are often presented as an offering in pursuit of blessings, protection, or certain gifts from the deity.

Brigid has numerous symbols herself, many of which come from lore and legends surrounding the goddess and other figures in her tales. Some symbols also come from the rituals that the ancient Celts used in the rites of worship of Brigid. She is typically represented by a wide array of symbols, especially those associated with farm animals, agriculture, and light. You may be surprised to learn that there are numerous things we associate with inspiration, love, and compassion that were originally symbols of the ancient goddess Brigid.

This chapter mainly focuses on two topics; the animals and symbols of the goddess Brigid. It explores the deep connection and bond the goddess had with animals, as well as the various creatures that are often associated with her. As for the symbols, you will learn the origins and the meaning behind the most important symbol: Brigid's Cross. Included is a step-by-step instruction manual for creating one along with the other symbols associated with Brigid.

Sacred Animals

Brigid's dominion over motherhood and fertility did not only include humans and deities but also extended to animals. Her duty as the protector of animals is eminent through the animals she had, which are as follows:

- Two oxen named Fe and Men. A field named Mag Femen, which is located in County Kildare, was named after them

- The *King of Boars* was named Torc Triath, made an appearance in Arthurian legend

- A strong ram named Cirb, also known as the *King of Sheep*

As mentioned in previous chapters, Brigid was labeled the goddess of agriculture due to her strong association with the sun. She was particularly the protector of animals. As you know, Brigid's eagerness to watch over mothers and their offspring, whether humans, deities, or animals, came from the fact that she lost her son in battle.

Since cattle were a very important part of Irish life, herdsmen strived for the blessings of Brigid to have her watch over and protect their animals. The goddess made them fertile and ensured their wellness and safe delivery of offspring.

There are many religions where deities are not immortal, and the Celtic religions are among them. There are many stories of deities dying in battle, through old age, or in other ways, and when this happens, another deity usually takes their place. When the smith god died, Brigid took his place and became the smith goddess. Many legends suggest that Brigid was the daughter of Danu. Danu was the mother goddess of the Tuatha De Danann, whose place Brigid appeared to take when she became the main mother of the pantheon.

Not much is known about Danu. However, there are some things we can garner from old texts and stories passed down. Just like Brigid, she was connected to water and the earth, acting as a mother to the world. The Danube River might have been named after her, though the similarity in the name could also be a coincidence. Brigid has taken her place as a protective archetype of motherhood, who was especially associated with Planet Earth.

Brigid was different from the other "motherly" goddesses in the sense that she didn't have as many children as they did. However, she was believed to take exceptional care of children, or the young, in general. Though, she was associated with the fundamental agricultural practices in her locale like many other Earth mother goddesses.

Ireland and Scotland do not have tropical climates, and much of the land is mountainous or carved through by rivers and lakes. It was hard to find a good place to grow crops, and while many root vegetables were traditionally grown, it was the livestock that took precedence. Animals did not only provide meat but gave clothing, tools, and vessels too. And the ingenious Celts always found ways to use the whole animal, like in the creation of haggis. Brigid, the goddess of agriculture, also contributed greatly to this.

Certain issues became a lot more serious during the colder months of the year. The Irish wondered whether there would be enough food to sustain them and their livestock. They also lived in fear of having disease affect their tribes, particularly the children, nursing mothers, and the elderly. They were always concerned with identifying the animals that were vital to the lives of humans.

However, the most pressing questions would surround pregnant ewes and cows as milk, cheese, and curds were considered essential aspects of life.

Animals typically give birth to their offspring and produce milk by Imbolc. Since milk was considered sacred food, cows were also a symbol of motherhood and its sacredness. Milk was deemed very pure and nourishing, and they thought that a mother's milk had healing powers. The Celts thought of cows as protective mothers who were concerned with the well-being of their offspring rather than a cow that merely produced milk.

Besides the cow and the ewe, which were Brigid's totemic animals, the goddess was also linked to the cockerel and the snake, which was a symbol of regeneration. This is essentially why she was linked to the fertility goddesses – as they were typically depicted holding snakes. Brigid was also similar to Minerva, as they shared symbols such as the spear, shield, and serpent crown. Serpents were a prominent theme when it came to Celtic jewelry (notice the link to smithing and craftwork). Many torcs paraded this symbol of divinity and power.

Aside from cows, ewes, and serpents, owls, bees, lambs, and hibernating animals were highly associated with Brigid.

Symbols and Animals

The following creatures act as prominent symbols of the goddess Brigid:

- **Birds:** The Falcon and the Raven have very strong connections to Brigid, as well as the festival of Imbolc. This is because birds are symbols of the end of winter and the renewal of spring. Around the time of the Imbolc festival, ravens start building their nests. Nesting is a symbol of fertility, rebirth, and new life.

- **Serpents:** Serpents are among Brigid's most popular emblems. They represent generation and renewal and are also associated with the coming of the spring. The Celts also believed that serpents were symbols of Brigid's domination and divine power, in general.

Brigid was also linked to swans. In Celtic mythology, swans had a connection to fertility, healing, and growth. The Druids believed swans represented the soul and thought they helped in traveling to the otherworld. In modern-day Ireland, it's still believed that killing a swan will result in death or misfortune.

Brigid the Bee Goddess

Many claim the Celts only came to Britain for the black bee and honey. The country was named *Isle of Honey* by the Welsh because of the great number of bees that flew to and from Britain.

According to Celtic myth, Bees were believed to possess a lot of wisdom. It was said that these creatures served as messengers between both realms. They traveled to the otherworld, bearing messages from the gods. The Scots believed that bees consolidated the knowledge of the Druids. This belief led to the creation of the lore that suggested bees had a secret type of knowledge. Highlanders thought that when a person fell asleep, bees that had embodied their souls left their bodies.

This ideology around bees made it into the rise of Christianity. Scottish and English folk tales suggested that on Christmas day's midnight, bees hum very loudly in honor of the birth of the Savior. The lore about the bees traveling from one realm to the other was modified to state that bees came to Earth directly from paradise.

There were numerous Celtic lore and tales that went on about how bees should be treated and even went as far as to say they should be informed about family events or occurrences.

Mead and honey, which are products of bees, were used for mystical, magical, and medicinal purposes. The Scots made potions out of cream, whiskey, and heather honey, all in equal portions, to cure ailments and diseases. It was customary to feed infants hazel milk and honey, which is where the modern tradition of feeding babies milk and honey comes from. Finn mac Cumhaill, a mythical Irish hunter-warrior, was tricked into marriage because he was given a goblet of mead which was intended to muddle his senses. You can also attain the blessings of the exalted deities on Beltane by offering them honey cakes. The recipe typically consists of white wine and honey. Mead is also an acceptable ingredient.

To Brigid, bees were sacred creatures. Her hives were thought to carry mystical nectar from Brigid's apple orchard of the other realm. In her lore, the rivers that ran all the way into the Otherworld were made of meat. St. Brigid was believed to protect her people with bees. She used them to fend off cattle thieves and used honey to heal victims of the plague. Dadweir Dallpenn's sow, Henwen, left three wheat grains and three bees in Gwen. It is a popular thought that this resulted in the production of the best wheat and honey on Earth to date.

St. Brigit and the Wolf

Centuries ago, St. Brigid built a little hut, which could be found under a huge oak tree in a location that we now know as Kildare. The rural area was very tranquil and quiet when she had first moved in. There were many wild animals, a dandelion meadow, and a forest, all of which St. Brigid loved greatly. Not long after, more and more people started to know about St. Brigid's healing powers and great kindness, which is why many pilgrims arrived in Kildare to meet her. Many of them decided to stay, growing a village around Brigid's small hut. Even the king went to visit her and built a hunting lodge in the forest.

Wolves were among the common wild animals that roamed around Kildare and Ireland's vast woodlands, which made the villagers scared. With the king and his men hunting down so many deer, the wolves had no choice but to eat more of the lambs, upsetting the villagers. The King, however, also started noticing that the deer were diminishing in number, and he also blamed it on the wolves. Wanting to punish them, the king offered a gold coin to those who killed a wolf and brought it to him.

Among the people who had delivered him dead wolves, a hunter brought back a cub along with the wolf (its mother) he had killed. The king trained the cub and was proud of his compliant wolf. He even brought it with him when he went to Kildare sometimes. Tragically, the wolf got loose in the village at one time. A woodcutter came across the wolf, not knowing who it belonged to, and shot it with an arrow. He took it to the King, awaiting his reward. The king, however, immediately recognized his pet by his markings. In a fit of boiling anger, he asked the guards to lock the woodcutter up in the dungeon.

The villagers found out about what had happened to the woodcutter when the king ordered that a gallows be built by the local carpenter. As a result, they went to Brigid, seeking her help. Brigid was very sad to hear about the death of the wolf and the oncoming death of the woodcutter and set off to visit the king after borrowing a villager's horse and cart.

On her way to the lodge, Brigit saw a white shadow moving between the trees. The horse immediately started spooking in fear.

However, the saint was able to calm him down with her words. The shadow started moving faster before jumping and landing on Brigid's lap. It turned out to be a large, white, friendly wolf.

They were welcomed into the King's chambers, where he stared greedily at the beautiful wolf. White wolves were very rare, which is why the king wanted to own one so badly. Brigid constructed a deal with the king where he would take the white wolf in exchange for the woodcutter's freedom. The king undoubtedly agreed, and Brigid whispered to the wolf that he'd be rewarded with incredible cuts of meat all his life as long as he remained a good servant to the king. The wolf laid his head on the king's lap as he stroked its ear.

Brigid took the woodcutter back and insisted it would be better to leave two wicked beasts to roam around freely than to punish an innocent one. It was said that no other wolf was ever killed in that area of Ireland again for as long as Brigid was alive.

Symbols

In addition to the swan, the serpent, and the bird discussed earlier, there are many other symbols associated with Brigid, which include:

- **Flowers:** Flowers and herbs are very popular symbols of Brigid. The most common symbols include the rowan, snowdrop, basil, heather, and angelica. It's customary to have bouquets that include several of these flowers and plants around during the festival of Imbolc. The herbs are representative of Brigid's renewal and healing powers, while the flowers are linked to fertility and the coming of spring.

- **Woods:** Both roles of Brigid, the goddess, and the saint, are highly associated with wands that are either made of willow or white birch. Oak forests were also symbolic of the goddess Brigid, according to the Druids. They believed these trees to be sacred to her. The Christians also preserved this tradition and built a church in a grove of Oak in honor of St. Brigid.

- **Milk:** Being the goddess of agriculture and the patroness and protector of domestic animals, milk is thought to be a prominent symbol that represents Saint Brigid. As we explained above, milk was of great importance to the Celts. This was especially the case during the wintertime when food and crops were scarce. Brigid can be seen with a stag in many pieces of artwork and paintings. Milk is also representative of the goddess's divinity and purity.

- **The Eternal Flame:** The goddess had flaming red hair similar to a fire, which is why she is usually represented by a flame. Additionally, Brigid is believed to be a fire goddess, which is why those who worship her use this symbol in her honor. The ancient Celts also burned a sacred flame in Kildare to pay homage to the goddess. Priestesses gathered up on the hill to tend to the fire and invoked her to protect the animals and provide fertility and abundant harvest.

- **Wells:** As you may recall, Brigid, the goddess of water, was in control of wells and rivers. She had two wells, one in Kildare and the other in County Clare, both in her name.

- **Cloaks and Mantles:** Brigid wore a healing cloak that protected whoever sought shelter underneath it. The goddess once hung the mantle on a beam of sunlight.

- **White Candle:** It is believed that the Saint blesses candles on Feill-Bride, Candlemas, or Brigid's feast day. This is why having a candle dedicated especially to Brigid on her altar makes a great symbol. It's recommended that you use a white candle that has three wicks.

- **Anvil:** Brigid is the goddess of craftwork and blacksmiths. This is why using an anvil or any other smithing tool is a great symbol to represent her.

- **Brigid's Cross:** Brigid's cross is among the most significant symbols associated with Brigid. While helping a dying chieftain, St. Brigid prayed while weaving an equal-arm cross using the rushes scattered all around the floor (As explained extensively in chapter 2). The saint told the man all about the salvation of Jesus Christ when he asked what she was doing, which is why he decided to be baptized before his death. Pre-Christianity, the Brigid cross served as Brigid's symbol as the goddess of the sun. The cross can be made with three or four legs.

People usually hang the Brigid Cross over the doors of their homes and businesses to keep them protected. The cross is also hung over a child's bed or an infant's cradle to ensure their safety and well-being. The Celts also hung the Brigid Cross over the byre in the barn. They used to burn it on St. Brigid's eve in the hearth fire. They then made a new one to receive the Saint's blessings for the New Year.

To make a Brigid Cross:

You will need:

- Reeds/straws – 16
- Small rubber bands – 4
- Scissors

Directions:

1. Hold a reed vertically and fold another one in half.
2. Place the first reed in the middle of the folded one.
3. Hold the overlapping middle tightly between your forefinger and thumb.
4. Turn the rushes anti-clockwise to 90 degrees. The open ends of the folded reed should be pointing upward.
5. Fold the third reed in half over the other folded reed. It should lie horizontally (left to right) against the first straw.
6. Make sure to hold tightly in the middle, turning all the pieces together anti-clockwise another 90 degrees. The open ends of the third reed should be pointing upward.
7. Fold the fourth reed in half and place it over and across all the reeds that point upward.
8. Rotate anti-clockwise another 90 degrees and add another folded reed. Keep repeating this process until you use up all your reeds.
9. Use the elastic bands to secure the cross's arms.
10. Trim the ends of the reeds so they're all the same length. Hang up your Brigid Cross for protection.

Having numerous roles in the Irish Celtic world, the goddess Brigid has numerous symbols. She is linked to various symbols representative of her role as the goddess of agriculture, patroness of domestic animals, and the protector of women, children, and animals.

Chapter 6: Celebrating Imbolc or St. Brigid's Day

Imbolc is celebrated on the 1st and 2nd of February in the Northern Hemisphere and on the 1st and 2nd of August in the Southern Hemisphere. Imbolc is the last of the winter festivals and the first of the summer celebrations. On the Wheel of the Year, it falls between Yule and Ostara.

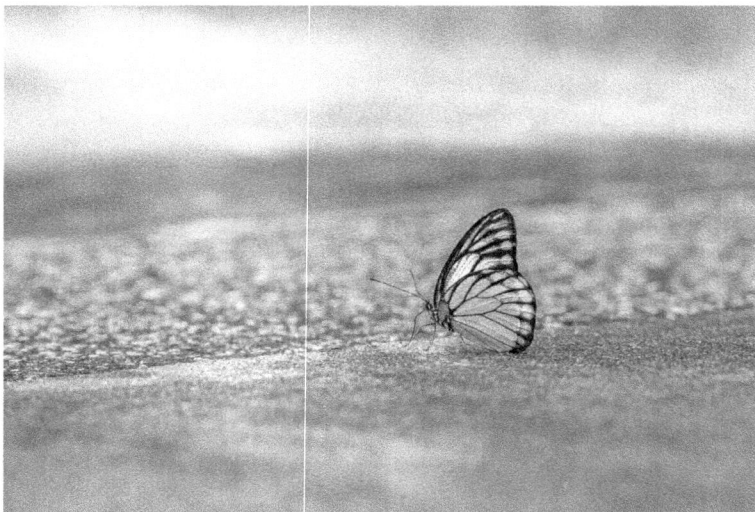

Today the Imbolc celebration is not as popular as it used to be, but it is still one of the four greater Sabbats. Back in the pre-Christian era, Imbolc was one of the most prominent celebrations because it came right after the most challenging part of the year, which was winter. It was a celebration that ushered in spring and signified the fact that winter was over, setting the stage for the most productive time of year: summer. The old European settlers, just like many people across the world, relied on farming and hunting to make ends meet. Winter in this region was and still is a very harsh time of year with little to grow and little to do. Summer was the most productive time of year when people could be out and about, growing crops, and this was the time to make all their preparations for the long, dark winter ahead. Therefore, Imbolc was a time that everyone looked forward to.

The word Imbolc means "in the belly" and references how things in nature are in the early stages of pregnancy during the late winter and early spring. Nothing has started to blossom as of yet, but the warm weather approaching has an impact on the earth's fertility as the winter dies down – the environment gets ready to produce in summer – which is why farmers plant crops during this time. Just like how pregnancy is associated with a new beginning, purity, hidden potential, and an awakening, Imbolc is the time of year when existence is getting a fresh start. This is the reward for the tough time that they endured during winter, but it is also the time to make the most of the available resources to better prepare for the next inevitable winter season. Alternatively, farmers use the wintertime to prepare for the upcoming summer, making sure they'll be ready when the time comes.

The Focus of Brigid on Imbolc

While there are many reasons to celebrate this festival, the main focus of Imbolc is on Brigid and honors her and all her contributions. In ancient times, people had different ways of celebrating the Goddess. One of the most common celebrations was to make a doll out of wheat straws or oat straws and dress it up. This doll would be placed in white flower bedding, and young girls would carry the doll from one house to another in their neighborhood and would receive gifts, much like how children trick-or-treat today. On the day of Imbolc, people would light large bonfires and have a large feast where people of all ages would gather to eat, dance, pray and spend time with the community.

In the modern-day, these celebrations are still used, but one of the most common ones is to decorate the altar with different symbols of Brigid, such as white flowers, a bowl of milk, candles, or even set up a small fire. Today people live in very different houses and in cities where it isn't always possible to have large community festivals, so celebrations may look a little different, but the spirit remains the same. Also, in the past, the celebration was more about preparing for the year ahead, celebrating the change of seasons, and moving into a different pace of life. In the modern-day, the focus is still on Brigid as people are looking to earn her blessings, though we are less reliant on the environment to earn our livelihood.

In the next chapter, we provide instructions on how to set up an altar for Brigid. This is important because it is a major part of the Imbolc festivities when celebrating the goddess – not only does it launch the festival, but it is also a ritual that people perform all year round. When setting up your altar at home to prepare for Imbolc, remember to make it a personal experience whether you want to seek her blessings or thank the deity for everything she has done specifically for you. We have covered everything about how you can set up a great altar at home for Imbolc and how you can use specific things to represent the different characteristics of Brigid, too.

St. Brigid's Day

Over the many centuries that pagan religions have existed alongside Christianity, certain elements have been carried over from each religion to the other – and there is a lot of common ground in the religions today. A good example of this is the concept of Saint Brigid in Christianity. The roots of the idea of Brigid come from pagan religions, as explained in Chapter 2.

Many of the things believed in Paganism about Brigid stand true in Christianity as well. There are identical celebrations between Imbolc and St. Brigid's day, and these can be found when researching the ancient Celtic festival of Imbolc. St. Brigid's day is also about embracing the fact that the warmer weather is ushering in brighter days, as well as welcoming new life and fertility with the growth of plants and the birth of farm animals. The only main difference is this was celebrated by Christians. Since these festivals are held on the same day and share the same purpose, they are almost interchangeable today. The great thing about this is that you can take elements from both festivities when celebrating the 1st of February today.

The history behind St. Brigid's day shows how Christianity embraced a lot of Brigid lore and how the goddess is honored – with a few tweaks here and there. The church imposed the celebration of St. Brigid's day on February 1st as a way to overwrite the more traditional Imbolc celebration. The Christians that celebrated this day used to make an effigy of St. Brigid and wash it in the fresh ocean water. Then, the effigy was placed in a circle of candles where it was left to dry. To accompany this, people would use stalks of wheat to make unique crosses known as Brigid crosses.

Activities for Imbolc

Modern-day celebrations for Imbolc have definitely evolved over the centuries. One of the major differences is the time it is celebrated. Since spring happens at different times in different places of the world, and practitioners of Paganism are spread out all over the globe, some hold Imbolc festivities at different times. Some people prefer to stick to natural seasons as a reference point – as it is a celebration of the transition from winter to spring and celebrate it in their region whenever springtime comes around. Others believe that February 1st is more symbolic and choose to stick to the date rather than follow the actual seasons of the year.

Some of the most common celebrations include the following:

Creating a Brideog/Straw Doll

Making an effigy of Brigid in the form of a straw doll is a common practice in both Christianity and Paganism. In Paganism, this is known as the Brideog. This depiction of Brigid represents fertility, fortune, and the awakening of nature. There are a few different ways to use these dolls. Traditionally, the dolls are placed in little beds decorated with white flowers and positioned next to the fireplace or a bonfire outside – this is believed to bring good fortune and light to the home. Some people prefer to wash the doll with water and then place it near a fire to dry, while others prefer to make the doll and keep it on their altar.

To make the doll:

You will need:

- Straw lengths are usually made with wheat straw, but you can use any kind of natural straw you find
- Some decorative garments such as hats, scarfs, red hair, shoes, a dress, or anything else you'd like to add
- Some yarn
- Dried herbs for decorations

Directions:

1. Begin by placing all your strips of straw into some warm water so they can moisten a bit. This will make them more pliable, and they won't snap in half when you bend them into different positions. They will also retain the final shape better when they dry out.

2. If you want a doll that is six inches tall, then you need a length of straw that is at least 12 inches long. You will fold this length of straw over itself lengthwise, so you have all the ends of the straw on one side and a bulb on the other end.

3. From this position, you want to tie a bit of yarn around the bulb portion of the straw. Tie this an inch or two down from the actual bend – this will be the head of the doll.

4. Spread the straws out from under the spot where you have tied them together and make some room to add some more straw horizontally here, as these will be the doll's arms. To make the arms, simply get some straw together and tie it at both ends so it is secure. Place this bundle of straws horizontally under the head and in between the straws that you have spread out.

5. Once placed, tie another bit of yarn under the arms on the main body of the doll so that the arms are held securely in place.

6. From there, spread the straw from below the second yarn not to resemble a dress. Now the structure of the doll is complete.

From here, you can start to decorate the doll as you wish. You can dress it in clothes and even glue on some hair to make it more appealing. Some people prefer to put a hat on the doll. You can use dried herbs such as lavender to decorate the skirt of the doll, and you can make it as colorful as you like. Since Brigid is associated with fire, most people make her hair red, but it's not compulsory.

Brigid Cross

The Brigid cross is commonly used as a decoration for the altar, and people also hang this at the entrance of their homes as a symbol of protection. If you would like to learn about the Brigid cross and how it's made, refer to the previous chapter, where it is explained in detail. Note this is an important aspect of Imbolc.

Spring Cleaning

Imbolc is characterized by change. Change in the seasons, change in the food, change in the lifestyle, and change through the emergence of new life. Just like you wouldn't want to eat fresh food out of a dirty plate, you can't expect good changes to happen in your life if you don't have a clean area to welcome these positive changes. It is also important to note that cleaning and showering were things that didn't happen very frequently for people in ancient times. So, periods of time that were dedicated to cleaning were taken very seriously and were often very desperately needed. Spring cleaning is one ritual that is common among all pagan religions and even Christians during the time of Imbolc.

To ensure thorough spring cleaning:

You will need:

- Some fresh water (you can also use distilled water if you like)
- Some sea salt
- Some precious oils such as rosemary oil, lavender oil, or a mix of both
- A spray bottle or a brush
- A candle

Directions:

The first thing to do is to prepare your mixture. For this, you are going to combine the water, salt, and essential oils into a bag or bowl if you plan on using a brush to smudge it around the house, or you can put it into a spray bottle and spray it all over. When you are going through the house to spray the water, you will also take the candle with you to expose parts of the house to the light of the candle.

To begin, you should just start clearing the house of clutter. Tidy up the space, vacuum if you need to, organize things that are out of place, then clean out the kitchen and the toilets, along with every other room you intend to clean that day. This is the time to assess the mess that has been piling up over the slow winter months so that you can clear your home of things you don't need and make room for what you do need for the year ahead.

With everything nice and tidy, you can move on to cleansing. It's a good idea to do this on a bright and sunny day when you can open all the doors and windows, allowing some fresh air into the structure.

To perform this cleansing, you will start at the front door and light the candle. You can spray the mixture around the perimeter of the door, or you can use your brush to smudge the corners of the door. Then move the candle around the corners of the door so as to illuminate all parts of the entrance. Then move through the different rooms of the house. The aim is to get the cleansing mixture into all those hard-to-reach areas that don't get the same maintenance and also get some light into these hidden corners that are often restricted from fresh air and light. You can go on to cleanse every room in your house, including the exterior of the house.

Some people prefer to say a prayer while they do this. If you like, you can say a prayer is asking for happiness, abundance, and cleanliness before you start the practice. You should also follow the spring cleaning with a prayer at the end of the process. Once you are done, simply discard any of the fluid you have left and wait for everything to dry out properly.

Bonfires

Like many other pagan celebrations, bonfires are also a big part of Imbolc. Some people who don't have access to a backyard can have a little fire indoors in the fireplace or opt for a fire on the roof. If you have space for a larger fire, then have a good-sized bonfire outside in the garden. Usually, this is celebrated in the late afternoon and early evening so people can gather around the fire to eat, pray, and dance. You can have a feast lined up for an early dinner, or you can stick to snacks for the guests while they attend the bonfire.

Family Activities for Imbolc

Imbolc is a time to connect with your friends and family and cherish the time you have together. In ancient times, it was clear to see why winter was a challenging time, and many people didn't survive the difficult weather. Imbolc gave families the opportunity to come together and try to overcome the losses they had faced while preparing for the year ahead. Some of the best things you can do as a family at this time include:

Crafts

There are many things to do related to crafts during Imbolc, such as making the Brigid doll, decorating the altar, making bonfires, and making all kinds of other decorations for their homes or for displaying on the altar. These are all fun activities you can do with your children rather than buying store-bought items. They are all very basic and can be made as advanced or complex as you like – or as advanced as your skills can handle. You can give children the tools they need and let them create something through their creative expression while staying within the requirements of Imbolc. It's a great way to spend time together, immersing yourselves in the arts while educating them on the celebration and teaching them a few skills.

Celebrate Health and Home

Brigid rules health, wellness, fertility, and fresh starts. As the season changes from a slow winter to a slightly faster-paced spring and summer, take this time to celebrate the changes with your children and give them the opportunity to appreciate their own health and the environment. Make them a part of your home cleansing ritual, invite them to build the altar with you, take them out for walks and hikes, and let them have fun at an outdoor bonfire. This is also a time to teach them how they can contribute to taking care of their environment, as many people are preparing for farming at this time. Educate them about the importance of the environment and how it plays a vital role in our well-being.

Magic

Imbolc is a magical time, and the changes that are taking place in the physical and spiritual world are nothing short of magical. Take this time to show your children how to use a pendulum, study the weather, or observe changes in the stars. Let them know how the energy of the world around us impacts us and the significance of magic in our lives. You can educate them on the different stones and other tools that are used in magic and give them some room to play with these items as they learn about them.

Imbolc Food

Imbolc feasts are known as being extremely delicious. It is the peak of winter comfort food, and it is served in generous quantities, usually in a serene environment like at the bonfire in the backyard. As Brigid is associated with milk and dairy, a lot of the recipes that are cooked at this festival tend to have a lot of dairy in them, with ingredients like butter, cream, cheese, and milk.

One of the best dishes to make for this occasion is lamb and barley. You can make it in a large batch as a complete meal without any need for sides. It's very easy to make and is best done when cooked slowly. Get started in the late morning to have the feast ready by dinner. Here is what you need to make the dish:

Lamb and Barley
Ingredients:

- 3 tbsp. oil or butter
- 1 kg Bone-in lamb (shanks work very well – if you don't like bone-in meat, you can use boneless)
- 1 cup of beef, lamb, or vegetable broth
- 1 large onion chopped
- ½ cup barley

- 2 tbsp. curry powder or a spice mix you prefer
- ½ cup golden raisins
- 1 tbsp. crushed garlic
- Salt and pepper to taste
- Coriander and lemon for garnish

Directions:

In a large pot that will fit in all the ingredients, start adding the oil, crushed garlic, and chopped onion. Sauté these till the onions are translucent and the garlic is fragrant. This should take no more than 5 minutes at a low flame to prevent the onion and garlic from burning or caramelizing.

Next, add in the meat and start to brown it on high heat. The aim is to brown the exterior of the meat to keep all the moisture in, not to cook it completely. Once browned, add in the broth, curry powder/spices, salt, and pepper, and allow it to come to a rolling boil. Once boiling, lower the flame to a low setting and cover. Let it cook slowly on low heat for the meat to cook evenly. If you are using bone-in lamb, it can take a couple of hours for the meat to be ready. If you are using boneless lamb that has been sliced into fine strips, it can take as little as twenty minutes. The thicker the meat, the longer it will take to cook all the way through.

If you are using bone-in lamb, let it cook till it is 75% done, and then add the barley and the raisins. You might need to add some more stock to adjust the proportions. This way, your meat and the barley will be completed together.

If you are using thin strips of boneless lamb, add the barley with the meat to allow them to cook together at the same time. When the barley and meat are three-quarters done, add in the raisins.

Once cooked, your lamb should be falling off the bone, the barley should be nice and fluffy, and you should have some thick gravy at the bottom of the pot that you can spoon over the meat and barley when you serve it. Have a taste to check how well it is seasoned at the final stage and adjust by adding more spices, as necessary.

To serve the dish, use bowls rather than plates. Make a base of barley in the bowl, place a piece of meat on top, and pour some gravy over the meat. Slice the coriander and sprinkle it over as a garnish, and finish with a squeeze of lemon. You can also serve wedges of lemon in the bowl as a garnish.

Some of the best meals to make at this time of year include dumplings, sowans, bannocks, barmbrack, and colcannon. It is also a tradition to make a plate for Brigid and leave some delicious food at the table for her spirit to enjoy.

Chapter 7: Building an Altar for Brigid

Altars are places of worship, sacrifice, and prayer. They have been a part of numerous religions and cultures ever since the beginning of time. Having an altar at home can help you draw strength and enhance your spirituality. Altars can provide us with opportunities we may not have been able to experience otherwise.

Altars open up a unique channel of a direct connection between an individual and the divine. Setting up your own altar enables you to choose your divine, forge a special spiritual connection with your deity, and personalize the overall experience. The practice allows you to view life situations and events through a different lens. It grants you the opportunity to approach unfortunate situations in a positive way, as connecting with your deity is always a relieving, constructive experience. Building an altar allows you to maintain a spiritual center, especially if you don't practice an organized form of religion. Those who do, however, can still benefit greatly from all the enriching elements home altars have to offer.

Setting up an altar is a form of art. It is not something you can throw together in just a few hours. Finding out what you want to include in your altar, where you want to place it, and how you want to use it takes a lot of time. The altar should be an ideal blend of things that work for you and your chosen deity to give you the desired outcome. This process requires contemplation and a deep understanding of symbolism, which brings us to our next point.

When you're setting up an altar, you accumulate a huge mental encyclopedia of symbolism and underlying meanings. You understand the symbols and underlying messages of each color, animal, and mythological figure. Not only is it an unmatchable learning experience, but it is also a very meditative activity. It provides a form of much-needed relaxation in today's world.

Having an altar at home provides a temporary escape from the busy nature of life. It serves as a safe space in which you can recollect your strength, reorganize your thoughts, and tap into your spirituality. This spiritual space can generate positive energy and regulate its flow in your home. Creating an altar is also a great way to bond with your family, teach your children about spirituality, and introduce them to the world of the divine.

Most people use altars to connect with deities and build a strong relationship with them. This way, the deities can offer you guidance and accept your requests. They won't necessarily ask for specific physical items. For the most part, it is your time and apparent willingness to put in the effort that matters. The gods want you to prove how keen you are about working with them. To know exactly what to include on your altar and offerings, you may need to look into their myths, tales, and lore. Fortunately, you'll be able to establish a strong connection with Saint Brigid using the knowledge you've accumulated on Brigid herself (and the guidance on how to build an altar for her) in this chapter.

Building the Altar

Creating an altar for Brigid is pretty much the same as setting one up to celebrate Imbolc. This is because, as you know, the celebrations of Imbolc were shaped to honor the goddess Brigid. Since the concepts of growth, fertility, purity, life, birth, virginity, rebirth, reunion and renewal are closely related to Brigid and Imbolc, incorporating elements that convey these themes into your altar would be a great idea. These include the following:

- **Brigid's Bed**

  You can make Brigid's bed using a cardboard box, a wooden box, or a wicker basket. Use paint, flowers, ribbons, essential oils, and herbs to decorate it (read on to find out which ones to use). This bed is a symbol of hospitality, signaling that you are welcoming the goddess into your home. You should place it near a hearth fire. In exchange for your invitation and kindness, Brigid blesses your home with healing, protection, and fertility. Place a soft blanket on it before you place the Brigid corn doll and the priapic wand on it. Chant a phrase that welcomes the goddess into your home.

- **Brigid Corn Doll**

  As you can infer from the name, this doll is made of corn. It is a symbol of good fortune, abundance, and fertility and should be placed on Brigid's bed along with the priapic wand. The Corn Mother of the Lammas holiday would make a good Brigid corn doll. Make sure to dress the doll up in the colors gold, white, and red.

- **Priapic Wand**

  A Priapic wand is to be made of fruitwood wrapped up in a ribbon with a pine cone attached to one end. This is a symbol of male fertility and, as we mentioned before, should be placed with the doll onto Brigid's bed.

- **Brigid's Cross**

If you recall from chapter 5, Brigid's cross is one of the most prominent symbols of the goddess and Imbolc. It is made of woven straw and is representative of the sun. These crosses are believed to bless your home with protection, fertility, luck, and prosperity. They are commonly hung over babies' cribs, doorways, near the hearth, in barns, or below the eaves.

- **Other Crafts**

You can make other crafts like a heart sachet, a rowan cross-protection charm, and candle wheels and incorporate them into your altar decor.

- **Sacred Flames**

The hearth fire is the sacred fire of the Imbolc season and of the goddess Brigid. It is representative of the increasing power of the sun. If you don't have a fireplace or hearth fire, you can burn a long-lasting candle someplace safe. Ancient people used to carry torches all around their pastures and fields to purify and ready them for the cultivating season. The pagan Italians, particularly in Rome, used to carry torches in a march in honor of Juno, the goddess of marriage.

- **Flowing Water**

Brigid, the goddess of water, had dominion over rivers and wells. Aside from having multiple of them in her name, she believed water to be sacred. It was customary to toss a coin in fountains, wells, or springs as an offering to Brigid. For this reason, you can also include cauldrons or chalices on your altar.

Other Symbols

- Faeries – According to lore, the goddess of light is the sister of the fae.

- A hammer or an anvil; Brigid is the goddess of craft and smith work.

- Poetry/creative writing/lyrics – Brigid is also the goddess of poetry.

- An image or statue of Brigid

Colors

The colors red and white are very prominent symbols of the goddess Brigid. The red is symbolic of the hearth fire. It also represents the blood that comes with giving birth. The color white is associated with snow and healing. Other significant colors include light green, pink, brown, yellow, and pastel colors.

Plants

- **Blackberries** – Blackberries are thought to be sacred to Brigid. Not only are they symbolic of prosperity, but they also possess healing properties. Blackberries are especially helpful when it comes to stomach-related ailments.

- **Hops and Grains** – Brigid's preferred drinks were beer and ale. Offering her favorite drinks every once in a while would be a great gesture.

- **Flowers** – You can decorate your altar using any early spring flowers, such as snowdrops, potted bulb flowers, daffodils, crocus, forsythia, or white or yellow flowers, in general.

- **Herbs** – You can use herbs like dill, red clover, rosemary, and chamomile to decorate your altar and Brigid's bed.

- **The Hazel** – Hazel is representative of keening. It is said to have been invented by the goddess Brigid herself when she wailed over the murder of her son, Ruadan.

- **The Oak** – Cill-Dara, which is otherwise known as the cell of the oak tree, was the place Brigid's abbey existed. The goddess was brought up by a Druid, who was considered an oak priest. Oaks are highly symbolic of Dagda, Brigid's father.

- **Willow** – Willows are sacred to February, which is the month of Imbolc. It also symbolizes the lunar cycle and feminine energy.

- **Rowan** – Rowans are also sacred to February. They are believed to provide protection against potential disasters and evil witchcraft or magic. It is best to keep a Rowan near the doorway.

- Celandine, Basil, Mugwort, and Coltsfoot, which Brigid is associated with, are also great healing plants. Using these leaves can help you attract prosperity, affluence, and healing into your home.

- Angelica, bay laurel, ginger, iris, tansy, heather, myrrh, and violets are other plants associated with Imbolc.

Animals

You can incorporate figurines of some or all of the following animals:

- **Cow** – Preferably, select a fairy cow (it should be white with red ears).

- **Boar** – It is a Celtic symbol of battle and aggression.

- **Snakes** – Snakes are said to come out of their lairs on February the 1st.

- **Fish** – Small spotted fish are believed to be a sign of healing, as they appear in the goddess' sacred springs.

- **Sheep** – Brigid protects the lambs as soon as they are born. She also serves as a midwife, protecting their mothers.

- **Badger, Wolf, and Bear** – These all come out of hibernation around Imbolc, which links them to Brigid.

- **Swan** – Swans leave Ireland during Imbolc and come back again during Samhain. The fact that they know exactly when to leave and return is what makes them so sacred to the goddess of knowledge, Brigid.

Incense

The benefits of incense have been known for hundreds of years. While the exact beliefs differ from one time, place, and culture to the other, one thing has always been clear. That is that incense stimulates and enriches the spiritual aspects of ourselves and our minds. Incense can be enjoyed as a means of self-care or as a tool to enhance spiritual and religious experiences. Either way, its sense can stimulate the brain and positively impact one's mood. It's incredible how a scent can promote positive energy and influence the general atmosphere of a room. Here are some of the scents associated with Brigid and Imbolc:

- Frankincense
- Camphor
- Basil
- Cinnamon
- Myrrh
- Wisteria
- Vanilla
- Jasmine
- Violet
- Lotus

Crystals

- **Pyrite** – Working with pyrite can be a great way to honor the role of Brigid as the goddess of smith work. This stone is made of iron and is associated with strength and success.

- **Citrine** – The fire of Imbolc is made of more light than it is of heat. This is why choosing the stone Citrine, which is otherwise known as the light make, is a great way to honor the goddess of life. Citrine is also associated with success and is a symbol of the goddess' fiery hair.

- **Bloodstone** – You can honor the goddess's midwifery skills by working with bloodstone. This stone is representative of everything having to do with blood and health.

- **Green Opal** – The crystal generates water content as it forms, which later results in the creation of opal. Opal, in that case, is a symbol of the goddess's water element.

- **Staurolite** – Staurolite is also known as a fairy cross. This crystal looks like fairy wings and is believed to bring the fairies' luck.

- Other crystals associated with Imbolc and Brigid include amethyst, garnet, ruby, onyx, and turquoise.

Food and Drink

- **Seeds** – Seeds are symbolic of the anticipated new life. You can either use sunflower seeds or pumpkin seeds on your altar.

- **Baked Goods** – The goddess favors freshly baked goods like bread, scones, poppy seed cakes, and muffins.

- **Dairy Products** – As you may recall, dairy products were sacred to the Celtic Irish. You can offer things like milk or cheese.

- Peppers, onions, garlic, raisins, herbal teas, and spiced wines are also associated with Brigid and her festival.

Where to Place It

You can place your altar anywhere you like. You can build it on top of a table or any other existing piece of furniture, mount it onto the wall, or even build a designated stand for it. The most important thing you should keep in mind, however, is its size and height. It is recommended to keep your altar above the height of your heart chakra, so you will need to consider the position in which you typically practice. For instance, if you like to work with the goddess in a meditative state, you would likely be sitting down on the floor. If you usually stand, make sure to position it higher. Placing your altar above your heart chakra is a symbol of your desire for oneness. If you'd like, you can also create a private space for your altar or place it behind curtains or a door. This way, you can keep it safe from children, pets, and accidents.

Using the Altar

You should try to connect or interact with your altar every day, in one way or another. This doesn't mean that you need to pray or provide offerings all the time. All it means is effort is required to tend to it, whether this means dusting it, tidying it, or even lighting up a candle. There will come days, however, when you will sit down for hours on end, connecting with the goddess Brigid. You can also use your altar to do rituals. For instance, you can use it to celebrate the seasonal cycles, especially Imbolc, or rite of passage. As explained above, it's all about building a relationship with your deity. This is why you'll have to put in the work every single day.

After you've created your altar and made sure that everything is in place, you need to give it life. To do that, you need to:

1. Close your eyes and bring your awareness to your heart. Feel the love, devotion, and longing you have towards Brigid. You can recite an invocation or a prayer that speaks to your deep admiration and appreciation for her. Allow your heart to sense the lobe.

2. Keep focusing your attention on yourself and visualize the goddess immersed in the love you have for her.

3. After a few minutes, open your eyes and externalize this love. Send it out to the image or statue of Brigid that you have on your altar. This serves as an invitation to Brigid to dwell in the space created for her. While her energy is present all around, your altar acts as the center point.

4. Make Offerings. The way you make the offerings depends largely on your personal experience and traditions. It will also be based on what you believe is suitable for you and enriches your connection with your deity, or in your case, Brigid. Many feel that offering Brigid beer, incense, dairy products, candies, baked goods, and even heavy cream is appropriate. After you close your eyes, feel in tune with your heartbeat, and feel and send out the love that you have for her. Make sure that you feel relaxed and grounded. Light your candle only when you feel calm and centered. Then, recite a chant or a prayer (you will come across numerous to choose from in the following chapter. Be careful to put your candle out when you have finished, and always keep it away from flammable surfaces. It's preferable that you put the lid back on it and snuff it instead of blowing it out when you need to. You need to dispose of your offerings safely when the goddess is done with them and doesn't need them anymore, especially if they consist of food and drinks. You can use them as compost or feed them to stray animals (if they will not harm them, of course) instead of throwing them down the drain or in the trash.

There is no better way to build your relationship with Brigid or any other deity for that matter than to build a dedicated altar. Altars are a great way to forge a personal connection with your deity. It also serves as a great opportunity to prove to your deity that you're keen on working with them.

Chapter 8: Honoring the Goddess Daily

There are various ways to celebrate the goddess on Imbolc. However, you can also honor her throughout the year in many ways. In this chapter, we provide information on ways you can celebrate Brigid daily in an acceptable way. It doesn't take much to show your appreciation and praise the goddess. You can consider tending to her altar regularly, researching about her, lighting candles, and visiting wells, among other ideas. Once you've chosen your method of choice, the last section of the chapter provides prayers, chants, and affirmations dedicated to Brigid.

Read about Brigid

There are several Irish myths about the Celtic Goddess Brigid. If you want to honor her, then you need to know her well enough. The best way to learn about Brigid is to read various books and other sources of literature dedicated to her. First and foremost, you should know the many names she has, including the following: Brigantia, St. Brigid, Brid, Bride, Briginda, Brigdu, Brigit, Breosaighit, Brigantia, and Bridey. As you learned at the start, the name Brigid means the "Exalted One."

To honor Brigid, equip yourself with the right tools to use, like various crystals, including citrine, moss agate, garnet, emerald, rainbow obsidian, and amber. Similarly, there are specific plants, such as oak, red clover, rushes, and shamrock, which you should use when you perform your rites. As explained in chapter 5, certain animals like a cow, boar, serpent, sheep, wolf, badger, pig, salmon, white bull, horse, and vulture are symbolic when you worship the Goddess Brigid. The following are other important symbols to keep in mind.

- **Brigid's Cross:** As you know, this is made of grass or reed and is commonly used as an offering to the Goddess. It is recommended to place your cross-over windows or doorways to protect your home from bad energy and evil spirits.

- **Serpent:** The popular symbol that represents renewal is another way to honor the Goddess Brigid.

- **Eternal Flame:** Since Brigid's flaming red hair is associated with fire and is often symbolized by flame, many worshippers use fire to pay homage to the Fire Goddess. Therefore, when you light your white candle, you invoke the element fire, which will help you feel her presence.

To celebrate Brigid, include the ideal offerings and gestures that she deems sacred such as water, milk, eggs, blackberries, coins, bread, spears and arrows, herbal teas, Brigid's crosses, and tying ribbons on trees. You can also leave food and drink for her and her cow on your doorstep. There are several homemade gifts you can present to the Goddess, and these will help you develop a strong relationship with her. For instance, Brigid's dolls are made from dried raffia and displayed on makeshift beds close to a fireplace. They are believed to bring fortune and light into your life.

Set Up a Small Altar

Brigid is a nurturing and loving Goddess. She appreciates her followers dedicating a small place in their homes to invoke her presence. You can achieve this by setting a small altar in a suitable spot. Use the previous chapter's guidance to build an appropriate altar.

Visit your altar daily to meditate, open yourself up to more experiences with Brigid, and chant prayers. On your altar, you must have items such as drawings or small statues that remind you of the Pagan deities. Make it a point to display items that honor Brigid on your altar – healing herbs and sheep are necessary since they are sacred. Every time you visit your shrine, cleanse it to get rid of negative energy as part of the ritual honoring your Goddess.

Tend to Her Sacred Flame

Whenever you speak to the Irish Goddess, you must burn a candle. During ancient periods, the priestesses of Brigid would keep a fire burning for hundreds of years. Because of the modern priestesses, the fire burns and is tended at Kildare today. However, the practice of lighting a candle as well as tending her sacred flame are ways to connect with Brigid.

With Brigid being the Lady of the Sacred Flame, you cannot overlook the importance of associating her with fire when honoring her. Therefore, if you have pledged yourself to this specific deity, you should light a candle before you recite prayers. Lighting a candle is a special way to declare your allegiance and faith in the Goddess. Make sure you choose the appropriate candle that suits a specific ritual you want to perform.

Visit Local Wells

On top of tending to Brigid's sacred fires, you should also acknowledge water, and you can achieve this by visiting a local spring or well. When you visit a natural water body, you must pray to the Goddess there. As discussed previously, Brigid is regarded as the goddess of water since she maintained dominion over wells and rivers. Therefore, when you visit a well, you need to offer your gratitude while asking for healing of the soul, mind, and body. She is a healer, and, as cited in the first chapter, she had two famous wells – one in County Clare, the other in Kildare. To this day, many people still visit these wells to seek blessings and pay their respects.

If you cannot visit these famous sites, you can choose any local natural water body to honor your goddess.

Write Poetry

Writing poetry is another crucial aspect you can consider honoring the Goddess Brigid. She is regarded as the goddess of poetry; the one poets used to follow. Many people still do, and they get inspiration from writing poetry. Therefore, it is crucial to learn the role of poets in ancient Ireland. The Goddess can help inspire you to express yourself. Take this opportunity to awaken your poetic side to honor her. Writing poetry, music, meditations, and other forms of art can help you know Brigid better. This can go a long way in helping you celebrate her.

Celebrate Brigid Using Food

Apart from celebrating the Celtic Goddess with a feast during Imbolc, you can use different types of food to honor Brigid today. The pagans continue to celebrate her by lighting bonfires and presenting a variety of offerings, including crosses. You can also do the same regularly, but you don't necessarily need to hold big events like feasts. There are different types of food you can eat to celebrate the goddess. But some food is more appropriate for honoring the Irish Goddess than others. For instance, you can include root vegetables such as carrots and potatoes in your diet since they are traditionally consumed at Imbolc festivals and associated with Brigid. Other foods you can eat to honor the goddess include dairy products like milk, cheese, yogurt, and cream.

Learn Traditional Prayers

There are several prayers for Brigid that you can use when worshipping her. Remember that the Goddess has many names, so when you learn her traditional names, make sure you honor all of her aspects. If you can recite a prayer, this is a great way of celebrating your Goddess. Another way of celebrating her is to honor and recognize the significance of your Irish ancestors. You need to set up a family tree to help you trace your roots to your Irish ancestry. You can also play traditional Irish or any act that honors Brigid.

Another thing you can consider is to dedicate your hearth fireplace to Brigid, who will bless the center of your home since she is the domestic Goddess as well. She also keeps the sacred and everyday fires burning. Create a mini altar for her on the hearth. If you don't have a hearth, you can dedicate a cauldron to her. As part of honoring your Goddess, you should offer some grains, dairy products, pieces of bread, or part of your family meals.

Prayers, Chants, and Affirmations Dedicated to Brigid

Whatever ritual or spell you do to honor the Irish Goddess Brigid should be accompanied by a prayer, chant, or affirmations. Consider the following when celebrating her to show your unwavering appreciation.

Sing Praises to Brigid

"Every day, every night
that I praise the Goddess,
I know I shall be safe:
I shall not be chased,
I shall not be caught,
I shall not be harmed.
Fire, sun, and moon cannot burn me. Not
lake nor stream nor sea
can drown me. Fairy,
the arrow cannot pierce me.

I am safe, safe, safe,
singing her praises."

Brigid Invocation Prayer and Offerings

"Celtic goddess of the hearth,
home, and inspiration.
Patroness of poetry,
healing, and smithcraft.
Weave a web and tell a story,
oh Brig, so that those who weave
as well may understand.
Blessed Brig, grant your peace and
patience across the land.
Every hill, every valley, every river
and stream shall sing your praise.
Lady Brig, I am calling you.
Come into my home
and sit upon my hearth.
Bless my home and family with the
protection you have to offer.
A bed is always here for you.
Lady Brig, if you would have it.
I call to you as I weave my web,
paint my picture, and write my story.
May your blessings be
ever-present in my life."

During this prayer to Brigid, you should light a red candle. The incense you can use includes Lavender, Jasmine, Chamomile, and Rosemary. Remember that you can also include water, coins, bread, milk, herbal tea, and blackberries as offerings.

Thank Brigid for Meal Blessing

"This is the season of Brigid,
She who protects our hearth and home.
We honor her and thank her

for keeping us warm as we eat this meal.

Great Lady, bless us and this food

and protect us in your name."

It is customary in other modern Pagan traditions to offer a blessing before a meal. As part of honoring Brigid, the goddess of the home and hearth, you should bless your food before eating it. This simple blessing of gratitude can go a long way in helping you celebrate the goddess of the home fire you use to prepare your food.

End of Winter Meal Blessing

"The winter is coming to an end

The stores of food are dwindling,

And yet we eat and stay warm

In the chilled winter months.

We are grateful for our good fortune,

And for the food before us."

Imbolc is not celebrated in winter, but it is good for you to honor the Goddess Brigid every season. When winter is about to end, many traditions are practiced as people look forward to spring. This is the time to appreciate the goddess' blessings that got you through the colder months now that winter is coming to an end, and you can do this by saying prayers.

Prayer to Brigantia, Keeper of the Forge

"Hail, Brigantia! Keeper of the forge,

she who shapes the world itself with fire,

she who ignites the spark of passion in the poets,

she who leads the clans with a warrior's cry,

she who is the bride of the islands,

and who leads the fight for freedom.

Hail, Brigantia! Defender of kin and hearth,

she who inspires the bards to sing,

she who drives the smith to raise his hammer,

she who is a fire sweeping across the land."

Brigid was known by several names, and in those places where she was known as Brigantia, she was also viewed as the keeper of the forge. From this perspective, she is associated with cauldrons and smithcraft. In some instances, she is known as Minerva or the warrior goddess (refer to chapter 1 for a reason behind her many names).

Prayer to Brigid, Keeper of the Flame

"Mighty Brigid, keeper of the flame,

blazing in the darkness of winter.

O goddess, we honor you, bringer of light,

healer exalted one.

Bless us now, hearth mother,

that we may be as fruitful as the soil itself,

and our lives abundant and fertile."

This prayer is dedicated to honoring Brigid for her specific role as keeper of the flame.

Prayer to Brigid, Bride of Earth

"Bride of the earth,

sister of the faeries,

daughter of the Tuatha de Danaan,

keeper of the eternal flame.

In autumn, the nights began to lengthen,

and the days grew shorter,

as the earth went to sleep.

Now, Brighid stokes her fire,

burning flames in the hearth,

bringing light back to us once more.

Winter is brief, but life is forever.

Brighid makes it so."

Brigid, the Celtic Hearth Goddess, was also known as the Bride of the Earth. She is the patroness of the home and domesticity, and this short prayer is meant to honor her for that role.

Hail Bríd

> "Hail Bríd,
>
> Exalted One,
>
> You teach me the greater skill of life's purchase,
>
> I welcome you into my heart, unfettered by reservation.
>
> Hail Bríd,
>
> Poet & Seer
>
> She who lights the labyrinth of lucidity inciting battles within the hearts of men,
>
> You spur to rise and be the victor over the disharmony within.
>
> Hail Bríd,
>
> Healer & Leech
>
> My Sacrifice I give to you of great importance,
>
> So do I commit to follow your will.
>
> Hail Bríd
>
> Blacksmith & Artisan
>
> Through your Gift, Transformation is ours,
>
> Guided by your Strength & Grace, from raw toward refinement.
>
> Hail Bríd
>
> Patron to the Poets, Physicians, and Artisans,
>
> Three Sisters, fire in the head, fire in the heart, and fire in hand,
>
> Bringer of the mead of inspiration,
>
> Let my words fall softly upon you, in splendor and truth.
>
> A Bríd, glacaigí lenár n-íobairt! (Bríd, accept our sacrifice!)
>
> Bíodh sé amhlaidh! (So be it!)"

O Gods

> "O Gods,
>
> In my deeds,
>
> In my words,
>
> In my wishes,

For my reason,
And in the fulfilling of my desires,
In my sleep,
In my dreams,
In my repose.
In my thoughts,
In my heart and soul always,
May the flames of Brid,
And the passage of fire, well, and tree-dwelling.
Oh! in my heart and soul always,
May the waters of Brid,
And the strength of land, sky, and sea dwell.
Oh! in my heart and soul always,
May the vision of Brid,
And the words of the Gods, Dead, and Sidhe dwell."

Nines Woods Sacred

"Sacred god, her triple fire,
Exalted one who imparts,
Keening out of rippled ire,
Her hand is seen well in arts.
Her sons, three gods of gifts,
Of Bres, their father the King,
He hosted his squads with thrift,
And still, his satire we sing.
Holy God of bard and smith,
Three Sisters of all bright flame,
Her wise touch is guarding pith,
Goddess is Bríd, magic wrights claim.
At starry Gate of heavens,
Curse of Fílid leave fools naked,
Number my blessings seven,
Hot flames on nine woods sacred."

Litany of Bríd

"Exalt the truth of the High One,

Who illuminates the dark and cold with her sisters,

She is in our homes, in the shop, and in our minds,

Her brightness is the healing that takes us through the gateway to the realm of gods.

When I hear her, I am sustained by her song,

When I walk with her, many stories I hear,

and when I ask of her name, my ancestors exalt her.

Standing there in the green field with the warmth of the sun on my back,

I face west upon one foot, with one arm, and see with one eye,

My prohibition ends,

My struggle ends,

My toil ends,

Guided by her hand."

Hymn to Brigid

"A Bhrid, ár gcroí, an-gheal Bheanríon;

lo de thoil é beannachta sinn.

Is sinn bhur leanaí, is tu ár mamaí;

bí ag isteacht dúinn mar sin.

Is tu an coire, anois inár doire *;

a Bhean-Feasa tinfím orainn.

A thine ghrá, a thine bheatha;

lo de thoil é ag teacht Bhrid dúinn!

O Bridget, our heart, o brightest Queen;

cast your blessings unto us.

We are your children; you are our mother;

so hearken unto us.

You are the cauldron, now in our grove *;

Wise Woman inspire us.

O fire of love, o fire of life;

---

please, Brigid, come to us!

A Bhrid, ár gcroí, an-gheal Bheanríon;

lo de thoil é beannachta sinn.

Is sinn bhur leanaí, is tu ár mamaí;

bí ag isteacht dúinn mar sin.

Is tu an coire, anois inár doire *;

a Bhean-Feasa tinfím orainn.

A thine ghrá, a thine bheatha;

lo de thoil é ag teacht Bhrid dúinn!" – Isaac Bonewits

The Irish Celtic Goddess, Brigid, is the healer, provider, and protector. Therefore, dedicated pagans, who are interested in getting blessings from her, honor her with the aforementioned methods. Today, you can still implement the same traditions with a modern twist. With the different prayers, chants, and affirmations provided in this chapter, you can honor your goddess during worship while presenting her with offerings. Now that you know what to do to celebrate Brigid, the next chapter focuses on rituals for seeking healing and protection from her.

Chapter 9: Rituals for Healing and Protection

Paganism is associated with a variety of rituals designed to suit the needs of different people. In this chapter, we outline some healing rituals and spells that use colors, herbs, and other elements that honor Brigid. We also provide step-by-step instructions on how to conduct the ritual or spell, as well as the chants to include when calling to the goddess.

Honoring a Deity Associated with Healing

This ritual is usually performed on behalf of an ill family member or friend. Before practicing magic or attempting a healing ritual, it is customary to seek permission from the individual who is not feeling well. It is important to follow the ethical standards and your tradition's belief system. However, an individual who is terminally ill may no longer wish to live as a result of the unbearable pain their illness may be causing them. In this case, you should not go against the wishes of the patient. If they are willing to accept help, then you can perform the ritual on their behalf. Note that the deity will consider the patient's feelings before offering help.

Deities and Healing

When you perform this ritual, you ask the goddess/god of your tradition to look after the sick individual and heal them. There are different forms of deities associated with healing in Brigid Paganism. You can work with other deities if your tradition does not have an effective goddess. The following are some of the deities you can consider for your ritual:

- **Celtic:** Aimed, Brigid, Maponus, Sirona
- **Norse:** Eir
- **Egyptian:** Heka, Isis
- **Yoruba:** Babalu Aye, Aja
- **Greek:** Artemis, Apollo, Hygaiea, Aesclepius, Panacea
- **Roman:** Febris, Vejovis, Bona

When you decide to call upon a deity, make sure you do your research to understand their requirements first. Alternatively, it might be a good idea to consult a professional practitioner.

Items Required:

To perform this spell, you will need the following items:

- A small white candle to represent the person whom you want to assist with the ritual
- Healing incense which can include yarrow, allspice, apple blossoms, bay, cinnamon, lemon balm

---

- A candle representing the goddess or god you want to invoke for assistance

Setup:

Depending on your tradition, you may need to cast a circle. Make sure you set up your altar the way you usually do and place the candle of your goddess/god in the ideal position. When you perform this ritual, you should recite the following:

"I call upon you, Brigid, in a time of need.

I ask your assistance and blessing for one who is ailing.

[Name] is ill, and she needs your healing light.

I ask you to watch over her and give her strength,

Keep her safe from further illness, and protect her body and soul.

I ask you, great Brigid, to heal her in this time of sickness."

Take the loose incense and put it on your brazier or charcoal disc, and then light it. The incense will begin to emit smoke, and this is the time you should envision your peer's illness drifting away with the fumes. While the incense is burning, you must say the following chant.

"Brigid, I ask you to take away [Name of the person]'s illness,

Carry it out to the four winds, never to return.

To the north, take this illness away and replace it with health.

To the east, take this illness away, and replace it with strength.

To the south, take this illness away, and replace it with vitality.

To the west, take this illness away, and replace it with life.

Carry it away from [Name], Brigid, that it may scatter and be no more.

The next step is to light a candle that represents the goddess or god. In this case, your Goddess is Brigid, so light your candle and say the following verse.

Hail to you, powerful Brigid, I pay you tribute.

I honor you and ask for this one small gift.

May your light and strength wash over [Name of the person],

Supporting her in this time of need."

Using the flame coming from the candle, light the small candle that represents your friend or your peer who is not feeling well. When you light the candle, say the following words.

"[Call the name of the person], I light this candle in your honor tonight.

It is lit from the fires of Brigid, and she will watch over you.

She will guide you and heal you, and ease your suffering.

May Brigid continue to care for you and embrace you in her light."

When you finish chanting these words, take a few minutes to meditate on all the good things you wish for your loved one. When you finish your ritual, leave the candles to burn out. They will go with the illness or ailment bedeviling the patient.

Ritual for Brigid

This rite is meant to invite Brigid into your house to become your hearth guardian to enjoy her presence and protection. You can also use it to renew your acquaintance with the goddess. To perform this ritual, find and place an image of Brigid in a strategic place so that you can place your oil lamp in front of it. If you don't have an image, however, you can skip this step since the flame can take its place.

If you have a fireplace, prepare a fire, but don't be in a rush to light it. Put a bowl and pitcher of milk in front of the fireplace. Find a place to sit or stand to be at eye level with the fire. While in this position, extend your arms – your palms should be facing forward, and your elbow should be slightly bent. This is known as the "orans position," which is commonly used for pagan prayer. Bow your head to the fire source and recite the following verse.

"I invite you into my home,

you who are the Queen of the Hearth,

you who are the fire's bright flame,

you who are the burning shining.

I call you, Brigid, to come to me.

I ask you, Brigid, for your bright presence.

Light the fire and say, "The fire of Brigid is the flame on my hearth."

Pick the pitcher with your right hand, and hold it before the fire, saying:

A gift for you,

Brigid of the cows,

A gift for you,

Brigid of the blessings."

Pour milk into the bowl, saying the following words, "My prayers are poured out with this milk. My words and deeds flow straight to Brigid."

Put your pitcher down and make your request. You can pray to Brigid for healing, protection, and inspiration. If you don't have any requests, stand or sit in a meditation position and visualize the fire burning in your heart. The mantra you should use is, *"The Brigid is the flame in my heart."* You can also use this mantra to establish or renew your relationship with the goddess.

When you complete the ritual, extinguish the candle saying, *"She ever burns, lady of fire, in my heart, in my home, or family."* Lastly, take up the orans position once again and bow your head to mark the end of the rite. If you choose to use a fireplace for your rite, use the same words, but leave the fire burning. You can spend some time enjoying the warmth of the fire. Leave your bowl of milk in its position for 24 hours, then put it outside for the spirits of the land.

A Group Brigid Ritual for Healing

This is a rite that is performed during group healings when a community is hit by a crisis. For instance, the outbreak of a pandemic or any other event that can lead to the loss of human life or animals. Many people believe that these misfortunes are caused by evil spells and are not taken lightly in many cultures. They also believe that the challenges can be resolved by performing exorcism and cleansing ceremonies. The following are some options you can consider when undertaking a group Brigid Ritual for the purpose of healing.

Materials Required:

- Vessel of water enough to anoint all participants
- A light tea candle for each participant
- A large candle for the altar
- One big candle for the altar
- An altar table that is decorated with white, green, and red cloths and ribbons
- Brigid's crosses, the image of Brigid (you can download it from the internet), and Brigid statues

To begin the ritual, assemble all the guests in a circle around the room. The candles should be unlit at first while you create a sacred space. The guests at this ritual should hold hands one at a time, and the leader petitions Brigid by saying: "*Brigid, Lady of the wells – we invite you to our space to heal. Brigid, Lady of the Bards, help our words...*"

Light the candle on the altar and anoint every individual at the rite with water after saying a prayer to the Goddess Brigid. The participants will light their tea candles from the big one on the table. This ceremony is mainly characterized by chanting, meditation, and prayers, where participants invoke the powers of Brigid to help them overcome the problems they are facing. The leader will signal the end of the rite when it has ended, and the remnants of the burning candles are buried.

Brigid Home Protection Ritual

To perform this ritual, you need Brigid's cross, which is a traditional Imbolc craft woven from reeds and weeds. Other people can decorate this item with pieces of cloth and spring flowers. When you make your cross, you should invoke the Goddess to bless it with a powerful light. To keep your home safe from different forms of negativity, place the cross on your front door. However, you still need to lock your doors. Some people prefer to hang this traditional cross above the hearth to invoke the power of the flame. They will keep it for the whole year until they make another one. The hanging of the cross is often accompanied by the following incantation.

"And perhaps if you admire,
That this great house ne'er take fire,
Where sparks, as thick as stars in the sky,
About the house did often fly,
And reach'd the sapless wither'd thatch,
Which dry like spunge the fire would catch,
And no chimney was erected,
Where sparks and flames might be directed,
St. Bridget's cross hung over the door,
Which did the house from fire secure,
As Gillo thought, O powerful charm,
To keep a house from taking harm,
And tho' the dogs and servants slept,
By Bridget's care, the house was kept."

If you cannot make your own St. Brigid's cross, you can buy one from a store. It is believed that painting the cross on your walls is one permanent method of bringing Brigid energy into your house. When you decide to repaint the wall, start by painting your cross first, then cover it with paint. The power of the cross will be present even if the cross is not visible.

You should use prayer to enchant the St. Brigid's cross to protect your home and life. The cross will let Brigid know that you wish for your home to be under her protection, and your desire will be fulfilled. You also need to reinforce these words annually. Additionally, when your hand-made cross is showing signs of weathering, you can replace it.

The Goddess Brigid is believed to possess strong healing and protective powers. Pagans often invoke her spiritual power to seek help with all kinds of problems. With the many different rituals we have explored in this chapter, you can consider which healing and protection rituals would solve your situation. Note that some of these rites should be performed under the guidance of an experienced pagan practitioner. If you do not need to acquire healing or protection, however, you may still want to practice divination with Brigid, which will be the focus of the next chapter.

Chapter 10: Practicing Divination with Brigid

Many pagans use divination to get answers and solutions to different issues they may have in life. To do this, they invoke the powers of the goddess Brigid, and several tools are used. In this chapter, you will learn how to gain insight into the future with the aid of Brigid. We explore the divination methods that work with Brigid as the goddess of both water and fire, as well as of wisdom and words. We cover methods such as ceromancy, bibliomancy, and tasseography, although you are free to choose whatever method suits your needs.

Ceromancy

Ceromancy is a method of divination that utilizes water and candle wax. By posing questions as the candle burns and then dripping the hot wax into water to cool and shape it, you can find answers to your questions. The burning of the candle has the power to manifest solutions to the problems you are facing in life, and the solutions usually come in easy-to-recognize shapes that can be easily interpreted.

There are a few ways to perform ceromancy, but let's start with the simplest. You can choose a variety of colored candles, but for this purpose, one is enough. Colored candles produce clear images and beautiful contrasts. You can also assign a different color for a specific aspect of your reading in your divination work. If you are looking for answers from the past, choose a blue candle; if you want to tackle a current problem, look for yellow or white candles; if you are focused on the future, use a green candle.

First, find a space where you can practice ceromancy uninterrupted. Light your candle, and place it somewhere away from flammable materials. You need liquid wax for the ritual, so allow the candle to burn down and produce the melted wax. While the candle is burning, fill a bowl with water (if you have not already). Any type of bowl will do, although some people have their preferences. With the candle burning and the bowl filled with water, take some time to form the questions in your mind, dwelling on them and how they can be answered. You can think deeply about the questions or try to meditate on them – it can be helpful to stare into the candle flame as you meditate. When you have enough wax (and this will become easier to judge over time), you can snuff out the candle.

Pour the wax into the water, paying attention to the shape it takes. As soon as the wax hits the water, it will harden and form an image. The image is not going to be picture-perfect, but it will give you what you need. You can leave the wax in the water or lift it out to study it. Look at the wax from all angles and see what is held there, the pictures ad thoughts contained.

When you carry out this exercise, the wax can harden to produce any image you can visualize. One thing you should know about this practice is that it does not provide any definite answer to your questions. When you look at the formed wax, you need to interpret it. It is not only about what you see – but also how you feel about it. The image is trying to communicate what is held inside of you.

There are books you can refer to that will help pinpoint what an image means in the context of your problem, so refer to dream, divination, or other books for help. Throughout time, certain images have been associated with specific things, and this can be a good starting point. However, do not limit yourself to a single meaning of a particular image since common symbols can mean various things to different people. We all come from different backgrounds, so our perceptions of many things can differ significantly. Symbols and images do not always mean what we think they mean. For instance, if you see an image connected to death, it is not necessarily a bad thing. Death can also mean rebirth, and the image needs to be resolved in context to the question asked.

You can also practice ceromancy divination while taking a bath in the tub. Put your candles around the tub, and light them. The flames around you will help to relax you, more so if you have scented candles, and the flickering of the flame can help you meditate. When you have enough wax, pour some into the bath and look for the images and symbols that will be presented. The images may appear bigger if you pour the wax on a large water surface compared to a small bowl. However, ceromancy requires patience if you want your answers to be as accurate as possible. If you rush it, you may end up missing the goal.

Bibliomancy

Poetry is connected to Brigid, and many poems have been written in her honor and with her guidance. If you are an ardent reader and often go through different types of literature, the art of bibliomancy will be closer to your heart. Just like the visual images that come with ceromancy, words can give you guidance when you have problems or need answers. Bibliomancy can be done by anyone and requires minimal preparation.

All you need is a book. Any book will do, but you should try to use a book that has lots of words. You might find your answers in a poetry book or picture book, but you are more likely to succeed with a novel. Start by concentrating on the problem or question at hand, asking for an answer or guidance. Open a page of the book at random and immediately place your finger on a random point of the book.

Read from where your finger landed, and look for an answer within the words. Do not be discouraged if there is not a concrete answer to your question; the text is there to help you unlock the answer. You may also need to take some time to reflect on what you have read to get appropriate answers. You may realize that the words you get from the book may have literal or implied meaning to what you are looking for.

You can read any type of book to perform bibliomancy divination. However, in some instances, you may find that specific books are more appropriate for certain forms of questions and readings that you want to conduct. For instance, poetry can be a good source of insight and inspiration when you want to find answers to questions about relationships. If your question is magical, spiritual, and pagan books are ideal.

You should not take yourself too seriously when you exercise bibliomancy. You can read any book – it doesn't have to be too specific or academic. However, there are certain books you should consider if you want to build a strong connection to Brigid.

Additionally, music can also be an effective source of inspiration if you want to be creative. Instead of books, you can use songs to get answers to your questions. If you have a media player, focus on your question, and play different songs randomly. See what messages or information you get from the song lyrics.

When looking for a meaning in the songs played, it is important to focus on the feeling of the song. Combine the feeling with the words being sung, the overall message of the song, the tone, the intent, the speed, and everything about the piece of music. You can also look at the name of the song and the artist – what can be discerned from them?

When you are done, be sure to thank Brigid, for she is the one who is guiding you through the process and leading you to answers. You can do this through prayer, chants, offerings, or talking to her directly to show your appreciation. Ask the fiery arrow of healing waters, inspiration, and words of wisdom to guide you in your divination.

Conclusion

Brigid is perhaps one of the most multifaceted Celtic goddesses – and she is also the most influential one. As told by the ancient myths, she arrived in Ireland as part of the ancient Tuatha Dé Danann tribe. Her roles spanned from being the patroness of fire and smiths to guiding healers and inspiring poets. Not only that, but Brigid united many different cultures and traditions, such as Paganism and Christianity. Therefore, it's easy to see how her lore managed to travel down through many generations and stay alive until modern times.

In popular culture, she is most popularly known as St. Brigid of Kildare, one of Ireland's patron saints. She is also commemorated in the highlands and islands of Scotland as the protector of midwives, babies, cattle, and dairymaids. In Haiti, Brigid is Maman Brigitte, a Vodou loa, and the wife of Baron Samedi. Here, she reigns over fertility, motherhood, life, death, and even cemeteries. Her roles in these religions stem from ancient Celtic traditions.

However, before her transformation, she was known as Brigid the Triple Goddess. Her name is probably the result of her contradictory roles, which are, once again, venerated in modern culture. Contemporary Paganism relies on her connection to the Sacred Flame, through which this goddess can help anyone who may call upon her. Whether someone needs a gentle healing hand or wants to ignite fire and passion for conceiving, they can rely on Brigid's aid on their journey.

Her sacred holiday, Imbolc, is still celebrated in the middle of the winter by people making generous offerings at wells and other water sources. The sabbat is preceded by lavish preparation that allows families and communities to connect with each other and plan for the coming season. Another way to honor Brigid is through the symbols often associated with her, including the Brigid's Cross and her sacred animals. Whether placing them on the altar or utilizing them in any other way, a practitioner can use these symbols to invoke Brigid's power and enhance their spells and rituals.

Nowadays, Brigid is often associated with Paganistic healing rituals. While this practice is centered primarily on self-healing, ultimately, it leads to greater compassion and the ability to provide assistance for others in need. Since having a sacred space also promotes the development of a much deeper spiritual connection with oneself, honoring the goddess every day will empower the practitioner to become better at their craft. Once you are able to manifest your intentions, your healing magic will be much more powerful. In this book, you will find detailed instructions on how to successfully master both parts of this process and begin using chants, calling for Brigid to heal others as well.

Lastly, you will have learned how to glimpse any part of the future with the help of the goddess of fire and wisdom. For Brigid is the best guide to turn to when you wish to seek answers through divination. And while each practitioner should use a divination method that feels right for them, doing it with the help of Brigid can ensure far better results. She will be particularly generous if you also practice honoring her on a daily basis.

Here's another book by Mari Silva that you might like

MARI SILVA

ELDER FUTHARK RUNES

UNLOCKING RUNE DIVINATION· NORSE MAGIC· SPELLS· AND RUNIC SYMBOLS

Your Free Gift
(only available for a limited time)

Thanks for getting this book! If you want to learn more about various spirituality topics, then join Mari Silva's community and get a free guided meditation MP3 for awakening your third eye. This guided meditation mp3 is designed to open and strengthen ones third eye so you can experience a higher state of consciousness. Simply visit the link below the image to get started.

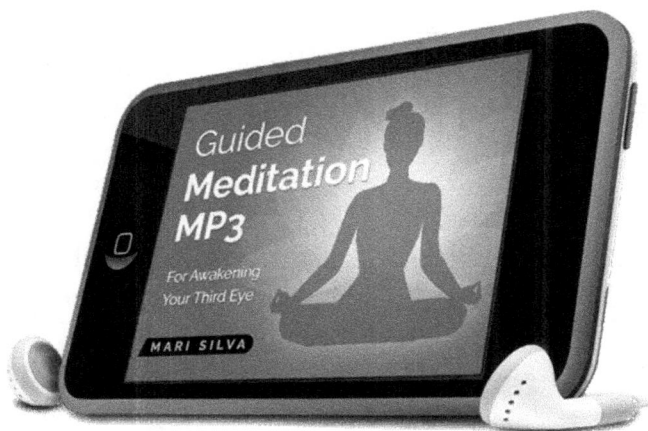

https://spiritualityspot.com/meditation

References

Cartwright, M. (2021a). Ancient Celtic Religion. World History Encyclopedia.
https://www.worldhistory.org/Ancient_Celtic_Religion

Cartwright, M. (2021b). Ancient Celts. World History Encyclopedia.
https://www.worldhistory.org/celt/

Duffy, K. (2000). Who were the Celts? Barnes & Noble.

Jarus, O. (2014, April 7). History of the Celts. Livescience.Com; Live Science.
https://www.livescience.com/44666-history-of-the-celts.html

May, A. (2019, November 14). Celtic Wicca - myths and secrets explained. Welcome To Wicca
Now. https://wiccanow.com/celtic-wicca-myths-and-secrets-explained

Putka, S. (2021, June 4). The ancient Celts: Iron age foes of Rome who left behind more than
weapons. Discover Magazine.
https://www.discovermagazine.com/planet-earth/the-ancient-celts-iron-age-foes-of-rome-who-left-behind-more-than-weapons

Flanagan, K. (2020, February 13). Aengus Óg: The Irish god of love. The Brehon Academy.
https://brehonacademy.org/aengus-og-the-irish-god-of-love

God Studies: Cernunnos. (n.d.). Sabrina's Grimoire. Retrieved from
https://sabrinasgrimoire.tumblr.com/post/622301491987906560/god-studies-cernunnos

Goddess epona. (2012, June 13). Journeying to the Goddess. https://journeyingtothegoddess.wordpress.com/2012/06/13/goddess-epona

Info. (2020, February 11). Ogma: The god of speech & language. Order of Bards, Ovates & Druids. https://druidry.org/resources/ogma-the-god-of-speech-language

Lugh. (n.d.). Wiccaneopagan.Com. Retrieved from http://www.wiccaneopagan.com/group/deities/forum/topics/2453436:Topic:59053

Mainyu, E. A. (Ed.). (2011). Belenus. Aud Publishing.

Mandal, D. (2018, July 2). 15 ancient Celtic gods and goddesses you should know about. Realm of History. https://www.realmofhistory.com/2018/07/02/ancient-celtic-gods-goddesses-facts

Mantrik. (2013, August 27). Introduction to Belenos. Wyrdfyre. https://belinus1.wordpress.com/2013/08/27/introduction-to-belinus

The Editors of Encyclopedia Britannica. (2017). Danu. In Encyclopedia Britannica.

The Editors of Encyclopedia Britannica. (2018). Belenus. In Encyclopedia Britannica.

Treanor, D., Elle, Walker, R., Roots, S., Fields, K., Duff, C., Latta, A. L., 30+ Types of Fairies Worldwide: Brownies, Elves, Gnomes, and More!, Celtic Deities: 10 Lesser-Known Celtic Gods and Goddesses, Tavernier, M., Are Fairies Real? Origins and Evidence that Fairies Exist, & Triple Goddess: Maiden, Mother, and Crone for Modern Practitioners. (2020, April 10). Celtic Goddess of War: 8 ways to work with The Morrigan. Otherworldly Oracle. https://otherworldlyoracle.com/celtic-goddess-of-war

Wigington, P. (n.d.-a). Cernunnos, the wild Celtic god of the Forest. Learn Religions. Retrieved from https://www.learnreligions.com/cernunnos-wild-god-of-the-forest-2561959

Wigington, P. (n.d.-b). The Dagda, the father god of Ireland. Learn Religions. Retrieved from https://www.learnreligions.com/the-dagda-father-god-of-ireland-2561706

Zuberbuehler, A. (1996). Fieldstones. Players Press.

Aos Sí – ancestors of Ireland. (2021, June 7). Symbol Sage. https://symbolsage.com/aos-si-ancestors-of-ireland/

Irish Pagan beliefs. (2018, September 25). Lora O'Brien - Irish Author &

Guide.

https://loraobrien.ie/irish-pagan-beliefs

Metalgaia. (2012, June 6). Why Wicca and Celtic Paganism are different things. Metal Gaia. https://metal-gaia.com/2012/06/06/why-wicca-and-celtic-paganism-are-different-things

Paganism in Scotland. (n.d.). Electricscotland.Com. Retrieved from https://electricscotland.com/bible/paganism.htm

Scott. (2017, April 24). Who the hell is Sidhe? – Fairy Faith and Animism in Scotland. A Challenge to Divinity. Cailleach's Herbarium. https://cailleachs-herbarium.com/2017/04/who-the-hell-is-sidhe-fairy-faith-and-animism-in-scotland-a-challenge-to-divinity

Scottish folklore - Cat Sìth & Cù-Sìth. (n.d.). Timberbush-Tours.Co.Uk. Retrieved from https://www.timberbush-tours.co.uk/news-offers/scottish-folklore-cat-sith-cu-sith

The Newsroom. (2016, March 31). The tale of Scottish banshees: Baobhan Sith. The Scotsman. https://www.scotsman.com/whats-on/arts-and-entertainment/tale-scottish-banshees-baobhan-sith-1479692

The tuatha D' danann - Ireland's greatest tribe. (n.d.). IrelandInformation.Com. Retrieved from https://www.ireland-information.com/irish-mythology/tuatha-de-danann-irish-legend.html

Dana. (n.d.). invoking awen – The Druid's Garden. The Druid's Garden. Retrieved from https://druidgarden.wordpress.com/tag/invoking-awen

Druids of California. (n.d.). CaliforniaDruids.Org. Retrieved from https://californiaDruids.org/pages/history.html

Former Student. (2019, July 18). Modern-day Druids: No animal sacrifices, but connected to community, history. Cronkite News - Arizona PBS.

https://cronkitenews.azpbs.org/2019/07/18/modern-Druids-arizona

Info. (2019a, November 27). Bard. Order of Bards, Ovates & Druids. https://druidry.org/druid-way/what-druidry/what-is-a-bard

Info. (2019b, November 27). Druid. Order of Bards, Ovates & Druids. https://druidry.org/druid-way/what-druidry/what-is-a-druid

Info. (2019c, November 27). Ovate. Order of Bards, Ovates & Druids. https://druidry.org/druid-way/what-druidry/what-is-an-ovate

Philip. (2019, November 21). Groups & groves. Order of Bards, Ovates & Druids. https://druidry.org/get-involved/groups-groves

Philip. (2020, March 16). The three functions of druidry. Order of Bards, Ovates & Druids. https://druidry.org/resources/the-three-functions-of-druidry

Rule of Awen. (n.d.). Aoda.Org. Retrieved from https://aoda.org/aoda-structure/gnostic-celtic-church-gcc/rule-of-awen

Shedding light on Stonehenge and the summer solstice. (2020, June 17). VisitBritain. https://www.visitbritain.com/au/en/media/story-ideas/shedding-light-stonehenge-and-summer-solstice-0

The order of bards ovates and Druids (OBOD). (2013, May 2). The Druid Network. https://druidnetwork.org/what-is-druidry/learning-resources/obod

All Answers Ltd. (2021, December 31). Trees in Celtic culture and art: An analysis.

Ukessays.Com; UK Essays. https://www.ukessays.com/essays/arts/trees-celtic-culture-art-analysis-3271.php

Hawthorn Tree in Celtic mythology. (2013, September 26). Ireland Calling. https://ireland-calling.com/celtic-mythology-hawthorn-tree

Festivals & Rituals. (n.d.). Retrieved from The Ancient Celtic Relgion website:

http://theancientcelticreligion.weebly.com/-festivals--rituals.html

Info. (2019, November 27). Oracles & divination in druidry. Retrieved from Order of Bards, Ovates & Druids website:

https://druidry.org/druid-way/teaching-and-practice/oracles-divination-druidry

Marketing The Conscious Club. (2019, November 13). Why ceremonies and rituals are still important today —. Retrieved from The Conscious Club website:

https://theconsciousclub.com/articles/2019/10/17/why-ceremonies-and-rituals-are-still-important-today

Ancient Irish spells and charms to celebrate Halloween. (2021, October 9). Retrieved from IrishCentral.com website: https://www.irishcentral.com/roots/ancient-irish-spells-charms

Campsie, A. (2019, October 17). 9 charms, spells, and cures used by Highland witches. The Scotsman. Retrieved from https://www.scotsman.com/heritage-and-retro/heritage/9-charms-spells-and-cures-used-highland-witches-1404985

Cath. (2021, May 4). 11 fascinating Celtic symbols and their meanings. Travel Around Ireland.

https://travelaroundireland.com/celtic-symbols-and-their-meanings

O'Reilly, L. J. (2020, May 7). Paganism: Ireland's contemporary shining light. Trinity News.

http://trinitynews.ie/2020/05/paganism-irelands-contemporary-shining-light

Irish Pagan beliefs. (2018, September 25). Lora O'Brien - Irish Author & Guide.

https://loraobrien.ie/irish-pagan-belief

Celtic religion - Beliefs, practices, and institutions. (n.d.). In Encyclopedia Britannica.

Culture Northern Ireland. (n.d.). Irish pagan gods. Culture Northern Ireland.

https://www.culturenorthernireland.org/features/heritage/irish-pagan-gods

Daimler, M. (2015). Irish Paganism: Reconstructing Irish polytheism. Moon Books.

Irish Pagan beliefs. (2018, September 25). Lora O'Brien - Irish Author & Guide.

https://loraobrien.ie/irish-pagan-beliefs

Joyce, P. W. (2018). The story of ancient Irish civilization. Outlook Verlag.

O'Reilly, L. J. (2020, May 7). Paganism: Ireland's contemporary shining light. Trinity News. http://trinitynews.ie/2020/05/paganism-irelands-contemporary-shining-light

Pizza, M., & Lewis, J. (Eds.). (2008). Handbook of contemporary Paganism. Brill Academic. https://doi.org/10.1163/ej.9789004163737.i-650

The snakes are still in Ireland: Pagans, shamans, and modern Druids in a catholic world. (2013, May 10). The On Being Project. https://onbeing.org/blog/the-snakes-are-still-in-ireland-pagans-shamans-and-modern-Druids-in-a-catholic-world

Top gods and goddesses from Celtic mythology. (2021, December 30). IrishCentral.Com. https://www.irishcentral.com/roots/history/celtic-mythology-gods-goddesses

Cartwright, M. (2021). Druid. World History Encyclopedia. https://www.worldhistory.org/Druid

Who were the Druids? (2017, March 21). Historic UK.

https://www.historic-uk.com/HistoryUK/HistoryofWales/Druids

A day in the life of a Celtic Druid - Philip Freeman. (2019, September 17). TED-Ed.

Crawford, C. (2020, July 14). A beginners guide to the Wheel of the Year – . The Self-Care Emporium. https://theselfcareemporium.com/blog/beginners-guide-wheel-of-the-year

The Pagan Grimoire. (2020, April 18). Wheel of the Year: The 8 Wiccan sabbats (2021 + 2022 dates). The Pagan Grimoire. https://www.pagangrimoire.com/wheel-of-the-year

Barry, B. (2017, October 12). What sparked our fear of witches – and what kept it burning so long? Washington Post (Washington, D.C.: 1974). https://www.washingtonpost.com/entertainment/books/what-sparked-our-fear-of-witches--and-what-kept-it-burning-so-long

Bradley, C. (2020, December 23). "pagan" vs. "Wicca": What is the difference? Dictionary.com website: https://www.dictionary.com/e/pagan-vs-wicca-pagan-vs-heathen

Lewis, I. M., & Russell, J. B. (2021). witchcraft. In Encyclopedia Britannica.

SelFelin, Fields, K., John, Ben, Medieval Magic: Alchemy, Witchery, and Magic from the Middle Ages, Jennifer, ... Morganwg, R. (2019, June 17). Welsh goddesses and gods: List and descriptions + how to honor them. Otherworldly Oracle website:

https://otherworldlyoracle.com/welsh-goddesses-gods

witchcraft - The witch hunts. (n.d.). In Encyclopedia Britannica.

Little, B. (2018, January 10). How medieval churches used witch hunts to gain more followers. HISTORY website: https://www.history.com/news/how-medieval-churches-used-witch-hunts-to-gain-more-followers

Celtic god of blacksmithing and hospitality goibniu. (n.d.). Worldanvil.Com.

https://www.worldanvil.com/w/tyran-jackswiftshot/a/celtic-god-of-blacksmithing-and-hospitality-goibniu-article

Gill, N. S. (n.d.). A list of Celtic gods and goddesses. ThoughtCo.

https://www.thoughtco.com/celtic-gods-and-goddesses-117625

Heritage, E. (2017, October 31). Legendary Irish Gods and Goddesses. Emerald Heritage. https://emerald-heritage.com/blog/2017/legendary-irish-gods-and-goddesses

Klimczak, N. (2021, June 4). Aine: Radiant Celtic goddess of love, summer, and sovereignty. Ancient-Origins.Net; Ancient Origins. https://www.ancient-origins.net/myths-legends/aine-radiant-celtic-goddess-007097

Mandal, D. (2018, July 2). 15 ancient Celtic gods and goddesses you should know about. Realm of History. https://www.realmofhistory.com/2018/07/02/ancient-celtic-gods-goddesses-facts

Perkins, M. (n.d.). Irish mythology: History and legacy. ThoughtCo. http://thoughtco.com/irish-mythology-4768762

The call of Danu. (n.d.). The Call of Danu. https://thecallofdanu.wordpress.com

The Celtic god Nuada. (n.d.). Thecottagemystic.Com. https://www.thecottagemystic.com/nuada.html

Whitecatgrove, V. A. P. (2010, July 27). Invocations to Goibhniu and Manannan. White Cat Grove. https://whitecatgrove.wordpress.com/2010/07/27/invocations-to-goibhniu-and-manannan

Williams, A. (2020, August 16). Cu Chulainn. Mythopedia. https://mythopedia.com/topics/cu-chulainn

Dewey, P. (2020, April 10). The story of The Mabinogion and its impact on Welsh literature and beyond. WalesOnline website: https://www.walesonline.co.uk/whats-on/arts-culture-news/story-mabinogion-impact-welsh-literature-18040842

SelFelin, Fields, K., John, Ben, Medieval Magic: Alchemy, Witchery, and Magic from the Middle Ages, Jennifer, ... Morganwg, R. (2019, June 17). Welsh goddesses and gods: List and descriptions + how to honor them. Otherworldly Oracle website:

https://otherworldlyoracle.com/welsh-goddesses-gods

Why mythology is still important today. (n.d.). Parmaobserver.com website:

http://www.parmaobserver.com/read/2013/02/01/why-mythology-is-still-important-today

20 modern traditions with pagan origins. (2019, September 5). TheEssentialBS.Com. https://theessentialbs.com/2019/09/05/20-modern-traditions-with-pagan-origins

John Halstead, C. (2015, October 2). We're not all Witches: An introduction to Neopaganism. HuffPost.

Wigington, P. (n.d.). The magic & symbolism of animals. Learn Religions. https://www.learnreligions.com/the-magic-of-animals-2562522

An Irish Pagan Altar - Lora O'Brien - Irish author & guide. (2018, October 22). Retrieved, from Lora O'Brien - Irish Author & Guide website: https://loraobrien.ie/irish-pagan-altar

Celtic Wicca altar setup. (n.d.). Deviantart.com website: https://www.deviantart.com/morsoth/art/Celtic-Wicca-Altar-Setup-539056829?comment=1%3A539056829%3A3879380538

The Goddess movement. (n.d.).
https://www.bbc.co.uk/religion/religions/paganism/subdivisions/goddess.s
html

The Irish Times. (2000, January 22). Something Wiccan this way comes.
Irish Times. https://www.irishtimes.com/news/something-wiccan-this-way-
comes-1.236955

McGarry, M. (2020, April 30). Fire, water, light, and luck: Bealtaine
traditions in Ireland. RTÉ website:
https://www.rte.ie/brainstorm/2019/0429/1046282-fire-water-light-and-
luck-bealtaine-traditions-in-ireland

Gardner, P. (2016). Wicca: The pan Gardner book of shadows - A
spiritual guide to spells, rituals, and Wiccan traditions. North Charleston,
SC: CreateSpace Independent Publishing
Platform.

Key ingredients to use for spells to bring someone back. (n.d.). Org. UK
website:
https://rfs.org.uk/articles/key_ingredients_to_use_for_spells_to_bring_so
meone_back.html

Claddagh Design. (2022, January 19). Celtic festivals: What is Bealtaine?
Claddaghdesign.com website:
https://www.claddaghdesign.com/history/all-about-bealtaine

Guardian staff reporter. (2000, October 28). The witching hour. The
Guardian.
https://www.theguardian.com/theguardian/2000/oct/28/weekend7.weeken
d3

Irish Pagan beliefs. (2018, September 25). Lora O'Brien - Irish Author &
Guide. https://loraobrien.ie/irish-pagan-beliefs

O'Reilly, L. J. (2020, May 7). Paganism: Ireland's contemporary shining
light. Trinity News.
http://trinitynews.ie/2020/05/paganism-irelands-contemporary-shining-
light

Morissette, A. (2015, October 11). Top 10 tools of divination. Alanis
Morissette website:
https://alanis.com/news/top-10-tools-of-divination

Wigington, P. (n.d.). 14 magical tools for pagan practice. Learn Religions
website:
https://www.learnreligions.com/magical-tools-for-pagan-practice-4064607

Info. (2020, February 11). Morrigan. Order of Bards, Ovates & Druids.
https://druidry.org/resources/morrigan

O'Hara, K. (2020, April 21). The Morrigan: The Story of the Fiercest Goddess in Irish Myth. The Irish Road Trip. https://www.theirishroadtrip.com/the-morrigan

Greenberg, M. (2020, December 29). Badb Irish Goddess of the Morrigan: The Complete Guide. MythologySource. https://mythologysource.com/badb-irish-goddess-morrigan

Mythologies, B. (2014, June 5). Macha. Bard Mythologies. https://bardmythologies.com/macha

Wright, G. (2020, August 16). Danu. Mythopedia. https://mythopedia.com/topics/danu

https://www.sciencealert.com/new-research-finds-crows-can-ponder-their-own-knowledge

Wigington, P. (n.d.). The triple goddess: Maiden, Mother, and Crone. Learn Religions. https://www.learnreligions.com/maiden-mother-and-crone-2562881

West, B. (2020, January 29). Eriu :: A great goddess of the feminine Trinity of ancient Ireland. Projeda. http://www.projectglobalawakening.com/eriu

The Morrigan: Phantom Queen and Shape-shifter. (n.d.). IrelandInformation.Com. https://www.ireland-information.com/irish-mythology/the-morrigan-irish-legend.html

Russo, L. (2015). The Morrigan. P'Kaboo.

Nemain – occult world. (n.d.). Occult-World.Com. https://occult-world.com/nemain

Muse, A. (2020, October 22). The Morrigan – faerie queen. Adamantine Muse. https://www.patheos.com/blogs/adamantinemuse/2020/10/the-morrigan-faerie-queen

CelticJourney, & View my complete profile. (n.d.). CelticJourney-gifts. Blogspot.Com. http://carmenceltcjourney.blogspot.com/2010/12/this-is-one-of-images-of-many-iv.html

Anu/Anann. (n.d.). Maryjones.Us. https://www.maryjones.us/jce/anu.html

Carmody, I. Ó. (n.d.). The mórrígan speaks – her three poems. Storyarchaeology.com website: https://storyarchaeology.com/the-morrigan-speaks-her-three-poems-2

Daimler, M. (2015). The role of the Morrigan in the Cath Maige Tuired: Incitement, battle magic, and prophecy.

https://www.academia.edu/15486900/The_Role_of_the_Morrigan_in_th e_Cath_Maige_Tuired_Incitement_Battle_Magic_and_Prophecy?pop_s utd=false

Fir bolg: An ancient people of Irish mythology. (2021, September 29). MythBank website: https://mythbank.com/fir-bolg

The Morrigan: Phantom Queen and Shape-shifter. (n.d.). IrelandInformation.com website: https://www.ireland-information.com/irish-mythology/the-morrigan-irish-legend.html

Williams, A. (2020, August 16). Morrigan. Mythopedia website: https://mythopedia.com/topics/morrigan

Animal symbolism in Celtic mythology - mongoose publishing. (n.d.). Mongoosepublishing.Com.

Garis, M. G. (2020, December 2). Waxing and waning moons affect your mindset and mood differently—here's what to know. Well+Good. https://www.wellandgood.com/waxing-waning-moon

hÉireann, S. na. (2016, December 11). The crow goddess – Morrigan. Stair Na HÉireann | History of Ireland. https://stairnaheireann.net/2016/12/11/the-crow-goddess-morrigan

History.com Editors. (2018, April 6). Samhain. HISTORY. https://www.history.com/topics/holidays/samhain

Kneale, A. (2017, June 17). Ravens in Celtic and Norse mythology. Transceltic - Home of the Celtic Nations. https://www.transceltic.com/pan-celtic/ravens-celtic-and-norse-mythology

MacCulloch, J. A., Gray, L. H., & Machal, J. (2018). Celtic Mythology. Franklin Classics

Morrigan - the ancient Irish Trinity goddess. (2020, September 14). Symbol Sage. https://symbolsage.com/morrigan-goddess-origin

Sacred symbols: Triquetra & the power of "3." (2019, October 1). The Spells8 Forum. https://forum.spells8.com/t/sacred-symbols-triquetra-the-power-of-3/233?_ga=2.185581673.1108131998.1644631994-818242194.1644631994

Triple moon symbol/Triple Goddess symbol meaning, and origins explained. (2021, March 11). Symbols and Meanings - Your Ultimate Guide for Symbolism. https://symbolsandmeanings.net/triple-moon-symbol-triple-goddess-symbol-meaning-origins

Wigington, P. (n.d.). The magic behind crow & Raven mythology, legends, and folklore. Learn Religions. https://www.learnreligions.com/the-magic-of-crows-and-ravens-2562511

O'Hara, K. (2020, April 21). The Morrigan: The story of the fiercest goddess in Irish myth. The Irish Road Trip website:

https://www.theirishroadtrip.com/the-morrigan

(1992). Whitcraftlearningsolutions.com website: https://whitcraftlearningsolutions.com/wp-content/uploads/2015/07/Animal_Symbolism.pdf

Daimler, M. (2014). Pagan portals - the Morrigan: Meeting the great queens. https://books.google.at/books?id=ckOQBQAAQBAJ

31 day of creative samhain day 5: Dark goddess Morrigan. (n.d.). Thecreativepriestesspath.Com. https://thecreativepriestesspath.com/31-day-of-creative-samhain-day-5-dark-goddess-morrigan

Cartwright, M. (2021). The Mórrigan. World History Encyclopedia. https://www.worldhistory.org/The_Morrigan

Clark, R. (1987). Aspects of the morrígan in early Irish literature. Irish University Review, 17(2), 223–236. http://www.jstor.org/stable/25477680

Garcia, J. (n.d.). The morrígan: Phantom queen of Celtic mythology the morrígan: Phantom queen of Celtic mythology. Chapman.Edu. https://digitalcommons.chapman.edu/cgi/viewcontent.cgi?article=1407&context=cusrd_abstracts#:~:text=Neiman%2C%20but%20is%20also%20associated%20with%20the%20goddesses%2C,of%20fate%2C%20the%20Morr%C3%ADgan%20is%20also%20one%20of

Morrigan. (2022, January 27). Gods and Goddesses. https://godsandgoddesses.org/celtic/morrigan

Morrigan and Danu. (n.d.). Livejournal.Com. https://mhorrioghain.livejournal.com/23009.html

Morrígan: Goddess offerings, signs, symbols & myth. (2021, September 17). Spells8. https://spells8.com/lessons/goddess-morrigan-signs

O'Hara, K. (2020, April 21). The Morrigan: The story of the fiercest goddess in Irish myth. The Irish Road Trip. https://www.theirishroadtrip.com/the-morrigan

Russo, L. (2015). The Morrigan. P'Kaboo.

Shaw, J. (2014, December 31). Morrigan, Celtic Goddess of sovereignty, war, and fertility by Judith Shaw. Feminismandreligion.Com. https://feminismandreligion.com/2014/12/31/morrigan-celtic-goddess-of-sovereinty-war-and-fertility

Tuatha Dé Danann explai ed and list of gods. ( ). Timeless Myths. https://www.timelessmyths.com/celtic/danann

Weber, C. (2021). The Morrigan: Celtic goddess of magick and might. Tantor Audio

Wigington, P. (n.d.). The Morrighan. Learn Religions. https://www.learnreligions.com/the-morrighan-of-ireland-2561971

Woodfield, S. (2011). Celtic lore & spellcraft of the dark goddess. Llewellyn Publications. https://books.google.at/books?id=CRN4w6g2mMwC

Morrigan, R. (2011, November 14). About The Altar (and how to set it up). Rowan Morrigan. https://rowanmorrigan.wordpress.com/2011/11/14/the-altar

Warren, Á. (2020). Altars for the Morrigan: the legitimizing agency of a goddess in the networked flow of authority of a YouTube sub-culture. Journal of Contemporary Religion, 35(2), 287–305. https://doi.org/10.1080/13537903.2020.1761632

Anonymous, Elder Futhark Runes: How to Read Runes for Divination, Medusa Goddess & Gorgon: 7 Ways to Work With Her Fierce Energy, Ciera, Water Scrying Ritual: Egyptian Magic and Divination, & Tarot Reading With Playing Cards: History and How-To With Examples. (2020, June 17). How to use tarot to work with gods and goddesses. Otherworldly Oracle website: https://otherworldlyoracle.com/how-to-use-tarot-to-work-with-gods-and-goddesses

Holmes, S., Lynch, S., Mcgrath, G., Castillo, M., Bethany, Russell, L., ... Burch, I. (2021, February 24). Celtic Runes. Predict My Future website: https://predictmyfuture.com/celtic-runes-everything-you-need-to-know

How do you Scry with a Black Mirror? (n.d.). Kelleemaize.com website: https://www.kelleemaize.com/post/how-do-you-scry-with-a-black-mirror

Tarot of the gods: The Morrigan. (2014, May 2). Áine Órga website: http://aineorga.com/2014/05/02/tarot-gods-morrigan

The morrigan's call. (2013, February 8). Coru Cathubodua Priesthood website: https://www.corupriesthood.com/the-morrigan/morrigans-call

Treanor, D., Elle, Walker, R., Roots, S., Fields, K., Duff, C., ... Triple Goddess: Maiden, Mother, and Crone for Modern Practitioners. (2020, April 10). Celtic Goddess of War: 8 ways to work with The Morrigan. Otherworldly Oracle website: https://otherworldlyoracle.com/celtic-goddess-of-war

What is Visualization & How do I do it? (n.d.). Witchy Things website: https://themanicnami.tumblr.com/post/160105192986/what-is-visualization-how-do-i-do-it

(N.d.). Llewellyn.com website: https://www.llewellyn.com/journal/article/2877

Maxberry, A. (2011). The Morrigan. Wisdom House Books.

Treanor, D., Elle, Walker, R., Roots, S., Fields, K., Duff, C., ... Triple Goddess: Maiden, Mother, and Crone for Modern Practitioners. (2020, April 10). Celtic Goddess of War: 8 ways to work with The Morrigan. Otherworldly Oracle website: https://otherworldlyoracle.com/celtic-goddess-of-war

Caro, T. (2020, December 21). Goddess Morrigan: Prayers, symbols, books & more [guide]. Magickal Spot website: https://magickalspot.com/morrigan

Wilson, A. (2018, May 11). The magic of the Morrigan: Shedding light on the Dark Goddess. Exemplore website: https://exemplore.com/paganism/The-Magic-of-the-Morrigan-A-Three-Part-Series

Meet goddess Morrigan: Shadow Work and Dark Magic With the Morrigan. (n.d.). Everyday Laurali Star website: https://www.everydaylauralistar.com/2021/09/meet-goddess-morrigan-shadow-work-and-dark-magic-with-the-morrigan.html

The Morrigan 2. (n.d.). Orderwhitemoon.Org. https://orderwhitemoon.org/goddess/morrigan-2/Morrigan2.html

Caro, T. (2020, December 21). Goddess Morrigan: Prayers, Symbols, Books & More [Guide]. Magickal Spot. https://magickalspot.com/morrigan

Daniel, S. (n.d.). Ritual for Banishing Depression. Tripod.Com. https://nemain.tripod.com/spells/BanishingDep.htm

Daniel, S. (n.d.). The Memory Ritual. Tripod.Com. https://nemain.tripod.com/spells/MemoryRitual.htm

Treanor, D., Elle, Walker, R., Roots, S., Fields, K., Duff, C., ... Triple Goddess: Maiden, Mother, and Crone for Modern Practitioners. (2020, April 10). Celtic Goddess of War: 8 ways to work with The Morrigan. Otherworldly Oracle website: https://otherworldlyoracle.com/celtic-goddess-of-war

Morrígan: Goddess offerings, signs, symbols & myth. (2021, September 17). Spells8 website: https://spells8.com/lessons/goddess-morrigan-signs

Rose, A. (2021, April 19). Signs of the Morrigan: The ultimate guide to the Morrigan goddess signs -. Occultmafia.com website: https://occultmafia.com/signs-of-the-morrigan-the-ultimate-guide-to-the-morrigan-goddess-signs

Caro, T. (2020, December 21). Goddess Morrigan: Prayers, symbols, books & more [guide]. Magickal Spot website: https://magickalspot.com/morrigan

anninyn. (2018, August 20). Morrigan worship in daily life – no altar required! Following The Dark Goddess website: https://fatqueerpagan.wordpress.com/2018/08/20/morrigan-worship-in-daily-life-no-altar-required

O'Hara, K. (2020, April 21). The Morrigan: The Story of the Fiercest Goddess in Irish Myth. The Irish Road Trip. https://www.theirishroadtrip.com/the-morrigan

Info. (2020, February 11). Morrigan. Order of Bards, Ovates & Druids. https://druidry.org/resources/morrigan

Bhride, C. (2015, June 7). The exalted ones. Clann Bhríde website: https://clannbhride.org/2015/06/07/the-exalted-ones

Brigid: Goddess of the Flame and of the well. (n.d.). Wicca-spirituality.com website: https://www.wicca-spirituality.com/brigid.html

Brigid: Goddess offerings, signs, symbols & myth. (2021, October 10). Spells8 website: https://spells8.com/lessons/brigid-goddess-symbols

Faireroseswitchygarden, V. A. P. (2019, January 30). Brigid, the goddess of Fire and Water. Fairerose's Witchy Garden website: https://faireroseswitchygarden.wordpress.com/2019/01/30/brigid-the-goddess-of-fire-and-water

Greenberg, M. (2021, January 12). Brigid, goddess of the Celts: The complete guide (2022). MythologySource website: https://mythologysource.com/brigid-irish-goddess

Info. (2020, February 11). Brigid: Survival of A Goddess. Order of Bards, Ovates & Druids website: https://druidry.org/resources/brigid-survival-of-a-goddess

MacGowan, D. (2016, December 9). Celtic goddess Brigid and her enduring deity. Historic Mysteries website: https://www.historicmysteries.com/celtic-goddess-brigid-saint-irish-myth

How Brigid went from a Celtic goddess to Catholic saint. (2022, February 1). IrishCentral.Com. https://www.irishcentral.com/roots/brigid-celtic-goddess-catholic-saint

Info. (2020, February 11). Brigid: Survival of A Goddess. Order of Bards, Ovates & Druids. https://druidry.org/resources/brigid-survival-of-a-goddess

Klimczak, N. (2019, March 30). A tale of two brigids: A Celtic goddess and a Christian saint. Ancient-Origins.Net; Ancient Origins. https://www.ancient-origins.net/history-famous-people/tale-two-brigids-celtic-goddess-and-christian-saint-006027

Legend of st. Brigid's cloak. (n.d.). Org.Au. https://brigidine.org.au/about-us/our-patroness/legend-of-st-brigids-cloak

St. Brigid of Ireland. (2018, August 16). Catholic Saint Medals. https://catholicsaintmedals.com/saints/st-brigid-of-ireland

Thompson, S. (2009, January 31). From goddess to saint and back again. Irish Times. https://www.irishtimes.com/news/from-goddess-to-saint-and-back-again-1.1238405

Thomson, C. (2006). Brigid of Ireland: A historical novel. Monarch Books.

Brigid: Goddess offerings, signs, symbols & myth. (2021, October 10). Spells8. https://spells8.com/lessons/brigid-goddess-symbols

Brigid: Lady of the sacred flame. (n.d.). The Goddess Circle. https://thegoddesscircle.net/visionary-writing/brigid-lady-sacred-flame

Brigid: Triple goddess of the flame (Health, hearth, & forge). (n.d.). Mimosa Books & Gifts. https://www.mimosaspirit.com/blogs/news/brigit-triple-goddess-of-the-flame-health-hearth-the-forge

galros. (2020, June 11). Is Brigid calling me? Brigid's Forge. https://mybrigidsforge.com/2020/06/11/is-brigid-calling-me

Goddess Brigit. (2012, February 1). Journeying to the Goddess. https://journeyingtothegoddess.wordpress.com/2012/02/01/goddess-brigit

Lighting the Perpetual Flame of Brigid – A brief history of the flame. (n.d.). Kildare.Ie. https://www.kildare.ie/community/notices/perpetual-flame.asp

Divine Ancestors: Find Out If You Descend From a Celtic God or Goddess, Celtic Deities: 10 Lesser-Known Celtic Gods and Goddesses, Triple Goddess: Maiden, Mother, and Crone for Modern Practitioners, & Jezebel: Ancient Queen, Pagan Priestess, and How to Work With Her. (2020, January 7). Celtic Goddess Brigid: How to work with the Irish Triple Goddess. Otherworldly Oracle. https://otherworldlyoracle.com/celtic-goddess-brigid

Wigington, P. (n.d.). Maman Brigitte, Loa of the dead in voodoo religion. Learn Religions. https://www.learnreligions.com/maman-brigitte-4771715

Watson, C. (2019, December 9). Meet the loa, the invisible spirits of Voodoo. History101.Com. https://www.history101.com/meet-the-loa-the-invisible-spirits-of-voodoo

Vidani, P. (n.d.). Shadow council. Shadow Council. https://shadowcouncil.tumblr.com/post/4445723165/maman-brigitte-maman-brigitte-surprisingly

Veve of Maman Brigitte. (n.d.). Symbols.Com. https://www.symbols.com/symbol/veve-of-maman-brigitte

Veve. (n.d.). Symbols.Com. https://www.symbols.com/group/72/Veve

Maman Brigitte. (n.d.). Myths and Folklore Wiki. https://mythus.fandom.com/wiki/Maman_Brigitte

Kathryn, E. (2019, January 16). Life, light, death, & darkness: How Brighid became maman Brigitte. The House Of Twigs. https://thehouseoftwigs.com/2019/01/16/life-light-death-darkness-how-brighid-became-maman-brigitte

Calann. (2019, June 9). Who is maman Brigitte? – Morrigan in the kitchen.

Morriganinthekitchen.Com.

Beyer, C. (n.d.). Vodoun symbols for their gods. Learn Religions. https://www.learnreligions.com/vodou-veves-4123236

Arrrados, (53), Street Yoga, (55), Skycae, (56), Treeplanter, (68), Steemitboard, (66), Blanca237, (49), Spalatino, (53), Wnfdiary, (68), Zen-Art, (68), Lunaticpandora, (69), Rodeo670, (61), Derosnec, (65), & Unshakeable, (49). (2018, February 28). Haitian Vodou – baron samedi & maman Brigitte – the lord and the lady of death and sexuality. Steemit. https://steemit.com/mythology/@arrrados/haitian-vodou-baron-samedi-and-maman-brigitte-the-lord-and-the-lady-of-death-and-sexuality

Brigid – Irish goddess (symbolism and significance). (2020, October 3). Symbol Sage website: https://symbolsage.com/brigid-irish-goddess-significance

Brigid: Goddess offerings, signs, symbols & myth. (2021, October 10). Spells8 website: https://spells8.com/lessons/brigid-goddess-symbols

BRIGID-symbols. (2019, June 3). Goddess Gift website: https://www.goddessgift.com/goddess-info/meet-the-goddesses/brigid/brigid-symbols

Crow, C. (2020, June 21). The Swan ★. Sanctuary of Brigid website: https://www.sanctuaryofbrigid.com/the-swan/

Greenberg, M. (2021, January 12). Brigid goddess of the Celts: The complete guide (2022). MythologySource website: https://mythologysource.com/brigid-irish-goddess

How to make a st. Brigid's cross. (n.d.). Scoil-bhride.com website: https://scoil-bhride.com/how-to-make-a-st-brigids-cross

Info. (2020, February 11). Brigit. Order of Bards, Ovates & Druids website: https://druidry.org/resources/brigid-2

Lighting the Perpetual Flame of Brigid – A brief history of the flame. (n.d.). Kildare.ie website: https://www.kildare.ie/community/notices/perpetual-flame.asp

Saint Brigid and the wolf. (n.d.). The Earth Stories Collection website: https://theearthstoriescollection.org/en/saint-brigid-and-the-wolf

Slaven, J. (2015, December 7). Celtic lore of the honey bee. Owlcation website: https://owlcation.com/humanities/Celtic-Lore-of-the-Honey-Bee

Symbols associated with Brigid. (n.d.). Moonlight and Flowers website: https://moonlight-and-flowerss.tumblr.com/post/182427854816/symbols-associated-with-brigid-since-imbolc-is

History.com Editors. (2018, April 5). Imbolc. HISTORY. https://www.history.com/topics/holidays/imbolc

Wigington, P. (n.d.). Celebrating Imbolc with kids. Learn Religions. https://www.learnreligions.com/celebrating-imbolc-with-kids-4118557

10 Benefits to Building Altars in Your home. (n.d.). AuthorsDen.com website: https://www.authorsden.com/visit/viewarticle.asp?id=21959

An Irish Pagan Altar – Lora O'Brien – Irish author & guide. (2018, October 22). Lora O'Brien – Irish Author & Guide website: https://loraobrien.ie/irish-pagan-altar

Brigid: Goddess offerings, signs, symbols & myth. (2021, October 10). Spells8 website: https://spells8.com/lessons/brigid-goddess-symbols

Brigit. (n.d.). Sacredwicca.com website: https://sacredwicca.com/brigit

How to create a home altar and keep it alive. (2019, January 25). Hridaya Yoga website: https://hridaya-yoga.com/how-to-create-a-home-altar

Kyteler, E. (2019, December 16). The ultimate guide to imbolc altar decor. Eclectic Witchcraft website: https://eclecticwitchcraft.com/the-ultimate-guide-to-imbolc-altar-decor

Offerings at home. (2020, January 23). The Spells8 Forum website: https://forum.spells8.com/t/offerings-at-home/807?_ga=2.121020747.218465654.1644054967-13729897.1643797479

Sisterlisa. (n.d.). Imbolc and the goddess Brigid. Intuitivehomesolutions.com website: https://intuitivehomesolutions.com/imbolc-and-the-goddess-brigid

Symbols associated with Brigid. (n.d.). Moonlight and Flowers website: https://moonlight-and-flowerss.tumblr.com/post/182427854816/symbols-associated-with-brigid-since-imbolc-is

What does incense do? Sacred smoke and spirituality. (2021, August 30). Spiru website: https://spiru.com/what-does-incense-do-sacred-smoke-and-spirituality

Chrysanthou, A. (2018, February 7). Pagans honor Gaelic goddess Brigid at Imbolc ritual, welcome returning of the light. The Daily Egyptian website: https://dailyegyptian.com/78486/uncategorized/pagans-honor-gaelic-goddess-brigid-at-imbolc-ritual-welcome-returning-of-the-light

Wigington, P. (n.d.). Brighid, the hearth goddess of Ireland. Learn Religions website: https://www.learnreligions.com/brighid-hearth-goddess-of-ireland-2561958

Brigid: Goddess offerings, signs, symbols & myth. (2021, October 10). Spells8 website: https://spells8.com/lessons/brigid-goddess-symbols

Hertzenberg, S., & Hertzenberg, S. (n.d.). 5 ways to celebrate Imbolc. Beliefnet.com website: https://www.beliefnet.com/faiths/pagan-and-earth-based/5-ways-to-celebrate-imbolc.aspx

Wigington, P. (n.d.-b). Pagan prayers to celebrate the Imbolc sabbat. Learn Religions website: https://www.learnreligions.com/imbolc-prayers-4122188

Wigington, P. (n.d.-b). How to hold a god/goddess healing ritual. Learn Religions website: https://www.learnreligions.com/god-goddess-healing-ritual-2562842

Goddess Bridget. (n.d.). Goddessschool.com website: http://www.goddessschool.com/projects/baywytch/brigid.html

Rach, Divina, Whitehurst, T., & Kim. (2019, January 28). 5 types of magic to work on Imbolc. Tess Whitehurst website: https://tesswhitehurst.com/5-types-of-magic-to-work-on-imbolc

---

Corak, R. (2020, February 8). Phoenix rising: Fire, water, and words: Divination with the goddess Brigid. Agora website: https://www.patheos.com/blogs/agora/2020/02/phoenix-rising-fire-water-and-words-divination-with-the-goddess-brigid

What is ancient divination? (n.d.). Actingcolleges.org website: https://actingcolleges.org/library/acting-questions/read/132957-what-is-ancient-divination

Info. (2020, February 11). Brigid: Survival of A Goddess. Order of Bards, Ovates & Druids.

https://druidry.org/resources/brigid-survival-of-a-goddess

Wright, G. (2020, August 16). Brigid. Mythopedia. https://mythopedia.com/topics/brigid

www.ingramcontent.com/pod-product-compliance
Lightning Source LLC
Chambersburg PA
CBHW071855090426
42811CB00004B/610